FREE Study Skills Vide

MW01136635

Dear Customer,

Thank you for your purchase from Mometrix! We consider it an honor and a privilege that you have purchased our product and we want to ensure your satisfaction.

As part of our ongoing effort to meet the needs of test takers, we have developed a set of Study Skills Videos that we would like to give you for <u>FREE</u>. These videos cover our *best practices* for getting ready for your exam, from how to use our study materials to how to best prepare for the day of the test.

All that we ask is that you email us with feedback that would describe your experience so far with our product. Good, bad, or indifferent, we want to know what you think!

To get your FREE Study Skills Videos, you can use the **QR code** below, or send us an **email** at studyvideos@mometrix.com with *FREE VIDEOS* in the subject line and the following information in the body of the email:

- The name of the product you purchased.
- Your product rating on a scale of 1-5, with 5 being the highest rating.
- Your feedback. It can be long, short, or anything in between. We just want to know your impressions and experience so far with our product. (Good feedback might include how our study material met your needs and ways we might be able to make it even better. You could highlight features that you found helpful or features that you think we should add.)

If you have any questions or concerns, please don't hesitate to contact me directly.

Thanks again!

Sincerely,

Jay Willis
Vice President
jay.willis@mometrix.com
1-800-673-8175

Praxis II

Health and Physical Education: Content Knowledge (5857) Exam

Secrets

Study Guide
Your Key to Exam Success

Mometrix
TEST PREPARATION

Written and edited by the Mometrix Teacher Certification Test Team

Printed in the United States of America

This paper meets the requirements of ANSI/NISO Z39.48-1992 (Permanence of Paper).

Mometrix offers volume discount pricing to institutions. For more information or a price quote, please contact our sales department at sales@mometrix.com or 888-248-1219.

Mometrix Media LLC is not affiliated with or endorsed by any official testing organization. All organizational and test names are trademarks of their respective owners.

Paperback
ISBN 13: 978-1-63094-939-6
ISBN 10: 1-63094-939-6

Ebook
ISBN 13: 978-1-5167-0282-4
ISBN 10: 1-5167-0282-4

Hardback
ISBN 13: 978-1-5167-1399-8
ISBN 10: 1-5167-1399-0

DEAR FUTURE EXAM SUCCESS STORY

First of all, **THANK YOU** for purchasing Mometrix study materials!

Second, congratulations! You are one of the few determined test-takers who are committed to doing whatever it takes to excel on your exam. **You have come to the right place.** We developed these study materials with one goal in mind: to deliver you the information you need in a format that's concise and easy to use.

In addition to optimizing your guide for the content of the test, we've outlined our recommended steps for breaking down the preparation process into small, attainable goals so you can make sure you stay on track.

We've also analyzed the entire test-taking process, identifying the most common pitfalls and showing how you can overcome them and be ready for any curveball the test throws you.

Standardized testing is one of the biggest obstacles on your road to success, which only increases the importance of doing well in the high-pressure, high-stakes environment of test day. Your results on this test could have a significant impact on your future, and this guide provides the information and practical advice to help you achieve your full potential on test day.

Your success is our success

We would love to hear from you! If you would like to share the story of your exam success or if you have any questions or comments in regard to our products, please contact us at **800-673-8175** or **support@mometrix.com**.

Thanks again for your business and we wish you continued success!

Sincerely,
The Mometrix Test Preparation Team

Need more help? Check out our flashcards at:
http://mometrixflashcards.com/PraxisII

TABLE OF CONTENTS

Introduction

Thank you for purchasing this resource! You have made the choice to prepare yourself for a test that could have a huge impact on your future, and this guide is designed to help you be fully ready for test day. Obviously, it's important to have a solid understanding of the test material, but you also need to be prepared for the unique environment and stressors of the test, so that you can perform to the best of your abilities.

For this purpose, the first section that appears in this guide is the **Secret Keys**. We've devoted countless hours to meticulously researching what works and what doesn't, and we've boiled down our findings to the five most impactful steps you can take to improve your performance on the test. We start at the beginning with study planning and move through the preparation process, all the way to the testing strategies that will help you get the most out of what you know when you're finally sitting in front of the test.

We recommend that you start preparing for your test as far in advance as possible. However, if you've bought this guide as a last-minute study resource and only have a few days before your test, we recommend that you skip over the first two Secret Keys since they address a long-term study plan.

If you struggle with **test anxiety**, we strongly encourage you to check out our recommendations for how you can overcome it. Test anxiety is a formidable foe, but it can be beaten, and we want to make sure you have the tools you need to defeat it.

1

Secret Key #1 – Plan Big, Study Small

There's a lot riding on your performance. If you want to ace this test, you're going to need to keep your skills sharp and the material fresh in your mind. You need a plan that lets you review everything you need to know while still fitting in your schedule. We'll break this strategy down into three categories.

Information Organization

Start with the information you already have: the official test outline. From this, you can make a complete list of all the concepts you need to cover before the test. Organize these concepts into groups that can be studied together, and create a list of any related vocabulary you need to learn so you can brush up on any difficult terms. You'll want to keep this vocabulary list handy once you actually start studying since you may need to add to it along the way.

Time Management

Once you have your set of study concepts, decide how to spread them out over the time you have left before the test. Break your study plan into small, clear goals so you have a manageable task for each day and know exactly what you're doing. Then just focus on one small step at a time. When you manage your time this way, you don't need to spend hours at a time studying. Studying a small block of content for a short period each day helps you retain information better and avoid stressing over how much you have left to do. You can relax knowing that you have a plan to cover everything in time. In order for this strategy to be effective though, you have to start studying early and stick to your schedule. Avoid the exhaustion and futility that comes from last-minute cramming!

Study Environment

The environment you study in has a big impact on your learning. Studying in a coffee shop, while probably more enjoyable, is not likely to be as fruitful as studying in a quiet room. It's important to keep distractions to a minimum. You're only planning to study for a short block of time, so make the most of it. Don't pause to check your phone or get up to find a snack. It's also important to **avoid multitasking**. Research has consistently shown that multitasking will make your studying dramatically less effective. Your study area should also be comfortable and well-lit so you don't have the distraction of straining your eyes or sitting on an uncomfortable chair.

 The time of day you study is also important. You want to be rested and alert. Don't wait until just before bedtime. Study when you'll be most likely to comprehend and remember. Even better, if you know what time of day your test will be, set that time aside for study. That way your brain will be used to working on that subject at that specific time and you'll have a better chance of recalling information.

Finally, it can be helpful to team up with others who are studying for the same test. Your actual studying should be done in as isolated an environment as possible, but the work of organizing the information and setting up the study plan can be divided up. In between study sessions, you can discuss with your teammates the concepts that you're all studying and quiz each other on the details. Just be sure that your teammates are as serious about the test as you are. If you find that your study time is being replaced with social time, you might need to find a new team.

2

Secret Key #2 – Make Your Studying Count

You're devoting a lot of time and effort to preparing for this test, so you want to be absolutely certain it will pay off. This means doing more than just reading the content and hoping you can remember it on test day. It's important to make every minute of study count. There are two main areas you can focus on to make your studying count.

Retention

It doesn't matter how much time you study if you can't remember the material. You need to make sure you are retaining the concepts. To check your retention of the information you're learning, try recalling it at later times with minimal prompting. Try carrying around flashcards and glance at one or two from time to time or ask a friend who's also studying for the test to quiz you.

To enhance your retention, look for ways to put the information into practice so that you can apply it rather than simply recalling it. If you're using the information in practical ways, it will be much easier to remember. Similarly, it helps to solidify a concept in your mind if you're not only reading it to yourself but also explaining it to someone else. Ask a friend to let you teach them about a concept you're a little shaky on (or speak aloud to an imaginary audience if necessary). As you try to summarize, define, give examples, and answer your friend's questions, you'll understand the concepts better and they will stay with you longer. Finally, step back for a big picture view and ask yourself how each piece of information fits with the whole subject. When you link the different concepts together and see them working together as a whole, it's easier to remember the individual components.

Finally, practice showing your work on any multi-step problems, even if you're just studying. Writing out each step you take to solve a problem will help solidify the process in your mind, and you'll be more likely to remember it during the test.

Modality

Modality simply refers to the means or method by which you study. Choosing a study modality that fits your own individual learning style is crucial. No two people learn best in exactly the same way, so it's important to know your strengths and use them to your advantage.

For example, if you learn best by visualization, focus on visualizing a concept in your mind and draw an image or a diagram. Try color-coding your notes, illustrating them, or creating symbols that will trigger your mind to recall a learned concept. If you learn best by hearing or discussing information, find a study partner who learns the same way or read aloud to yourself. Think about how to put the information in your own words. Imagine that you are giving a lecture on the topic and record yourself so you can listen to it later.

For any learning style, flashcards can be helpful. Organize the information so you can take advantage of spare moments to review. Underline key words or phrases. Use different colors for different categories. Mnemonic devices (such as creating a short list in which every item starts with the same letter) can also help with retention. Find what works best for you and use it to store the information in your mind most effectively and easily.

3

Secret Key #3 – Practice the Right Way

Your success on test day depends not only on how many hours you put into preparing, but also on whether you prepared the right way. It's good to check along the way to see if your studying is paying off. One of the most effective ways to do this is by taking practice tests to evaluate your progress. Practice tests are useful because they show exactly where you need to improve. Every time you take a practice test, pay special attention to these three groups of questions:

- The questions you got wrong
- The questions you had to guess on, even if you guessed right
- The questions you found difficult or slow to work through

This will show you exactly what your weak areas are, and where you need to devote more study time. Ask yourself why each of these questions gave you trouble. Was it because you didn't understand the material? Was it because you didn't remember the vocabulary? Do you need more repetitions on this type of question to build speed and confidence? Dig into those questions and figure out how you can strengthen your weak areas as you go back to review the material.

 Additionally, many practice tests have a section explaining the answer choices. It can be tempting to read the explanation and think that you now have a good understanding of the concept. However, an explanation likely only covers part of the question's broader context. Even if the explanation makes perfect sense, **go back and investigate** every concept related to the question until you're positive you have a thorough understanding.

As you go along, keep in mind that the practice test is just that: practice. Memorizing these questions and answers will not be very helpful on the actual test because it is unlikely to have any of the same exact questions. If you only know the right answers to the sample questions, you won't be prepared for the real thing. **Study the concepts** until you understand them fully, and then you'll be able to answer any question that shows up on the test.

It's important to wait on the practice tests until you're ready. If you take a test on your first day of study, you may be overwhelmed by the amount of material covered and how much you need to learn. Work up to it gradually.

On test day, you'll need to be prepared for answering questions, managing your time, and using the test-taking strategies you've learned. It's a lot to balance, like a mental marathon that will have a big impact on your future. Like training for a marathon, you'll need to start slowly and work your way up. When test day arrives, you'll be ready.

Start with the strategies you've read in the first two Secret Keys—plan your course and study in the way that works best for you. If you have time, consider using multiple study resources to get different approaches to the same concepts. It can be helpful to see difficult concepts from more than one angle. Then find a good source for practice tests. Many times, the test website will suggest potential study resources or provide sample tests.

Practice Test Strategy

If you're able to find at least three practice tests, we recommend this strategy:

UNTIMED AND OPEN-BOOK PRACTICE

Take the first test with no time constraints and with your notes and study guide handy. Take your time and focus on applying the strategies you've learned.

TIMED AND OPEN-BOOK PRACTICE

Take the second practice test open-book as well, but set a timer and practice pacing yourself to finish in time.

TIMED AND CLOSED-BOOK PRACTICE

Take any other practice tests as if it were test day. Set a timer and put away your study materials. Sit at a table or desk in a quiet room, imagine yourself at the testing center, and answer questions as quickly and accurately as possible.

Keep repeating timed and closed-book tests on a regular basis until you run out of practice tests or it's time for the actual test. Your mind will be ready for the schedule and stress of test day, and you'll be able to focus on recalling the material you've learned.

Secret Key #4 – Pace Yourself

Once you're fully prepared for the material on the test, your biggest challenge on test day will be managing your time. Just knowing that the clock is ticking can make you panic even if you have plenty of time left. Work on pacing yourself so you can build confidence against the time constraints of the exam. Pacing is a difficult skill to master, especially in a high-pressure environment, so **practice is vital**.

Set time expectations for your pace based on how much time is available. For example, if a section has 60 questions and the time limit is 30 minutes, you know you have to average 30 seconds or less per question in order to answer them all. Although 30 seconds is the hard limit, set 25 seconds per question as your goal, so you reserve extra time to spend on harder questions. When you budget extra time for the harder questions, you no longer have any reason to stress when those questions take longer to answer.

Don't let this time expectation distract you from working through the test at a calm, steady pace, but keep it in mind so you don't spend too much time on any one question. Recognize that taking extra time on one question you don't understand may keep you from answering two that you do understand later in the test. If your time limit for a question is up and you're still not sure of the answer, mark it and move on, and come back to it later if the time and the test format allow. If the testing format doesn't allow you to return to earlier questions, just make an educated guess; then put it out of your mind and move on.

On the easier questions, be careful not to rush. It may seem wise to hurry through them so you have more time for the challenging ones, but it's not worth missing one if you know the concept and just didn't take the time to read the question fully. Work efficiently but make sure you understand the question and have looked at all of the answer choices, since more than one may seem right at first.

Even if you're paying attention to the time, you may find yourself a little behind at some point. You should speed up to get back on track, but do so wisely. Don't panic; just take a few seconds less on each question until you're caught up. Don't guess without thinking, but do look through the answer choices and eliminate any you know are wrong. If you can get down to two choices, it is often worthwhile to guess from those. Once you've chosen an answer, move on and don't dwell on any that you skipped or had to hurry through. If a question was taking too long, chances are it was one of the harder ones, so you weren't as likely to get it right anyway.

On the other hand, if you find yourself getting ahead of schedule, it may be beneficial to slow down a little. The more quickly you work, the more likely you are to make a careless mistake that will affect your score. You've budgeted time for each question, so don't be afraid to spend that time. Practice an efficient but careful pace to get the most out of the time you have.

Copyright © Mometrix Media. You have been licensed one copy of this document for personal use only. Any other reproduction or redistribution is strictly prohibited. All rights reserved. This content is provided for test preparation purposes only and does not imply an endorsement by Mometrix of any particular political, scientific, or religious point of view.

Secret Key #5 – Have a Plan for Guessing

When you're taking the test, you may find yourself stuck on a question. Some of the answer choices seem better than others, but you don't see the one answer choice that is obviously correct. What do you do?

The scenario described above is very common, yet most test takers have not effectively prepared for it. Developing and practicing a plan for guessing may be one of the single most effective uses of your time as you get ready for the exam.

In developing your plan for guessing, there are three questions to address:

- When should you start the guessing process?
- How should you narrow down the choices?
- Which answer should you choose?

When to Start the Guessing Process

Unless your plan for guessing is to select C every time (which, despite its merits, is not what we recommend), you need to leave yourself enough time to apply your answer elimination strategies. Since you have a limited amount of time for each question, that means that if you're going to give yourself the best shot at guessing correctly, you have to decide quickly whether or not you will guess.

Of course, the best-case scenario is that you don't have to guess at all, so first, see if you can answer the question based on your knowledge of the subject and basic reasoning skills. Focus on the key words in the question and try to jog your memory of related topics. Give yourself a chance to bring the knowledge to mind, but once you realize that you don't have (or you can't access) the knowledge you need to answer the question, it's time to start the guessing process.

It's almost always better to start the guessing process too early than too late. It only takes a few seconds to remember something and answer the question from knowledge. Carefully eliminating wrong answer choices takes longer. Plus, going through the process of eliminating answer choices can actually help jog your memory.

Summary: Start the guessing process as soon as you decide that you can't answer the question based on your knowledge.

How to Narrow Down the Choices

The next chapter in this book (**Test-Taking Strategies**) includes a wide range of strategies for how to approach questions and how to look for answer choices to eliminate. You will definitely want to read those carefully, practice them, and figure out which ones work best for you. Here though, we're going to address a mindset rather than a particular strategy.

Your odds of guessing an answer correctly depend on how many options you are choosing from.

Number of options left	5	4	3	2	1
Odds of guessing correctly	20%	25%	33%	50%	100%

You can see from this chart just how valuable it is to be able to eliminate incorrect answers and make an educated guess, but there are two things that many test takers do that cause them to miss out on the benefits of guessing:

- Accidentally eliminating the correct answer
- Selecting an answer based on an impression

We'll look at the first one here, and the second one in the next section.

To avoid accidentally eliminating the correct answer, we recommend a thought exercise called **the $5 challenge**. In this challenge, you only eliminate an answer choice from contention if you are willing to bet $5 on it being wrong. Why $5? Five dollars is a small but not insignificant amount of money. It's an amount you could afford to lose but wouldn't want to throw away. And while losing $5 once might not hurt too much, doing it twenty times will set you back $100. In the same way, each small decision you make—eliminating a choice here, guessing on a question there—won't by itself impact your score very much, but when you put them all together, they can make a big difference. By holding each answer choice elimination decision to a higher standard, you can reduce the risk of accidentally eliminating the correct answer.

The $5 challenge can also be applied in a positive sense: If you are willing to bet $5 that an answer choice *is* correct, go ahead and mark it as correct.

Summary: Only eliminate an answer choice if you are willing to bet $5 that it is wrong.

Which Answer to Choose

You're taking the test. You've run into a hard question and decided you'll have to guess. You've eliminated all the answer choices you're willing to bet $5 on. Now you have to pick an answer. Why do we even need to talk about this? Why can't you just pick whichever one you feel like when the time comes?

The answer to these questions is that if you don't come into the test with a plan, you'll rely on your impression to select an answer choice, and if you do that, you risk falling into a trap. The test writers know that everyone who takes their test will be guessing on some of the questions, so they intentionally write wrong answer choices to seem plausible. You still have to pick an answer though, and if the wrong answer choices are designed to look right, how can you ever be sure that you're not falling for their trap? The best solution we've found to this dilemma is to take the decision out of your hands entirely. Here is the process we recommend:

Once you've eliminated any choices that you are confident (willing to bet $5) are wrong, select the first remaining choice as your answer.

Whether you choose to select the first remaining choice, the second, or the last, the important thing is that you use some preselected standard. Using this approach guarantees that you will not be enticed into selecting an answer choice that looks right, because you are not basing your decision on how the answer choices look.

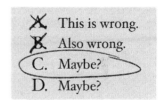

This is not meant to make you question your knowledge. Instead, it is to help you recognize the difference between your knowledge and your impressions. There's a huge difference between thinking an answer is right because of what you know, and thinking an answer is right because it looks or sounds like it should be right.

Summary: To ensure that your selection is appropriately random, make a predetermined selection from among all answer choices you have not eliminated.

Test-Taking Strategies

This section contains a list of test-taking strategies that you may find helpful as you work through the test. By taking what you know and applying logical thought, you can maximize your chances of answering any question correctly!

It is very important to realize that every question is different and every person is different: no single strategy will work on every question, and no single strategy will work for every person. That's why we've included all of them here, so you can try them out and determine which ones work best for different types of questions and which ones work best for you.

Question Strategies

⊘ Read Carefully

Read the question and the answer choices carefully. Don't miss the question because you misread the terms. You have plenty of time to read each question thoroughly and make sure you understand what is being asked. Yet a happy medium must be attained, so don't waste too much time. You must read carefully and efficiently.

⊘ Contextual Clues

Look for contextual clues. If the question includes a word you are not familiar with, look at the immediate context for some indication of what the word might mean. Contextual clues can often give you all the information you need to decipher the meaning of an unfamiliar word. Even if you can't determine the meaning, you may be able to narrow down the possibilities enough to make a solid guess at the answer to the question.

⊘ Prefixes

If you're having trouble with a word in the question or answer choices, try dissecting it. Take advantage of every clue that the word might include. Prefixes can be a huge help. Usually, they allow you to determine a basic meaning. *Pre-* means before, *post-* means after, *pro-* is positive, *de-* is negative. From prefixes, you can get an idea of the general meaning of the word and try to put it into context.

⊘ Hedge Words

Watch out for critical hedge words, such as *likely, may, can, sometimes, often, almost, mostly, usually, generally, rarely,* and *sometimes*. Question writers insert these hedge phrases to cover every possibility. Often an answer choice will be wrong simply because it leaves no room for exception. Be on guard for answer choices that have definitive words such as *exactly* and *always*.

⊘ Switchback Words

Stay alert for *switchbacks*. These are the words and phrases frequently used to alert you to shifts in thought. The most common switchback words are *but, although,* and *however*. Others include *nevertheless, on the other hand, even though, while, in spite of, despite,* and *regardless of*. Switchback words are important to catch because they can change the direction of the question or an answer choice.

⊘ Face Value

When in doubt, use common sense. Accept the situation in the problem at face value. Don't read too much into it. These problems will not require you to make wild assumptions. If you have to go beyond creativity and warp time or space in order to have an answer choice fit the question, then you should move on and consider the other answer choices. These are normal problems rooted in reality. The applicable relationship or explanation may not be readily apparent, but it is there for you to figure out. Use your common sense to interpret anything that isn't clear.

Answer Choice Strategies

⊘ Answer Selection

The most thorough way to pick an answer choice is to identify and eliminate wrong answers until only one is left, then confirm it is the correct answer. Sometimes an answer choice may immediately seem right, but be careful. The test writers will usually put more than one reasonable answer choice on each question, so take a second to read all of them and make sure that the other choices are not equally obvious. As long as you have time left, it is better to read every answer choice than to pick the first one that looks right without checking the others.

⊘ Answer Choice Families

An answer choice family consists of two (in rare cases, three) answer choices that are very similar in construction and cannot all be true at the same time. If you see two answer choices that are direct opposites or parallels, one of them is usually the correct answer. For instance, if one answer choice says that quantity x increases and another either says that quantity x decreases (opposite) or says that quantity y increases (parallel), then those answer choices would fall into the same family. An answer choice that doesn't match the construction of the answer choice family is more likely to be incorrect. Most questions will not have answer choice families, but when they do appear, you should be prepared to recognize them.

⊘ Eliminate Answers

Eliminate answer choices as soon as you realize they are wrong, but make sure you consider all possibilities. If you are eliminating answer choices and realize that the last one you are left with is also wrong, don't panic. Start over and consider each choice again. There may be something you missed the first time that you will realize on the second pass.

⊘ Avoid Fact Traps

Don't be distracted by an answer choice that is factually true but doesn't answer the question. You are looking for the choice that answers the question. Stay focused on what the question is asking for so you don't accidentally pick an answer that is true but incorrect. Always go back to the question and make sure the answer choice you've selected actually answers the question and is not merely a true statement.

⊘ Extreme Statements

In general, you should avoid answers that put forth extreme actions as standard practice or proclaim controversial ideas as established fact. An answer choice that states the "process should be used in certain situations, if..." is much more likely to be correct than one that states the "process should be discontinued completely." The first is a calm rational statement and doesn't even make a definitive, uncompromising stance, using a hedge word *if* to provide wiggle room, whereas the second choice is far more extreme.

⊘ Benchmark

As you read through the answer choices and you come across one that seems to answer the question well, mentally select that answer choice. This is not your final answer, but it's the one that will help you evaluate the other answer choices. The one that you selected is your benchmark or standard for judging each of the other answer choices. Every other answer choice must be compared to your benchmark. That choice is correct until proven otherwise by another answer choice beating it. If you find a better answer, then that one becomes your new benchmark. Once you've decided that no other choice answers the question as well as your benchmark, you have your final answer.

⊘ Predict the Answer

Before you even start looking at the answer choices, it is often best to try to predict the answer. When you come up with the answer on your own, it is easier to avoid distractions and traps because you will know exactly what to look for. The right answer choice is unlikely to be word-for-word what you came up with, but it should be a close match. Even if you are confident that you have the right answer, you should still take the time to read each option before moving on.

General Strategies

⊘ Tough Questions

If you are stumped on a problem or it appears too hard or too difficult, don't waste time. Move on! Remember though, if you can quickly check for obviously incorrect answer choices, your chances of guessing correctly are greatly improved. Before you completely give up, at least try to knock out a couple of possible answers. Eliminate what you can and then guess at the remaining answer choices before moving on.

⊘ Check Your Work

Since you will probably not know every term listed and the answer to every question, it is important that you get credit for the ones that you do know. Don't miss any questions through careless mistakes. If at all possible, try to take a second to look back over your answer selection and make sure you've selected the correct answer choice and haven't made a costly careless mistake (such as marking an answer choice that you didn't mean to mark). This quick double check should more than pay for itself in caught mistakes for the time it costs.

⊘ Pace Yourself

It's easy to be overwhelmed when you're looking at a page full of questions; your mind is confused and full of random thoughts, and the clock is ticking down faster than you would like. Calm down and maintain the pace that you have set for yourself. Especially as you get down to the last few minutes of the test, don't let the small numbers on the clock make you panic. As long as you are on track by monitoring your pace, you are guaranteed to have time for each question.

⊘ Don't Rush

It is very easy to make errors when you are in a hurry. Maintaining a fast pace in answering questions is pointless if it makes you miss questions that you would have gotten right otherwise. Test writers like to include distracting information and wrong answers that seem right. Taking a little extra time to avoid careless mistakes can make all the difference in your test score. Find a pace that allows you to be confident in the answers that you select.

⊘ Keep Moving

Panicking will not help you pass the test, so do your best to stay calm and keep moving. Taking deep breaths and going through the answer elimination steps you practiced can help to break through a stress barrier and keep your pace.

Final Notes

The combination of a solid foundation of content knowledge and the confidence that comes from practicing your plan for applying that knowledge is the key to maximizing your performance on test day. As your foundation of content knowledge is built up and strengthened, you'll find that the strategies included in this chapter become more and more effective in helping you quickly sift through the distractions and traps of the test to isolate the correct answer.

Now that you're preparing to move forward into the test content chapters of this book, be sure to keep your goal in mind. As you read, think about how you will be able to apply this information on the test. If you've already seen sample questions for the test and you have an idea of the question format and style, try to come up with questions of your own that you can answer based on what you're reading. This will give you valuable practice applying your knowledge in the same ways you can expect to on test day.

Good luck and good studying!

Content Knowledge and Student Growth and Development

Transform passive reading into active learning! After immersing yourself in this chapter, put your comprehension to the test by taking a quiz. The insights you gained will stay with you longer this way. Scan the QR code to go directly to the chapter quiz interface for this study guide. If you're using a computer, simply visit the bonus page at **mometrix.com/bonus948/priihpeck5857** and click the Chapter Quizzes link.

Motor Development Processes

ANN GENTILE'S MOTOR LEARNING STAGES

Gentile's learning model has two stages. In stage 1, the learner is **getting the idea of the movement.** In stage 2, the learner focuses on **fixation**, or working on consistency and closed skills (e.g., executing the skill in isolation) and **diversification**, or working on open skill in changing environments. In stage 1, the learner is getting a grasp on the movements that are required for the skill. The learner decides on the regulatory and nonregulatory conditions needed to perform the movement. **Regulatory conditions** are important to the movement skill, whereas **nonregulatory conditions** are not. However, nonregulatory conditions, such as crowd noise, can be distracting. Regulatory conditions include things like equipment type, positions of players, and the proximity to the goal. These aspects must be considered before a learner can be proficient. Learners who are more skilled and have more experience are better able to ignore nonregulatory conditions. In contrast, it is difficult for novice learners to ignore nonregulatory conditions. Once learners are proficient, they move on to stage 2.

FITTS AND POSNER'S MOTOR LEARNING STAGES

Fitts and Posner's three motor stages of learning are the cognitive stage, the associative stage, and the autonomous stage**.** In the **cognitive**, or beginner, stage, the learner makes lots of errors, is inconsistent, and focuses heavily on the skill cues. During this stage, the teacher is more direct with instructions, which include both verbal instructions and demonstrations, to help the learner understand the movements. This first stage is similar to Gentile's stage 1 (getting the idea of the movement). In the **associative**, or intermediate, stage, the learner has a grasp on the skill and understands the skill movement patterns. This learner will start to become more consistent in movement patterns. As such, they will rely less on skill cues and begin to refine movement by trial, error, and feedback, which aids in the development of self-correction skills. During the associative stage, the teacher designs the practice activities after identifying the errors and providing corrective feedback. In the **autonomous,** or advanced, stage, the movements become automatic and the student can perform skills independently. The learner is able to self-correct during the autonomous stage. During this stage, the teacher should focus on motivation and design activities that refine the movements.

OPEN AND CLOSED SKILLS

While no skill is completely open or closed, **open skills** occur in dynamic environments where things are always changing, like during team sports. There are players, a ball (or object), coaches, and spectators, all of which create an unpredictable environment and impact performance. There

15

are also closed skills within team sports, like a free throw in basketball or a penalty kick in soccer, that illustrate the open-closed continuum. **Closed skills** occur in environments that are stable and predictable, like golf. Closed skills are often introduced when teaching novice learners, so that they can focus solely on the skill, or when teaching a closed and controlled activity, like archery. Activities that are open in team sports are often taught in progression from closed (e.g., dribbling in isolation) to open skills (e.g., dribbling during game play) to increase competency.

BERNSTEIN'S DEGREES OF FREEDOM PROBLEM

Bernstein's motor learning stages focus on the **degrees of freedom problem**. The degrees of freedom problem refers to the variations that can take place in a **complex movement** because of the number of **isolated types of movement** involved in accomplishing a movement skill. For instance, when a pitcher throws a baseball, his feet, legs, torso, arms, and hands are involved in throwing the ball. Therefore, the goal is to reduce the number of problems that can arise from degrees of freedom that may impede success to achieve the desired movement. Two concepts integral to Bernstein's learning stages are the coordination and regulation of movement. Coordination is the ability to move fluidly with complex movement skills. In throwing a ball, a pitcher starts by winding up the upper arm and back and smoothly translating the throw through the whole arm so that all of the arm muscles involved can contribute to the motion. Regulation is the ability to control individual movements in joints, limbs, and muscles. This usually means working a particular muscle in isolation. To work on regulating motions involved in throwing a baseball, one might attempt to throw a baseball by only using the forearm, or work on the associated footwork without throwing a ball.

BERNSTEIN'S MOTOR LEARNING STAGES

Bernstein's motor learning stages revolve around breaking down motor tasks into smaller pieces to develop **regulation** of individual movements, then integrating them to develop **coordination** between those movements. **Stage 1** is freezing the limbs, which involves regulating as many degrees of freedom necessary to produce the desired movement. For example, the leg and foot action of an overhand throw might be restricted so that the novice learner can focus on the arm motion of the throw. **Stage 2** is releasing the limbs as degrees of freedom gradually increase as skills become more proficient. **Stage 3** is exploiting the environment, (expert stage), which is when the learner is able to perform the tasks in a variety of situations. For example, throwing at different speeds, throwing while running, throwing at various distances and levels, and throwing with defenders all exploit the environment in different ways. Developing skills on each of these levels helps to isolate inefficient movements and develop the fluidity of movements involved in a complex skill.

MOTOR LEARNING AND MOTOR PERFORMANCE

Motor learning is the study of skill acquisition processes and includes the factors that help or hinder motor skill performance. Motor learning can be a permanent or semi-permanent change. Once a person learns how to ride a bike, they will not forget—even after a long absence of riding. Motor learning cannot be observed directly. Instead, performance is observed over time to evaluate consistency and proficiency in a movement skill, which aids in making a determination about whether or not learning has occurred. **Motor performance** is the demonstration of a skill or set of skills. In contrast to motor learning, motor performance is not permanent, as it is contingent upon other factors. While one may have learned how to perform a jump shot in basketball, the success of the jump shot will differ based on the changing environment. Further, the individual's fitness level, fatigue, stress, and other factors impact performance. In contrast to motor learning, motor performance can be observed.

KNOWLEDGE OF PERFORMANCE AND KNOWLEDGE OF RESULTS

Knowledge of performance is the quality of a performance. It is often felt by the learner while executing the movement or observed while watching the movement. These feelings or observations help to identify either errors that need correction or actions that need to be replicated to promote consistent performance, a process known as **descriptive feedback**. For example, the hand positions and release of a basketball during a free throw can be observed. If the hand position and release of the basketball are to the left, the ball will likely go in that direction. This observation of performance would warrant a change in technique or positioning to improve performance. The feedback given to correct the error in performance is **prescriptive feedback.** In contrast, the **knowledge of results**, or terminal feedback, is the outcome feedback that occurs after a skill has been performed. An example of the knowledge of results is evident during a free throw shot in basketball or a penalty kick in soccer where the outcome is that the ball either goes in or out. When only outcome feedback (knowledge of results) is given, there is little improvement of motor skills. Conversely, knowledge of performance feedback appears more impactful for improving motor skill acquisition and performance.

SKILL TRANSFER

The three types of skill transfer are positive, negative, and zero. **Positive transfer** is when a previously learned skill benefits the performance of another skill. An example of positive transfer may include performing a forehand in racquetball after learning a forehand in tennis. **Negative transfer** is when a previously learned skill impedes the performance of another skill. An example of negative transfer is someone's knowledge of how to properly swing a baseball bat impeding their ability to learn how to properly swing a golf club. **Zero transfer** is when a previously learned skill has no impact on the learning of a future skill. The skills are usually unrelated (though not always). For example, dribbling in basketball has little to no impact on dribbling in soccer. However, positive transfer is often evident during invasion games (team sports that involve two teams with the goal of scoring an object into a goal) such as these because the offensive and defensive concepts and strategies in basketball and soccer are the same.

THEORY OF DELIBERATE PRACTICE

"Practice makes perfect" is a common phrase often used in physical education. This concept is included in the five tenets of **deliberate practice** described here.

1. Skills must be developed through practice, even among those with natural ability. While it is often assumed that some students have "natural talent," practice is still necessary for improvement and permanency.
2. The frequency of practice and the opportunities to respond must be high for students to master a skill.
3. Short duration and high quality practice tends to yield better results, so variety in activities is beneficial. This also keeps students on task.
4. Goals or objectives must be established to give students focus and to aid in assessment.
5. Direct, early feedback is given to both prevent errors and redirect students towards the goal.

PROVIDING FEEDBACK FOR MOTOR SKILLS

Feedback is the information that teachers provide to students to improve motor skills. Types of feedback include general, specific, positive, negative, and constructive. **General** feedback is vague and not focused on the skill performance. It includes statements like "good job" and "nice shot." **Specific** or descriptive feedback is explicit and focuses on the skill action. An example of specific feedback is, "You demonstrated early preparation of your racket by moving it behind you before

17

striking the ball." **Positive** feedback is praise and focuses on what is correct, while **negative** feedback focuses on what is wrong. Both positive and negative feedback can be either general or specific. **Constructive** feedback gives specific details on what the student is doing incorrectly and explicit details on how to improve. An example of constructive feedback is, "You are standing up too straight during your golf swing. You need to keep your knees bent as you make contact with the ball." Students often perceive constructive feedback as negative, therefore, the three-step **sandwich method** of providing feedback is recommended:

1. **Positive specific feedback** is given on what the student is doing well.
2. **Specific constructive feedback** is given on what is wrong and why or how it impedes success.
3. **Positive specific feedback** completes the feedback loop by giving explicit cues on how to correctly perform the skill.

TYPES OF FEEDBACK

When giving student feedback, multiple approaches should be employed, including verbal (e.g., talking), visual (demonstration, images, video), and kinesthetic (student practice). As students move kinesthetically in physical education, it is often recommended to use the **tell-show-do** method to ensure that verbal (tell), visual (show), and kinesthetic (do) types of feedback are reinforced to optimize student learning. This approach is further enhanced by providing video feedback, a type of visual feedback that has shown to have a significant impact on student learning. Similar to other types of feedback, video feedback works best when accompanied by verbal and visual cues, and must be used consistently to have the greatest impact.

Perceptual-Motor Development

FLEISHMAN'S PERCEPTUAL-MOTOR ABILITIES AND PHYSICAL PROFICIENCY ABILITIES

Fleishman's taxonomy of motor abilities consists of perceptual-motor abilities and physical proficiency abilities. **Perceptual-motor abilities** are the sensory motor aspects of how the body interprets and responds to the environment. These perceptual-motor abilities include reaction time, rate control, aiming, manual and finger dexterity, control precision, and arm-hand steadiness. In contrast, Fleishman's **physical proficiency abilities** include both skill-related and health-related fitness components or the physiologic aspects of motor ability. The abilities are less dependent on the environment. Health-related examples of physical proficiency abilities include muscular strength, muscular endurance, flexibility, and cardiovascular endurance. Skill-related examples include coordination, power, speed, and balance. Both motor ability categories influence skill development and motor performance. Optimal performance is increased when both are utilized, which can be developed and refined through practice and training. Further, the rates of development and improvement depend on one's abilities, which are determined by biological and physiological influences.

PERCEPTUAL-MOTOR DEVELOPMENT

Perceptual-motor skills are needed to perform the fundamental movement skills. While perceptual motor abilities are genetic, they are developed according to stage of development and through practice. Perceptual-motor development is impacted or enhanced by auditory, visual, and kinesthetic discrimination. **Auditory discrimination** is the ability to differentiate between sounds (e.g., loud or soft, the sound of a cow versus the sound a dog). **Visual discrimination** allows students to differentiate between images (people, sizes, shapes, colors, objects). **Kinesthetic discrimination** is the ability to detect small changes in muscle movement, which involves large gross motor movements. The ability to discriminate in all of these areas will foster perceptual-motor development, whereas the inability in one or more of these areas of discrimination will make it more difficult to develop perceptual-motor skills.

VISION AND COORDINATION

Vision is a perceptual ability that aids in balance and coordination, as the information received through the eyes is transmitted to the muscles and the inner ear, which informs or detects movement and a movement response. As such, vision helps with equilibrium, which then helps during physical activities. Performing an activity such as standing or walking with the eyes closed illustrates the impact that vision has on coordination, as the ability to see the environment reduces the difficulty of movement. Vision training helps with other perceptual-motor skills, including eye tracking, movement precision, reaction time, peripheral vision, improved hand-eye coordination, and improved visual discrimination.

HEARING AND PERCEPTUAL MOTOR DEVELOPMENT

Similar to vision, the ability to hear also impacts perceptual-motor skills, including reaction time, as the sound alerts or prepares the body for the response (e.g., hearing a ball thrown outside the peripheral view). Activities that start with sound (e.g., verbal command, whistle, bell, horn) require auditory senses to transmit information to the brain, which informs movement. Hearing impairments slow down perceptual motor response. Using audition to improve perceptual-motor skills often combines verbal cues in unison with tactile learning, or learning through touch, especially for fine motor activities (e.g., catching a ball after hearing "hands out in front" or "get ready").

RELATIONSHIP BETWEEN AWARENESS AND PERFORMANCE

The kinesthetic system (sensory) involves proprioception and joints, muscles, and tendons, as well as receptors of the skin, ears, and eyes. It is largely responsible for body awareness and spatial awareness. Exposure to activities that involve gross motor movements combined with multiple sensory experiences (touch, sound, sight) enhances perceptual-motor performances. Perceptual-motor performances include an awareness of the body's position when stationary (e.g., upright, seated) and during movement (e.g., hands out front when falling forward to prevent injury), which requires balance. This is also developed through a variety of kinesthetic experiences.

Factors Affecting Motor Development and Performance

CONSTRAINTS AND MOTOR PERFORMANCE

Constraints are boundaries that limit or promote movement options. **Individual constraints** have two sub-categories: 1) structural constraints, which include physical body structures (e.g., height, weight, gender), and 2) functional constraints, which include psychological (e.g., arousal) and cognitive (e.g., IQ) conditions. **Task constraints** include movement goals, game rules, and equipment used in movement and games. Examples of task constraints include ball size (e.g., women's vs men's basketball size) and game rules (e.g., regulation or modified rules). Adjusting ball size can make the task easier or more difficult. **Environmental constraints** include external factors and also have two sub-categories: 1) **physical environment**, which includes the space (e.g., indoor or outdoor), lights, temperature, and weather, and 2) **sociocultural environment**, which includes social and cultural aspects that impact physical activity engagement and may include gender (e.g., beliefs that girls should not be engaged in physical activity or develop muscular bodies), race, ethnicity, religion, and social class.

ALBERT BANDURA'S SOCIAL LEARNING THEORY

Social or observational learning theory acknowledges that one's behavior influences others and vice versa. Three elements of social learning theory are **modeling** (watching others), **reinforcement** (rewarding or penalizing), and **social comparison** (the evaluation of skills to the model or a peer). For example, demonstrations, which include learning through observation or the ability to follow a model, are social learning theory methods used in physical education settings. The downside of this theory is that teachers are unable to control all observational learning, since students can learn or observe motor skills outside of class. To ensure effectiveness of observational learning, Bandura suggests a four-step process:

1. **Attention:** students must focus instructional or skill cues
2. **Retention:** students need to remember the demonstrated model (reinforced by skill cues and mental imagery)
3. **Motor reproduction:** students must practice or try to replicate the demonstration
4. **Motivation:** the teacher needs to motivate students to increase their desire to imitate the performance. Reinforcement is often used at this stage.

By including these steps, students are better able to achieve both the psychomotor and cognitive aspects of motor skill acquisition.

IMPACT OF EMOTIONAL DEVELOPMENT ON MOTOR PERFORMANCE

The ability to control and recognize emotions (e.g., anger, happiness) impacts motor performance. **Emotional self-regulation** is the control of emotions that starts to develop during infancy and becomes more refined by the age of six. **Emotional knowledge** is the awareness of emotions in other people. **Emotional development** is important because students need to manage emotions in order to focus on instruction. Physical activities that foster positive emotions contribute to positive self-esteem. **Self-esteem** is how one feels about themselves. Positive self-esteem can lead to **competence motivation**, which is the desire to continue to engage in physical activities even when difficult. **Self-efficacy** is the belief in one's ability to perform motor skills. Experiences that foster negative emotions can result in low competence motivation, low self-efficacy, and even disengagement or non-participation in physical activities. As such, increasing student successes in physical education classes fosters the development of competence motivation and self-efficacy.

PSYCHOLOGICAL STIMULATION AND PERFORMANCE

Arousal is the activation of physiological and psychological responses that vary in intensity from resting to extreme happiness. **Anxiety** is a collection of negative feelings that include fear, worry, and nervousness. A person in a state of anxiety is in a state of arousal, but a person in a state of arousal may or may not be in a state of anxiety. As arousal increases, motor performance tends to increase. According to the Yerkes-Dodson **inverted-U hypothesis**, however, after arousal exceeds the performer's highest level of arousal, performance tends to regress. Some individuals are able to perform well in high-arousal situations, which is dependent on skill level and experience. Those who are predisposed to **trait anxiety**, or anxiety in non-threatening environments, don't do well in high-arousal environments. **State anxiety,** on the other hand, is a temporary state of anxiety and is only triggered in certain situations (e.g., experienced when serving a volleyball in front of others but not when serving alone). Those with high trait anxiety, however, tend to have high state anxiety in high-pressure situations when compared to those with low trait anxiety.

EVALUATING MOTOR SKILLS

Techniques used to evaluate motor skills include observation and comparison to the model or skill cues. Video analysis software (e.g., Coach's Eye) is also effective, as students' skills are performed

and recorded, then replayed simultaneously with the model performance or skill cues, which is used to evaluate strong and weak performance areas. Self-assessments, in which the student checks their performance according to the model or cues, can also be used. Pre-assessment and post-assessments of skills is another way to evaluate improvement in motor skills. Tracking student performance over time also provides information on the consistency or stability of a performance and evaluates whether students are able to transfer skills or adapt to other situations.

Detecting Errors in Motor Performance

Techniques used to detect errors in motor performance include familiarizing students with the appropriate skill tasks. Using videos tends to work best, as they can be replayed. Students should practice skills, observe their performance, and compare it to the desired outcome (self-assessment and reflection). During this strategy, students should be encouraged to identify and solve their own skill problem and follow it with practice. Attentional focus cues would accompany the video analysis of the skills so that students can develop an understanding and vocabulary for error detection. This technique helps students pay attention to relevant information and begin to detect and correct errors independently.

Providing Corrective Feedback

Research shows that the best approach to providing effective **error-based** or **corrective feedback** is to surround the error-based feedback with positive feedback, which is widely known as the sandwich method. The focus should be on the desired outcome rather than the error. Therefore, providing skill cues to direct students to the appropriate movement pattern should be given. For example, if a student does not pivot the back foot during the overhand throw, the cue might be "squish the bug" for younger students or "pivot the back foot" for older students—both cues tell the students what to do rather than focus on what they are doing incorrectly.

Delivering Effective Feedback

To provide effective feedback, the developmental stage or level of the student must be considered. After consideration of the student's level, the activity (or sport), and the feedback schedule, frequency, timing, and precision should all be considered. The interests and motivations of students are also important. For example, a beginner is more likely to respond well to error correction feedback to help improve the action or skill, while this type of feedback would be ineffective for an advanced student because they are able to self-detect and correct their own errors. For **unmotivated** or disinterested students, feedback that focuses on the performance of correct actions or skills is more beneficial because this type of feedback fosters engagement in the activity. The amount and precision of feedback varies according to student level, where more feedback is generally given to beginners and tapers off as students progress to higher levels. Feedback should also be vague during the beginner stage and become more precise as students improve.

Elements and Characteristics of Movement

Locomotor Movement

Locomotor movements are fundamental movement skills that allow an individual to move from one place to another. There are eight locomotor movements: walking, skipping, jumping, hopping, leaping, sliding, galloping, and running. Children perform most locomotor movements naturally, however, they are developed through play and practice. Most children are proficient in the locomotor movements by age eight. Learning these skills helps students learn how and where the body moves and aids in movement efficiency. Locomotor movements are used to teach movement concepts, including **pathways** (e.g., straight, zigzag), **directions** (e.g., forward, backward), and **time** and **speed** (e.g., fast and slow).

NON-LOCOMOTOR MOVEMENT

Non-locomotor skills are fundamental movements that consist of moving without traveling. Bending, twisting, curling, stretching, reaching, pulling, turning, and swaying are types of non-locomotor movements. **Movement concepts** often taught with non-locomotor movements include personal space, levels (e.g., low, medium, high), directions (e.g., clockwise and counterclockwise), and relationships with the body (e.g., shape formation like round, narrow, twisted, symmetrical, and asymmetrical). In addition to bending and twisting, **skill themes** that complement non-locomotor movements include balancing, jumping and landing, and transferring weight. As students become proficient in non-locomotor skills, they combine them with locomotor and **manipulative skills** to develop mature patterns of movement (e.g., run while jumping; walk while twisting, shuffling, or sliding; and stretching to catch a ball).

RHYTHMIC ACTIVITIES

Rhythmic activity is the combination of body movements and music or sounds. Common rhythmic activities in physical education include creative movement, dance, and gymnastics. **Creative movements** use the body (with or without sound) to communicate. Creative movement is the cornerstone for dance and gymnastics. Creative movements or creative rhythms are designed to give students the freedom of expression to move to their own beat without the pressures of formalized dance or gymnastics (e.g., staying on beat to music, performing steps correctly, performing a routine). By design, there are no mistakes when students move creatively, which helps foster **self-efficacy**, or the belief in one's ability to perform motor skills.

GENERAL SPACE AND PERSONAL SPACE

The two types of space in spatial awareness are general space and personal space. **General space** is the space that does not belong to anyone and is used for students to travel during activities. It is the area in gymnasiums and athletic fields where students have plenty of room to move freely without touching someone or something. **Personal space** belongs to the individual—no one should invade another person's personal space. Personal space is private and is often described as an "arms-length" distance. It is recommended that personal space is taught first because this concept can be taught using non-locomotor movements (bending, twisting, marching in place), which gives students time to focus on and develop awareness of how their bodies move without distraction or interference.

KICKING AND DRIBBLING

Kicking and dribbling are **manipulative skills** because the learner manipulates a ball or a piece of equipment. Manipulative skills are more difficult to grasp because they are used alongside locomotor and non-locomotor movements. Kicking is the act of striking an object, such as a ball, with one foot. Kicking is used in games and sports like soccer, kickball, football, and three-ball kick baseball. Foot dribbling, which is small, rapid kicking used to advance the ball forward, which occurs in soccer and speedball. Hand dribbling, which uses the hands to advance the ball forward, is evident in basketball and team handball. When manipulative skills are developed, students are likely to be more engaged in physical activities and sports that use these skills.

MATURE MOTOR PATTERNS FOR JUMPING AND LANDING

Jumping is one of the eight locomotor movements. During the jump, the body becomes airborne after pushing off of a surface with two feet and then returns to the surface with a two-foot landing. The two basic jumps include the vertical jump and the horizontal jump (broad jump). A mature horizontal jumping pattern is when the learner bends the knees, swings the arms back, and then swings the arms forward in unison with the jump. These actions help the jumper propel forward. Bent knees and the arm swing are the same for the vertical jump, however, the jumper's arms swing upward instead of forward. These actions help the jumper propel upward. The **landing** in both jumps require soft or bent knees to absorb the force of the ground and protect the knees. Learning the basic jumps helps with positive transfer of jumps used in sports and other physical activities. Jump patterns and techniques vary among sports and sometimes are actually hops (one-foot take off) like in the long jump, triple jump, and high jump sporting events. Other types of jumps include jumping jacks and tuck jumps. Jumps are also present in jump rope, basketball, volleyball, baseball, diving, and jumps that are performed on a trampoline.

OVERHAND THROW

The **overhand throw** is a manipulative skill that involves propelling an object (usually a ball) with one hand above the shoulder. There are generally three phases to the overhand throw: the preparation phase, the execution phase, and the follow-through. In the **preparation phase**, the non-throwing side faces the target and the arm is back with a high elbow. The action of bringing the arm back with the elbow leading is often referred to as the **wind-up phase**. During the **execution phase**, a step is taken with the opposite foot as the elbow leads the arm forward. During this phase, the trunk of the body rotates internally towards the target. The final phase of the overhand throw is when the arm **follows through** diagonally across the body. A one-handed overhand throw is used in several sports, including baseball, softball, basketball, football, and team handball.

STRIKING SKILLS

Striking with an implement is a manipulative skill where an object (e.g., ball) is struck with another object (e.g., racket, paddle, baseball bat, golf club). The implement becomes an extension of the user's body. Striking with implements is taught during the latter part of elementary school as hand-eye coordination and visual tracking are needed to produce mature motor patterns. Further, there are two objects that students have to focus on: the implement and the ball. This increases the complexity of the skill. To prepare students to strike with an implement, striking with body parts (e.g., hands) followed by rackets and paddles is the recommended progression. Longer implements (baseball bat, golf club) increase the difficulty of the skill and should be taught last. There are a variety of physical activities that involve striking with an implement, including golf, baseball, tennis, pickleball, badminton, cricket, and racquetball.

Promoting Student Motor Development

USING ANIMAL WALKS TO AID IN THE DEVELOPMENT OF MOVEMENT SKILLS

Animal walks are fun, simple activities that help students develop gross motor skill movements (locomotor and non-locomotor). Animal walks help students gain understanding of body awareness, body control, spatial awareness, effort, directions, and levels as only the body is needed to accomplish them. Animal walks also allow students to use their imaginations by drawing on previous animal movement knowledge and experiences. Teachers can also check for movement concept understandings by how students respond to animal cues. Examples of animal walk cues include "walk like a sloth," to illustrate the concept of slow movement; "move like a cheetah," to illustrate the concept of fast movement; "show me how an elephant moves," which illustrates a large shape and slow speed; and "slide like a snake," which illustrates a low level and curved pathway. Students also develop strength ("crawl like a bear"), cardiovascular fitness ("run like a fox"), and improve flexibility ("stretch like a dog") from engaging in animal walks, which are needed for more complex skills (chasing, fleeing).

PROMOTING STUDENTS' DEVELOPMENT OF MANIPULATIVE SKILLS

Manipulative activities require the interaction of gross motor and fine motor skills. Strategies used to build manipulative skills include using a variety of manipulable objects. For example, when teaching catching and throwing, different sizes, shapes, and textures of throwing objects should be used with varied distances, targets, and speeds. Performing manipulative skills without locomotor movements before adding locomotor movements also aids in the development of manipulative skills and provides a foundation for game-play actions. An example of this would be to have students start by playing a stationary passing game, then follow that with a game that requires students to run three steps before passing.

CHASING, FLEEING, AND DODGING GAMES

Students should be introduced to chasing, fleeing, and dodging skills after they have demonstrated proficiency in the locomotor movements. Students should also have an understanding of spatial awareness, as chasing, fleeing, and dodging are more complex due to combination movements that often include manipulative skills. It is ideal to teach these activities outdoors to give students a lot of space for safety. Clear boundaries also help facilitate these skills. Tag games are often used to develop chasing, fleeing, and dodging skills where there are one or more chasers, while others are fleeing (running) and dodging (bending or ducking) to avoid getting tagged by the chaser. These movements further promote and enhance the movement concepts of **effort** (speed), **relationships** (with others), and **space** (movement with others within boundaries), which are the skills needed to participate in manipulative games (e.g., basketball, soccer, tennis). As such, these are the foundational elements of defensive and offensive strategies.

USING PARTNER ACTIVITIES TO TEACH LOCOMOTOR AND NON-LOCOMOTOR MOVEMENTS

Strategies used to teach locomotor and non-locomotor movements during partner activities include mirroring, matching, and leading and following. **Mirroring** is when partners are positioned face-to-face and one partner copies the other, **matching** is when partners are positioned side-by-side and one partner copies the other, and **leading and following** is when one partner leads and the other follows. Traveling while mirroring, matching, and leading and following are other strategies used to teach locomotor and non-locomotor movements in pairs. It can be beneficial to have students who are proficient in the movements lead first in order to help the developing students learn the mature movement patterns.

REFINEMENT OF MANIPULATIVE SKILLS

Developmentally appropriate techniques that can aid in the **refinement of manipulative skills** include demonstrations, written and verbal cues, feedback (peer, self, teacher), and video analysis. To further aid in the refinement of manipulative skills, multiple objects with various shapes, textures, and sizes should be used, as well as combination fine and gross motor activities. Student choice and gradual progressions (easy to difficult tasks) increase student motivation to participate in skill development activities. There should also be several opportunities for students to practice, or opportunities to respond, in order to refine skills, which requires an adequate amount of equipment (2-1 ratio). Station practice can be used to facilitate the refinement of skills in isolation at various learning stages, and small-sided games allow students to put skills into practice.

REFINEMENT AND INTEGRATION OF RHYTHMIC ACTIVITIES

Teacher-led movements aid in the refinement and integration of rhythmic activities. This technique allows students to follow the movements of the teacher. Students can also create their own movement patterns or routines by incorporating the movement concepts and integrating locomotor, non-locomotor, and manipulative skills. For example, students might be given 6 to 12 criteria that include the fundamental movement skills and movement concepts. These may include tasks such as four locomotor movements, two rolls, two body shapes, two levels, four balances with different bases of support, and ending on two feet. This example includes both locomotor and non-locomotor movements and several movement concepts, but may also include equipment like balance beams, balls, and ribbons. For students struggling in any of the respective skills, **modifications** or **remediations** should be used. For example, if a student is unable to perform a forward roll, a cheese mat may be useful to give the student more force to turn around the axis of rotation while providing more cushion than regular mats. A student might also use a beanbag between the chin and chest to keep the ball-shaped position needed for the forward roll, which makes it easier to rotate. For students who excel in the forward roll, they should be given additional challenges or **extensions**, like performing a dive roll or multiple rolls in succession.

LOCOMOTOR SKILL INTEGRATION AND REFINEMENT

Using **movement concepts** (spatial awareness, effort, relationships) along with locomotor movements will aid in skill integration and refinement. Adding movement concept tasks helps move students from the basic locomotor movements to more mature movement patterns that are used in games, sports, and other physical activities. Examples of movement concept tasks include walk fast, walk slow, walk on your tip toes, walk on the low beam, walk on the high beam, walk in a circle, walk in a zigzag pattern, walk clockwise, walk counterclockwise; jump high, jump low, jump over, jump alone, jump with a partner; crawl under, crawl in a circle; hop on top, hop over. Another technique is to combine locomotor and non-locomotor movements. For example, run to the cone, touch your toes, leap and hold, jump and turn. Participation in **small-sided and tag games** also aid in the refinement of locomotor skills by giving students optimal opportunities to practice skills. Students are also challenged to transfer movements performed in isolation to performing the skills with obstacles, defenders, boundaries, and rules. Game play criteria requires students to integrate locomotor and non-locomotor movements and movement concepts independently, which fosters thinking and decision-making.

REFINEMENT AND INTEGRATION OF NON-LOCOMOTOR SKILLS

Incorporating the movement concepts (spatial awareness, effort, relationships) will aid in the refinement of non-locomotor movements. Movement concepts help students move from the basic non-locomotor movements to more mature movement patterns that are used in dance, gymnastics, and other physical activities. Examples of non-locomotor movements and (movement concept) tasks include bend one leg, bend two legs, bend one arm, bend your fingers, bend your head up and down (relationship with the body, personal space, and levels); balance on one or multiple body parts; balance on your tip toes; balance in a squat position; twist right, and twist left (relationships with the body and objects, direction, levels). Another technique is to combine non-locomotor movements, which helps with skill integration. For example, balance on one foot while bending the support or non-support leg, or raise and extend (levels and balance) one arm and the opposite leg forward (direction).

COMBINATION MOVEMENT PATTERNS

The overhand throw is a multi-action skill that combines non-locomotor actions with a manipulative skill. Without a ball, all of the movements in the overhand throw are non-locomotor (e.g., non-traveling position, with bending and extending the arm, twisting the torso, and pivoting the foot). The rear or throwing foot pivots simultaneously as the arm, hips, and trunk rotate towards the target. Body weight is evenly distributed on both feet before throwing actions start. The lead foot lifting prior to taking a step forward causes the body to lean slightly sideways, which transfers the thrower's body weight to the rear foot and the body is balanced momentarily on one

foot. As the lead foot takes a step and lands, the balance and weight transfer to the lead foot until the follow-through motion is completed.

BALANCE AND WEIGHT TRANSFER DURING THE FORWARD ROLL

The forward roll combines non-locomotor and traveling skills. Movement concepts involved in the forward roll include shape formation (C-shape), balancing on different bases of support and weight transfer (hands, feet, back), and effort (speed). Students should be competent in basic weight transfer tasks before performing the forward roll. Students can practice weight transfer tasks that include foot to foot, from the feet to the hands, and in rocking motions. These actions can progress to being performed on or with equipment or being held (balancing) longer. Rolls that are generally taught before the forward roll include sideways (log and pencil rolls) and the forward shoulder roll. Before teaching the forward roll, students should be strong enough in the arms to support their bodies to reduce the risk of neck and back injuries. Cues to help students perform the forward roll include: 1) squat or crouch down in a C-shape, 2) chin to chest, 3) hips up, 4) push-off hands and feet, 5) body tight, 6) roll onto feet.

AGILITY AND BALANCE

Agility is the ability to move quickly in various directions while maintaining control. Agility is evident in most physical activities and sports. An example of agility is running or shuffling quickly in a zigzag shape, which is a common skill pattern performed in basketball and soccer. Agility is also evident during invasion games when players quickly transition from offense to defense. Agility requires coordination, speed, and balance. **Balance** is what keeps the body stable and upright, which helps keep the body in control. Balance is often highlighted in dance and gymnastics. However, agility is also evident in these activities when performers quickly change directions during sequences.

COMMON COMBINATION STEPS AND SEQUENCING USED IN LINE DANCES

Line dances are dances that can be performed in large groups without a partner, and include locomotor and non-locomotor movements. Basic line dance steps include steps forward, backward, clockwise, counterclockwise, diagonally (three steps and tap), right and left (step touch), or sideways (step-together-step). The grapevine, shuffle, rock steps, taps, and half-turns and quarter-turns are also frequently used. The music used for most line dances is a 4/4 beat, which is a medium to fast tempo. Steps are counted to a 4/4 beat, which usually ends with a tap before changing directions.

An example of a basic step sequence is:

1-4 counts/beats	Walk/step forward and tap
5-8 counts/beats	Walk/step forward and tap
9-12 counts/beats	Grapevine right
13-16 beats	Grapevine left
Repeat	

VERBAL CUEING

Verbal cues reinforce desired movement outcomes and help students perform and improve movement skills. **Verbal cues** are action verbs that should be just a few words or less, usually three or four words, as students are better able to focus their attention and remember short phrases.

Example cues for the overhand throw:

Cue	Desired skill outcome
Squash the bug	Reminds students to pivot as they conduct overhand throw
Pick up the telephone	Wind up phase for the overhand throw
Buckle your seatbelt	Follow-through diagonally across the body

Verbal cues are more effective when coupled with demonstrations and written or visual cues.

KINESTHETIC FEEDBACK

Kinesthetic feedback utilizes proprioception to relay messages from muscles, tendons, and joints to the spinal cord to respond to movement commands. Intrinsic feedback or the knowledge of performance are other terms used for kinesthetic feedback. Kinesthetic feedback allows the performer to feel the movement, which helps skilled performers correct errors. Performers can only correct feedback for slow movements, which occurs at subconscious and conscious levels. When movements are slow, smooth, and continuous, like walking on a balance beam, they are subconsciously compared to previous motor patterns, which aids in the refinement of the skill or routine. At the conscious level, the movements are slow, jerky, or both slow and jerky, like when performing a squat. As such, the kinesthetic feedback is conscious and coupled with visual feedback. Therefore, if one squat was ill-performed, the performer has time to correct the errors before performing another squat. Kinesthetic feedback can be improved through practice and refined by also providing visual feedback (pictures, video) and verbal cues to help with the execution.

VIDEO ANALYSIS FOR FEEDBACK

Video recordings have shown to be more beneficial than other types of feedback because students can watch a demonstration or see their actions and movements, especially when slowed down. Videos can also be replayed. When students are able to view their own performance, it provides instant feedback on the quality or knowledge of performance (technique, skill execution), which other visual aids cannot do. Further, students often believe that they are performing a skill correctly until they view their performance. Video analysis is often considered the gold standard when giving feedback, but to increase effectiveness, it should be used consistently and be paired with verbal feedback. Teachers can also post video demonstrations and analysis online for students for ongoing review to further develop skill competencies.

Movement Concepts and Biomechanical Principles

MOVEMENT CONCEPT OF FLOW

Flow is the contrast between smooth and jerky movements, and the contrast between free and bound movements. **Smooth** movements are fluid, and cues often used to convey this concept are "glide," "melt," and "ooze." In contrast, **jerky** movements are rigid, and cues used to describe this include "rough" and "bouncy." Another type of smooth movement is **free**, in which the movements appear as if the movement is controlling the body rather than the body controlling the movement. An example of free movement is a dancer or an ice skater who spins effortlessly, or someone running downhill without the ability to stop. These movements tend to be fast, which reduces the amount of control the performer has over their movements. In contrast, **bound** movements are always voluntary and controlled and appear tense or stiff at times, like when lifting a heavy object.

BIOMECHANICAL PRINCIPLES INVOLVED IN THE LEAP

Biomechanical principles that are evident during the leap include **power** and **force.** The movement concept categories that are evident are **spatial awareness** (moving through general space), **effort** (force of the leap), and **relationships** with the body and surface. **Power** is strength multiplied by speed (strength × speed), which is generated by the amount of leg force (effort) used during the push-off phase of the leap. The **center of mass** is the equal distribution of the body's weight, which is illustrated during the airborne and landing phases of the leap. Children need to be aware of the relationship of their bodies in-flight and at a medium or high level (spatial awareness).

MOVEMENT CONCEPTS OF TIME AND FORCE

Effort is the movement concept category that includes time, force, and flow. **Time** is either fast or slow, which is the speed, beat, or pace in movement. Fast and slow are often illustrated through dance movements to different music tempos. Distance events like cross country or 100-meter runs and the timing of actions when striking a pitched ball are also evidence of time in physical activity and sports. Changes in time are elicited when the teacher provides opportunities for students to increase (acceleration) and decrease (deceleration) speed at different rates. Force is either strong or light. **Force** is evident in every physical activity because skeletal muscle force is required to move the body. However, the appropriate amount of force to use when performing a certain task (e.g., striking a pitched ball) is learned through practice. Example cues of force are: "stomp hard when you walk," or "walk like a feather" to illustrate and contrast strong and light forces.

SPATIAL AWARENESS AND THE MOVEMENT CONCEPT OF SPATIAL DIRECTIONS

Direction is one movement concept under **spatial awareness** (where the body moves). There are several **directions** or routes the body can take that include traveling forwards and backwards; clockwise and counterclockwise; right and left; up and down, and diagonally. **Spatial directions** are often grouped and taught in pairs (e.g., forwards and backwards) for better conceptual understanding. Proficiency in the directions helps build a strong foundation for combining movement patterns that occur during rhythmic activities and team sport transitions (offense to defense), which often require agility or the quick change in direction.

MOVEMENT CONCEPT OF RELATIONSHIPS WITH OBJECTS

Similar to directions, **relationships with objects** are often grouped in pairs and include on and off, under and over, behind and through. Relationships with objects are taught before relationships with people because there is more predictability with objects. Objects used in physical education include balls, balloons, scarves, cones, ropes, hula hoop boundaries, goals, discs, and targets. These skills are taught alongside locomotor (e.g., walk behind your ball) and non-locomotor (e.g., stand behind your ball) movements. Activities that involve objects allow for fine and gross motor developments that are needed in more complex manipulative activities and games (soccer, basketball).

BIOMECHANICAL PRINCIPLES IN SPORTS AND PHYSICAL ACTIVITIES

Exercise biomechanics and **sport biomechanics** involve the study of forces (internal and external) that impact human movement during physical activity and sports with the goal to improve performance. To help improve performance, biomechanics focuses on improvements in technique, equipment, training, injury prevention, and rehabilitation. Common units of measure used in biomechanics include length (how far or long), time (how much time it takes to complete a task), and mass and inertia (weight and resistance of a body or a piece of equipment), all of which can promote or impede performance.

BUOYANCY AND DRAG IN SWIMMING

Buoyancy is the ability to float in water or air. **Drag** is the amount of resistance that occurs in the air, water, and the body that can negatively impact one's buoyancy. **Body type,** or the amount of muscle mass and fat mass in the body, is critical for buoyancy. For example, fat mass floats more easily than muscle mass, therefore, students with more muscle mass and little fat will have a more difficult time staying afloat and an easier time sinking than students with less muscle mass and more fat mass. To compensate for drag from the water and body, swim techniques are designed to keep the body afloat, including arm strokes, leg kicks, body position, and breathing techniques. Staying in a **streamlined**, or straight, position and synchronizing breathing with strokes also helps one stay afloat. Relaxing muscles and not fully filling the lungs with air also aids in buoyancy and reduces drag.

PHYSICAL LAWS IN MOVEMENT

Newton's first law of motion is the **law of inertia**, which states that the objects or the body will continue to move or remain unmoved until met with an unbalanced force. The **moment of inertia** is the difficulty in getting a body or object to rotate around an axis. The goal is to reduce the moment of inertia. During the forward roll, the performer pushes off, or applies **force**, with the hands and feet, which moves the body forward and increases **angular velocity,** or the increase in speed around an axis (or the angle turned through per second). The **moment of inertia** will depend on the position, size, and speed of the performer to determine how easy or difficult it will be to roll. Making the body small and compact, with the chin tucked in, and pushing off with great force makes it easier to roll forward because this increases the **angular momentum**, or the **angular velocity** multiplied by the **moment of inertia**. The rolling motion will continue until met with greater force (law of inertia) of the feet or body landing on the floor or mat.

ROLE OF GRAVITY IN BALANCE AND STABILITY

Gravity is an external force that attracts a body or object towards the earth's center and is commonly referred to as the gravitational pull. **Balance** is the ability to stay in an upright position or maintain equilibrium and an equal distribution of body weight on all sides. **Stability** is the body's ability to regain balance after displacement. Stability is impacted by the size of the base of support, weight of the object, and the height of the center of gravity. Since the body is dynamic, its center of gravity can change. As such, the body is able to accomplish stability by changing stances and body positions during movement activities. For example, while surfing, the surfer (body weight) has to bend the legs and extend the arms (a change in body position) with a wide stance (a change in stance) on a surfboard to maintain stability and prevent from falling.

FORCE PROJECTION AND ABSORPTION

Absorption is the body's ability to absorb or reduce the kinetic energy of an object by applying negative force (e.g., catching a ball). The force is absorbed in the muscles, which helps protect the body (bones). Another example of absorption is when landing from a jump. However, the distance or height of the jump can impact the amount of force that can be absorbed, and if too great (e.g., jumping from a 10-story building or into an empty swimming pool), injury and potential death can occur. For some activities, the body is unable to safely absorb kinetic energy, therefore, additional absorption is created. For example, sand is added to the long and triple jump pit, and a mat is used for high jump landing, which are safety measures used to prevent injury.

BIOMECHANICAL PRINCIPLES IN THE OVERHAND THROW

Biomechanical principles used during the wind-up, release, and follow-through phases of the overhand throw include force, torque, acceleration, and the angle of release. **Force** is mass multiplied by acceleration ($F = m \times a$), or the amount of push or pull of an object or body. **Torque** is the force used during twisting actions that often cause rotation. Torque is evident at the shoulder joint during the wind-up phase or external rotation. Torque is also evident during the twisting action or internal rotation of the abdominal trunk during the follow-through phase. **Acceleration** is an increase in speed and **deceleration** is a decrease in speed. Acceleration occurs during the release of the ball, which is often called the speed of release. The **angle of release** is also evident, which is the point that the ball is released at the shoulder joint.

BIOMECHANICAL ERRORS FOR AN OVERTHROWN BALL

An overthrown ball is often the result of throwing too hard (applying too much force), the angle of release being too large, performing little to no follow-through, or a combination of these errors. To correct the overthrown ball, right-hand students should release the ball at the 2 o'clock position as if facing a clock on the wall, and 10 o'clock for left-hand students to adjust the angle and the timing of the release. "Buckle the seat belt" is a cue that can be used for students to follow through diagonally across the body of the throwing arm, or at the 7 o'clock position for right-hand throwers and 5 o'clock for left-hand throwers. The follow-through helps with speed, but also keeps the ball in line with the target.

BIOMECHANICAL ERRORS IN A FREE THROW

A missed free throw can be the result of the shooter lacking upper body strength or leg strength, thus the force applied is not enough for the ball to reach the rim. There may not be enough flexion in the knees to aid in more power. The shooter may be shooting from the palm of the hands rather than rolling the ball upward and across the hand. The student might also be shooting upward instead of up and outward. If maturation is the problem, the student can try to shoot the ball underhanded between the legs (aka the "granny shot"), as more power will be generated, thereby giving the ball more lift force. If maturation is not the problem, the student can be cued to "bend the knees," "bend and jump," or "bend and extend" for more power. Releasing the ball between 50 and 60 degrees may also help the student achieve the goal.

BIOMECHANICAL PRINCIPLES IN THE FOREHAND IN TENNIS

The biomechanical principle most evident in the tennis forehand is torque. **Torque** is the twisting force shown in the external and internal rotation during the racket preparation phase of reaching back (external rotation) to the contact and follow-through phases (internal rotation). **Force** is also evident when the racket makes contact with the ball, which is also under the movement concept **effort.** The striking of the ball sends or projects the ball forward (**projectile motion**). The **timing** of the strike is also a movement concept under the effort category. **Spatial awareness** is evident as the player needs to position themselves to make contact with the ball, and the player illustrates relationships with the self (body awareness); the racket and ball (objects); and, if playing against an opponent, the relationship with another. The player may further illustrate spatial awareness by the direction, pathways, and levels based on the angle of the stroke and desired placement of the ball.

SPATIAL CONCEPT OF PATHWAYS

Pathways is a movement concept under the space and spatial awareness (where the body moves) movement concept category. There are three pathways or patterns the body can create when traveling:

- straight, meaning to walk in a straight line
- curved, or moving in a C-shaped or bent pattern or motion
- zigzag, or moving in a Z-shaped or alternating diagonal pattern or motion

These movement concepts are taught alongside locomotor, non-locomotor, and other movement concepts (e.g., speed, directions, levels). To help students conceptualize and apply pathways, pictures of pathways should accompany the definitions, cues, and phrases used. Associating pathways with previously known information like animals, letters, and gym floor lines also aids in understanding. For example, "walk in a circle" conceptualizes a curved shape, whereas "travel in a 'Z' shape and repeat" would help students understand a zigzag shape.

SPATIAL CONCEPT OF LEVELS

Levels are a movement concept under the space and spatial awareness (where the body moves) movement concept category. The body can move at three levels: low, or below the knees (crawling on the ground); medium, or between the knees and shoulders (walking); and high, or above the shoulders (walking on tiptoes). This movement concept is taught alongside non-locomotor movements first, then progresses with locomotor and other movement concepts (e.g., pathways and direction). To help students conceptualize and apply the concept of levels, pictures of examples of the three levels should accompany the definition, cues, and phrases used. Associating the levels with previously known information like animals or the other concepts aid in understanding. For example, "stretch your hands high towards the sky" conceptualizes a high level, while "lie down on your back like a mat" illustrates a low level.

QUALITATIVE BIOMECHANICAL ANALYSIS

Qualitative biomechanical analyses are commonly used by physical education teachers and coaches. There are generally four steps in a qualitative biomechanical analysis that are used to improve movement skills:

1. Develop a description of the best technique and decide on the desired movement to be observed.
2. Observe the student's performance to determine how the student performs.
3. Compare the student's performance to the desired movement and identify and assess errors.
4. Provide feedback and inform the student with skill cues and other information to correct the errors.

BIOMECHANICAL PRINCIPLES NEEDED TO MAINTAIN BALANCE

The key biomechanical principles involved in **balance** are the stance, base of support, and the center of gravity. The **base of support** is the area below a person that involves each point of contact or the parts of the body that are in contact with the surface. For example, when standing (stance), the base of support is the area where the feet are in contact. In a push-up position (stance), the base of support is the area where the hands and feet are in contact. A narrow base of support (e.g., standing on tiptoes) raises the center of gravity and reduces the area of support, thus limiting stability or balance. Adjustments (leaning forward or backward) are made during different activities (forces) to prevent falling. A wide base of support with bent knees is the ideal position for balance as the center of gravity is lowered, thus aiding in stability and the prevention of falling.

IMPROVING BODY MECHANICS FOR SAFE AND EFFICIENT MOVEMENT

Injury prevention, rehabilitation techniques, and equipment are improvement areas of focus under the study of biomechanics. Sporting injury prevention techniques identified through biomechanics research include bending the knees on landings during gymnastics and adapting the tennis backhand technique to include a neutral wrist position that reduces tennis elbow (overuse). An advance in equipment includes running shoes that provide more cushion to absorb more force. Teachers and coaches also demonstrate an understanding of these principles by taking measures

31

such as requiring the use of mats when students practice tumbling skills and the wearing of shin guards during soccer.

MOVEMENT CONCEPTS AND CREATIVE MOVEMENT

Movement concepts help students take simple movements (locomotor and non-locomotor) and make them more dynamic and interesting to create an aesthetic appeal. The movement concepts give students additional guidance on how and where the body can move. For example, walking in a zigzag pathway allows for more dimension of the movement than walking in a straight line. Forming different shapes (V-shape, X-shape, round shape) while combining locomotor and non-locomotor movements also helps with the aesthetics of movement. Further aiding in the aesthetics of creative movements are the concepts of fast, slow, high, medium, low, jerky, and soft. These concepts help students get comfortable with and refine the fundamental movement skills necessary for dance.

RUNNING PATTERNS IN TEAM SPORTS

In team sports, running patterns are forward and straight and forward and zigzag. Running or jogging backwards may occur during transition play (offense to defense and vice versa). At times, a runner's path may be curved into a clockwise or counterclockwise direction when a player maneuvers to receive a pass or to avoid a defender. Running tends to be fast, but may slow down to a jog or walk. There are also a lot of start and stop patterns (e.g., run-stop-run, run-walk-run, run-jog-run), so runs are intermittent. Runs often change directions quickly, which illustrates agility skills used in these sports.

THROWING PATTERNS IN BASKETBALL AND TEAM HANDBALL

While both basketball and team handball are invasion games that use throwing (or passing) to advance a ball down a court or field, the throwing actions used in each game differ. In basketball, most throws are two-handed chest, bounce, or overhead passes. Sometimes players use one hand to bounce or chest pass, but this technique reduces the power of the pass and is often discouraged. Although a one-handed overhand pass can be used to advance the ball far down the length of the court, it is seldom used. In basketball and team handball, a player has the option to shoot, dribble, pass, fake, or pivot after receiving the ball. In team handball, one-hand overhand throws are most common, however, players sometimes use underhand throws. One-hand bounce passes, chest, and baseball passes are also used. Unlike basketball, which uses jump shots and layups to score, the overhand throw is used to score in team handball against a goalie. The scoring differences are due to the position, size, and height of the goals in each respective sport.

JUMPING PATTERNS USED IN SPORTS AND PHYSICAL ACTIVITIES

Jumping occurs in volleyball, basketball, and jumping rope. It is also central to the high jump, long jump, and triple jump in track and field. Most jumps are vertical, including jump shots and rebounds in basketball, blocking and spiking in volleyball, and while jumping a rope, which consists of an up-and-down motion. Horizontal jumps, however, occur during the standing broad jump, long jump, and triple jump, where the body is propelled forward during the jump. Although the long and triple jumps have a one-foot take-off and two-foot landing, they are still considered jumps. Similar to the track and field jumps, the layup shot in basketball has a one-foot take off and two-foot landing pattern.

Jumping is both an offensive and defensive skill. It can be used to score points in basketball (jump shot) and volleyball (spike). Jumps are also used to prevent opponents from scoring and to gain or maintain possession of the ball (e.g., blocked shot, spike, rebound). Some jumps have a runup or step approach like a layup or spike, while others do not (e.g., jumping rope).

KICKING PATTERNS USED IN SPORTS

Kicking is a manipulative skill that involves striking a ball, object, or body with the foot. Kicking is evident in soccer, kickball, and football. The basic kicking pattern consists of using the top of the foot (shoelaces) to strike behind the ball. Making contact in the center of the ball keeps it on the ground, while contact below the ball propels it in the air. Like throwing, there is a follow-through motion in kicking, however, the kicking follow-through is upward and forward. The hop-step taken by the support, or non-kicking, leg and leaning forward slightly help with power. The placement of the support foot also determines the direction. For example, if the support toes are pointing left, the ball will go in that direction. Soccer skills also include foot dribbling or rapid kicks back and forth between the feet to advance the ball forward. The insides and outsides of the feet are used to dribble in soccer. Punting is a type of kick done for height and distance and is used in soccer and football. The punt consists of kicking a dropped ball and making contact at a 45-degree angle. A step-hop pattern is also used for punting, although the stride is longer.

Individual, Dual, and Team Sports and Activities

CONDITIONING PROGRAMS AND SKILL PROGRESSION TECHNIQUES

Conditioning is the process of getting the body prepared for the physical demands of physical activity and exercise. Conditioning practices are designed to increase health-and skill-related fitness. A general conditioning program consists of a warm-up, health-related movements, skill-related training, and a cooldown with stretching. The intensity of conditioning sessions should gradually progress to reduce the risk of injury or overtraining. This gradual increase is call **progressive overload**, where the intensity of the exercise or activity is above the normal limits. Skill progressions are also used to teach sports, where the easiest form of the skill is introduced and gradually gets more difficult. Skill progressions start at the beginner stage and progressively increase to the advanced stage. A skill progression example for kicking the ball in soccer would be to kick a non-moving ball before kicking a ball in motion or with a partner. In softball, one would strike a ball off of a tee before striking a pitched ball. Each skill builds on the previous skill.

RULES AND SAFETY PRACTICES IN INDIVIDUAL AND DUAL SPORTS

Individual and dual sports often include handheld equipment (tennis racket, golf club) that can increase the risk of accidental injury if not used carefully. Students need to look to make sure that people or objects are not in their personal space or striking distance so that they do not hit someone or something. Cones or poly spots are items that can be used to space and mark off waiting and playing areas. Spacing and positioning away from target areas is also crucial during target activities (archery, darts). A proper warm-up should be conducted, and the proper shoes should be worn to reduce injury (ankle strain or sprain). All safety rules must be explained, and consequences for safety violations must be enforced.

DEFENSIVE STRATEGIES IN INVASION GAMES

Defensive strategies used during invasion games include reducing open space, shuffle steps, drop steps, and fast transitions. Strategies used to reduce open space include staying close to the opponent when they are near the goal. The body should be positioned on the goal side to make it more difficult for the opponent to score. The player should also begin with a large angle for passing and gradually decrease it, executing a technique known as closing the passing lanes. Footwork is also important to help the defender travel faster. Shuffle steps are used because they are quick and crossing the feet over one another slows down lateral movement. Drop steps towards the pass are also used to try to intercept or steal the ball. The defensive player should also leave upon the release of the opponent's pass to increase the likelihood of stealing the ball or forcing a turnover.

OFFENSIVE STRATEGIES IN INVASION GAMES

Invasion games are team sports where the objective of the game is to advance an object (ball, puck, Frisbee) down a field or court to score a point into the opponent's goal. While the specific skill actions differ, offensive movements and strategies are similar. Common offensive strategies used are passing, getting open, or creating space, which are used to advance the ball forward and maintain position in order to attack the opponents' goal. Passing strategies include ball or body fakes, or body feigns, to slow down the opponent. Passes should also be quick to avoid getting trapped or defended. In order to receive a pass, players should get open or create space. To create space, sharp movements, or cuts, are made that may include L-cuts and V-cuts to keep steady motion to avoid the defense stealing the ball. Movement in these letter formations help draw the defense away or in the wrong direction. Body fakes and feigns are also effective because they slow down the opposition by confusing the opponent on the direction of the player. To aid with maintaining possession, screens or picks should be used, which is when a teammate uses their body to block an opponent. All of these strategies aid in the goal of attacking or scoring a goal.

EQUIPMENT IN NET AND WALL SPORTS

Net sports have a net that divides the court in half and include striking an object like a ball (volleyball) or shuttlecock (badminton). Some net sports also use rackets (tennis). Wall sports use a ball that is hit off a wall, and some also include rackets (racquetball, squash). Standards (portable poles) are often used to set up volleyball and badminton nets, although some gyms are equipped with built-in standards that lift and lower from the floor. Some schools have outdoor courts, but sports typically played outside can also be played inside gymnasiums. Nets are sometimes interchanged. For example, if volleyball or tennis nets are unavailable, badminton nets might be used and vice versa. Sometimes play occurs without nets or with net substitutes, such as PVC pipes arranged between two cones to represent the height of the net. If court lines are not available, floor tape and cones can be used to establish boundaries.

EQUIPMENT IN COMBATIVE ACTIVITIES

Combative activities include fencing, wrestling, and martial arts. Cardio-kickboxing is a type of combative activity that derived from martial arts. Rather than kicking, punching, or fighting an individual, air punches and kicks are used to improve and maintain health-related and skill-related fitness. Equipment, including punching gloves, mitts, bags, and shin guards, can be used. If equipment is limited, station work can be employed or movements can be done without equipment. For example, while one student uses gloves to punch a punching bag, another student can air punch. Students can switch roles after the allotted time so that all have an opportunity to use the equipment. Equipment should be cleaned after each use or session to avoid passing germs. Fencing is an extracurricular activity that involves a sword or weapon (foil, epee, and saber), a face mask, and a head-to-toe uniform or outfit to protect the body. Wrestling is also an extracurricular activity that involves a thick, large mat, and players wear a singlet and male players wear a groin cup.

RULES FOR PARTICIPANTS AND SPECTATORS

Rules are important to maintain order and promote good classroom management, which helps keep participants, classmates, and spectators safe. Game rules outline the objectives of the game; player positions; movements allowed; boundaries; and fouls or consequences for infractions, like game ejection after committing a flagrant foul. Game rules also govern the expected attire, including clothing, jewelry, and the type of shoe. For example, athletic clothes and shoes are expected to be worn during sporting events and at fitness or workout centers. These expectations are also evident in many physical education programs. Class or gym rules also foster a safe and positive learning environment. Students should be taught the rules and routinely reminded of them. Rules should also be posted for students, players, and spectators. Coaches also have expectations of following the rules and can suffer consequences as well. For example, when coaches exhibit negative behaviors (e.g., yelling at the officials, throwing things, standing when required to sit, or coaching on the court or field), consequences of these violations include team or technical fouls (basketball), yellow and red cards (volleyball and soccer), and ejections from the game (basketball, volleyball, soccer).

DISCIPLINE IN SPORTS

Discipline in sports is the adherence to the game rules and the expectations of the coach or teacher. Discipline also involves actions or practice used to improve skill and fitness. Some players and students have great self-discipline and follow all of the rules and the training involved in sport participation. However, most of the discipline relies on the teacher or coach to enforce consequences for undisciplined behaviors. Physical punishment (e.g., running laps, push-ups) is a form of discipline sometimes used in sports, however, this type of consequence is discouraged. Other types of consequences include the temporary or permanent removal of the activity or a reduction in playing opportunities.

ETIQUETTE IN SPORTS

Etiquette refers to the unwritten rules of conduct that participants and spectators are expected to adhere to. Etiquette helps to promote safety, fair play, and values. **Sportsmanship** is a term associated with sports etiquette, which includes following the rules, "playing hard but fair," accepting the officials' decisions, shaking the opponents' hands after play, and refraining from outbursts and the taunting of players. Wishing the opponent "good luck" and losing without anger are also examples of sportsmanship, as the enjoyment of the game supersedes the outcome. Sports etiquette also includes remaining silent during a free throw, volleyball or tennis serve, and before the start of a track or swim event.

TEAMWORK IN SPORTS

Teamwork is the collective effort of a group to reach a common goal. In dual and team sports, teammates work together to score or win a game. The level of teamwork is dependent on the players, the coach, leadership (e.g., captains and managers), the size of the team, and the amount of time a team has been together. For example, teams of two have fewer distractions and attitudes to manage than teams of six, 11, or 25. Teams that have been together a long time tend to have better social cohesion (the degree to which groups get along) than newly formed groups. Further, the more things that players have in common (skill, age), the more likely a team is to work together. Task cohesion also helps establish teamwork, as the desire to win is so important that the team is more likely to cooperate with each other.

APPROPRIATE PARTICIPANT AND SPECTATOR BEHAVIOR IN SPORTS

Participants are expected to follow the rules of the sport, accept the coaches and referees' decisions, and engage in fair play. In team sports, spectators are expected to make noise and to cheer for their team except during penalty shots or kicks. There are exceptions, such as the fact that spectators tend to make noise during basketball free throws. Spectators are expected to be quiet during golf strokes, tennis and volleyball serves, and at the start of track and swim events. Spectators are also expected to refrain from jeers and profanity.

DIFFERENCES IN ETIQUETTE BETWEEN SINGLE, DUAL, AND TEAM SPORTS

Etiquette differences between single, dual, and team sports are noise level, attire, and warm-up procedures. In team sports, crowd participation is encouraged, therefore there is a high level of noise during game play. In contrast, in individual and dual sports, crowd participation is not encouraged during game play, therefore, the noise level is much lower. The attire also varies. For example, a collared polo shirt is expected to be worn while playing golf, but jerseys are worn in team sports. Jewelry is not worn during team sports, but may be worn during individual and dual sports. Warm-ups also differ. For example, in team sports, opponents tend to have separate warm-up sessions, but in tennis, the opponents warm up with each other (warm-up strokes and practice serves are done collaboratively).

ELEMENTS OF SUCCESSFUL PERFORMANCE IN INDIVIDUAL SPORTS

Self-efficacy is belief in one's ability to perform motor skills. Building a performer's self-efficacy positively impacts performance. According to Bandura, self-efficacy can be enhanced through performance accomplishments, vicarious experiences, persuasion, and physiological state. Goal setting also aids in improving self-efficacy. **Performance accomplishments** include the individual reflecting on previous and current performances to set goals on the desired performance. **Vicarious experience** is learning by observing others complete the desired task (modeling). **Persuasion** is a strategy used to encourage the individual, but the individual must respect and value the person (coach, teacher) who is doing the persuading for it to be effective. Last, the **physiological state** is dependent on the individual's arousal levels and their ability to focus on important tasks. Therefore, for a successful performance, the individual needs to be able to focus on important factors and ignore meaningless information (selective attention) to improve performance outcomes. These elements are also effective in dual and team sports, although there are more variables that affect performance to consider (e.g., teammates).

ELEMENTS OF SUCCESSFUL PERFORMANCE IN DUAL AND TEAM SPORTS

Successful performance in dual and team sports is enhanced with team cohesion, established team roles, and goal setting, which fosters cooperation. Team cohesion is when all members of the group or team have the same goal (to win), which has shown to positively impact team performance. Cooperation can be developed by having identified roles (captains, positions) and acknowledgement of the benefits of informal roles. Also aiding in cooperation is sharing individual goals, formulating group goals, and including everyone in the decision-making process. Training should also be fun but challenging, which contributes to an athlete's performance and satisfaction. Collectively, these factors are the elements of successful performance in dual and team sports.

IMPROVING STUDENTS' PERFORMANCE IN INDIVIDUAL SPORTS

Modeling, mental practice, and physical practice are strategies used to improve students' performance in individual sports. **Modeling** is observing the desired performance skill(s) with the goal of replicating the movements. This can be done by observing a teammate, coach, teacher, or by watching a video demonstration. **Mental practice**, also referred to as mental imagery and mental rehearsal, is visualizing or thinking about the performance or skills to be executed. Mental practice is more effective when used in conjunction with **physical practice**, or performance of the skills.

IMPROVING STUDENTS' PERFORMANCE IN TEAM SPORTS

Practice helps students improve performance in team sports. There are several practice types, including variable practice, massed practice, distributed practice, blocked practice, and serial practice. While all of these types of practices can benefit students' performance in team sports, variable practice has shown most effective. **Variable practice** is performing the same skill in a changing or dynamic environment as it would occur in a game setting. For example, when practicing receiving a pass in soccer, basketball, or flag football, the coach would create different angles and distances for receiving the pass, as the environment is constantly changing. As such, students are better able to respond to the dynamic situations that occur during game play, thus improving performance.

DEVELOPING TEAMWORK

Strategies that help improve teamwork include program structure, communication, goal setting, and shared responsibilities. The **structure of the program** (practices and games) is designed by the coach and includes team organization (time, day, and location of practices; rules; positions; playing time). **Input** (communication) from all members in the group on goal setting (individual and team), **shared responsibilities** (everyone sets up and breaks down the equipment), and team building activities are additional strategies that improve teamwork. Team building activities include trust falls, high-ropes courses, tug-of-war, the human knot, and spending time together in non-sporting activities, which are often done before sports practices begin.

IMPROVING SKILL COMBINATIONS

Part practice is a strategy used to improve skill combinations that are low in organization but high in complexity. **Part practice** is the process of breaking down each segment of the skill before combining the whole movement. For example, the overhand volleyball serve has several parts: the stance, toss, footwork, contact, and follow-through. When using a part practice approach, each part of the serve would be taught in isolation. Each element would build on another before combining all of the elements to perform the serve. Small-sided games also help improve skill combinations, as the combination of isolation skills are put into practice and the opportunities to respond are increased. For example, in a two vs. two game of basketball, players have more opportunities to practice combination skills like dribbling and shooting, dribbling and passing, or shooting and rebounding.

SELECTING SPORTS ACTIVITIES THAT PROMOTE PERFORMANCE

The selection of developmentally appropriate sports activities helps promote performance. The national and statewide physical education standards and physical education curricula are organized by scope and sequence. **Scope and sequence** are a gradual building of concepts and skills that consider the development rather than the age of students. Once skills or concepts are learned, they continue to be promoted, thus refining performance. For example, when striking with an implement, starting with a short-hand implement is introduced before a long-hand implement due to the increase in difficulty. As students learn these skills, the skills are revisited and performed in small-sided or real game play to promote skill refinement, which in turn promotes performance.

SIMPLIFICATION TO PROMOTE PERFORMANCE IN SPORT ACTIVITIES

Simplification is a method used to break down skills to promote performance. An example of simplification for the overhand volleyball serve would be to use a larger or lighter ball such as a beach ball, move closer to the net, or slow down the pace of the serve to allow more time to perform the serve. As students become proficient with the simplified versions, modifications would be gradually eliminated. Simplifying game rules also helps promote performance. For example, during a volleyball rally, a simplified rule may be to allow the ball to hit the floor one time before making a play to help students work on footwork and reaction time needed to make contact with the ball. This simplification slows down the pace of the game to promote passing skills without a lot of interruptions.

ADAPTATIONS AND MODIFICATIONS TO PROMOTE PERFORMANCE IN SPORTS

Adaptations and **modifications** are things that make tasks easier to promote performance. In net activities like tennis, badminton, and volleyball, adaptations and modifications that can be used include lowering the net. In volleyball, the rules can be modified to allow the ball to bounce once on the floor during play to give students more time and opportunities to respond. In tennis, the ball can similarly be allowed to bounce twice. During target activities (archery, throwing), there can be

37

various target distances to accommodate all student levels and abilities. In team sports, the number of players can increase or decrease. Multiple balls can also be used to give more opportunities to respond, and boundaries can be eliminated in both individual and team sports to promote continuous play.

TACTICAL GAMES APPROACH

The **tactical games approach** is a strategy used to teach team sports. The goal is to develop the cognitive aspects of team sports that includes skills, decision-making, and strategies, thus fostering understanding. There is an intentional focus on developing intrinsic motivation. Rather than the direct teaching of skills in isolation that eventually lead up to game play, the tactical games approach uses a whole-part-whole method in which students play the game first after an objective has been presented ("Today, we will focus on how to get open"). The teacher observes student behaviors to determine areas of growth. However, feedback is given in the form of questions (inquiry-based) to the group to help guide the students in solving problems. For example, the teacher might state, "I noticed that Team A had a difficult time getting open. What are some things we can do to get open?" With the teacher's guidance, students brainstorm and share techniques, then implement them during the next game play session. Game play is paused for a debrief session to discuss if and how the objective was met. Students then practice the identified problem(s) and return to play to work on implementing concepts, skills, or strategies in the game that were discussed during the debriefing session.

SPECIFICITY IN PRACTICE

Practice specificity is the practice of skills and movements as they appear in a game rather than in isolation. Practice specificity is often accomplished through small-sided games. For example, in basketball where a game consists of five vs. five, a small-sided game may consist of two vs. two or three vs. three. Instead of 11 vs. 11 in soccer, there may be three vs. three or five vs. five games. A three vs. three game of keep-away could also be used to teach passing and movement skills used in a real game, as the dynamic movements in the skills mimic game play. The inclusion of a referee or line judge also provides a game-like situation where calls, fouls, and other infractions are being made.

Performance Activities and Non-traditional Recreational Activities

JAZZ AND MODERN DANCE

Jazz and modern dance are social dances that require good posture and body alignment, as this is the foundation used in dance. These dances involve constant changes between neutral movements (static or isometric movements that are held for a period of time such as in a stretch) and dynamic movements (active, controlled movements through a full range of motion).

Basic dance skills used in most dance forms include locomotor and non-locomotor movements:

- Bending (non-locomotor)
- Stretching (non-locomotor)
- Rising (non-locomotor)
- Sliding (locomotor)
- Jumping, or leaping (locomotor)
- Darting (locomotor)
- Turning (non-locomotor)

While the steps in jazz and modern dance are similar, as both consist of free and creative movements, jazz dance has faster tempos and more elaborate movements than modern dance, and may include ballet and hip-hop movements. Modern dance tends to include several dance forms, but the movements are more connected to or guided by the music.

DANCE SEQUENCES IN FOLK DANCE AND SQUARE DANCE

Folk dance is a dance form that is the expression of cultural traditions and customs. Folk dances tell stories about a particular group of people, and are part of rituals and ceremonies like weddings, births, funerals, holidays, and social events. Folk dances also express the trials and tribulations marking certain time periods or eras. Sequences and steps used in folk dance include the basic dance steps, but they are performed in accordance to the beat of the music. Folk dances are often performed by several couples (pairs) at one time. Steps include step close, step-cross-step (grapevine), step point, step hop, slide steps, and step swing, and the steps repeat along with the music. While some folk dances may be ethnic dances, **ethnic dances** are associated with or originate from a specific ethnic group's culture (African, Asian, European). **Square dance** has explicit dance moves that are verbally called out (by a caller) along with music. Square dance is performed with four couples, called a set, who are numbered 1, 2, 3, and 4. Couples 1 and 3 are the head couples and face each other, and couples 2 and 4 face each other. Square dances start by bowing or honoring your partner and corner. Some movements are performed as a group, including grand marches. Other movements involve changing partners, such as swing your corner, or steps, including forward and back, do-si-dos, promenades, and circling left or right.

CONDITIONING PROGRAMS FOR DANCE

Conditioning for dance is similar to other forms of physical activity and sport, and should include exercises that address the health-related fitness components. For building cardiovascular endurance and stamina, aerobic dance is effective because it continuously engages large muscle movements needed for dance. Dance also requires muscular strength, muscular endurance, and flexibility, and so a dance conditioning program should incorporate activities that involve muscle contraction and muscle relaxation. Core strength (abdominals and back) is essential for good posture and body alignment is needed for dance. Depending on the goals and needs of the dancer, cardiovascular activities should be done three to five days a week, strength training two or three days a week, and flexibility training four to six days a week.

SAFETY PRACTICES WHEN TEACHING DANCE

Safety considerations in dance include posture and body alignment training; a warm-up (to prepare the body for more vigorous activity); dancing on non-slip floors; having students wear the appropriate footwear; providing water breaks before, during, and after dancing; using damage-free equipment; and a cooldown (to return the body back to normal). Other safety considerations include maintaining adequate spacing so that students do not bump into each other, having the instructor positioned to where all students can be seen, or performing dance in a space that has mirrors for multiple angles of visibility.

EQUIPMENT USED IN DANCE

One of the most common types of equipment used in dance is a sound system or device to play music and speakers or amplifier to project the music. Metronomes can also be used to help keep students on beat. Drums, other percussion tools, and musical instruments can be used to create sounds that accompany dance. A microphone aids in voice projection that can be heard while the music is playing. A wireless microphone allows the teacher to move around during instruction. Dances that involve jumps, leaps, and tumbling may be done on mats. Although not required, dance studios or gyms with mirrors provide a visual of the performer and during teacher-led instruction,

39

allowing for all to be seen. Circus arts such as aerial dances require a high level of expertise, as dancers perform while suspended in the air.

WALKING, JOGGING, AND HIKING

Walking, jogging, and hiking are recreational activities that can be done over a lifespan. These cardiovascular activities are non-competitive, and most people are able to participate with little or no equipment. To improve fitness, these activities should be done several days a week and get progressively more challenging. Increasing the frequency (how often), time (duration), or intensity (effort and speed) of an activity, along with setting goals, can help aid in improving outcomes. For example, a beginner may start with walking for 10 minutes and gradually increase the time by 5-10 minutes every two weeks. To increase the intensity, they might walk faster or hike. One may also start with a 20-minute walk and incorporate intermittent bouts of jogging in between (interval training), which also increases the intensity. Accountability measures also help with improving fitness that involve walking, jogging, and hiking, like the use of pedometers or activity trackers to track or monitor step count, calories burned, distance covered, and elevation (for hiking, walking, or jogging upwards).

ORIENTEERING

Orienteering is an outdoor adventure activity designed to teach students how to use maps and a compass by following routes and finding checkpoints. Each checkpoint has a score, with higher point values for increased difficulty (rough terrain, longer distances). Orienteering involves physical activity (running), and students have to learn how to pace themselves (walk, jog, or run without getting fatigued or "running out of gas"). Maps should be in paper format and a handheld compass is used. Teamwork and decision-making are also involved and can be designed for cooperative and competitive engagement. To help build students' skills with maps and compasses, partners or teams can be given short routes. Students can also create their own maps to use throughout the unit. Because an efficient use of time is critical in orienteering, students must know how to pace themselves. Distance by pace is a common technique used to help students establish a proper pace. Set up practice courses of 100 feet and have students count the number of times one foot (right or left) touches the ground. The number of times the foot touches the ground should be divided by 100, or the course length, to get a pace count. Varying the terrain by distance (e.g., a half-mile to one or two miles) can also help students work efficiently, which is called distance by terrain. In descriptive orienteering, maps are not used. In lieu of maps, bearing (the degrees between map points), distance, and descriptive clues are given to help complete the routes.

SWIMMING SAFETY

Water safety guidelines should be taught before swimming skills. Water safety includes the following:

- Never swim alone
- Jump in water feetfirst
- Avoid attempting to save someone from drowning if untrained
- Do not run on pool decks
- Wear life jackets on boats
- Avoid playing breath-holding games
- Wear proper swim attire

Introductory swimming skills should be taught first and include pool entry and exit, blowing bubbles, opening eyes under water, floating, treading water, and motions or land demonstrations of the swim stroke. The front crawl or freestyle stroke is generally taught first, using the part method because it is a multi-limb activity that includes arm strokes, kicks with the legs and feet, and breathing.

As such, skills are broken down. Examples of skill progression include:

- Floating, both on the front and the back
- Treading water
- Breathing (blowing bubbles from the mouth and nose, alternating breathing)
- Alternating arm action (on land, standing in water, and with flotation device)
- Kicking action (holding onto pool wall and with kickboard)
- Front crawl or freestyle practice – putting the skills together

PERIODIZATION IN SPORTS CONDITIONING

Periodization is a structured training program used by athletes that is broken down into three phases.

1. Phase 1 is the **transition** or **post-season stage**, when athletes are tired and take time off to recover from the season for about three or four weeks. To maintain fitness during this stage, athletes continue to work out, however, they engage in cross-training activities that differ from their regular sports training.
2. Phase 2 is the **preparation** or **pre-season stage.** This is a stage, lasting three to six months, where athletes prepare for competition. There are two sub-phases:
   a. The **general preparatory** phase, where the focus is on fitness
   b. The **specific preparatory** phase, where training is specific to the skills and techniques needed for the sport.
3. Phase 3 of periodization is the **competition phase,** where the athlete maintains fitness and works on sports skills and techniques that enhance competitive play.

BOWLING

Bowling is a recreational activity that involves rolling a ball down a lane with the goal of knocking down 10 pins. It is also a manipulative activity. While bowling pins can be set up in the gym or outside on the ground to help students learn, bowling is generally played at a bowling alley. The bowling ball has three holes, two in the middle for the middle and ring finger and one to the side for the thumb. The **grip** (ball hold) of the bowling ball can cause stress on the forearms, so forearm exercises can be used to strengthen this area. An underhand motion is used to roll the ball using a delivery (approach and release) of one to five steps. The one-step delivery is taught before the other deliveries in progressive order, as it is easier. Students should aim for the pins using an imaginary line from the delivery to the targeted pins. Markers are on the floors at bowling alleys to help guide bowlers. A skills progression example is: stationary, two-hand ball roll; stationary, one-hand ball roll; one-step delivery; and so on. The distance of the pins can also be progressed by starting the pins closer and gradually increasing the distance until they reach regulation distance (60 feet). Lane width can be adjusted as well, from wider to narrower, until reaching regulation bowling width (42 inches).

IMPORTANCE OF RULES AND SAFETY PRACTICES IN VARIOUS RECREATIONAL ACTIVITIES

In swimming and other aquatic activities, rules are important because people can drown quickly in bodies of water. Pool rules also help keep patrons and participants safe (e.g., prohibiting running to avoid slipping and falling, avoiding swimming in extremely cold water to prevent hypothermia). For road activities (cycling, in-line skating) wearing a helmet protects the skull from subsequent injuries (and possibly death) should an accident occur. Individuals engaging in road activities should follow all traffic rules to prevent accidents. Appropriate attire helps protect the body from the elements (e.g., light and loose clothing during the heat, and wick-away layers during the cold). Drinking fluids helps prevent dehydration. For hiking, following hiking trails monitored by park rangers, competence in using a map and compass, and hiking with others are important safety measures that prevent one from getting lost. Sharing the hiking itinerary with someone not hiking is a safety measure that can be used in case one does get lost or injured on the trail. Proper hiking gear (boots, socks, and clothing) prevents slippage and weather-related issues (e.g., sunburn, wind, precipitation). It is also best to stay visible and move to the right so faster hikers can progress. Carrying a cell phone, when possible, is another safety measure to use when hiking.

DISCIPLINE IN VARIOUS RECREATIONAL PURSUITS

To engage in recreational activities, self-discipline is required, especially when no officials, leaders, teachers, or coaches are monitoring practice, training, or safety. Discipline requires that the individual follow the rules of play and engagement along with consistent fitness and skill training that have shown to lead to successful outcomes in recreational activities. Discipline fosters the motivation to train, practice, study the activity, and observe behaviors that will improve performance or outcomes of consistent performance (e.g., cardiovascular fitness). Focusing on the outcome or creating measurable goals and accountability measures (tracking progress, fitness testing, planning) helps instill discipline.

GENERAL SPORTS ETIQUETTE

General sports etiquette practices include:

- Listen to the coach
- Know the game rules
- Put forth effort
- Respect all participants
- Discuss disagreements, don't yell
- Be fair (keep score, admit fouls and infractions, make the right call)
- Do not use profanity
- Be a gracious winner and loser (e.g., no bragging after a win and no sulking after a loss)
- Shake hands at the end of a game or match
- Help teammates and opponents if they fall or injure themselves
- Provide words of encouragement to teammates
- Thank the coach after games and practices

SAFETY PRACTICES AND CONSIDERATIONS IN RECREATIONAL ACTIVITIES

Safety practices reduce or eliminate injury or traumatic experiences that may occur when walking, jogging, or running outdoors. Safety considerations include wearing proper athletic shoes to support the feet and ankles. Clothes that do not restrict movement should be worn. Running with a buddy or in high-visibility areas is recommended to avoid potential harm. Wearing sunscreen and hats can prevent or limit sun damage and lower skin cancer risks. In extreme heat, the coolest part of the day should be chosen to engage in activities. Drinking fluids (water) before, during, and after activity keeps the body hydrated and reduces the risks of dehydration, which can lead to heat exhaustion and heat stroke. More fluids are needed in hotter temperatures. When cold, layering clothes and wearing wicking materials keeps the body warm and dry, which prevents hypothermia.

SUPERVISING STUDENTS IN RECREATIONAL PURSUITS

Issues and procedures to consider when supervising students in recreational pursuits include students changing clothes, locker room or change room duties, hygiene, classroom management of large or multiple classes, equipment, taking attendance, and safety. To promote a safe environment, the national physical education recommendations for teacher-student ratio is 1-25 for elementary; 1-30 for middle school, and 1-35 for high school. For class sizes larger than this, a request should be put in for a teacher's aide. Routines (roll call, or attendance; warm-up; squad lines, teams, or groups) will aid in classroom management, but consistency should be employed. Further, positive reinforcement should be used to encourage favorable behaviors, and consequences should be issued for not adhering to routines. If students change clothes, it is important to adhere to all local and state guidelines to ensure that students are safe but have an appropriate level of privacy. As such, a time limit should be allotted, and if a locker room is used, there should be adult supervision to help students move quickly and prevent theft or bullying. Student hygiene can be problematic because students might not shower after physical activity. Providing adequate time and a private space to shower are ways to address this issue.

INSTRUCTIONAL TRANSITIONS

Issues with instructional transitions involve time and students finishing early. To help expedite transitions, transitions should be planned and written out ahead of time. Clear, quick, and concise start and stop signals ("Go," or a single whistle blow) help speed up transitions. Students who complete activities early can continue and rotate to the next station and repeat until the cue to stop has been given. This transition strategy keeps students engaged. Timing activities instead of giving a repetition prompt can also help manage transitions. For example, students might engage in the activity for two minutes until they are cued to stop instead of completing 10 jumping jacks or kicks, as students will finish at varying times.

EQUIPMENT MANAGEMENT PRACTICES

The lack of equipment, cost, transportation, storage, distribution, cleaning, and repairing are common equipment issues that impact physical education programs. Procedures to help with transporting equipment include setting up or organizing equipment in the space one or two days prior to the lesson. Equipment transition time and distribution procedures can also be built into the lesson. Students can help set up, distribute, and break down equipment by groups, teams, or partners. Students can also be assigned or taught to wipe down equipment after each use. If there is not enough equipment to teach an activity or unit, equipment can be made or modified, or multiple activities can go on simultaneously to give students opportunity to engage in the activities regardless of equipment availability. Requesting funding for equipment from a PTA or PTO can also be considered. Storage facilities should be easy to access and secure, and old or damaged equipment should be discarded and replaced when possible. Keeping an inventory to avoid repeat orders should aid in maximizing equipment budgets. Assessing what students want can also aid in utilizing equipment.

LOGISTICS REGARDING FACILITIES, SPACE, STAFF, AND TECHNOLOGY

Physical education facilities and teaching spaces are often shared by other classes. Classes also tend to be large and understaffed with limited technology. Team planning should occur to determine who will teach, what will be taught, and where (in the gym or outside field) the class will occur. Team teaching might also be employed for large classes so that one teacher is leading instruction while the other is monitoring student behavior. To accommodate technology needs, professional development with instruction technology (IT) personnel should be requested to discuss the desired technology uses (videography, LCP projector). When recording students, parental permission needs to be granted. Physical education teaching spaces are often interrupted for school assemblies and other non-PE curriculum activities. To reduce the number of interruptions, a yearly teaching plan with a calendar should be made, compared to the school's calendar, and shared with school leadership to avoid scheduling conflicts.

Selecting, Adapting, and Modifying Activities

SELECTING AND MODIFYING ACTIVITIES BASED ON STUDENT CHARACTERISTICS

Students are diverse and vary in abilities and learning styles. It is important to use a variety of teaching methods to increase effectiveness. Asking students their preferred methods of learning might assist with student engagement and learning. Observations and assessment of abilities should help with the differentiation of instruction. From observation and student data, **modifications** (aka adaptations) should also be used to accommodate diverse learners by making tasks easier or more challenging. For example, allowing students to walk during activities that require a jog, or increasing the speed for students who find jogging too easy. Another modification example is to allow novice students to strike a ball from a stationary tee instead of a pitched ball, whereas a student on the baseball team might practice striking a ball from a pitching machine. The teacher can also incorporate students' personal goals into activities throughout the unit or academic year.

> **Review Video: Adapting and Modifying Lessons or Activities**
> Visit mometrix.com/academy and enter code: 834946

SELECTION OF ACTIVITIES AND GAMES BASED ON INSTRUCTIONAL GOALS

Instructional goals are dependent on national, state, and district standards. Content standards help guide the instructional framework, thus they set the objectives or instructional goals. There are three objective domains:

- psychomotor
- cognitive
- affective

The psychomotor domain is where most PE objectives are derived, as the focus is on the motor development of skills (throwing, kicking). The cognitive domain is the knowledge and understanding component that should align to the psychomotor domain (explaining or identifying the cues for throwing or kicking). The affective domain focuses on values, feelings, and attitudes (assisting with cleanup or helping a classmate perform a skill).

SELECTING, ADAPTING, AND MODIFYING ACTIVITIES BASED ON A RANGE OF SKILL LEVELS

Differentiation is tailoring education to meet each student's needs. During times when individualized instruction is impossible (large class sizes, little instructional time), teachers can create a variety of learning opportunities and experiences to help meet objectives. For example, a teacher can set up beginner, intermediate, and advanced activities that students can choose from. Students may be in all three groups depending on the skill(s). To ensure that all students are able to work on each skill, the class can be divided into groups that rotate through the type of activity. The difficulty level for practicing can be self-targeted by the student.

Basketball examples:

Skills	Beginner	Intermediate	Advanced
Dribbling	Stationary dribble	Walk and dribble	Run and dribble
Jump shots	5-foot jump shot	10-foot jump shot	15-foot jump shot
Applied practice	Two vs. two	Three vs. three	Five vs. five

In this situation, students would cycle through three stations. When they go to the jump-shot station, students can pick the distance that they think they need to practice to appropriately meet their current skill level. Coaches standing nearby can help students make a better choice if they pick a target that is too easy or too hard for them. This style of variation allows for both differentiation of skill type and adequate variety for each student's skill level.

SELECTING, ADAPTING, AND MODIFYING ACTIVITIES AND GAMES BASED ON EXCEPTIONAL NEEDS

There are students already competent in the motor skill objectives planned, while others are still developing or may have a disability. **Extensions** are a type of modification that makes tasks more challenging for students with high ability or who are competent in the tasks. For example, a student on the volleyball team may work on jump serves or target serving rather than the underhand and overhand serves during the service unit. These students can also peer-teach to demonstrate their understanding of the skills and movement concepts. There are also simplified versions (**remediations**) of the skill for students who need more time and direction to grasp the tasks or concepts. There are also students who need additional supports or adaptations that include playing basketball in a wheelchair or using a ramp to assist a wheelchair-bound student in bowling. Modifications or adaptations can be task specific (e.g., use a two-handed, underhand basketball free throw for students who have not developed their upper-body strength), equipment specific (e.g., lower or raise the net in volleyball, or use different size balls), or boundary, or space, specific (e.g., increase or decrease boundaries).

Major Body Systems and Physical Activity

MUSCULOSKELETAL SYSTEM AND PHYSICAL ACTIVITY

The musculoskeletal system is a combination of the muscular and skeletal systems that is comprised of muscles, bones, and joints. The skeletal system includes bones, cartilage, ligaments, and joints, and provides the body with protection, support, and movement. There are several types of joint movements, but the most common used during physical activity are synovial joints, which are moveable joints. There are three types of muscles (smooth, cardiac, skeletal) that make up the muscular system. However, skeletal muscle (voluntary movement) is responsible for mobility and movement via muscular contraction. Muscles are attached to bones and cause them to move, which changes the angle of the joint (increases, decreases, rotates, extends). These components work in unison for movement to occur, thus they are the components responsible for physical activity. Repetitive and consistent use of the musculoskeletal system has a positive impact on fitness, which translates to better health.

CIRCULATORY AND RESPIRATORY SYSTEMS AND PHYSICAL ACTIVITY

The circulatory system is responsible for blood transport around the body through blood vessels to the heart and lungs. The respiratory system is primarily contained in the lungs and is responsible for oxygen transport and excreting carbon dioxide from the body during physical activity, which is also known as gas exchange. During exercise, respiration increases to accommodate the oxygen demands of the muscles, and circulation also increases to bring more blood to the working muscles. During respiration, oxygenated air is inhaled through the nose or mouth and travels through the windpipe (trachea), to the bronchial tubes, and then to the lungs. The alveoli in the lungs are where gas exchange occurs (deoxygenated blood for oxygenated blood) and carbon dioxide (waste product) is exhaled.

DIGESTIVE AND EXCRETORY SYSTEMS AND PHYSICAL ACTIVITY

The digestive and excretory systems work in unison. The digestive system is responsible for converting food into energy and transporting nutrients to the body via blood and other tissues. The excretory system is responsible for removing waste, including blood, from the body. The digestive tract includes the mouth, esophagus, stomach, and the small and large intestines and is responsible for excreting urine and feces. During physical activity, the excretory system rids the body of water through sweat and the lungs of carbon dioxide through exhalations. Physical activity strengthens the digestive track, which makes it easier to remove waste.

IMMUNE, ENDOCRINE, NERVOUS, AND INTEGUMENTARY SYSTEM AND PHYSICAL ACTIVITY

Engaging in regular physical activity helps boost **immunity** by increasing white blood cells, which help fight off disease. Getting a cold or the flu also become less likely as the body flushes bacteria from the lungs more efficiently. The **endocrine system** is comprised of the pituitary gland (increases bone and muscle mass), thyroid (regulates heart rate, blood pressure, and body temperature; also increases alertness), adrenal gland (aids in anti-inflammatory response and helps regulate hydration), and the pancreas (helps transport glucose to the working muscles). It also regulates insulin, a process that is improved by physical activity. The **integumentary system** is the function of the skin, which is the point where sweat is released, therefore aiding in thermoregulation. As the body heats up during physical activity, the body releases water (in the form of sweat) to cool off and maintain homeostasis. When the body gets too cold, the skin contracts to retain heat. During physical activity, the **sympathetic nervous system** responds and is responsible for the increase in heart rate. As physical activity diminishes or slows down, the **parasympathetic nervous system** slows down respiration and heart rate.

Cardiovascular Endurance and Aerobic Activities

ACUTE RESPONSES TO AEROBIC EXERCISE

Acute responses when performing aerobic exercise include an increase in ventilation, cardiac output, heart rate, and stroke volume. However, after longer durations of continuous aerobic exercise, cardiac output occurs at a constant rate. Blood flow is also redistributed during aerobic exercise because during rest, about 83 percent of the blood is distributed between the muscles, liver, kidneys, and brain. During aerobic exercise, 84 percent of the blood is redistributed towards the working muscles. This is able to occur because **vasodilation**, or the widening of the of blood vessels, allows for greater blood flow to the muscles.

DIFFERENTIAL PHYSIOLOGICAL RESPONSES TO AEROBIC ACTIVITY

At rest, aerobically conditioned or trained individuals will have lower blood pressure, lower resting heart rate, greater stroke volume, and slightly lower resting cardiac output than an untrained individual. During sub-maximum exercise, the trained individual will have a lower heart rate, higher stroke volume, and lower cardiac output than the untrained individual. During maximum exercise, the trained and untrained individual will have about the same maximum heart rate. The trained individual, however, will have a higher stroke volume and cardiac output. To train aerobically, one can gradually increase the distance, intensity (moving faster or adding power), and frequency of aerobic activity for improvement. Interval training, in which one would engage in

46

short bouts of high-intensity activity, followed by short bouts of rest or lower intensity activity, is also effective.

EXERCISES THAT PROMOTE AEROBIC CONDITIONING

Exercises that promote aerobic conditioning include running, jogging, swimming, walking, biking, aerobic dance, jumping jacks, and jumping rope performed continuously for at least 20 to 30 minutes. However, high-intensity interval training has also shown effective in promoting aerobic conditioning. **High-intensity interval training (HIIT)** is a combination of high-intensity aerobic and muscular fitness activities performed in short bouts followed by a short rest period. **Tabata** is a type of HIIT training with a work interval of 20 seconds followed by a rest interval of 10 seconds. Repeating these intervals for four minutes has shown to be as effective as a 60-minute aerobic session. A general rule for aerobic interval training is the rest time should be half the work time. Other HIIT work-rest intervals include 30/15, 40/20, and 60/30 seconds.

METABOLISM AND AEROBIC CONDITIONING

Metabolism is the process of breaking down foods and converting them to energy (carbohydrates, fats, proteins) that is needed to sustain life. Carbohydrates are the primary source of energy, followed by fats, which are the back-up system once carbohydrate stores (glucose and glycogen) are depleted. After the glucose (carbohydrates) and glycogen (stored glucose) stores are used during aerobic activity, fat stores become the fuel source needed to continue aerobic activity because it is long lasting. This process is called **fat oxidation,** which is a metabolic process that helps create the energy. Monounsaturated and polyunsaturated (plant-based fats, liquid at room temperature) fats are easier to break down than saturated fats (mostly animal fats, solid at room temperature) due to the slower metabolic and oxidation processes of saturated fats. This is the reason that limiting saturated fats is recommended, especially among those who want to lose weight or avoid adding additional weight. To burn fat in an effort to lose weight, aerobic activity needs to occur long enough or at high-intensity levels to reach the stored fat in the adipocytes (fat cells).

CARDIOVASCULAR RECOMMENDATIONS FOR ELEMENTARY-AGED CHILDREN

It is recommended that elementary students between the ages of five and 12 engage in cardiovascular activities 5 to 7 days a week in sessions of 15 minutes or more several times throughout the day to an accumulated 60 minutes. Activities should vary and students should engage in low (stretching, yoga), moderate (walking), and vigorous (biking, jumping rope, games that involve running or chasing) physical activities. Continuous activity and working towards a specific heart rate goal are discouraged, as the goal at these ages is to encourage and promote physical activity.

CARDIOVASCULAR RECOMMENDATIONS FOR SECONDARY SCHOOL-AGED CHILDREN

Moderate and vigorous cardiovascular activities are recommended for secondary-aged students (aged 11-18 years) three to seven days a week in bouts of 20-60 minutes. Middle school-aged students are not expected to have target heart-rate goals, but are encouraged to use rate of perceived exertion scales to monitor effort and intensity. This is also the stage where target heart concepts are introduced. High school students are encouraged to work at 60-90 percent of their target heart rate because the goal is not only to promote physical activity, but to teach students how to plan for exercise as adults. Activities should vary and may include participation in individual, dual, and team sports; speed walking; jogging; dancing; swimming; skating; cycling; and mowing grass.

CONTINUOUS TRAINING

Continuous training is also known as steady state training because the same activity is performed at long durations or several minutes without rest (e.g., jogging, swimming, walking). Although continuous training is not encouraged for students in elementary school, continuous activities that range from three to five minutes with rest is appropriate for the primary years (grades K-2) or unfit students, 10-minute bouts are appropriate for upper elementary (grades 3-5), and 20-minute and longer sessions are appropriate for middle and high school students. A gradual increase in intensity should occur for all groups, and students should be able to take rest and water breaks when they need to. There should also be a gradual decrease in intensity.

FARTLEK TRAINING

Fartlek training, also known as "speed play," is a type of interval training that consists of performing aerobic and locomotor movements over natural or rough terrain at varied intervals. For example, if students are running on a cross-country trail or on grass, the teacher or student may randomly decide when to run hard and when to slow down to a jog and walk. This differs from the traditional interval training that has a set work-rest ratio (20 seconds of work followed by 10 seconds of rest). It is a method used in lieu of continuous training that helps students increase aerobic capacity, maintain a steady pace, increase speed, and develop mental toughness. It is appropriate for older elementary-aged students (grades 3-5) and middle and high school-aged students. All locomotor movements are used during Fartlek sessions in elementary school, and the teacher generally controls the intensity and pace. In secondary school, students are expected to control their intensity and pace based on fitness goals, and the locomotor movements consist of running, jogging, or walking.

USING HEART RATES TO PACE ACTIVITY

Instead of working at a particular pace, **heart rate training** involves changing intensities based on heart rate. A heart rate monitor is used throughout the activity to ensure that the desired heart rate zone is maintained. For example, if the goal is to work between 70 to 80 percent of the maximum heart rate, the exerciser would slow down their speed when the heart rate exceeds 80 percent, and increase their speed when the heart rate drops below 70 percent. This is a fair training method to use among students because heart rate is unique to the individual. Drastic or abnormal increases in heart rate can indicate an illness, such as a cold or fever, or a potential for sudden cardiac death. Therefore, heart rate training can also alert the performer of a problem to slow down, stop, or seek medical attention.

HEART RATE MONITORING METHODS

Heart rate is used to monitor intensity levels during aerobic activities. Methods used to assess heart rate include manually taking the pulse rate or heart rate and using devices that monitor heart rate. Manual heart rate methods include measuring the pulse at the wrist (radial artery) or the neck (carotid artery), which can be done by placing two fingers (first and middle fingers) at the artery locations and calculating the beats per minute, either by counting for 10 seconds and multiplying the pulse count by six, 15 seconds multiplied by four, 20 seconds multiplied by three, 30 seconds multiplied by two, or for 60 seconds. In every instance, the calculation equates to the number of beats in one minute. Ten seconds is preferred after engaging in physical activity or exercise because it is fast and accurate. A 60-second count is preferred to determine the resting heart rate. Elementary students should monitor heart rate by placing their right hand over the heart. To help elementary students understand the concept of intensity, various activities can be set up with pictures and words to convey low ("move like a turtle"), medium (brisk walking), and high-intensity (running) activities.

TALK TEST AND RATE OF PERCEIVED EXERTION

The talk test and rate of perceived exertion scales are easy alternatives to measuring heart rate that are used to establish exercise intensity. If one can talk but not sing during an activity, then the intensity level is appropriate; if one can sing, then the intensity is too low; and if one cannot talk or sing, then the intensity is too high. Rate of perceived exertion (RPE) scales are estimates of how one feels while engaging in aerobic activities. RPEs use a rating scale from 0 (extremely easy) to 10 (extremely hard). There are RPE scales designed for children and adults, and the most common are the OMNI and Borg scales.

Rating	Difficulty	Indicator
0	Rest	No effort
2	Easy	Very minimal effort, walking, able to talk and do other things.
4	Moderate	Not too hard. Activity can be done for extended time, and should still be able to talk while performing activity.
6	Hard	Able to sustain for some time, but pushing the cardiorespiratory limit, meaning they won't be able to talk while performing or sustain for long periods of time.
8	Very hard	Not quite full effort, but nearing that level of intensity. Unable to talk or do anything else while performing. Not sustainable for more than a few minutes at the most.
10	Maximum	Short bursts only. When finished, will be breathing very hard and unable to talk until they catch their breath.

TRACKING DURATION AND DISTANCE OF AEROBIC ACTIVITIES

Techniques used to measure the duration of aerobic activities are timetable devices that include watches, activity trackers, stopwatches, cell phone timers, and clocks. Techniques used to measure distance include performing aerobic activities in marked areas (e.g., standard track at 400 meters per lap, swimming pool at 50-100 meters per length) or built-in capabilities (e.g., treadmill, stationary bike, elliptical trainer). For aerobic activities that do not have standard measures or equipment (e.g., aerobic dance, walking or running on the street or unmarked area), a pedometer or accelerometer can be used. The purpose of monitoring the duration and distance is to track progress. For instance, at the start of an exercise program, a brisk 20-minute walk may be difficult, but with consistency and time, the brisk 20-minute walk will likely get easier as the body has adapted to the physical stress. Therefore, one will need to either walk longer or increase the pace (jog) to experience similar physiological responses (e.g., increase in heart rate).

MAXIMUM HEART RATE AND TARGET HEART RATE ZONE

Maximum heart rate (MHR) is the maximum number of beats the heart pumps per minute and is dependent on age. The formula for computing MHR is 220 minus the subject's age, so the MHR for a 15-year-old is 205 beats per minute (bpm). The **target heart rate zone (THRZ)** is a percentage of the MHR and has a range of low-intensity and high-intensity that is generally between 60 and 90 percent. As the model below demonstrates, the THRZ for a 15-year-old is 123 bpm to184.5 bpm (formula below).

	Moderate intensity	High intensity
Base number	220	220
Age	-15 years old	-15 years old
Difference	205	205
Intensity	× 0.60 (60 percent)	× 0.90 (90 percent)

THRZ	123 bpm	184.5 bpm

Beginners and unfit individuals should work at the 60 to 70 percent range of their THRZ and gradually increase over time. Fit individuals should work at the 80 to 85 percent range of their THRZ, athletes or those with high levels of fitness should aim for 90 percent, and some elite athletes can aim for 95 percent. However, working at this intensity for long periods can be dangerous, so interval training is recommended when working at high intensities.

KARVONEN METHOD FOR CALCULATING TARGET HEART RATE ZONE

The Karvonen method (aka maximum heart rate reserve) for calculating the target heart rate is one of the preferred methods because it takes fitness as measured by resting heart rate (RHR) into account. It is often used as the method for training. The preferred target heart rate under the Karvonen method is 60 to 75 percent because working at higher rates can produce lactic acid via anaerobic systems, thus causing fatigue. Using an individual's resting heart rate ensures that the correct intensity is used for adaptations to occur.

A worked example of the Karvonen formula illustrates the differences between a 15-year-old with a resting heart rate of 72 bpm and a 15-year-old with a resting heart rate of 60 bpm.

Age 15 with 72 BPM RHR		Age 15 with 60 BPM RHR	
60 Percent	90 Percent	60 Percent	90 Percent
$220 - 15 = 205$	$220 - 15 = 205$	$220 - 15 = 205$	$220 - 15 = 205$
$205 - 72 = 133$	$205 - 72 = 133$	$205 - 60 = 145$	$205 - 60 = 145$
$133 \times 0.60 = 79.8$	$133 \times 0.90 = 119.7$	$145 \times 0.60 = 87.0$	$145 \times 0.90 = 130.5$
$79.8 + 72 = 151.8$	$119.7 + 72 = 191.7$	$87 + 60 = 147$	$130.5 + 60 = 190.5$

USING RESTING AND EXERCISE HEART RATES TO ASSESS CARDIO-RESPIRATORY FITNESS

Tracking resting heart rate and exercise heart rates over time can aid in determining cardiovascular fitness progress and physiological adaptations. With consistent cardiorespiratory training, the resting heart rate should slow down. The exercise heart rate should also slow down at similar work rates done previously. The exerciser would use heart rate data to determine if and what changes need to be made. For example, at the start of a fitness program, the resting heart rate is 85 bpm. If there has been no change after six weeks of training, then the individual either needs to increase the exercise time, frequency, intensity, type, or a combination of those variables. The participant may also want to get a physical examination to ensure that there are no underlying conditions (e.g., high blood pressure, illness).

RECOVERY HEART RATE AND CARDIOVASCULAR FITNESS

Recovery heart rate is the time it takes for the heart to return to normal after engaging in cardiorespiratory activities. As the body becomes more conditioned by adapting to the physiological stresses of engaging aerobic activity, the heart will return to normal faster than someone who is not conditioned. A common recovery heart rate assessment is the three-minute step test, which is also used to predict VO2 max. The **Queen's College step test** is commonly used where a continuous step cadence (up, up, down, down) on a 41 centimeter (16.142 inches) high box or bench at a rate of 88 bpm for females and 96 bpm for males for three minutes. After three minutes has elapsed, a 15-second pulse should be taken and multiplied by four to equate 60 seconds, which corresponds to recovery heart rate and VO2 max estimates. Ranges to aim for are 128-156 bpm for females and 120-144 bpm for males. Students can track their recovery heart rates over time to see if they decrease.

HEALTH RISKS WHEN ENGAGING IN CARDIOVASCULAR ACTIVITIES IN THE HEAT

Engaging in cardiovascular activities in the heat increases the risks of dehydration, heat cramps, heat exhaustion, and heat stroke. **Dehydration** (aka hypohydration) is the when the body does not have enough fluids to maintain the body's processes. **Heat cramps** are painful spasms in the muscles due to fatigue or sodium lost via sweat. **Heat exhaustion** is the result of the increase of a negative balance of water resulting from dehydration, and heat stroke is the result of dehydration and thermoregulation failure (the ability to sweat). These conditions can cause **hyperthermia** (overheated body with thermoregulation failure) and lead to death. To prevent these heat and endurance-related conditions, it is best to hydrate before, during, and after activity, and take more frequent water and rest breaks. Engaging in activity during the coolest part of the day and lowering the intensity and time of activity can also reduce risk. Light-colored clothing is recommended because light colors reflect more wavelengths of light and therefore absorb less heat. Exercising in the shade and wearing a hat with a visor is also recommended.

RISK REDUCTION AND CARDIOVASCULAR TRAINING

A risk reduction technique to consider when preparing for cardiovascular endurance training is to have a physical examination from a licensed medical professional (e.g., doctor, nurse) to ensure that there are no underlying health conditions that can be exacerbated by physical activity. Another risk reduction technique is to complete the Physical Activity Readiness Questionnaire (PAR-Q), which asks questions used to determine if one is prepared to engage in physical activity. This survey consists of yes and no questions, and if one or more yeses are checked, a visit to the doctor for medical clearance is typically recommended. Once activity starts, conducting a warm-up, a gradual increase in intensity, wearing a heart rate monitor, and performing a cooldown after activity are risk reduction techniques.

HEALTH RISKS WHEN ENGAGING IN CARDIOVASCULAR ACTIVITIES IN THE COLD

Engaging in cardiovascular activities in the cold increases the risks of skin and body temperature dropping, thus creating heat loss that can lead to hypothermia. Another potential health concern is the increased possibility of inducing an asthma attack for those who suffer from exercise-induced asthma. Conducting cardiovascular activities in cold water exacerbates the effects of the cold and can increase the risk of tachycardia (abnormal resting heart rate) and hyperventilation (higher-than-normal respiration rate), both of which are cold shock responses. A rapid drop in skin temperature (jumping into a cold body of water) increases cold shock responses. When swimming in cold water, vasoconstriction (when the blood vessels narrow) and blood flow to the muscles are reduced, which makes movement stiff and more difficult. **Frostnip** (superficial skin tissues freeze) and **frostbite** (cooling and freezing of cells) are other cold-related concerns. To reduce risk, insulated, breathable clothing that draws sweat away from the body is recommended. When performing activities on dry land, layering clothes and removing layers as the body warms up is recommended. A longer warm-up should also be employed.

ALTITUDE AND CARDIOVASCULAR EXERCISE

Most physical activities are performed at sea level, or zero feet of altitude. Altitude training is training at least 7,874 feet above sea level (2,400 meters). There are three main physiological changes that occur when altitude training: 1) red blood cell count increases, allowing increases in the oxygen-transport change, which increases blood flow to the working muscles, which helps the body move more efficiently, 2) breathing rate increases, which reduces the amount of carbon dioxide, thus reducing fatigue, and 3) there is an increase in myoglobin, which is a temporary substance that acts as oxygen when oxygen delivery is compromised (e.g., during long, strenuous activities). These physiological changes, due to acclimatization from training at a different altitude, have a positive effect on cardiovascular performance when returning to sea level.

CARBOHYDRATE LOADING

Carbohydrates consist of sugars and starches that are the body's primary source of energy (aka fuel). Carbohydrates are broken down into glucose (sugar) to be used for energy. Any overage of carbohydrates (glucose) is stored in the muscles as glycogen, which is easy energy to recruit during cardiovascular endurance activities. Therefore, the purpose of carbohydrate (pasta, potatoes, rice) loading before endurance activities is to provide sustained energy for longer periods of time without accessing fat storage, which takes longer to recruit. Carbohydrate loading has shown effective for longer-duration cardiovascular events, such as 90 minutes of running and other long-duration cardiovascular activities. The negative side to carbohydrate loading is the athlete or performer may increase body weight because more water is retained to adequately store the extra glycogen. Carbohydrate loading is not recommended for most activities because shorter activities do not last long enough for the body to need to metabolize more carbohydrates, so the extra calories will actually work against a person who is trying to lose weight through shorter activities.

TREADMILLS AND STATIONARY BIKES

Treadmills promote options for walking, jogging, or running without the need for space. Treadmills are great when it rains or is too hot or cold for outdoor exercise, as they replicate or are specific to the motions that are performed outdoors. Treadmills also allow for inclines and declines to train different parts of the muscle used when walking, jogging, or running. The speed and resistance can also be adjusted. Stationary bikes work in a similar fashion but for biking. The downside of using treadmills and stationary bikes is they are not performed on the same terrain as when performing outside, but are still effective in improving cardiovascular fitness.

MODIFICATIONS FOR CARDIOVASCULAR ENDURANCE ACTIVITIES

Modifications for cardiovascular activities can make the activity easier, more challenging, or less impactful. For example, modifications for jogging include brisk or power walking (lowers the intensity and reduces the impact on the knees), running (increases the intensity), or a combination of all three (interval training). All modalities can increase cardiovascular endurance. However, in order to meet similar cardiovascular outcomes as jogging, one would need to engage in walking longer. Modifications for swimming include using a flotation device to stay buoyant to work on arm strokes and kicks, performing the doggy paddle, and water aerobics. One could also hold onto the wall of the pool and practice kicking and breathing. Endurance and interval sports activities can be used in lieu of traditional exercise activities or programs. They can also be used to cross-train and give the body a break from normal routines.

Muscular Strength and Endurance

ABDOMINAL STRENGTH

Muscles in the abdomen are part of the **core muscles**, which also includes muscles in the back, which work in agonist and antagonist pairings. Often referred to as the abdominals, or abs, these muscles aid in stability and posture. A strong core helps with other exercises. The abdominals should be engaged (contracted, pulling the navel towards the back) during abdominal activities. Exercises to work the abs include curl-ups, plank holds, and variations of these exercises. When performing curl-ups and sit-ups, exhalation should occur in the up position when the muscles contract (the work phase). Inhalation should occur when lowering to the down position when the abs relax. To keep contraction throughout the exercise, the head and shoulder blades should be

slightly off the surface on the down phase. Bending the neck should be avoided to prevent neck pain. Holding the arms across the chest is a safer option. Plank holds are an isometric exercise that is measured by time (seconds or minutes). Planks also engage the muscles of the back (erector spinae), the deltoids, and the glutes. Ab exercises are usually done at two to three sets until fatigue or a predetermined rep count. Abs are generally trained three or four days a week, and are usually incorporated into a complete workout program. However, they are also indirectly trained as they act as synergistic stabilizers during other exercises.

LOWER BACK STRENGTH

The **lower back** is used for most activities, as it provides stability. Exercise recommendations for the lower back include plank holds, Superman's exercise, pelvic tilts, bridges (glute raises), reverse curls, deadlifts, leaning back, leg lifts, low rows, stretching (cat and cow, lying on back alternating knees to the chest), and windshield wiper with knees. However, it is important to note that lower back injuries are common, so care should be taken to protect it. When lifting items off the floor, the knees should be used to lift and the hips and glutes should be kept back, rather than bending over and lifting with the back. Lower back exercises should be done in a slow and controlled motion. Inhalation occurs during the contraction portion and exhalation occurs during the relaxation portion. For isometric exercises, inhalation and exhalation are maintained throughout the hold (e.g., plank). Lower back exercises should be trained three to four days a week, although lower back stretches can still be performed daily.

UPPER BODY AND TRUNK STRENGTH

The **upper body** includes the arms, chest, back, and shoulders. The chest, back, shoulders, and abdominals comprise the **trunk** (body parts above the waist and below the neck). Muscles in these areas should be trained two to three times a week, with at least one rest day between sessions. Types of exercises, the associated muscles, and common exercises are indicated below.

Major Group	Muscle	Recommended Exercises
Arms	Biceps	Dumbbell curls, barbell curls, hammer curls, cable curls, preacher curls
	Triceps	Seated dips, dips, tricep kickbacks (extensions), overhead extensions
Chest	Pectorals (major and minor)	Push-ups, bench press, cable crossovers
Back	Latissimus dorsi and rhomboids	Lat pull downs, seated row, bent row, one-arm row
	Erector spinae	Reverse curls, Superman's exercise, deadlifts
	Trapezius muscles	Shrugs, shoulder blade squeezes
Shoulders	Deltoids	Front/lateral/rear deltoid raises, shoulder press – dumbbells, barbells.

Many of the exercises for these muscle groups are also performed on exercise equipment, which tends to be a safe option because machines have more support than free weight exercises.

LEG STRENGTH AND ENDURANCE

To train muscles in the legs for strength, high weight and low reps (3 to 5, 6 to 8, or 8 to 10) should be employed. For endurance, low weight and high reps (10 to 12, 12 to15, or 15 to 20) should be employed. Sets generally range from one to five, depending on the goal(s). One to three sets are often conducted for endurance and three to five sets are often done for strength. Shorter rest times between sets are taken for endurance, and longer rest times between sets for strength. Alternating workouts between strength and endurance allows for focus on each health-related fitness component.

Common exercises that work the muscles in the legs include:

- **Quadriceps**: <u>Squats,</u> lunges, leg extensions
- **Hamstrings**: Deadlifts, hamstring curls
- **Soleus/gastrocnemius**: heel/toe/calf raises (double or single-leg), seated calf raises.

Flexibility and Posture

PROMOTING GOOD POSTURE AND FLEXIBILITY IN THE HIPS, ANKLES, AND KNEES

Hip flexors are the muscles that, with proper flexibility, make it possible to bring the knees upwards and towards the body (chest). The hip flexors also help with good posture because they aid in spinal stabilization. Sitting for long periods can reduce flexibility, while engaging in certain physical activities (dance, soccer, cycling) can improve it. To increase flexibility in the hip flexors or alleviate "tight hips," hip flexor stretches should be conducted using the hip hinge motion (leading with the glutes moving backwards while the chest leads the forward bending motion) to prevent lower back injury.

Mobility in the ankles work in unison with the hip flexors to maintain posture. As the body stands from a seated position (chair) or bends, the hips hinge while the ankles dorsiflex (toes toward the body). Exercises that help build strength and flexibility in the ankles include alternating between dorsiflexion and plantar flexion (toes pointing downward), ankle rotations, hopping side-to-side on one foot, and balancing on one foot while the other one swings forward and back, then switching sides.

The knees also aid in good posture. To maintain good posture when standing, the knees should be soft (slightly bent), the feet should be placed shoulder-distance apart, the arms should be relaxed and hanging, and the body should stand straight and tall with the shoulders back. During exercises, the knees should also be soft, and locking the knee joint should be avoided. When performing squats and lunges, the knees should be aligned or behind the toes. To protect the knees, avoid hanging them over the toes.

PROMOTING GOOD POSTURE AND FLEXIBILITY IN THE LOWER BACK AND TRUNK

Lower back stretches that promote good posture and flexibility include child's pose, cobra, upward facing dog, supine twist, and lying on the back and bringing the knees to the chest. Trunk exercises that aid in good posture and flexibility include back extensions, spinal twist, crunches, crunches with a twist, and wood chops. Trunk stretches for flexibility include upper trunk rotations, trunk flexion rotation, standing and seated lateral trunk stretch, seated trunk rotation stretch, and dolphin stretch. For the chest and upper back parts of the trunk, reaching (stretching the arms) back aids in posture by keeping the chest lifted, shoulders back, and back upright. This is a counter-balance stretch because the shoulders and posture can be compromised (shoulders rounded forward, curve in the upper back) when the muscles on the anterior side are stronger than the posterior muscles.

PROMOTING GOOD POSTURE AND FLEXIBILITY FOR THE SHOULDERS AND NECK

Shoulder exercises that promote good posture and flexibility include reaching the arms back, reverse plank, threading the needle, dolphin, eagle arms, sphinx, and alternating shoulder stretch (hands touching behind the back in opposition). The following exercises are used to increase strength and flexibility in the neck, which also aids in good posture. Neck exercises include tilting the head forward (chin towards the chest), bending or tilting the head towards the left and right (side to side), and rotating the head to the right and left. These stretches should be held for 5 to 10 seconds and repeated up to five times each. Bending or tilting the head back is not recommended.

RESISTANCE TRAINING TO PROMOTE FLEXIBILITY

While static stretching is effective for increasing flexibility, it is not the only option for doing so. Weight and resistance training also increase range of motion, thus increasing flexibility. In fact, recent research suggests that strength training is just as effective at increasing range of motion as stretching is. During weight training, especially exercises that include a full range of motion (e.g., push-ups, squats, pull-ups, deadlifts), stretching occurs while building strength. Foam rollers (compressed tubes) are also effective in improving flexibility since they can apply pressure that is able to penetrate deep inside the muscle tissue, which aids in muscle lengthening.

Evaluating Strength, Endurance, and Flexibility

EVALUATING MUSCULAR STRENGTH

The steps used to conduct a one-repetition max (1RM) test are listed below.

Pectoral strength measured by the bench press:

1. Warm-up the area evaluated: light-weight bench press for two to five sets
2. Use two or three spotters
3. Select a heavy weight within the limits of the student
4. The student will bench press the amount of weight as many times as possible. If they can bench press one time in good form without assistance, then that is the 1RM. If they can bench press the selected weight more than one time, they should stop, add more weight, and repeat three to five minutes later. This would continue until the 1RM is achieved.

A safer method to use is the estimated 1RM. Two methods of estimated 1RM are below.

1. Use an estimated 1RM table to determine what the 1RM would likely be. For example, students select a weight that they can lift for six repetitions but cannot lift for more than 10 repetitions (chart dependent). If a student performed eight reps at eight pounds, they would use the estimated 1RM table corresponding chart and would find that their estimated 1RM would be 10 pounds.
2. Another method is to use the 1RM estimated max formula: (weight lifted × 0.03 × repetitions) + weight lifted = estimated 1RM max. Using the example of a student performing eight reps at eight pounds: (8 reps × 0.03 × 8 pounds) + 8 lbs = 9.92 pounds, which rounds up to 10 pounds.

EVALUATING ENDURANCE

There are two types of **endurance**: muscular endurance and cardiovascular endurance. At times, they work together, like when jogging or swimming—although these activities require muscular and cardiovascular movements, they are classified as aerobic because they use large amounts of oxygen. The amount of time engaged in the activity is how both are measured. For example, timing how long one can engage in continuous movement and tracking trends helps to determine improvement. When participating in locomotor endurance activities, tracking distance is another method used to evaluate endurance. For example, if someone jogs for 30 minutes a day, they can track the distance covered in the amount of time. If the distance increases, the data would suggest they are getting faster and the heart, lungs, and muscles are working more efficiently. Common cardiovascular endurance assessments include the 1-mile run, multi-stage progressive runs, 12-minute runs, and three-minute step tests. Common muscular endurance (and strength) tests are the curl-up test, push-up test, and plank hold. The amount of reps completed over a certain amount of time (e.g., two minutes) is another method of evaluation. Muscular endurance activities performed in isolation are classified as anaerobic because little to no oxygen is required to engage in the activity.

EVALUATING FLEXIBILITY

Flexibility is often evaluated by length or a decrease in joint angle. For example, the sit-and-reach is a test commonly used in physical education programs to measure lower back and hamstring flexibility. The test is usually performed on a box to protect the back, but can also be performed on the floor. In a seated position with the legs extended forward, the goal is to reach towards the feet as far as possible with slight tension but without pain. A tape measure on the floor or ruler on the box measures the distance or the length of the stretch. The back saver sit-and-reach is conducted with one leg at a time (while the other is bent upward). A tape measure is not required, as reaching an area on the body also provides information on progress. For example, one may only be able to reach their shins, but with practice can eventually reach their toes or go beyond their toes, indicating improvement.

Safe and Appropriate Activity for Improving Fitness

ACTIVITIES FOR IMPROVING MUSCULAR STRENGTH

Muscular strength can improve with and without equipment. Body weight exercises are generally introduced first because they are safer than exercises that use equipment. Body weight exercises also allow students to become familiar with what the body can do (e.g., body awareness). Some body weight exercises that help build strength are push-ups, curl-ups, planks, squats, lunges, and several variations of these exercises. Exercise tubes, resistance bands, and stability balls also improve strength because they add a little more resistance than body weight training alone. For faster strength gains, kettlebells, medicine balls, and dumbbells can be used. These types of equipment allow the body to complete exercises that mimic regular movements. Weight lifting machines (e.g., hamstring curl, leg press, lat pulldown) allow for heavy weight to be lifted, but restricts some natural movements, which makes it a safe option. Over time with consistency, exercises should get easier as the body adapts, and the load (weight) will need to either increase or more repetitions will be required to see further progress. It usually takes between four to six weeks for adaptations to occur. If the intensity remains the same, the body may plateau, which means there will be no more improvement gains.

ACTIVITIES FOR IMPROVING ENDURANCE AND INDICATORS OF IMPROVEMENT

The cardiorespiratory system needs to be challenged at least three days a week for 20-60 minutes for endurance to improve, increase, or maintain cardiovascular fitness. With consistency, the body adapts to the exercises and becomes more efficient and capable of meeting the cardiovascular demands on the body. Activities that help improve endurance include jumping rope, walking, jogging, running, swimming, aerobic dance, HIIT training, road and stationary biking, elliptical trainers, rowing, and high-repetition muscular fitness activities. Indicators of improvement include lower resting and working heart rates, faster recovery heart rate, longer durations, and a decrease in fatigue response. The activities will also get easier to do over time. Using a variety of these activities (aka cross-training) will prevent a plateau effect by putting different challenges across all body systems (e.g., musculoskeletal, circulatory, respiratory).

ACTIVITIES TO IMPROVE FLEXIBILITY AND POSTURE

A warm-up lasting five to 10 minutes is recommended prior to engaging in flexibility and posture activities. Selecting activities depends on the goal. Range of motion (ROM) exercises can be done every day to increase flexibility. ROM exercises are static holds (e.g., touching the toes, grabbing one foot, spinal twist) where the position or posture is maintained for 20 to 60 seconds. **Proprioceptive neuromuscular facilitation (PNF)** stretching, which is comprised of static holds with a person or object applying pressure to help deepen the stretch, has been shown to be most effective for increasing flexibility. These stretches should be used in intervals of stretch-relax-stretch. Static and PNF stretches are good for physical therapy (rehab for an injury) and are often done at the end of a workout. Static stretching is also preferred for students in elementary school as they learn body awareness. Dynamic stretches are introduced in middle school. Dynamic stretching is often used in warm-ups because it increases blood flow while stretching in positions and movements similar to the workout or sport. In this way, dynamic stretches prepare the body for the specific work.

PROGRESSIVE-PARTNER-RESISTANCE EXERCISES

Partner exercises allow for greater isolation of the muscle than when performing exercises alone. These exercises are also good for students who are too small to use exercise machines. Ideally, partners should be the same height, weight, and ability level (e.g., strength, flexibility). Communication is essential to prevent injury, therefore, the student performing the exercises needs to inform or cue the partner with how much pressure should be applied. The partner that is assisting should provide feedback on technique and form to ensure safe, correct movements. Equipment that can aid in partner-resistance exercises include exercise tubes, bands, and towels.

PRINCIPLES, SAFETY PRACTICES, AND EQUIPMENT FOR WEIGHT TRAINING

When engaging in weight training, weight selection should take into account the concept of progressive overload (start with a light weight and gradually increase) to prevent injury. A warm-up should also be conducted to prevent the risks of injury. Warm-ups usually consist of performing the same activities with little to no weight and is commonly referred to as a "warm-up set." For example, when conducting the biceps curl, a warm-up set might consist of 20 reps at five pounds before performing the biceps curl at the desired weight of 20 pounds at 10 reps for three sets. General principles include training the same muscle group at least two days a week; high weights with low reps for strength and size; low weights with high reps for endurance; rest between sets (30 seconds to three minutes), taking longer rests for size and shorter rests for endurance; and including at least one rest day between weight training workouts for the targeted body part or muscle group. Below are two **splits**, or weight training workout schedules. Depending on the segmentation and muscle groups to exercise, splits can come in hundreds of different variations.

Sunday	Monday	Tuesday	Wednesday	Thursday	Friday	Saturday
Legs	Arms, shoulders	Chest, back	Legs	Rest	Arms, shoulders	Chest, back

Sunday	Monday	Tuesday	Wednesday	Thursday	Friday	Saturday
Legs, arms	Chest, back	Shoulders, core	Rest	Legs, arms	Chest, back	Shoulders, core

PRINCIPLES, SAFETY PRACTICES, AND EQUIPMENT FOR CIRCUIT TRAINING

Circuit training is a combination of cardiovascular and non-cardiovascular activities performed at stations for a certain number of minutes or repetitions. Circuit training exercises may only include body weight exercises, free weights, resistance equipment (bands, suspension trainers), or a combination. In addition to the normal exercise safety (e.g., warm-up, cooldown, hydration), there are additional safety concerns that must be considered for young children (elementary school-aged). During physical activity and exercise, teachers should be aware that young children's bodies are less able to thermoregulate due to a lower sweat response than adults, therefore children may overheat faster than adults. As such, young children should be given more frequent rest and water breaks (before, during, and after activity). Their breathing capacity is also lower than older children and adults, which can cause them to hyperventilate, so the intensity should be moderate, not high.

DETERMINE APPROPRIATE INTENSITY OF TRAINING

Appropriate measures used to determine cardiovascular endurance training include training in one's target heart rate zone. The target heart rate zone is a percentage (60 to 90 percent) of an individual's maximum heart rate. Once the target heart rate has been computed, it can be monitored by taking the pulse or by wearing a heart rate monitoring device. The goal is to stay within the 60 to 90 percent range; beginners should stay in the 60 to 70 percent range and gradually advance to the 85 to 90 percent range. The talk test is another way to determine intensity: if the subject is able to talk, but not able to sing during the activity, then they are working at an appropriate intensity. If they are unable to talk, then the intensity is too high, and if they are able to sing, then the intensity is too low. For muscular fitness activities, gauging how one feels during the activities is a method used to determine the intensity of exercises. Whether training for strength or endurance, the last few reps in each set should be challenging but doable. When the last few reps are easy, it is an indication that the weight or rep count needs to increase, thus increasing the intensity.

APPROPRIATE DURATION OF TRAINING

The duration of training is dependent on the goal. For example, if the goal is to complete a 5-kilometer (3.1 miles) race, a gradual increase in distance should occur until the 5-kilometer goal is met. Running or swimming slightly over 5 kilometers can help train the body so that the stress response during the 5-kilometer run is easier. On the other hand, if someone is training for a marathon (42.185 kilometers, or 26.22 miles), multiple longer runs leading up to the marathon are recommended. Given the distance of a marathon, however, it is not recommended to train at or beyond the marathon distance. A few 20-mile runs are a general recommendation when training for a marathon. These recommendations are based on the principle of specificity. If one is training at shorter distances (e.g., 100-meter run), the duration should be short and explosive with repeated trials or attempts. It would be inappropriate to train in short bouts for activities that take a long time to complete and vice versa.

APPROPRIATE FREQUENCY OF TRAINING

The frequency of training depends on goals, fitness level, and the time available to train. For beginners, a training program consisting of two to three days a week at low-intensity activity is recommended. For intermediates, frequency recommendations are three to four days a week of moderate activities. For advanced exercisers, four to seven days a week of vigorous activities. A gradual increase over time has shown the most effective in exercise adherence. For weight training, it is generally recommended to perform two or three sets of each exercise (e.g., push-ups in three sets of 10) two to three days a week. More sets are recommended for those who are focused on size, and the frequency of workouts could be once a week because it will take longer for the body to recover and repair after heavy loads.

SAFETY, EFFECTIVENESS, AND CONTRAINDICATIONS OF THE TYPES OF TRAINING THAT PROMOTE STRENGTH

Safe and effective training that promotes strength in children and adolescents includes body weight training and lifting weights. It is a myth that children should not engage in strength training as it was once thought doing so would stunt their growth. Research shows that elementary-aged children benefit from strength training activities, however, the activities should vary to reduce the risk of injury and prevent overtraining. Since children and youth's bones (epiphyseal plate, or growth plate) are still developing, a slow progression should occur. Non-strength activities should be included (e.g., those that improve cardiovascular performance and flexibility). Specialization in training should not occur until later adolescence (e.g., high school-aged). Although multi-joint activities have shown safe for young children, proper form and technique that include slow and controlled movements are a must, as these types of exercises can put additional stress on the shoulder joint and lower back. To ensure safety, and in addition to progressive overload, the teacher should be trained, students should be taught about the benefits and risks, a warm-up should be conducted, frequent water breaks should be given, and rest days or non-strength activities should follow strength-training days. **Contraindications** or risky movements to avoid include jerky movements, locking of the joints, hyperextension, and fast and uncontrolled movements.

SAFETY AND EFFECTIVENESS IN ENDURANCE TRAINING

Most endurance activities (walking, jogging, running) conducted during physical education are appropriate for K-12 students, however, because of developmental stage, modifications should be made. For example, elementary-aged children should engage in bouts of endurance activities not to exceed 15 minutes at a time, while middle and high school students can engage in longer durations (20 minutes or longer). HIIT training can be used across grade levels, but it is only recommended for students who are moderately fit and should be avoided by students who are not. Swimming activities are effective, although specialized training among personnel is required and a certified lifeguard should be on duty during instruction. Students need to be proficient in floating and swimming or need flotation devices that keep non-swimmers buoyant. Endurance machines are also effective, but are unsafe for elementary-aged students due to size and developmental stage.

SAFETY AND EFFECTIVENESS IN STRETCHING

Static stretching and yoga poses are effective in promoting flexibility and enhancing posture. A warm-up should be conducted prior to stretching to reduce the risk of injury. To be effective, stretching should occur at least two days a week and be held for 10 to 60 seconds to the point of tension (not pain), followed by relaxation and repeat. There should be a gradual increase (progressive overload) in the amount of time the stretch is held. Regular breathing should occur, and during exhalation is the time to try to go deeper or reach farther (in small increments) in the stretch. No more than four stretches per muscle group at three sets each are recommended. Static stretching is recommended for elementary-aged children because it is more controlled and they are still learning how to move the body. Furthermore, dynamic stretching (with movement) can increase injury in young children because they can easily overstretch. Caution should also be used among older populations because static stretching can restrict blood flow and increase blood pressure, as the majority of blood is pooled to the area being stretched. Athletes and students in secondary school tend to warm-up using dynamic stretches, which are mobility exercises that mimic sporting movements and prepare the body for more intense motion specific to the activity.

Diet and Nutrition

MACRONUTRIENTS

Macronutrients (large amounts) include carbohydrates, proteins, and fats. Macronutrients are energy-yielding nutrients because they provide the body with energy to fuel exercise and physical activity. Water is not an energy-yielding macronutrient, but it does it help transport the energy-yielding nutrients. Water is the most essential nutrient because the body cannot survive without it. Carbohydrates (sugars and starches) are the primary source of energy, followed by fats and proteins. Fiber is a substrate of carbohydrates and comes from plant-based foods (vegetables, fruits, and grains). Fiber is either soluble (digestible) or insoluble (indigestible). Carbohydrates are either simple and easy to break down (table sugar, fruits) or complex (pasta and bread), which are more filling and supply longer energy than simple sugars. Fats supply long lasting energy after energy from carbohydrates (glucose, glycogen) have been used. Fats are either saturated (semi-solid at room temperature) or unsaturated (liquid at room temperature). Unsaturated fats are better for health. Protein's main role is muscle building and repair. Proteins are found in animal products like meats and eggs. There are also plant-based proteins, including beans, legumes, and soybeans (tofu). Proteins are made up of 20 amino acids, 11 of which are non-essential as the body can produce them, while the remaining nine are essential and can only be obtained through food.

Micronutrients

Vitamins and minerals are micronutrients (small amounts) and are responsible for growth, development, and maintaining the body's processes. Vitamins have two categories: 1) fat soluble (vitamins A, D, E, and K) and 2) water soluble (vitamins B, C, and all others). Having an overabundance of fat-soluble vitamins can be toxic. However, vitamin D deficiency is a concern in the United States, especially among people of color. Vitamin D helps with calcium absorption and is responsible for bone, skin, and immune health, and serves as a protective factor against cancer and other health conditions. Sources of vitamin D include dairy, salmon, and other fatty fish. Sources of vitamin A include carrots, sweet potatoes, spinach and liver. Vitamin E sources include almonds, sunflower seeds, and peanuts. Sources of vitamin K include broccoli, brussels sprouts, and spinach. Minerals also have two categories:

- Macro (calcium, potassium, sodium)
- Micro, or trace minerals (copper, fluoride, iron)

Ingesting too many minerals can lead to life-threatening conditions (e.g., too much sodium can lead to hypertension), so one should follow the recommended daily allowances based on age, gender, pregnancy status, and illnesses or predisposed conditions. Minerals are found in meats, fruits, vegetables, nuts, dairy, and fortified foods (cereals).

BASIC PRINCIPLES OF WEIGHT MANAGEMENT

The energy balance equation shown below is a simplified formula to describe weight management. Energy in is the amount of **calories** (unit of energy or unit of measure for fuel) consumed from foods and substances, and energy out is the amount of calories burned from movement or physical activity.

Energy in = Energy out = No change in weight
Energy in > Energy out = Weight gain
Energy in < Energy out = Weight loss

Physical activity patterns impact the equation. For example, individuals who engage in more physical activity will need more calories as fuel. In contrast, sedentary individuals will need fewer calories because inactivity consumes calories at a much slower rate. For individuals who want to gain weight, the energy in would need to exceed the energy out. Those who want to lose weight would need to burn more calories than they consume.

DIET AND EXERCISE PATTERNS

Generally, it is recommended that 45 to 65 percent of our diet comes from carbohydrates, which is the primary source of energy. Complex carbohydrates (vegetables and grains such as sweet potatoes and brown rice) are preferred over simple carbohydrates (fruits, desserts, sugar, fructose) because they take longer to break down, thereby providing longer bouts of energy. 20 to 35 percent of a person's diet should come from fats. Unsaturated fats (oils that are liquid at room temperature, includes plant-based oils like olive oil and canola oil) are preferred over saturated fats (solid or semi-solid at room temperature such as animal fats, lard, and butter) because too much saturated fat increases the risks of heart disease and obesity. Saturated fat should account for less than 10 percent of total fat intake. 12 to 20 percent should come from proteins, which are made up of 20 amino acids (building blocks of proteins), 11 of which are non-essential (the body can produce) and the remaining nine of which are essential (obtained from the diet foods consumed). The ranges take into account the needs and patterns of the exerciser and include the type of the activity. For example, someone who wants to increase muscle mass should take in more protein, while someone who wants to train for endurance may increase or consume more carbohydrates. In addition to physical activity, calorie intake and the way the body burns fuel is also dependent on genetics, gender, age, and body size and structure. There are online calculators that can provide an estimate of what is needed based on these factors.

BASIC NUTRITION PRINCIPLES

The basic nutrition principles include getting food from multiple food groups for a balanced diet. The five food groups include:

1. Dairy or dairy alternatives (e.g., milk, cheese, yogurt, soy) – should be low or reduced fat
2. Proteins – fish, poultry, lean meats, eggs, tofu, nuts, beans, legumes, seeds
3. Vegetables, including beans and legumes
4. Fruit
5. Grains – rice, bread, cereal, pasta, noodles

Intake of foods from the food groups ensures that the body is getting essential nutrients for the body's processes (systems). Low consumption of fat and moderate consumption of sodium and sugars are recommended because consuming too much of these can lead to obesity, obesity-related illness, high blood pressure, high cholesterol, and type 2 diabetes.

BODY MASS INDEX

Body mass index (BMI) is the most widely used measure of body composition. It is the relationship between weight and height squared. The BMI formula is: weight (kg)/height (m²), and is used to determine or predict the body fat of an individual.

BMI Categories
Underweight $\leq$ 18.5 Normal weight = 18.5 to 24.9 Overweight = 25 to 29.9 Obese $\geq$ 30

BMI is the most commonly used body composition measure because it is easy to calculate and non-invasive. However, there are several limitations. BMI is an indirect measure of body fatness because it does not measure the amount of fat in the body. There are also race, ethnicity, gender, and structural differences (mesomorph, ectomorph, and endomorph) to consider. **Ectomorphs** tend to be extremely thin and have a difficult time gaining weight. However, these individuals can also be "skinny fat" and have more fat on the body than appearances suggest. **Endomorphs** tend to be short and stout and have large bones, which can elevate or positively skew BMI. While these individuals carry larger amounts of fat, they are able to build muscle. **Mesomorphs** have athletic builds, tend to be lean, and have large muscle mass, but may register as obese even when they actually have low levels of body fat.

SKINFOLDS AND WAIST CIRCUMFERENCE FOR MEASURING BODY FAT PERCENTAGE

Skinfolds are a common measure of body fat percentage which involves pinching certain areas (e.g., biceps, triceps, subscapular, suprailiac, chest, abdomen, thigh) on the body using a skinfold caliper. This method is accurate and inexpensive, but involves touching the skin. The three-site and seven-site skinfolds are commonly used and vary by gender and age. The sum score (measured in millimeters) of the sites corresponds to a body fat percentage. Waist circumference is another measure of body composition and health risks as abdominal fat poses greater threats to good health. Although there are race, ethnicity, age, gender, and body structure differences in appropriate body fat percentages and waist circumference, general guidelines suggest to keep these low and small on respective criteria.

Waist circumference is another measure of body composition, which is also easy and accurate to measure and involves taking a spring-loaded tape measure above the iliac crest to measure the circumference of the waist. Too much fat around the abdominal area increases the risk of metabolic conditions. It is recommended that women maintain a waist circumference less than 35 inches and men should aim for less than 39 inches to minimize health risks.

DIET AND EXERCISE PLANS FOR WEIGHT MANAGEMENT

A combination of physical activity, low-fat, and high-fiber diets aid in maintaining a healthy body composition. Physical activities should include cardiovascular, muscular-strength, and muscular-endurance exercises conducted most days of the week. Cardiovascular activities help burn fat during the activity, and muscular-fitness activities help burn calories during and up to one to three days after. Diets that include consuming vegetables tend to have a positive effect on body composition because these foods are low in calories but are nutrient dense (vitamins, minerals, fiber). Eating lean proteins also aids in maintaining a healthy body composition. Limiting sweets, high-fat foods, and alcohol will help maintain a healthy body composition because these contain large amounts of sugar, fat, and empty calories.

CALORIC APPROACH TO WEIGHT MANAGEMENT

Counting calories is a strategy used to help maintain a healthy body composition. To do this, one needs to calculate their basal metabolic rate to determine their caloric needs. The **basal metabolic rate (BMR)** is the number of calories needed to keep functioning at rest. To compute BMR, height, weight, gender, and age are needed. A revised version of Harrison Benedict's BMR formula is below.

Male: $(88.4 + 13.4 \times$ weight in kilograms$) + (4.8 \times$ height in centimeters$) - (5.68 \times$ age$)$

Female: $(447.6 + 9.25 \times$ weight in kilograms$) + (3.10 \times$ height in centimeters$) - (4.33 \times$ age$)$

Once BMR is established, calories consumed would be counted not to exceed the BMR if the desired body composition is met. For weight loss, either fewer calories or more physical activity is recommended for desired body composition. For weight gain, more calories (ideally from lean proteins) or heavy muscular fitness activities are recommended.

Effects of Various Factors on Health and Fitness

REST AND NUTRITION

Resting the body is essential for peak physical performance and good health. Rest includes taking a break (a day off) from training and getting adequate amounts of sleep. Rest allows the body to recover and rebuild from the physical stress put on the body. When the body and muscles are well-rested, performance tends to be more efficient, whereas little to no rest can impede progress. Nutrition is also important for physical performance and good health because poor nutrition (high fat, high sodium, no fiber) negatively impacts growth, energy, exercise recovery, and a healthy body weight. Good nutrition (vegetables, grains, lean protein, low fat) provides energy and allows for greater demands on the body.

ALCOHOL AND TOBACCO

Consuming alcohol and tobacco can negatively impact physical performance and health. Alcohol contains empty calories (7 calories per 1 gram of alcohol) and no nutritional value, which can cause unwanted weight gain. Alcohol is metabolized before carbohydrates and fat, which disrupts weight-loss goals. Alcohol is a depressant drug that slows down the central nervous system, so movement responses (e.g., reaction time) are slower. Alcohol also lowers inhibitions and impairs judgment, and when working out, an injury may occur. Excessive alcohol consumption can lead to cirrhosis of the liver (scarring) and alcoholism (addiction). Nicotine is the addictive substance that is found in tobacco products. Smoking tobacco increases the risk of cardiovascular disease (hypertension, stroke) and makes it more difficult to breathe, especially during physical activity since blood flow is restricted due to the narrowing of blood vessels. Chewing tobacco increases the risks of tooth loss and throat and mouth cancers. When people stop smoking and drinking, many of the ill effects diminish over time.

HEREDITY

Heredity (genetic characteristics) impacts physical performance and is the foundation of one's health. For example, abilities (power, reaction time, muscle fibers) are hereditary, and some have more ability than others. While all can improve, improvement will only go as far as one's genetic abilities. The same is true for health, as some people are predisposed or have a higher risk of poor health if conditions and illness run in their family. For example, if a parent has hypertension or

diabetes, the offspring are at greater risks. Physical activity and nutrition can help mitigate negative heredity aspects.

PERSONAL HEALTH RISK FACTOR ASSESSMENTS

Health risk assessments (HRA) are commonly used to evaluate personal health risk. HRAs contain a battery of questions to help determine areas of health risk. HRA questionnaires tend to ask the age, gender, race, ethnicity, history of depression, physical activity, emotional health, social activities, pain, seatbelt usage, tiredness, injuries, smoking, alcohol consumption, and other questions that pertain to health. Based on the results of the questionnaire, physicians may administer a corresponding health assessment. Today, however, there are also online versions of HRAs that can help one evaluate their own health and make changes according to the results. Another option is to get an annual physical with blood work to receive an annual report on cholesterol, lipid, blood glucose, red and white blood cell profiles, and a host of other factors that can be determined by blood tests. Results provide information on how to maintain or improve health and reduce health-risk factors.

Healthy Choices and Behaviors

SELF-DETERMINATION IN MAKING HEALTHY CHOICES

As children transition from childhood to adulthood, they need to be capable of making healthy choices for themselves. In early childhood, nutrition, sleep, hygiene, and fitness are almost solely in the hands of parents. As children age and make more decisions for themselves, they can vary the amount and types of food they eat, time they sleep, and what types of activities they participate in. Usually by middle school or high school, students have enough decision-making power over their own lives that they are really controlling their own fitness and health. It is essential to provide students with the knowledge of what types of choices there are to make and how their choices affect them in the short term and in the long term. For instance, students may not consider how sleep habits affect them, but may decide to make better choices if they realize that sleep deprivation has powerful effects on one's mood, weight management, and stress level. Self-monitoring strategies, such as a health journal or calorie-tracking applications, may be helpful in encouraging students to increase their own self-awareness and pick good goals for themselves.

PATTERNS IN HEALTH CHOICES

Habits are when a behavior choice becomes repeated enough that those choices become the default way of acting. As good habits are formed, the choice involved becomes less difficult to make, as it becomes the natural pattern. Many healthy choices are difficult to make because they require effort or sacrificing something, such as time or instant gratification. Most health choices involve short-term sacrifices to achieve a long-term result, such as losing weight from skipping snacks or candy bars every day. The ultimate result is usually very rewarding, but requires considerable effort in the short-term. Key elements to successful habit-forming is to make sure that the goal is visible and that the behavior is consistently repeated. For example, if a student wants to lose weight by skipping sugary snacks, it is best not to cheat on the diet and occasionally have a candy bar. Cheating on the diet would undercut the development of a desired good habit. The goal also must be visible. If a student cannot see progress from their efforts, then they will not feel rewarded by their hard work and will struggle to maintain it. In this situation, it should be encouraged that the student keeps records of their initial weight or size and track the changes over time to see how well their behavior choices are affecting their outcomes.

MAINTAINING A HEALTHY WEIGHT

Choices that aid in maintaining a healthy weight include engaging in regular physical activity rather than sitting, taking stand-up breaks or moving every hour instead of sitting for very long periods throughout the day, choosing a low-fat diet over a high-fat diet, and eating baked foods instead of fried foods. Taking the stairs instead of the elevator or parking the car far away from a destination rather than close can increase physical activity, which burns calories and helps with weight management. Choosing to have at least three vegetables a day instead of none will increase fiber and nutrients, which also aid in weight regulation. Choosing to eat sweets in moderation (once a week instead of seven days a week) and adhering to serving size recommendations (rather than all-you-can-eat consumption), or eating smaller portions, further support healthy weight maintenance.

Effects of Stress and Stress Management

STRESS AND ITS EFFECTS ON THE BODY.

Stress is the body's response to the demands placed on it. Stress can be either physical or psychological (mental, emotional), and it can be either positive (eustress) or negative (distress). The stress response is usually fight (confront and deal with the stress) or flight (run away or avoid the stress). Chronic stress can have damaging mental and physical effects on the body, including high blood pressure, obesity, diabetes, heart disease, heart attack, stroke, anxiety, body aches, insomnia, irritability, fatigue, chest pain, sadness, depression, and a sense of being overwhelmed.

TECHNIQUES FOR MANAGING STRESS

Techniques or strategies that help manage stress include getting adequate sleep (8 to 10 hours per day), meditation, daily physical activity, deep breathing, yoga, tai chi, laughter, and mindfulness (awareness of behaviors and responses). Progressive relaxation (alternating between tensing and contracting muscles or releasing and relaxing muscles), guided imagery, and visualization also help to manage stress. Connecting with friends and family, engaging in hobbies, listening to music, and reading a book have proven effective in managing stress. Talking to a trusted friend or a therapist is another way to help manage stress. Avoiding illicit drugs, non-prescribed prescription drugs, excessive alcohol, and excessive caffeine also helps reduce the effects of stress because such substances exacerbate the effects of stress. Too much screen time (TV, computer, video games) can also increase the effects of stress.

BENEFITS OF STRESS MANAGEMENT

Physiological benefits of stress management include increased blood flow, an ache-free body, less muscle tension, lower resting and exercise heart rate, lowered blood pressure, lowered sweat response when confronted with stress, increased concentration, lowered release of stress hormones (e.g., cortisol), and improved mood. Psychological benefits of stress management include improved mood, positive self-esteem, enhanced quality of life, positive thoughts, increased confidence in handling stressful events, lowered stress response, and reduced risk of anxiety and depression. A combination of both physiological and psychological benefits can lead to overall better health.

Common Misconceptions in Health and Fitness

COMMON MISCONCEPTIONS REGARDING PHYSICAL ACTIVITY, EXERCISE, AND HEALTH

A common misconception is that exercise and physical activity can ward off the ill-effects of a poor diet or poor nutrition. While physical activity and exercise can burn additional calories from high caloric diets, the negative effects of diets that are high in fat and sugar remain. Another misconception is that lifting weights (barbells, dumbbells, medicine balls) is the only way to get stronger, as one can also get strong by using bodyweight. This misconception is linked to the belief that a gym is needed for exercise, even though exercise can be done at home or outdoors. There are also gender misconceptions that include the belief that girls should not participate in strength training and boys should not participate in cardiovascular activities. Both types of activities are beneficial for all gender groups. The belief that one has to exercise for long bouts of time to be effective is also erroneous because research shows that health benefits can result from short bouts of intense activities that last for as little as seven minutes.

COMMON MISCONCEPTIONS ABOUT BODY SIZE AND PHYSICAL ACTIVITY, HEALTH, EXERCISE, AND DIET

Two common misconceptions about body size in relation to physical activity, health, exercise, and diet are that 1) a large body size or thick frame is unfit and unhealthy and 2) a small body size or thin frame is fit and healthy. In reality, it is difficult to assess fitness and determine health simply by looking at someone. A large person can be fit, healthy, and lean, whereas a thin person can be unfit, unhealthy, and overfat. It depends on the behavior and genetics of an individual. For example, a large body or a person classified as overweight can engage in regular physical activity and eat a healthy diet and have a better fitness level and metabolic profile than a sedentary (inactive) thin person who eats poorly. A fitness assessment and medical exam (e.g., blood work) are required to determine fitness, fatness, and health. These misconceptions are attributed to the war on both childhood and adult obesity, which is responsible for weight loss misconceptions, such as the effects of fad diets. Fad diets are temporary programs that usually involve the extreme restriction of one or more food groups (no carbs, no fat, one meal a day) and are designed for fast weight loss. This short-term solution is not sustaining and once the fad diet stops, the lost weight is regained, and sometimes more weight is gained than prior to starting the fad diet.

EDUCATING STUDENTS ON HEALTH, PHYSICAL ACTIVITY, EXERCISE, DIET MISCONCEPTIONS, AND FAULTY PRACTICES

Teaching students about nutrition and the functions of nutrients at rest and during physical activity is a strategy for combating diet **misconceptions**. Using simulations and videos that accompany the misconceptions has also shown effective. Conducting **mini-research projects** by evaluating fad diets and weight loss products gives students practical opportunities to see the effects of health and fitness misconceptions. Students can also learn how to calculate their caloric needs and shop for foods (online or in-person) that promote optimal functioning, rather than the foods and calories needed for fad diets. Illustrations of the harmful effects of certain behaviors, foods, and practices are also helpful. Students should also learn how to read food labels and ingredients lists. Contraindicated exercises and joint movements and their harmful effects should also be taught (e.g., a lat pull behind the neck can damage the neck, shoulders, and back) because the risks of some exercises supersede the benefits.

Evaluating Health and Fitness Products and Services

QUACKERY AND FALSE INFORMATION IN HEALTH

Quackery is exaggerated, non-scientific claims (testimonials) about the benefits or effectiveness of a product. Quackery is used to sell quick-fix solutions to health and fitness problems. Quackery products tend to use actors to sell the items or testimonials from individuals who had atypical results. The adage "it's too good to be true" is a common and accurate response to quackery. Strategies used to avoid quackery and evaluate health and fitness products include reading labels and ingredients and researching where the content originates. Health and fitness products should originate from or be supported by scientific evidence or medical experts. The Food and Drug Administration (FDA) is the evaluating agency for food, drugs, medical devices, and other substances to ensure that products are safe for Americans to consume or use. Only FDA-approved items have gone through rigorous scientific evaluation that includes thousands of trials before dissemination to the public. Some FDA products require a doctor's prescription (controlled) and some are over-the-counter (e.g., aspirin, ibuprofen). The FDA further ensures safety by continual tracking of effectiveness and side effects, and will remove substances and devices from the public if the risks outweigh the benefits. Many over-the-counter health and fitness substances are neither FDA approved nor supported by scientific research.

EVALUATING INFORMATION RELATED TO HEALTH AND FITNESS PROGRAMS

One strategy to use to evaluate health and related fitness programs is to determine the reputation of the source. For example, programs developed by health and fitness agencies that are accredited to grant certifications are more reputable than programs that are not because they have experts from diverse fields engaged in research on the most effective practices and go through a rigorous process to become accredited. Agencies with strong health and fitness programs include the American College of Sports Medicine, the American Council on Exercise, the National Academy of Sports Medicine, and the National Strength and Conditioning Association, although there are others. Nutrition programs should also be endorsed by reputable agencies, and nutrition plans should only be prescribed by licensed nutritionists or dietitians.

EVALUATING HEALTH AND FITNESS FACILITIES AND SERVICES

Visiting several health and fitness facilities is one strategy used for evaluation to determine the best option. Things to consider during visits include evaluations of facility size; equipment, including the type, age, safety, and maintenance; the location; dates of operation; parking; the distance to travel; fitness class offerings and schedule; day care options; costs; cleanliness; showering and changing facilities; members (coed, same-sex, age, general fitness, body building, power lifting); and personnel. Personal trainers and group fitness instructors should be certified by reputable agencies and certified in first aid, CPR (cardiopulmonary resuscitation), and AED (automated external defibrillation). A serviced AED and fire extinguisher should be visible, and emergency plans posted or available.

Legal and Ethical Responsibilities

CONFIDENTIALITY ISSUES IN PHYSICAL EDUCATION

There are certain legal and ethical considerations in regards to keeping student confidentiality. Any information shared in meetings about students, including students with individualized education plans (IEP) and medical or health conditions, should be kept confidential. When students share confidential information with a teacher, the teacher must weigh the risk involved and report any information a student tells them that may cause physical harm to the student or another person. For example, if a student is homicidal or suicidal, the teacher must report this immediately to the counselor and an administrator. If a student shares that they are harming themselves (e.g., cutting), this too must be shared with the counselor. However, the teacher should both encourage the student to tell the counselor themselves and inform the student of their intentions. Teachers must adhere to any school and district policies and also to local and state laws. If the student discusses a sexuality issue (gay, lesbian, transgender), pregnancy, or relationship status in confidence, while not illegal, disclosing this type of information may eliminate student trust and could possibly pose physical or psychological harm to the student, depending on the environment.

SUPERVISION, LIABILITY, AND NEGLECT

Providing a safe environment is a top priority for teachers. To keep the environment safe, adequate supervision is essential. The teacher should position themselves where they can see all students and be aware of unsafe behaviors. The teacher should also be first to arrive in the teaching space, and should put rules in place if students arrive first. For instance, students should not touch any equipment or engage in physical activity until the teacher arrives and provides instructions. The teacher should check the equipment for damage, and review and post safety rules. Teachers should be aware of their students' strengths and limitations to ensure that activities are safe and appropriate. Accidents and injury are more frequent in physical education settings than other subject areas, thus prevention is critical so that teachers are less likely to be held liable or deemed negligent. **Liability** is a violation of responsibilities (aka duty) usually attributed to negligence. **Negligence** is misconduct that includes failure to create a safe environment that eliminates or reduces the risk of harm. For example, if students are playing soccer without using shin guards and a student gets injured (fractured shin), that would be considered negligence and the teacher could be held liable.

LEGAL AND ETHICAL ISSUES AND RESPONSIBILITIES IN REGARDS TO THE STANDARDS OF CARE

It is the responsibility of school personnel, including the teacher, to ensure that the teaching environment is safe and that standards of care procedures are in place. It is expected that teachers identify or foresee risks and take actions to eliminate or minimize those risks. Teachers should be aware of all legal liability policies, as they are expected to provide a reasonable standard of care according to their professional expertise. Lawsuits may occur if standards of care were not provided, in which negligence would have to be proven. **Malfeasance** is a type of negligence when a teacher engages in misconduct by committing an unlawful act. For instance, a teacher may give a student two negative discipline choices (corporal punishment or run a mile) after misbehaving, but because both choices can cause physical harm, emotional harm, or both, the teacher is liable. **Misfeasance** is the type of negligence where the teacher adheres to proper protocols, but implements them inappropriately (improperly spotting a student during the bench press). **Nonfeasance** is when a teacher fails to act (aka act of omission). For example, if the teacher knows how to spot a student performing the bench press but does not do so, they can be held liable if an injury occurs.

ABUSE AND EXPLOITATION

Abuse is the misuse of another person or treating another person with cruelty. **Exploitation** is using someone unfairly for personal gain. It is against the law to abuse and exploit children. Examples of abuse include physical (e.g., hitting, spanking), verbal (profanity, derogatory words), mental or emotional (humiliation, sarcasm, name calling), and sexual abuse (touching students inappropriately). Physical activity should not be used as punishment (e.g., 10 push-ups for misbehaving) because doing so is considered physical abuse. If it is suspected that a student is experiencing abuse (bruises, broken bones, unexplained injuries, inappropriate contact), the teacher should make record of it and notify the school counselor or psychologist immediately. An example of exploitation would be having students do the teacher's work for free (e.g., supervising students, locker room duty).

TEACHER RESPONSIBILITIES IN RELATION TO STUDENT RIGHTS

Other **student rights** include free speech, the right to wear certain clothing and hairstyles, immigration status, speaking English as a second language (ESL), and the freedom from racial, ethnic, and religious discrimination. At times, schools have policies that are discriminatory (no dreadlocks or long hair allowed, English proficiency required for entry), or illegal practices (asking for students' social media and cell phone information) that infringe on freedom of speech and expression, with the latter infringing upon privacy laws—all of which can cause lawsuits. Teachers have the responsibility to ensure that the environment is **safe and equitable** to meet all students' needs. For instance, a female Muslim student should be allowed to wear a head covering (hijab) at school and in physical education, since the prevention of this would be a violation of the student's religious freedom. Schools and teachers are required by law to provide assistance to students who are not proficient in English. Teachers should also not engage in racist behaviors (treating students negatively based on race or ethnicity).

SEX AND GENDER DISCRIMINATION LAWS (TITLE IX)

Title IX is a federal law enacted in 1972 to end sex and gender discrimination in education and athletics, as girls had less physical education time, less equipment, and fewer sporting opportunities than boys. Prior to Title IX, physical education classes were segregated by gender. After Title IX was enacted, physical education classes became coeducational (coed) with a few exceptions. Title IX was later expanded to protect other groups, including individuals who identify as LGBTQ. Teachers need to make sure that they balance privacy and protection while also maintaining accountability and safety for themselves and other students. For instance, if the only alternative location for a student to change clothes is unsupervised, then the teacher will have to conduct a risk-benefit analysis on the steps to take.

INCLUSION LAWS AND GUIDELINES FOR STUDENTS WITH DISABILITIES

The Individuals with Disabilities Education Act (IDEA) is a federally sanctioned law that ensures a quality educational experience for students with disabilities. Teachers should ensure that accommodations are implemented to meet the needs of students with disabilities. Disabilities can be mental, physical, or both. In physical education settings, adapted physical education (APE) focuses on students with disabilities. To make sure that the learning environment is inclusive, teachers must design instruction to serve all students. As with students without disabilities, teachers should plan intently on helping the students with disabilities to be successful or able to meet the outcomes with modifications and adaptations.

> **Review Video: Medical Conditions in Education**
> Visit mometrix.com/academy and enter code: 531058

PRIVACY LAWS INVOLVING MEDICAL AND PERSONAL INFORMATION

Privacy laws are mandated by the federal government. States can also have independent privacy laws, but they cannot deviate from the federal mandates. The Federal Education Records and Privacy Act (FERPA) indicates that any school receiving federal funding cannot share student records or any other identifiable information without consent (permission) of the student or parent of a minor. This includes individual education plans (IEPs), health and medical issues, and other personal information about the student. However, IEPs and some health issues (such as attention deficit disorder, or ADD, and attention deficit hyperactivity disorder, or ADHD), may be shared with teachers of the student to best meet the student's needs. Students also have the right to see their records or personal school files. Photos and videos of students should not be shared or posted without student or parent permission and consent. Students, however, only have moderate levels of privacy in situations where supervision is still required to ensure student safety and minimize bullying risk, such as in locker rooms.

Chapter Quiz

Ready to see how well you retained what you just read? Scan the QR code to go directly to the chapter quiz interface for this study guide. If you're using a computer, simply visit the bonus page at **mometrix.com/bonus948/priihpeck5857** and click the Chapter Quizzes link.

Management, Motivation, and Communication

Transform passive reading into active learning! After immersing yourself in this chapter, put your comprehension to the test by taking a quiz. The insights you gained will stay with you longer this way. Scan the QR code to go directly to the chapter quiz interface for this study guide. If you're using a computer, simply visit the bonus page at **mometrix.com/bonus948/priihpeck5857** and click the Chapter Quizzes link.

Student Motivation and Lifelong Physical Fitness

MOTIVATING STUDENTS TO PARTICIPATE IN LIFELONG PHYSICAL ACTIVITY

Teachers who role model or engage in physical activity have shown to motivate students to engage in physical activity for life. Students who are skilled or proficient in the fundamental movement patterns are also more likely to engage in physical activities as adults. Positive feedback with explicit acknowledgement of effort and improvement is another effective strategy that encourages regular physical activity. Furthermore, activities that promote self-efficacy and autonomy, which are better achieved with student goal-setting, also helps foster physical activity engagement. Students who have knowledge of the benefits of physical activity and the consequences of not engaging in physical activity further fosters motivation to engage in physical activity over the lifespan.

EFFECTS OF SELF-ASSESSMENT AND PROGRESS TRACKING ON STUDENT MOTIVATION

Self-assessment aids in motivating students to participate in lifelong physical activity as it allows students to evaluate their own performance. From the assessment, students evaluate and reflect on their performance and will either continue, revise, or update goals. As students revisit goals and create a plan to achieve those goals, they will track progress over time to determine growth or the lack thereof. Ongoing self-assessment and reflection allows students to take ownership and responsibility in their performance and develop a plan suitable for their needs. These activities help develop intrinsic motivation, which has shown more effective than extrinsic motivation in promoting lifelong physical activity.

SELF-EFFICACY

Self-efficacy is belief in one's ability to perform motor skills. The development of self-efficacy leads to self-motivation and is strongly associated with engaging in physical activity over the lifespan. There are four circumstances that have shown to increase self-efficacy listed below.

1. Past performance: previous experience of accomplishment or success in a performance task or skill (success in one sport increases the self-efficacy of learning a new sport)
2. Observing others (vicarious learning): watching someone else perform the task or exhibit the skill, which fosters confidence to attempt and perform the task or develop the ("If they can do it, so can I")
3. Verbal persuasion: encouragement from a teacher, parent, or peer ("You can do it!")
4. Physiological cues: kinesthetic responses to the environment (body position or sensory awareness, which is enhanced through repetition and practice)

71

Classroom and Resource Management

ORGANIZING TIME, LOCATION, AND EQUIPMENT

Planning ahead and providing clear and concise instructions will reduce classroom management and behavioral issues. A schedule of teaching space should be known long before the semester begins. Once the location has been determined, the dimensions of the space and knowledge of the type, amount, and location of equipment should also be known. If there are other teachers on staff, communication on teaching rotations and activities should be discussed to avoid conflicts and time wasting. Establishing routines from student entry and exit, attendance, warm-up, equipment distribution, and equipment cleanup helps students move quickly without losing instructional time or allowing time for students to get off task. A strategy for entrance and attendance is to have students walk to assigned squad lines and conduct an active warm-up while attendance is taken. The teacher can take attendance or assign a squad line leader. Squad lines make it easy to see who is absent. Another management strategy is to have students conduct an instant activity (IA) as soon as they enter the gym or field that can be posted for students to read upon entry. Attendance should be taken during the IA, which allows students to immediately engage and reduces time for off-task behaviors. This IA can also serve as a warm-up or an opportunity to pre-assess or post-assess students' skill levels and performance.

ALLOCATING TIME, LOCATION, AND EQUIPMENT

Every minute of instructional time should be accounted for. All tasks and activities, including transitions, should have an allotted time when lesson planning (e.g., three minutes, five minutes). The equipment should be out and ready for easy retrieval (e.g., on the sidelines, in the corners of the teaching space). If outside, a backup plan (go to the gym, multi-purpose room, classroom) should be in place in case of inclement or unsafe weather (e.g., rain, heat, cold). Students should be trained and assigned roles to help put equipment away. This saves time and promotes personal responsibility and teamwork, which will minimize disruptions in the future. When sharing teaching space, communication and planning are extremely important because conflicts are likely to occur when there is a communication breakdown. Teachers who teach at the same time, in the same place, and use the same equipment should meet before the school year to map out activities, equipment usage (setting up and breaking down), teaching space (one-half or one-third of the court or field), rules, routines, duties, and protocols (e.g., locker room, attendance, and warm-up procedures) to optimize the learning experience. Some teachers elect to team teach, where one teacher leads while the other helps facilitate. This is often done so teachers can teach to their strengths and to reduce management issues.

CLASSROOM MANAGEMENT APPROACHES

Large class sizes, minimal space, and lack of equipment are limitations of taking attendance, physical activities, and managing time. Large classes require more time to move and take attendance, and they require extra safety measures in cramped spaces. Squad lines (students arranged in rows or lines of 5 to 10, forming a box shape) are more effective than instant activities for large groups because students are more contained, which reduces the risk of injury. Large class sizes, minimal space, and the lack of equipment do not give students the opportunity to engage in all of the same activities at the same time. For example, a common approach is to have half of the class in the center of the court or field engaging in activities, while the other half are doing activities on the sidelines. While this approach increases safety, it does not allow students to fully engage in the learning objectives and decreases practice time for refinement and improvement. Large class sizes also make it more difficult for the teacher to see all students and provide appropriate feedback.

> **Review Video: Classroom Management - Rhythms of Teaching**
> Visit mometrix.com/academy and enter code: 809399

Maintaining a Positive Learning Climate

GENDER DIVERSE CLASSES

To avoid gender favoritism and gender disparities in physical education, teachers should expect all students to engage in the activities and work towards the performance goals. Teachers should create coeducational activities and incorporate student preferences into the curriculum and activities. All students should be included in gender stereotypic games activities (e.g., boys engaging in dance and gymnastics and girls engaging in team sports like football). Teachers should not use or allow stereotypic language like, "You throw like a girl." The teacher should also monitor time given to all groups to ensure equal time is given and that one group does not dominate another. The teacher can also reflect on their behaviors to make sure that they are not responding to one gender group over another.

MIXED-ABILITY CLASSES

A cooperative environment helps foster inclusion in mixed ability classes. Depending on the objective, groups can contain students of mixed abilities, but sometimes students with the same abilities need to be grouped. For example, novice learners may need to be grouped together to focus on skill levels because grouping these novices with more skilled students may intimidate and discourage them from participation. The skilled students may get frustrated as beginner skills and activities below their more advanced skill level become boring and causes them to go off task. However, sometimes mixed groupings may be beneficial when peer coaching or teaching is practiced and advanced students work with beginners, since there is evidence that students learn best from peers.

DIFFERENT CULTURAL BACKGROUNDS

Strategies that promote a healthy social climate for students of various cultural backgrounds include offering diverse curricula, activities, and teaching approaches that include all student groups. If English is a second or additional language for students, cues and assignments should also include the student's first language. Respect and understanding of other cultures should be the standard, and derogatory language and behaviors should not be tolerated. The teacher should explore cultural practices, differences in discipline, and physical activity expectations. For instance, in some cultures, it is disrespectful to look teachers or authority figures in the eyes. In other cultures, and in some religions, physical activity is discouraged. In these instances, asking questions about cultural and physical activity expectations and conveying the facts (not opinions) about the benefits of physical activity and social engagement in American culture should be shared with students and parents. Additionally, some cultures and religions do not allow for bare skin to be exposed, so students should not be penalized if these factors prevent them from changing out of their clothing and into the school PE uniform.

Developing Positive Interpersonal Skills in Physical Education

DEVELOPING CONFIDENCE THROUGH PHYSICAL ACTIVITIES

Games and sports promote the development of confidence through leadership in both the various roles involved and accomplishing a goal. For example, in team sports, everyone has a role and a responsibility that helps the team work towards a goal. Games and sports also involve competition, which provides opportunities to develop competence, which has shown to increase motivation and confidence. Successful students, players, and teams tend to have greater confidence than unsuccessful students, players, and teams. Therefore, the learning environment should be challenging yet attainable to help build confidence. Dance helps promote confidence as students are able to move freely without judgment or competition. In dances that involve steps, learning or mastery of these dances helps build confidence through accomplishing the task of learning the dance steps.

FAIRNESS AND RESPECT FOR DIVERSITY

Games and sports are governed by rules that involve fair play. Fair play has to be taught and includes personal responsibility, showing respect to self and others, giving full effort, and being helpful. Diversity is promoted through games and sports as teams and opponents tend to include different types of individuals (gender, race, ethnicity, ability, learning styles), and sport and games allow for interactions across groups that can aid in a better understanding of similarities and differences. A respect for diversity can also be developed and promoted through dance as individuals have the opportunity to engage in freedom of expression. In PE curricula, dances from around the world and from different cultures are taught (the Virginia reel, polka, African dance, folk dances, square dance), exposing children to other people's cultures and fostering inclusion, diversity, and respect for others.

CONFLICT RESOLUTION SKILLS

Outdoor pursuits help develop conflict resolutions skills by having students engage in challenging tasks like high ropes courses and partner or group activities like trust falls. Partner and group activities require frequent communication to problem solve or accomplish a task. Dual and team sports are also avenues that promote conflict resolution skills, as communication is needed for the team's success. It is customary for a player to apologize when they make an error. Players also communicate how to strategize against an opponent, which is an example of solving a problem. For example, when a teammate keeps losing to his or her opponent, the team will need to communicate with each other to either switch roles, provide assistance, or utilize a different defensive strategy to solve the problem.

TURN TAKING AND TEAMWORK

Games and sports require cooperation and collaboration, thus the promotion of teamwork. Teamwork is shown through working together to score a point, playing defense and offense, and communicating to accomplish these tasks. Taking turns is evident in games and sports when players have to substitute in and out of a game. In softball and baseball, batters have to wait for their turn. Taking turns is also evident in group games like jumping rope, where the jumpers have to wait for the person in front to complete their jump before entering. The rope turners also take turns. Students or players on the sidelines also demonstrate teamwork by cheering and encouraging other active students or players.

TREATING OPPONENTS WITH RESPECT AND LEADERSHIP SKILLS

Sport and game etiquette are promoted and teach how players should treat their opponents. For example, if a player from the opposing team falls, a respectful act would be to assist the opponent with getting up. During a sport, it is common to take a knee out of respect when a player gets injured. This knee position is held until the player gets up or is taken off of the field or court. Calling personal fouls and apologizing if one causes harm are other examples of treating opponents with respect that are developed and promoted through games and sports. Wishing the opposition good luck before the game and shaking hands at the end of play are other examples of how to treat opponents with respect. Opportunities for leadership are promoted in roles including team captain and positions played. For example, in basketball, the point guard is usually responsible for bringing the ball up the court and calling the offense, making this player the leader in this capacity. Other players also have a role and lead in their respective positions.

EXAMPLES OF LEADERSHIP, TAKING TURNS, AND LOYALTY IN OUTDOOR ACTIVITIES

Examples of teamwork, taking turns, and loyalty are evident in outdoor activities. For instance, rock climbing activities in physical education require a climber and three to four belayers (anchors who support the climber). The belayers work and communicate as one unit and provide safety (loyalty) and leadership for the climber. The belayers also provide encouragement to help the climber reach the top of the climb, which illustrates leadership. If the belayers are not focused while supporting the climber, injury can occur. Climbers and belayers change roles, which illustrates taking turns. In partner or couples' dances (foxtrot, tango, salsa), there is a leader and follower, which gives students opportunities to engage in leadership. These roles are usually switched, which illustrates taking turns in the leader and follower roles. The climber in rock climbing and the follower in dance have to trust that the belayers and leader know what they are doing, and consistency in performance helps students demonstrate loyalty.

Promoting Self-Management Skills

Self-assessment (evaluating performance) and **self-monitoring** (observation of self) are used to help students reflect on and evaluate their own performance by identifying strengths, weaknesses, and the learning process. These self-monitoring methods are self-regulation strategies or self-management skills that help students take ownership of their learning. Self-management skills include the ability to identify successes and failures and to create goals for improvement, which promotes intrinsic motivation to engage in physical activity. Of these strategies, goal setting is considered the most important because students are choosing their own specific focus and outcome. As such, goals should be specific and measurable, which helps students determine the next steps for practice, remediation, or growth.

STUDENT RESPONSIBILITY AND SELF-CONTROL

Assigning roles to students helps them develop responsible behaviors and self-control. Common roles in physical education include line or squad line leader, exercise or warm-up leader, equipment manager, and attendance taker. Behavioral rules and expectations help promote self-control. A common behavioral method used in physical education is Don Hellison's teaching personal and social responsibility (TPSR) model, which aims to teach personal and social responsibility. The TPSR model has five levels listed below.

1. Respect for others' rights and feelings (manage temper, work towards peaceful conflict resolution)
2. Effort: practice and learn persistence and intrinsic motivation, take on challenges
3. Self-direction: goal-setting, refraining from peer pressure
4. Helping others
5. Behaviors are carried over outside of the gym: the goal of having values learned in class transfer to other environments (e.g., home, playground)

These behaviors can be the focus during an individual lesson, unit, or every lesson. However, students are often taught each level and evaluate where they were on a particular day or lesson. It is recommended that this model is embedded with other instructional models because stand-alone use is not effective for behavior change.

HELLISON'S TEACHING PERSONAL AND SOCIAL RESPONSIBILITY (TPSR) MODEL

Hellison's **Teaching Personal and Social Responsibility** (TPSR) model seeks to promote students' ability to take responsibility for their actions in the physical education classroom and carry that responsibility into the students' lives. This model, therefore, is useful in helping to develop students' ability to **manage success** and **failure** well. The elements of the TPSR model apply to both success and failure. Students who may care too much about winning or losing may lose their temper when losing, and therefore may need to work on improving their **respect** for others' rights and feelings. Other students may not care enough about success and may not put in the necessary **effort** to perform well. Alternatively, a student who succeeds in sports on talent may have a poor attitude about their abilities and not respect other students who are not as skilled. Another consequence might be that a talented student may not put forth the effort required to further develop their skills. The **self-direction** stage may be a good focal point for a student who remains unchallenged without specific goals. Helping the student to **self-evaluate** and target particular skills may help to keep the student motivated and able to grow more efficiently. Ultimately, the goals of TPSR are skills well suited to learning through physical education, but apply to the whole life of a student.

STUDENTS' GOAL-SETTING ABILITIES

To help students develop goal-setting abilities, they must be taught that goals should be specific and measurable. An example should be given, such as, "I can hit the target 6 out of 10 times." Students should be told to create a moderately challenging goal. A goal that is too easy lacks challenge, and a goal that is too difficult can create frustration. Students should also be encouraged to set short-term and long-term goals. When students set their own goals, they gain a sense of accomplishment and personal satisfaction, which fosters intrinsic motivation and competence.

PROBLEM-SOLVING SKILLS

Teachers can help students analyze and problem-solve through guided discovery and cooperative learning. **Guided discovery** is when the teacher structures the environment to where students can figure out or solve the problem on their own. Using this method, the teacher asks students questions to help "guide" them to accomplish predetermined tasks. This has also been called a **problem-solving approach.** Rather than having one right answer, there are usually several options to complete the tasks. For example, a task may be to get from one obstacle to another without walking. Students would then analyze the obstacles, make a decision on what they think is the best method, and attempt the tasks. If the students are successful, they have solved the problem. To further aid in analyzing and problem-solving, the teacher may follow up and ask if there is another way to complete the task, at which time students would have to continue with their analysis and attempt to solve the problem another way.

DECISION-MAKING SKILLS

Tactical learning approaches help students with decision-making skills used in individual, dual, and team sports. In sports, every move made or action performed is a decision. Practicing sports skills during modified game play (e.g., the tactical approach) allows students opportunities to consistently make decisions. Depending on the outcome of the decision, students will either continue or do something different. For example, if a student conducted a fake before kicking the ball into the goal, he or she may try to do the same thing the next time. However, if the fake was

unsuccessful and the ball got stolen, the student will likely make another choice. If a student continues to make the same error, the teacher may have to ask questions to help the student do something different. Experiencing the tactics helps students develop an inventory of things to do and what decision to make according to the environment.

Chapter Quiz

Ready to see how well you retained what you just read? Scan the QR code to go directly to the chapter quiz interface for this study guide. If you're using a computer, simply visit the bonus page at **mometrix.com/bonus948/priihpeck5857** and click the Chapter Quizzes link.

Planning, Instruction, and Student Assessment

Transform passive reading into active learning! After immersing yourself in this chapter, put your comprehension to the test by taking a quiz. The insights you gained will stay with you longer this way. Scan the QR code to go directly to the chapter quiz interface for this study guide. If you're using a computer, simply visit the bonus page at **mometrix.com/bonus948/priihpeck5857** and click the Chapter Quizzes link.

Principles and Benefits of a Physically Active Lifestyle

CARDIOVASCULAR ENDURANCE

Cardiovascular endurance is one of five health-related fitness components. Cardiovascular activities involve engaging in continuous gross motor movements that work the heart and lungs. Cardiovascular activities include walking, jogging, swimming, cycling, hiking, and aerobic dance. It is recommended that youth engage in at least 60 minutes of cardiovascular activities three to six days a week. Adults should engage in at least 30-minute exercises five days a week, or 150 to 225 minutes per week. Cardiovascular outcomes are enhanced with muscular fitness and flexibility training because they have a synergistic effect (work together in unison).

BENEFITS OF LIVING A PHYSICALLY ACTIVE LIFESTYLE

The benefits of living a physically active lifestyle include lowering the risk of diabetes, heart attack, and heart disease, which are the foremost killers in the United States. Blood pressure and blood cholesterol are also lowered. Further, bones and muscles are strengthened, which lowers the risks of falling or developing osteoporosis. Physical activity increases metabolism, helps maintain a healthy body weight, and helps improve immunity needed to fight off infections, including some cancers. Physical activity also improves mood, reduces stress, increases energy, improves sleep, and has shown to improve academic outcomes.

CIRCUIT TRAINING

Circuit training is a great way to introduce students to multiple types of exercises. Circuit training is a fitness activity made up of 6 to 10 stations that are used to improve the health-related fitness components (cardiovascular endurance, muscular strength and endurance, flexibility, body composition) and skill-related fitness components (agility, speed, power). Students participate in each activity for a designated time or number of repetitions before rotating to the next exercise. Circuit training tends to be enjoyable because it is non-competitive, provides variety, and allows students to work at their own pace. Music usually accompanies circuit training, which has shown to positively impact student intensity and engagement.

LEARNING OPPORTUNITIES THAT PROMOTE PARTICIPATION IN PHYSICAL ACTIVITIES

Learning opportunities that promote participation and enjoyment of physical fitness activities include engaging in a variety of activities and developing individualized programs that include personal goal setting, feedback, encouragement, enthusiasm, and role modeling. Variety in activities reduces boredom and allows students to engage in activities they will find enjoyable. Individualized programs with personal goals give students ownership of want they want to work on or improve, which increases the likelihood of participation. Encouragement and providing feedback with a positive attitude foster positive feelings among students, which in turn can elicit student buy-in. Students are also more likely to engage in physical activity if the teacher also engages in physical activity.

PHYSIOLOGICAL ADAPTATIONS IN RESPONSE TO REGULAR PHYSICAL ACTIVITY

Physiological adaptations that occur from regularly engaging in cardiovascular physical activity include increased perspiration, stronger and more elastic smooth muscles, decreased heart rate, and an increase in both the size and strength of the heart, which increases blood flow and volume. Oxygen transfer (gas exchange) becomes more efficient due to an increase in alveoli and capillaries in the lungs, which aids in an increase in VO2 max or aerobic capacity. There is also an increase of nutrients and glucose to the muscles performing the work. Exercise recovery also improves as it becomes easier to remove lactic acid. Slow twitch fibers (responsible for slow continuous movements) become more efficient as they are easier to recruit by regularly engaging in cardiovascular physical activity. These adaptations aid in lowering the risks of hypokinetic diseases and obesity-related conditions (e.g., diabetes, heart disease, metabolic syndrome).

HEALTH BENEFITS OF REGULARLY PHYSICAL ACTIVITY

Engaging in **regular physical activity** increases life expectancy, improves mood, reduces the risk of some cancers, lowers blood pressure, aids in weight loss, and helps maintain a healthy body composition. Physical activity strengthens bones, which lowers the risk of developing osteoporosis, improves mobility and flexibility, and reduces the risk of falling. Regular physical activity has shown to improve mental alertness, judgement, learning, and relieve some symptoms of depression. Heart rate is also lowered by engaging in regular physical activity, and the risk of heart disease goes down. Blood glucose and insulin are also regulated, and diabetes and other metabolic conditions can be managed by engaging in regular physical activity.

HYPOKINETIC DISEASES AND METABOLIC SYNDROME

Hypokinetic diseases result from inactivity or living a sedentary lifestyle. Hypokinetic diseases include heart disease, obesity, diabetes, and stroke. **Metabolic syndrome** is a collection of diseases or risk factors, including high blood glucose, high blood pressure, excessive fat around the waist, and high cholesterol, which increases the risk of heart attack, stroke, and diabetes. Hypokinetic diseases and metabolic syndrome are often referred to as lifestyle diseases or conditions because most can be prevented by engaging in regular physical activity, eating a healthy diet, avoiding or limiting certain foods (sodium, fried foods) and substances (smoking tobacco and excessive alcohol intake). Engaging in regular physical activity lowers these risks.

Components of Health-Related Fitness

MUSCULAR STRENGTH AND MUSCULAR ENDURANCE

Muscular strength is the amount of force (push, pull, lift) exerted by the muscles, as shown in lifting weights and performing push-ups. **Muscular endurance** is the ability for the muscles to work continuously or repeatedly without excessive fatigue. Muscular endurance is measured through assessments such as the curl-up test. Although these are two separate health-related fitness components, improvement in one will improve the other. For example, if the fitness goal is to increase size and strength in the quadriceps, training would include lifting heavy loads at low rep counts. Muscular endurance would also improve, but endurance would be gained at a slower rate than size and strength. To train for muscular endurance in quadriceps, the load would be lighter and the rep count higher. Again, the quadriceps will get stronger, but would not likely increase in size due to the low weight and high rep count.

CARDIOVASCULAR ENDURANCE

Cardiovascular endurance is the ability to engage in continuous physical activity that increases the heart rate and sweat response. Cardiovascular activities use the heart and lungs, which become more efficient with regular engagement. Engaging in cardiovascular activities lowers the risk of heart disease (coronary artery disease, high cholesterol, heart attack), hypertension, obesity, and metabolic conditions such as type 2 diabetes. Cardiovascular activities also improve mood as endorphins ("happy hormones") are released. Blood also flows more freely, which increases oxygen levels, thus making it easier to breathe. The benefits of cardiovascular activities increase as the frequency and time increases.

BODY COMPOSITION AND FLEXIBILITY

Body composition is the measure of muscle, bone, and fat in the body. It is commonly associated with a measure of body fatness (e.g., body mass index, body fat percentage). Maintaining a healthy body composition reduces the risks of obesity and obesity-related conditions. Engaging in muscular and cardiovascular fitness activities along with good nutrition help with the maintenance of a healthy body composition. **Flexibility** is the range of motion at the joint. The lengthening or stretching of muscles helps increase flexibility, which helps increase mobility. Flexibility is often overlooked, but it should be developed just as the cardiovascular and muscular fitness components are. Flexibility contributes to more efficient mechanical movements in these health-related fitness components. In addition to increasing mobility, flexibility helps with posture, body awareness, reduces muscle soreness after engaging in other vigorous activities, and reduces the risk of debilitating back pain. Deep stretching along with deep breathing (e.g., yoga) has also shown to also improve mental health and wellbeing. A lack of flexibility increases the risk of poor health, including pain, stiffness, and difficulty performing daily tasks.

FITT PRINCIPLE

The **FITT** acronym stands for frequency, intensity, time, and type. It is a simple guide to fitness training principles deemed appropriate for children and sedentary adults. **Frequency** is how often one engages in physical activity or exercise. **Intensity** is the difficulty or challenge of the activities (heart rate, load and weight, reps). **Time** is the duration or how long one engages in physical activity per session (20 minutes, 60 minutes). **Type** is the kind of activities chosen (weight training, cardiovascular activities, yoga). When using the FITT principle, favorable physiological outcomes can occur, as engaging in a variety of physical activity several days a week has shown to promote good health.

WARM-UP AND COOLDOWN IN EXERCISE

Conducting a **warm-up** before engaging in exercise prepares the body for more vigorous activity and may reduce the risk of injury. Warm-ups generally consist of bouts of low-intensity activities and dynamic movements, lasting 5 to 10 minutes, to increase blood flow to the muscles and heart. The warm-up should reflect or be specific to the activities that will be performed. A cooldown also consists of low-intensity activities and helps return the body back to pre-exercise or normal conditions to restore the body's homeostasis (equilibrium, or bringing heart rate and other systems back to normal). The **cooldown** is the gradual slowing down of the more vigorous exercise session. Stretching may or may not be involved in the cooldown, although stretching during the cooldown, when the muscles are still warm, is best. To increase flexibility, static stretching (holding the stretch for several seconds) is preferred during the cooldown as well.

OVERLOAD AND PROGRESSION IN EXERCISE

Overload is performing more work than is normal or putting stress on the body's systems, either of which can produce physiological adaptations. For example, if one mile of walking is the normal activity done throughout the day, then to increase cardiovascular fitness, one would have to walk more than one mile a day or adapt the routine to include jogging or running, either of which would put more stress on the body than what is normal, thus increasing the intensity. **Progression** (aka progressive overload) is the gradual increase in overload to reduce the risk of injury and to prevent overtraining or overuse, which can demotivate individuals to continue in an exercise program.

Fitness Goals and Planning

SMART GOAL-SETTING METHOD

The **SMART** goal-setting method is designed to help individuals create goals, track progress, and have accountability measures. When setting fitness or exercise goals, they should be specific, measurable, achievable, relevant, and timely. For example, a weight loss goal for someone who is 10 pounds overweight might be to lose five pounds (specific, attainable, and measurable) in 12 weeks (attainable within in the time frame). Based on this goal, the person would design a physical activity program that complements the goal and take an inventory of foods that negate this outcome. A pre-assessment and post-assessment of weight would be taken on a scale (measurable) to determine if the goal was met. They could also measure their weight once a week to track progress over time, especially if the goal is met sooner. If the goal is met before the timeline, a new goal would be created.

DESIGNING EFFECTIVE HEALTH AND FITNESS PLANS

In order to reap the rewards or experience of the physiological adaptations that occur as a result of engaging in physical activity and exercise, the activities must be performed with **regularity**, or consistency. The activities should also be performed with **specificity**, which is achieved by participating in activities that address the desired outcomes. For example, if the goal is to increase muscular strength, then the activities should involve lifting weights (resistance training) at least two to three times a week. For cardiovascular goals, one should engage in cardiovascular activities for 150 minutes a week. To increase flexibility, one should engage in stretching activities at least twice a week. The principle of **individuality** is also important, as it is recognized that fitness training is personal and a host of factors influence engagement and outcome goals (sport, baseline fitness levels). Factors to consider under the principal of individuality include genetics (gender, muscle fiber type), body type and size, fitness levels, personal preferences, personal goals, and different abilities in reaching fitness goals. Given the understanding that students are individuals with different needs, students should have the opportunity to use the FITT principle and teacher's guidance to develop their own goals and the activities that they want to engage in.

SELECTING AND EVALUATING PHYSICAL ACTIVITIES

Creating SMART goals is the first step that should be taken before selecting activities. Once goals are set, activities should be chosen based on enjoyment and proficiency in the skills needed to perform the activities. For example, playing a game of basketball or soccer can also meet cardiovascular goals instead of traditional cardiovascular activities like running or swimming. Monitoring heart rate (e.g., working in the target heart rate zone) is one way to evaluate the intensity and the effectiveness of training, as the resting heart rate lowers as fitness improves. When initially selecting weight training activities, light weight(s) should be used to ensure proper form and reduce the risk of injury. If the weight is too easy, gradually increase weights until the last few reps in a set are challenging. Lifting at a percentage of a one-repetition max (1RM), the maximum amount of weight that can be lifted one time with excellent form, or a predicted 1RM can be used to select an appropriate weight. Although a 1RM can be used to evaluate strength gains, they are discouraged unless the teacher and students have advanced training and understanding. Reflection journals and workout logs also help evaluate progress.

Self-Assessment of Health and Fitness

ACTIVITY TRACKERS

Activity trackers are devices that record step count, distance traveled, minutes engaged in activity, calories burned, and heart rate. **Pedometers** are activity trackers worn around the waist or wrist that track step count and distance traveled. **Accelerometers** measure acceleration, and most also track step count or distance traveled. **Heart rate monitors** measure heart rate or the intensity of activity through heart rate. Some activity trackers measure all of the above, including body position, and some are waterproof and can be used for aquatic activities. Students may not only be challenged and motivated by activity trackers, but they may even have fun using them. Activity trackers also provide instant and continuous feedback that can help students monitor their engagement and make decisions on the frequency, intensity, and duration of their physical activity, which holds them accountable. Heart rate data is specific to the user, which creates potential for a fair environment where students can work in their own target heart rate zones. Data is also objective, which reduces teacher bias in assessments.

JOURNALS AND FITNESS LOGS

Maintaining **journals** and **fitness logs** are writing activities that help students make connections to concepts and apply them. Journals require students to reflect on skills, performance, fitness, and feelings. Journals can also be used for students to respond to questions regarding the relationships between FITT and behaviors to fitness outcomes. Students can also describe how they felt during the exercise ("The workout was easy, so I need to increase my weight," or "I was exhausted and did not complete the exercises because I had little sleep."), which further aids in their understanding of the interrelated components of health and physical activity. Fitness logs record or document activity over time. Students can log minutes engaged in activity (10 minutes on the treadmill), sets, repetitions, and weight (two sets of 12 reps at eight pounds), and types of activity engaged in (weight training, swimming). Logs also provide students with a visual of progress, which can be adjusted as goals are met.

SELF-ASSESSMENT

Self-assessments help students track their progress, which helps them develop competence in creating their own fitness programs. Self-assessments may include fitness tests (e.g., number of push-ups completed in a certain time frame to evaluate upper body strength or measure endurance) that students can conduct on their own. Self-assessments may also be performance-based (e.g., the quality of the push-up: hands below shoulders, arms extended, 90-degree angle, body flat). The latter is most important because it helps students gain an understanding of the movements before focusing on fitness outcomes. Self-assessments also remove stress, demotivation, and the unhealthy competition that is often associated with group fitness testing and assessments.

Identifying and Addressing Various Student Needs

IDENTIFYING AND MEETING ALL STUDENTS NEEDS

Assessments are used to determine if students have met, not met, or are making progress towards their objectives. The teacher needs to make sure that assessments both measure the objective and are specific. For example, a general objective is being able to perform the overhand throw; however, the elements of the overhand throw (e.g., wind-up phase, follow-through) are what should be assessed. For instance, if there are five elements or critical skill cues that make up a skill, the student would need to meet four or five of the cues to meet or exceed the objective. A student who can perform two or three of the critical skill cues may indicate that they are making progress towards meeting the objective, but performing only one or none of the cues would indicate that the student is not meeting the objectives. Based on how the student is performing, corrective feedback would be given to help the student meet the objective. If a student is already proficient with all five cues, the teacher should provide instruction to make the task more challenging (e.g., run, throw, and hit the target) to keep the student progressing and to reduce boredom and off-task behaviors.

ROLE OF STUDENT CHOICE IN PHYSICAL EDUCATION

Student choice is another way to differentiate and provide equitable instruction. **Equity** is defined as providing equal opportunity, sometimes through modification, whereas **equality** is treating everyone the same regardless of individual needs. While these terms are often used interchangeably, equity is the goal during instruction because not everyone has the same needs. For example, giving each student a basketball to shoot at a 10-foot basketball goal is equality, but equity is lowering the goal for students who are much shorter than their peers (e.g., four feet tall when other peers are five feet tall and taller), which makes the distance proportional to height. Student choice has shown to motivate students to engage in physical activity settings. By offering choice, students can select activities based on their strengths. Allowing student choice also reduces embarrassment for students who are unable to perform the desired outcome. Student choice also allows students to select activities that they are comfortable with and take greater challenges if desired. During choice activities, the teacher should provide progressive activities from the beginner stage to the advanced stage as students become more proficient or comfortable moving through the tasks.

> **Review Video: Equality vs Equity**
> Visit mometrix.com/academy and enter code: 685648

EQUITABLE INSTRUCTION PRACTICES

Teaching practices that contribute to equitable instruction include taking an inventory of student's needs through assessment and asking students questions. Tracking teacher and student behaviors can also aid in equitable instruction to determine if there are unconscious biases. For example, a teacher might call on or help boys more than girls in a class, may discipline one ethnic group harsher than another, or give more attention to athletes than non-athletes. Tracking teacher behaviors allows for the teacher to reflect and make changes to instruction. **Reflection** is when the teacher has an opportunity to think about the lesson(s) and determine what went well and what needs improvement. When a teacher makes a change that benefits all students, equitable instruction can be achieved.

Designing and Implementing Instruction

SAFETY CONSIDERATIONS FOR DESIGNING AND IMPLEMENTING INSTRUCTION

Safety practices to consider when designing and implementing instruction include a warm-up and stretching before physical activity engagement. The equipment used should be damage-free and spaced where students can move about freely. **Protective equipment** should be used to prevent injury (e.g., shin guards, helmets, weather-appropriate clothing). When instruction is outside in the heat and sun, protective clothing, hats, and sunscreen should be encouraged, and water should be easily accessible. Students should be informed of precautions to take when engaging in road activities (walking, jogging, cycling, skating). The teacher should watch for **overexertion** and students who have a **medical condition** (e.g., asthma). An **emergency plan** should be in place and teachers should be certified in first aid and CPR or have knowledge of actions to take for common injuries in physical education. Teachers should also know when to call 911 and who will make the call in the event of an emergency.

MOTIVATION CONSIDERATIONS FOR DESIGN AND INSTRUCTION

Teachers can create an environment where all students can succeed, which helps build student confidence in the ability to complete more difficult tasks. This is known as **self-efficacy**, which fosters intrinsic motivation. Teachers should provide positive feedback, allow for student choice, and have students set goals. The teacher can also set up the environment where students are encouraged and allowed to make mistakes by allowing multiple non-accessed opportunities to practice or engage in the activities. The teacher can design healthy competitive activities (e.g., no one is eliminated, ability group for fair and equal teams, don't take score) as some students do not enjoy competitive activities, which can demotivate students. If available, the teacher can also recommend that higher performing or competitive students enroll in sport-specific or competitive physical education courses. The teacher can give rewards (e.g., student choice, stickers, pencils), which has shown effective, although these should be used with caution because they can negatively impact intrinsic motivation, especially when not related to learning. The teacher should design lessons that allow for social interaction and provide students with a rationale (objectives) for tasks to aid motivation.

STUDENT PROGRESS AND PHYSICAL EDUCATION

Instructional strategies that aid in ensuring students' progress includes high expectations, providing adequate learning time to engage in activities, giving students maximum opportunities to respond, providing students with cues and corrective feedback (e.g., "Look up," "Keep your eyes on the ball," "Use a wider stance"), differentiation in instruction (written, oral, physical, video), and accommodating students' learning styles (verbal and auditory, visual, and kinesthetic instruction). Assessments also ensure students' progress (self, peer, formative, homework, quizzes), which should vary and appropriately address the objectives. Students can be motivated by incorporating curriculum that is developmentally appropriate (larger size equipment for students in the primary grades) and encourages student social responsibility and social skills (putting equipment away, team work). A safe, equitable, inclusive, and cooperative environment have all shown to help students improve.

VARYING INSTRUCTIONAL APPROACHES

There are various approaches and accompanying models used in physical education, including skill development (skill themes approach), team sports (sport education model, tactical games), and physical fitness and health-related fitness education. The skill themes approach is primarily used in elementary school and focuses on building the fundamental movement skills used in individual and dual sports. There are two common approaches when teaching team sports. The **sport education**

model is where students not only play the sport, but are also responsible for leadership roles, including coaching, refereeing, keeping score, calculating statistics, managing equipment, and other roles specific to the sport which foster team cohesion and leadership. This model provides students with details involved in all aspects involved in sports rather than focusing only on skills and game play. In contrast, the **tactical games approach** is designed to promote cognitive connections with the physical aspects of play and focuses heavily on building students' decision-making skills. Fitness education models are designed for students to engage in health-related fitness to prevent disease and increase the quality of life. Fitness curriculums are generally introduced during middle school with increased focus during high school.

MOVEMENT EDUCATION FRAMEWORK

Movement education is the foundation of physical education programs and is where the direct physical application of psychomotor, cognitive, and affective domains derived, as well as the movement concepts of spatial awareness, effort, and relationships of the body. Movement education is another approach used often in elementary physical education programs and is most evident in creative movement, dance, and gymnastics curriculums. Movement education is not common in secondary schools because middle school physical education involves team sports and high school focuses on health-related fitness. However, movement concepts are evident in other models. When adopting a movement education approach, it is understood that students must have an understanding of how, what, why, and where the body moves and be able to demonstrate the fundamental movement skills in order to progress to more complex movements (manipulatives, games, and movement skills used in individual, dual, and team sports). A criticism of movement education is that it lacks structure as students are guided through activities to come to their own conclusions, but this criticism fails to recognize that student creativity is one of the strengths of movement education.

MATERIALS AND TECHNOLOGIES

There are many materials and technology tools that help students meet objectives and address their needs. A common tech tool is the heart rate monitor, which assesses the intensity of cardiovascular activities to ensure that students are working within their target heart rate zone. Heart rate monitors also add a safety element, as students can monitor when they are above their target heart rate zone and slow down activity accordingly. The pedometer is another technological tool that helps students track step count and meet activity or step count objectives. Other effective technologies include slideshows and videos of concepts and skills, which provide students with visual tools that support verbal instruction. Recording students on a device (iPad, smartphone) can provide students with visual feedback of their performance, and corrective feedback can be given for improvement. Written assignments (e.g., worksheets) and journals are materials that can be used to assess student learning and understanding. Posters or boards with objectives and cues can aid as reminders for students of the focus of the lesson.

Physical Education Models

TACTICAL GAMES APPROACH

The **tactical games approach** is a teaching model used to teach team sports. The goal is to develop the cognitive aspects of team sports that include skills, decision-making, and strategies, thus fostering understanding. There is an intentional focus on developing intrinsic motivation, which has shown to increase metacognition (the knowledge of how someone knows something). Rather than the direct teaching of skills in isolation that eventually lead to game play, the tactical games approach uses a whole-part-whole method where students play the game after an objective (how to get open) has been presented. The teacher observes student behaviors to determine areas of growth. However, feedback is given in the form of questions (inquiry-based) to the group to help guide the students in solving problems. For example, the teacher might state, "I noticed that Team A had a difficult time getting open. What are some things we can do to get open?" With the teacher's guidance, students brainstorm and share techniques, then implement during the next gameplay session. Gameplay is paused for a debrief session to discuss if and how the objective was met. Students then practice the identified problems and return to play to work on implementing concepts, skills, and strategies discussed during the debriefing session.

COOPERATIVE LEARNING

Cooperative learning is a teaching approach used in physical education settings. **Cooperative learning** is a student-centered, non-competitive approach that develops tasks around group work or through collaboration. Cooperative learning complements the affective domain that includes values, feelings, and sportsmanship. The fostering of collaboration (teamwork) is a strength of this approach because it requires students to work together to meet goals. This is one of many approaches that can be used to teach team sports (e.g., basketball, lacrosse), as group members share a common goal and work together to accomplish it. Using this approach alone may limit the amount of motor skill development needed to perform the skills necessary for team sports, as the learning environment is designed so students can solve problems rather than listen to the teacher explicitly provide the information.

SKILL THEMES APPROACH

The **skill themes approach** is an elementary physical education framework that aids in the development of the fundamental movement skills (locomotor, non-locomotor, and manipulative) with an overarching goal to ensure that students are proficient or competent in these areas. There are four characteristics that underpin the skill themes approach:

1. Competence in the fundamental movement skills, where students are able to perform locomotor, non-locomotor, and manipulative skills
2. Providing ample student experiences to perform and develop these skills is important, as more opportunities to practice increases skill competency
3. Scope and sequence (progression) ensures that developmentally appropriate movements start from easy movements to progressively more challenging, complex movements. This is done because the more successes students have, the more likely they will continue to engage in physical activities. The scope and sequence characteristic focuses on stage of development rather than the age or the grade of the students
4. Instructional alignment is intentional instruction that includes objectives and assessments. Teachers explicitly plan for students to learn the fundamental movement skills by setting goals (objectives), providing activities that support the objectives, and administering ongoing assessments (formative) and cumulative final assessments (summative) to ensure students are competent in the skills or have reached mastery.

Modifying and Adapting Activities for All Students

ACADEMIC LEARNING TIME IN PHYSICAL EDUCATION

Academic learning time in physical education (ALT-PE) is a strategy used to create an equitable learning environment. ALT-PE is an observation and evaluation tool in which the teacher can analyze instructional time, student activity time in games, time off-task, learning and practice time, opportunities to respond, and equipment usage opportunities. Analysis can occur for a few students, the entire class, or an analysis of teacher behaviors to determine what is transpiring in

86

class and to make any necessary changes. For example, the teacher may identify that a student or some students never get possession of the ball during a three vs. three basketball game. From this data, the teacher can modify the rules to require all players to touch or have possession of the ball at least three times before scoring or other parameters to ensure equal opportunity. The teacher may also observe an imbalance in teams by numbers or abilities and can modify the rules, change team rosters, or provide extra equipment to level the playing field.

DEVELOPMENTALLY APPROPRIATE MODIFICATIONS

Game rules, equipment, and activities should be **modifiable** to ensure that all students participate, learn, and succeed. For example, beginners may be allowed to travel with a basketball when learning how to dribble as stop-and-go action limits the opportunity to practice and learn. The teacher can also use basketballs of different sizes to accommodate varying hand sizes or use balls that include the correct hand and finger-pad placements (palm print) to help guide the students with proper technique. **Developmentally appropriate game modifications** include limiting the number of rules, skills, and strategies to help build competence before more difficult tasks. Increasing the amount of balls used in team sports also creates more equity in skill development. For example, using three to five soccer balls of different colors during game play, whether with the same or different criteria for each ball (dribbling, passing, etc.), allows for more students to get involved. Targets and goals can also be positioned closer, farther, higher, wider, or narrower to accommodate various abilities.

ADAPTATIONS TO ACTIVITIES

Adaptations that promote equity in opportunities for students to participate, learn, and succeed include using lighter weight equipment, making goals wider and larger (for students having difficulty) or shorter and narrower (for students who need more challenge as they are proficient with the normal goals), decreasing target distances (for students unable to reach the target), allowing peers to assist students who may have physical challenges (e.g., wheelchair-bound), and including more frequent rest or water breaks (for unfit or obese students). Other adaptations include how objects are manipulated to ensure equitable activity. For example, some students may be able to kick a moving ball, while others may need to kick a stationary ball or drop kick a ball. A lighter ball can also be used for students with less muscular strength (e.g., a student with muscular dystrophy or muscular atrophy). Adaptations should be student specific. For example, if one or two students need an adaptation, the entire group should not be required to engage in the adaptation, as it may not meet their needs and could possibly impede the progress of others, which can increase off-task behaviors.

Providing Appropriate and Effective Feedback

PROVIDING POSITIVE FEEDBACK

Positive feedback increases student motivation and performance. Specific positive feedback is more effective than general feedback. For example, "Good job" is general feedback that does not inform the student of what went well or what was good about the performance. A more effective example is, "Good job, I like that you kept moving during the entire aerobic session. Next time, try to march in place with high knees rather than walk in place with low knees to increase your heart rate and reach your target heart rate zone. By increasing the intensity, you will increase your cardiovascular endurance, which leads to a healthy heart and better overall health." In this example, the teacher provides positive feedback on something they are doing well and provides an explicit suggestion on how to improve in this area along with its own rationale. Not all students will need corrective or improvement feedback, however, feedback is necessary to increase the challenge for students who meet or exceed the objective.

VERBAL AND NONVERBAL TEACHING CUES

Verbal and nonverbal teaching cues help with student performance. Verbal cues are descriptive words or phrases that help students perform a skill or task. Verbal cues should be short and brief (no longer than three to four words) for ease in delivery and student retention. Cues that are too long are difficult to remember and may confuse students and impede progress. Common verbal cues include "follow-through" (overhand thrown), "squish the bug" (pivot), "t-shape" (forming a "T" with the body), and "move like an airplane" (locomotor movement and speed). Teachers can make up cues designed for the student population, region, or based on the school's mascot (e.g., "Tiger high-five"). To cue (lead) a group fitness or aerobics session, verbal cues should be given in advance to give students time to respond, as there is a brief delay while the brain processes the verbal information. Nonverbal teaching cues include hand gestures (pointing in a direction, as when leading a group fitness or aerobic dance session), moving the head and eyes in different directions, facial expressions (smiling at a correct behavior or frowning when a student does something inappropriate), and thumbs up, down, and sideways can be used for cues and to provide behavioral or performative feedback. Written cues (nonverbal) posted around the gym or teaching space that support the verbal cues students refer to when needed are useful to reinforce the concepts and address the various learning styles.

Assessment in Physical Education

TYPES OF FORMAL ASSESSMENTS

Assessment	Advantages	Disadvantages	When to use
Observational checklists	Fast and easy (Y/N)	Non-descriptive	During large class sizes; can be used as pre-tests or post-tests.
Performance assessments	Descriptive and student-specific; allows the teacher to evaluate if students are able to put skills and concepts into practice.	Can take up a lot of time; without recording and reviewing, the teacher can miss performances.	During game or activity play; when assessing one or two concepts (e.g., getting open, shooting).
Fitness tests	Fitness tests assess health-related and skill-related fitness; fitness tests are often easy to administer; fitness tests have a competitive element, which is great for high-performing, competitive students.	Fitness tests can take up a lot of instructional time; some students may get embarrassed, especially if they are unfit, overweight, or non-competitive students; fitness tests have a competitive element, which has shown to demotivate some students; shown ineffective when not connected to learning and fitness principles	To measure fitness before, during, and after instruction, practice, or training to evaluate growth and deficits and to adjust programming.

INFORMAL ASSESSMENTS

Assessment	Advantages	Disadvantages	When to use

Journals	Students can reflect and see their growth over time; there are no right or wrong answers; students can write in journals at home; students take ownership of their learning.	Writing time can take away from physical activity time; journals can be difficult to mark or assess.	At the end of each class or unit, or assigned for homework.
Peer coaching	Increases student learning opportunities, as this requires explaining, correcting, or identifying correct and incorrect performances; after students are trained, assessment time can decrease; promotes social interaction; all students get to lead (coach) and follow (receive coaching).	Reliant on students who may provide inaccurate information or do not fully understand; can take up instructional time as students have to be taught how to use and what to look for; some students may give improper feedback (e.g., higher or lower marks because of friendship status.)	Large class sizes; limited space where half the class is performing while the other half is coaching; when focusing on the affective domain.

SELECTING, CONSTRUCTING, ADAPTING, AND IMPLEMENTING ASSESSMENTS

Standards, objectives, students' needs, class size, facilities, and equipment should all be used to select, construct, adapt, and implement assessments in physical education. Pre-assessments should occur at the beginning of a new lesson, unit, or concept to determine the ability and needs of the students, which should consist of the objectives or the desired outcome by the end of the lesson. For example, if the goal is to have students engage in 10 or 20 minutes of continuous aerobic activity, then the pre-assessment would consist of asking students to perform cardiovascular activities (jogging, team sports, step aerobics) to the best of their ability for as long as they can. Some students will complete this objective, while others may tire before the time expires. Based on these data points, the teacher will construct or design cardiovascular activities that help students reach the goal. Progress can be tracked over time. Longer rest breaks are an adaptation to accommodate students with low ability, while shorter rest breaks would accommodate students with high ability. While the cardiovascular activities should vary in class for improvement, the activity used for the assessment should be practiced regularly and used as the post-assessment.

Technology in Fitness Assessment

HEART RATE MONITORS AND PEDOMETERS FOR MONITORING ACTIVITY LEVELS

Technological devices used in physical education to assess progress in fitness and performance include pedometers and heart rate monitors. These devices help the teacher and students track and analyze performance to include step count (pedometers), intensity, and duration (heart rate monitors). For example, 10,000 steps a day is a good goal to ensure that moderate levels of physical activity are achieved. Teachers and students can track and examine daily, weekly, or monthly step count to determine if students have improved, regressed, or maintained their level of activity. Steps achieved during class can also be used, and pedometers can be worn during most physical activities, not just walking or running. Tracking heart rate also aids in determining student progress in cardiovascular fitness, as engaging in consistent cardiovascular activities usually leads to lower resting heart rates. Heart rate monitors can also track when students are working too hard or not hard enough.

ACTIVITY TRACKERS, FITNESS APPLICATIONS, AND WEBSITES FOR TRACKING ACTIVITIES

In addition to heart rate monitors and pedometers, other activity trackers are found on fitness and computer applications (apps) via smartphones, tablets, devices worn on the wrist, and website platforms. When using website platforms, students can enter the types, duration, and frequency of activities that they engage in. Recommendations are given based on anthropometric measures (height, weight), gender, age, activity levels, and fitness goals. Many platforms allow for the entry of nutrition intake, which further aid in activity recommendations. Activity trackers worn around the wrist or carried on a cell phone have accelerometers which, in addition to tracking step count, measure speed and distance traveled. Many activity trackers also have the ability to measure heart rate. There are also weight training apps where students can enter the amount of weight lifted, reps, and sets. As with cardiovascular tracking, the amount of reps, sets, or weight lifted should increase over time.

INTERPRETING PERFORMANCE DATA

Cardiovascular data analysis and interpretation includes tracking resting and exercise heart rates (HR) over time, as both provide insight on health risks and improvement and should decrease over time with participation in frequent cardiovascular activities. A normal resting HR is between 60 and 90 beats per minute (bpm). Individuals who engage in regular physical activity may have resting heart rates lower than 60 bpm. For instance, if a student starts with a resting heart rate of 90 bpm, with consistent training, the resting heart rate should decrease. A resting HR over 90 bpm is considered high. Students over 90 bpm should be referred to a physician. Muscular fitness data analysis and interpretation includes tracking the amount of weight lifted and the number of repetitions over time. The weight and reps should increase, which illustrates growth and improvement. For example, if a student went from lifting 3 sets of 8 pounds at 10 repetitions at the beginning of the semester to lifting 3 sets of 15 pounds at 10 repetitions, that indicates an improvement in strength. However, going from lifting 3 sets of 8 pounds at 10 repetitions to lifting 3 sets of 8 pounds at 20 repetitions indicates an improvement in muscular endurance, and the student will likely need to increase the weight for greater improvement and challenge.

FITNESS FEEDBACK AND RECOMMENDATIONS FOR STUDENTS

Fitness feedback is often given in the form of a recommendation or suggestion. For all types of feedback, it is helpful to start with a positive comment on what the student is doing well. For example, "I love that you are trying this out!" Next, state the issue: "I noticed that you are just below your target heart rate zone." Instead of giving the student the answer(s), ask students questions that can help guide them to an appropriate answer while also checking for understanding: "What can you do to increase your exercise heart rate?" Pause for student response(s). If they are accurate, support and commend their response. The teacher can also make a few suggestions: "Try to engage or move your arms," or "Incorporate high-impact movements and take larger steps." Students who do not challenge themselves or who have not grasped fitness concepts may be encouraged to choose a heavier weight (intensity), conduct more repetitions (duration), engage in physical activity an additional day or two each week (frequency), or find an activity they enjoy (sport, hiking).

Cultural Influences on Student Physical Activity

EFFECTS OF PEER PRESSURE AND MEDIA MESSAGES

The media has a strong influence on children and adolescents and can positively or negatively impact students' attitudes regarding engagement in physical activity. The same is true for pressure from peers, which is especially strong during adolescence. Media messages and images tend to focus on thinness and unhealthy methods to achieve it, including extreme calorie restriction and extreme exercising. Awareness of these factors have improved and include positive messages from the National Football League (NFL) to "Play 60," which encourages children to engage in 60 minutes of physical activity every day. Positive and negative peer pressure also impact student attitudes and engagement in physical activity. For example, peers who value and appreciate physical activity can sometimes convince friends to engage in physical activity. In contrast, peers who do not value and appreciate physical activity can undermine positive messages given by the teacher and influence classmates not to engage.

EFFECTS OF CULTURAL INFLUENCES

Culture, family background, and community all influence student attitudes on physical activity engagement. For example, if a student is in a family that does not value physical activity, they may adopt those same beliefs and vice versa. Sometimes families do value physical activity, but they may not have the privilege of leisure time to engage in physical activity because they may work long hours, have an additional job (or jobs), or have childcare responsibilities. Some families and communities are unaware of the benefits of physical activity. Furthermore, there are some cultures and religions that are not keen on physical activity, especially for girls and women, which will influence students' attitudes and engagement in physical activity. To combat some of the negative messages surrounding physical activity that some students may receive at home, share the benefits of physical activity with parents by inviting them to school events, creating family fun activity nights or weekends, or sending emails or newsletters with tips for improving health and exercise to keep them informed and engaged. It may possibly change their negative perceptions of physical activity engagement.

GENDER EXPECTATIONS IN PHYSICAL EDUCATION

Title IX, introduced in 1972, provides equal access to physical activity and sports to female students. Prior to its introduction, girls were more culturally discouraged from engaging in vigorous physical activities which were considered less feminine. Instead, females who wanted to participate in athletics usually only had options in activities such as dance and gymnastics and were steered away from team sports. While more female students participate in sports today, there are still differences in cultural expectations for males and females. Females tend to have lower expectations to participate in competitive athletics, whereas males are generally expected to participate as a rite of passage into manhood. This distinction can act as a cultural gender stereotype that leads to unhealthy habits or tends to exclude students who want to participate in sports or force students to engage in activities to a higher degree than is reasonable to expect.

EFFECTS OF BODY IMAGE EXPECTATIONS

Body image and skill level both have a powerful impact on student attitudes and engagement in physical activity. Students who are highly skilled tend to enjoy physical education and physical activity, whereas low-skilled students have less enjoyment. Negative concepts of body image also impact attitudes and engagement in physical activity. When students do not feel good about their bodies, they are less likely to engage in physical activity due to a fear of being judged for their appearance. This fear is common among obese students. Alternatively, students may suffer from anorexia nervosa, an eating and mental disorder where one starves themselves because of an irrational fear of gaining weight, and may engage in extreme and unhealthy levels of physical activity.

Physical Education and the General Curriculum

RELATIONSHIP BETWEEN PHYSICAL EDUCATION AND THE GENERAL CURRICULUM

The **integrated physical education model** incorporates other subject areas to aid in the understanding of concepts in a real-world setting and their application. Also known as **interdisciplinary learning** or an **interdisciplinary teaching model**, physical education is inherently aligned to other subject areas. For example, physical education teachers use and teach the principles of physics and biomechanics when teaching throwing, jumping skills, and most other physical activities. History is also taught in physical education when students learn about physical activity, sports, dance, and gymnastics history during the physical components of these activities. Robin J. Fogarty asserts that physical education is the leading field of integration and has identified the following four integration methods:

- Sequenced integration, where two or more subject areas focus on one topic
- Shared integration, or the overlap of subject areas
- Webbed integration, the use of themes to guide instruction
- Threaded integration, which combines cognitive and social domains in every subject area

PHYSICAL EDUCATION CONCEPTS ACROSS THE CURRICULUM

Physical education teachers often collaborate with teachers in other subjects to determine the best approaches to meet students' needs. Sometimes physical education teachers are required to integrate by school districts or personnel. For example, some schools have DEAR (Drop Everything and Read) programs to help foster literacy and reading comprehension. Physical education teachers can select books that are related to physical education but are categorized under another subject area. Some schools choose a book or movie to integrate across all subjects and grade levels. For example, Harry Potter, the popular book and movie series, has been used in schools to teach literacy, history, math, science, art, choir, and physical education. In fact, a physical education teacher implemented the game of Quidditch from Harry Potter into his classes in response to a school's interdisciplinary approach to Harry Potter. Quidditch has become a competitive, sanctioned sport played in many physical education programs and on several college campuses.

INTEGRATING PHYSICAL EDUCATION CONCEPTS IN OTHER SUBJECT AREAS

Physical education teachers can take the initiative and contact teachers in other disciplines to explore ways to incorporate physical education in other subject areas. For example, English language arts teachers can use physical education objectives to teach nouns and verb tenses. Math teachers can have students compute and analyze sports data or use sports and physical activity examples in word problems. Science teachers can incorporate exercise physiology for human physiology concepts or sporting examples to use in biomechanics. History teachers can incorporate the history of sports and physical activity, especially during events like the Olympics.

Safety and Risk-Management

GENERAL SAFETY RULES AND CONSIDERATIONS

Teachers should be competent in what they teach. Teachers can invite a visiting instructor (another PE teacher or coach) to help teach a unit where the teacher is untrained (e.g., swimming, gymnastics). Teachers should ensure that they are able to adequately supervise all students. Physical education teachers are usually required to hold first aid, CPR, and automated external defibrillation (AED) certifications. Teachers should inform students of the rules and any hazards or risks. Rules should be revisited regularly and posted in high-visibility areas (gym walls, locker rooms, high-risk areas). Dangerous areas should be roped or coned off. Lesson plans should be written to include safety guidelines in language that a substitute teacher (non-PE teacher) can understand. Students should be required to wear appropriate and safe athletic attire. Students wearing unsafe clothing (e.g., high-heeled shoes) should not engage in physical activity. Court and field surfaces should be inspected for dust and spills (slippage), glass and other sharp objects, and rocks. Ensure students have frequent breaks when engaging in moderate to vigorous activities and when exercising in the heat.

RISK MANAGEMENT PLANS

A risk management plan is designed to prevent, minimize, or prepare for any problems (e.g., injury). Risk management plans in physical education include being trained and certified in first aid and cardiopulmonary resuscitation (CPR), eliminating hazards (e.g., sharp objects), and being aware of any medical conditions (e.g., asthma). Teachers should maintain an equipment safety checklist to identify broken equipment. Emergency phone numbers should be posted and easy to locate. Schools often have risk management flowcharts that should be reviewed and posted. Fire and intruder drills help prepare students on safe routes to take and places (rooms) to go to in the event of an emergency. Safeguards should be put in place for high-risk physical activities (e.g., mats for gymnastics, additional spotters, trained personnel).

EMERGENCY PLANS

A school-wide emergency plan is often developed in advance and should be on file in writing. Furthermore, students and teachers should be aware of the basic procedures of the plan. Most emergency plans include emergency exits, routes, and phone numbers (911, principal, school and district numbers, school resource officer). The telephone numbers of parents should be easily retrievable. First aid kits and ice should be available and replenished after each use. Student health records (medical conditions, allergies) should be up-to-date. Student medications (e.g., inhaler, insulin) should be listed with administration guidelines, properly stored (some require refrigeration), and easily accessible to students in need. Teachers are usually trained in administering certain medications (e.g., EpiPen for allergies).

PROTOCOLS FOR INJURIES IN CLASS

In the event of an injury, the teacher should follow the emergency care plan. After an assessment of the injury, the teacher should ensure that the student is in a safe location. If the injury is minor (e.g., open cut from a student's fingernails), the teacher should administer first aid (clean the wound and put on a bandage). Gloves should be worn before touching any blood or bodily fluids and hands should be washed both before and after treatment. If there is an illness that requires over-the-counter (OTC) medication (e.g., high temperature or fever), the student should be sent to the school nurse or other personnel, who will usually call the parents for permission to administer OTC medication. Sometimes parents give permission for students to take OTC at the beginning of the school year. For major injuries (e.g., broken limb), the teacher should make a phone call to the emergency system (e.g., 911 or school required number) and a call to the parents. An injury report should be provided for minor and major injuries and kept on file. The injury report should provide an accurate description of the injury; the cause, time, location, and treatment of the injury; and a list of any witnesses. The teacher should also notify the principal and school nurse of the injuries and give them a copy of the report.

PHYSICAL DANGERS ASSOCIATED WITH PHYSICAL ACTIVITIES

There are inherent risks associated with physical activities. Potential risks include injuries such as overstretching the muscles, overexertion, and muscle sprains, strains, and spasms. Trips and falls due to shoe laces, equipment, and other objects may occur, which can cause cuts, scrapes, bruises,

fractures, and broken limbs. Students may also slip or fall on exercise equipment (e.g., treadmills) or get their fingers smashed by a weight room apparatus. Fingers can also get jammed when catching sports balls (e.g., basketball). Students also acquire bruises and nose bleeds after getting struck by an object or a classmate, and collisions may occur during game play. There is also cardiovascular risk that includes cardiac arrest. Proper supervision, however, can reduce or eliminate many risks.

ENVIRONMENTAL RISKS INHERENT IN PHYSICAL ACTIVITIES

Environmental risks that are inherent when engaging in physical activities include the weather (rain, sleet, snow), the temperature (too hot, too cold), and road-related issues (gravel, slick roads). In hot environments, risks include hyperthermia (overheating), which can lead to heat exhaustion and heat stroke. It is easy to lose fluids and become dehydrated when engaging in physical activities in the heat. In cold environments, risks include hypothermia (low body temperature) and risks of frostbite. Traffic and pedestrians can also be potential hazards when engaging in physical activity outdoors, including bumping into others or getting hit by an automobile. Precipitation (rain, sleet, snow) can increase the risks of slipping, and can speed up cold-related conditions. Other risks include tripping on uneven pavement or stepping on glass, which can lead to physical injuries. Precautions to take against environmental risks include checking the weather forecast, wearing protective clothing appropriate for the weather, having an emergency plan, using the buddy system by never engaging in physical activity alone, finding alternative routes when visibility is low (fog) or concentration is high (too much traffic, too many people in the area), and hydrating before, during, and after activity. Teachers will need to use their judgement. For example, physical activity can occur outdoors with a small amount of precipitation (rain drizzle), but engaging in physical activity when lightning is present requires a safe, indoor shelter.

LIABILITY IN PHYSICAL EDUCATION

Liability is an obligation or the responsibility to perform the duties required in a job. Liability in the legal aspect is a failure to perform the duties as a result of negligence. **Negligence** is a breach of duty that increases the risk of harm. Actions that increase a teacher's liability or acts of negligence in physical education include having students participate on broken or defective equipment, failure to cover or protect sharp objects, and failure to report an injury. Other acts of negligence include the failure to block off unsafe areas, not providing students with rest and water breaks, and failure to incorporate a warm-up. Failure to maintain first aid, CPR, and AED training is another potential liability. Failure to supervise students, review and post safety rules, and form an awareness of students' strengths and limitations are also potential liabilities. Teachers could also be held liable if they allow or ignore student misconduct that can lead to injury.

DISCLOSING RISKS

Students and families should be informed that the benefits of engagement in physical activity outweigh the risks associated with physical activity. Obtaining informed consent will ensure that parents are aware of the risk. Requiring liability waivers will also provide some legal protection should an injury occur. Students should be informed of the risks through lecture, video, practical labs, or simulations. Risks and safety guidelines should be posted in the teaching and learning space (e.g., risks of weight training equipment or risks of not using a spotter) and reviewed with students regularly.

ROUTINE INSPECTIONS OF EQUIPMENT

Equipment that is not in use should be stored and secured. Routine inspections of equipment include checking for loose screws and making sure sharp or blunt edges are removed or covered with protective padding. Professional-grade equipment often used in school weight rooms and

94

fitness centers should have scheduled maintenance in addition to the daily checks of equipment. Students should be informed of gym etiquette rules, which include wiping down equipment after use to keep it clean and reduce germ transmission and returning equipment to its proper location to prevent injury. When students perform tasks such as these, the teacher should inspect to ensure safety guidelines were followed. Any broken or malfunctioning equipment should be roped off and have an "out of service" sign. The floor and field should be routinely inspected for damage, objects, glass, and uneven surfaces to minimize injury risks and liabilities.

RISK CONSIDERATIONS FOR AGE, SIZE, MATURITY, AND SKILL

Because students develop at different rates, the developmental stage (maturity and size) of students should inform teaching and instruction, rather than age. For instance, a boy in grade six might be six feet tall (early maturation in physical size means the boy's skeletal age is greater than chronological age), while another boy in the same class is four feet tall (late maturation, meaning his skeletal age is less than his chronological age). To minimize injury risks and liabilities, early-maturing students should be paired with other early-maturing students, as the larger and stronger student might inadvertently hurt the smaller student. In addition to the physical advantage that the early-maturing student has, the imbalance can also cause psychological harm to the less-developed student. Students should also be matched by skill and cognitive development (maturity) to minimize risks and liabilities, including safe engagement, as the four-foot-tall student might have a higher skill level and greater cognitive abilities than the six-foot-tall student, which would again be an unfair pairing and could pose psychological harm to the student with lower cognitive abilities. Equipment should also be developmentally appropriate and scaled to the sizes for diverse learners (e.g., the early-maturing student may need larger pieces of equipment).

MATCHING PLAYERS TO MINIMIZE RISK

Matching players based on skill level minimizes risks and liabilities. For instance, higher-skilled players tend to engage in more advanced and aggressive play because they are faster and stronger (more muscle and bone) than lower-skilled players. A mismatch in skill can lead to bullying from players with more skill or an increase in accidents as novice players may make errors that put them or others at risk for injuries. As such, the teacher could be held liable for not foreseeing potential risks of the mismatched skill levels or the recognition that students vary in skill development. For example, a novice player may be unaware of certain infractions (fouls, pushing, and the types of physical contact that are acceptable and unacceptable) that could put other players at risk.

CONFLICT RESOLUTION

There are generally three types of behavior evident in conflict situations: the **cooperator** (gets along with everyone), the **appeaser** (pleaser and conflict avoider), and the **dominator** (conflict starter, bully). Bullying and fights increase the risk of harm, which increases potential liabilities, so teachers should teach and model conflict resolution strategies as a prevention measure. Strategies shown effective in conflict resolution include stopping aggressive behaviors immediately, collecting information to establish the cause of the conflict, collaborating with students on possible solutions, incorporating the solutions that the students agree on, implementing a plan, and debriefing with the students to determine the plan's effectiveness. Using these steps both teaches and empowers students to solve their own conflicts. However, if the plan does not work, the teacher can step in to modify. This approach also helps the teacher refrain from taking sides or choosing a solution, which does not encourage students to think about their actions.

FIRST AID AND INJURY PREVENTION

The purpose of **first aid** is to provide immediate care to an injured person to reduce further injury or deterioration and sometimes even to prolong life or prevent death. The person administering first aid should ensure a safe environment and keep both the victim and bystanders calm. If an ambulance is required, the person in charge will have to call the authorities if they are alone, or should have someone else call if others are present. Prevention techniques for cuts and scrapes include tying shoelaces and removing objects to prevent tripping. Wearing long pants and sleeves can minimize risks to prevent burns, and hot items that are not in use should be turned off and removed from areas where students might touch them accidentally. Inspecting and repairing hardwood flooring and other wooden objects can reduce the risks of splinters, fractures, muscle sprains and strains, and dislocated joints.

MODIFICATIONS TO IMPROVE SAFETY

- **Equipment**: cover hard objects and equipment with padding (e.g., volleyball standards and polls) to avoid painful collisions.
- **Environment**: sweep floors before class, make sure that students have their shoelaces tied to prevent slips and falls, review and post the rules to remind students to avoid dangerous areas and to abstain from dangerous behaviors (e.g., tumbling off of the mat, tripping a classmate), have sunscreen available and encourage students to wear hats or visors when outdoors to prevent sun or heat-related conditions, have an emergency plan on file to expedite care when needed, and ensure that first aid and CPR trainings and certifications are current.
- **Activity-related**: ensure students engage in a warm-up and cooldown to prevent muscle-related injuries, allow students to get water to prevent dehydration, allow for appropriate breaks to avoid overexertion.

RICE PROCEDURE

RICE is a first aid treatment best used for sprains, strains, and muscle aches. RICE stands for **rest** (stop use), **ice** (wrapped in protective coating or an ice pack), **compression** (gentle pressure, usually with an elastic bandage to the injured area), and **elevation** (to move blood away from the affected area to reduce swelling). RICE reduces swelling, inflammation, and pain, that could otherwise prolong healing time. **NSAIDs** are non-steroidal anti-inflammatory drugs that include pain and inflammation reducers like ibuprofen and naproxen sodium. NSAIDs are often used in conjunction with RICE to also reduce inflammation, pain, and speed up recovery time. Acetaminophen is a common over-the-counter (OTC) drug which is also used to reduce pain, but because it does not reduce inflammation, it is not an NSAID. NSAIDs and acetaminophen also reduce fever.

CPR PROCEDURE AND EMERGENCY RESPONSE

Check, call, and care are emergency steps to take in the event that a victim is unconscious. **Check**: Shout and tap the victim's shoulder and ask if they are ok. If there is no response, the next step is to check for consciousness (check for breathing, pulse). **Call**: After this initial assessment, a call should be made to 911 that includes the symptoms. If another person is present and able, it is best to have them call 911, rather than the person attending to the victim. For example, the person checking the victim would point to a bystander and instruct them to call 911 and describe the victim's ailment to the first responders. **Care**: If the victim has a pulse but is not breathing, someone trained and certified in CPR should provide two rescue breaths to see if air goes in (e.g., chest rises) or if there is a blockage causing the victim to choke. They should then look, listen, and feel for breathing and a pulse. A protective mask is recommended to reduce transmission of any illnesses or infections. If there is still no breathing, rescue breaths should occur for two minutes before checking again. If there is no pulse, 30 CPR compressions should be administered, followed by two rescue breaths. This process should be repeated for two minutes (about five cycles) or until the victim is breathing and has pulse, until an AED or emergency care arrives, or when the person administering CPR is too tired to perform it effectively.

Chapter Quiz

Ready to see how well you retained what you just read? Scan the QR code to go directly to the chapter quiz interface for this study guide. If you're using a computer, simply visit the bonus page at **mometrix.com/bonus948/priihpeck5857** and click the Chapter Quizzes link.

Collaboration, Reflection, and Technology

Transform passive reading into active learning! After immersing yourself in this chapter, put your comprehension to the test by taking a quiz. The insights you gained will stay with you longer this way. Scan the QR code to go directly to the chapter quiz interface for this study guide. If you're using a computer, simply visit the bonus page at **mometrix.com/bonus948/priihpeck5857** and click the Chapter Quizzes link.

Goals, Trends, and Philosophies of Physical Education Programs

PURPOSE OF PHYSICAL EDUCATION PROGRAMS

The main purpose of physical education programs is to ensure that students are physically literate. According to the Society of Health and Physical Educators of America (SHAPE), **physical literacy** is "the ability to move with competence and confidence in a wide variety of physical activities in multiple environments that benefit the healthy development of the whole person." With the goal of physical literacy, physical education programs are designed to promote physical activity over the lifespan. To do this, quality physical education programs ensure that students are engaged in psychomotor (movement), cognitive (thinking), and affective (social and emotional) domains, thus influencing the development of the whole person.

ROLE OF THE SOCIETY OF HEALTH AND PHYSICAL EDUCATORS OF AMERICA (SHAPE)

SHAPE America is the oldest and largest physical education professional organization in the United States. SHAPE is the national governing body of physical education, and each state and US territory has a SHAPE (aka AAHPERD) equivalent (e.g., Texas Association for Health, Physical Education, Recreation and Dance, or TAHPERD). There are five SHAPE districts which combine states and territories by region. For example, TAHPERD is in the Southern District along with 12 other states. SHAPE America sets the national physical education standards and learning outcomes; however, each state can decide whether to adopt SHAPE standards, devise their own, or use a combination of SHAPE and state-level standards. For example, Texas has its own standards called the Texas Essential Knowledge and Skills (TEKS). SHAPE America and state-level organizations require membership, but both advocate for physical education, disseminate best teaching practice information, provide professional development, and manage state and national policies—usually for free. They also hold annual conferences where teachers and experts hold teaching workshops and training.

STATE-LEVEL PHYSICAL EDUCATION PROGRAMS

Physical education programs in each state and US territory are governed by state-level law and policy. These laws and policies include setting physical education requirements that concern the format (in-class or online), amount, and frequency of physical education; the time allocated for physical education; and fitness testing, teacher certification requirements, and class size. These are usually minimums or recommendations that school districts should aim to achieve. For example, the state of Texas requires that students in elementary school engage in structured physical activity for at least 135 minutes every week, and at least 30 minutes a day for students in middle school. High school students must earn 1.0 physical education credit, but each school district determines the implementation. The state also decides on waivers, exemptions (Texas does not allow for waivers and exemptions), and activities that can be substituted for physical education (e.g., athletic sports team participation, JROTC, dance teams).

LOCAL SCHOOL DISTRICT PHYSICAL EDUCATION PROGRAMS

While the state sets physical education standards and determines the number of minutes students should be actively engaged in elementary and middle schools, schools have flexibility in the structure of the physical education program. For instance, schools are responsible for scheduling, teaching models and modalities, class size, and curriculum approaches. For example, the state of Texas requires a maximum of 45:1 student-teacher ratio in physical education, however, districts and schools may choose to endorse SHAPE America's 25:1 student-teacher ratio for elementary grades, 30:1 for middle school grades, and 35:1 for high school grades. Some states do not require physical education teacher certification for school districts, but most public school districts require a degree in physical education and physical education teacher certification. Private and parochial schools are governed independently and do not have to adhere to district policies.

TRENDS IN PHYSICAL EDUCATION

Due to an increase in childhood obesity related to poor dietary habits and sedentary lifestyles, many physical education programs have shifted to health-related fitness curriculums instead of team sport curriculums in efforts to prevent obesity. Fitness and physical activity have also shown to improve brain functioning and learning. This is especially true in high school, when students are preparing for adulthood and making independent choices. Many schools now have fitness centers and weight rooms to meet the needs of this trend. Alongside fitness is the use of technology to monitor fitness, including heart rate monitors, pedometers, and activity trackers. Another trend is the focus on social and emotional learning (SEL) due to increased mental health concerns of youth and the understanding that physical education and physical activity can aid in reducing and managing mental health risks. As a result, there has been an increase in yoga and mindfulness in physical education programs.

COMMON ISSUES IN PHYSICAL EDUCATION

Common issues that affect physical education programs are financial cuts, large class sizes, little or reduced instructional time, and the lack of value in its role of educating and developing the whole child. Other issues include the lack of equipment or teaching space and frequent, unexpected teaching interruptions (e.g., the gym is needed for an assembly). Assessment and grading are also topics of debate in physical education programs, as some believe students should get an A grade for participation while others believe that students should meet learning outcomes. Fitness testing has been and continues to be an issue in physical education, especially when used for a grade. While fitness testing can be a good assessment tool and provide educational and motivational opportunities, fitness testing takes time and may embarrass some students. Other issues with fitness testing are that students are often unaware of the rationale or that they are not working on the fitness measures throughout the year.

BEHAVIORISM, COGNITIVISM, AND CONSTRUCTIVISM PHILOSOPHIES

Behaviorism takes on a repetitive approach. Teachers who engage in behaviorist practices focus on repetition of the ideal movement, or gold standard. The goal is to have students repeat tasks until they achieve mastery. This approach is best used for students who need more direction, as it could demotivate high-performing students. Cognitivism was developed out of disagreement with behaviorism, as the cognitive domain is not addressed. The beliefs that underpin **cognitivism** are that students will be unable to master movement without an understanding of the movement, therefore, emphasis needs to include both cognitive and psychomotor domains. As such, information processing must occur in the brain before movement can occur. **Constructivism**

evolved out of cognitivism and is evident in physical education programs as constructivists believe in getting students actively involved during the learning process. For example, students who engage in and learn the history of dance will better understand movement concepts. Constructivism includes the psychomotor, cognitive, and affective domains and takes on an interdisciplinary approach. As such, students learn the skills for a game (e.g., lacrosse), the rules, the history, and the values of the game.

HUMANISM PHILOSOPHY

Constructivism underpins **humanism**, which focuses on the affective and cognitive domains, takes a student-centered and holistic approach, and was derived out of criticisms of behaviorism and cognitivism. Teachers who operate from a humanist framework believe in the facilitation of learning by creating optimal learning environments. These teachers provide constant encouragement and positive feedback with the aim to help students grow at their own pace and in their own time. These teachers also focus on the good (effort, persistence) of students rather than the bad (use of profane language, pushing or shoving), and try to foster the positive aspects of students. Abraham Maslow and Carl Rogers were well-known humanists who created Maslow's hierarchy of needs, which posits that when the basic needs are met (physiological, safety, belongingness, and esteem), self-fulfillment, or self-actualization, can be achieved.

CHARACTERISTICS OF EFFECTIVE PHYSICAL EDUCATION PROGRAMS

An effective physical education program is student-centered and attempts to balance short-term goals with lifelong health and fitness. The ultimate outcome of a physical education program is to help students fully develop their motor skills, to inform them about health and fitness principles, and help them to develop the skills to make good decisions for themselves as they transition to adulthood. The use of high expectations and standards-based instruction helps to keep students in a mode of progress toward particular goals that are generally developmentally appropriate. Instruction needs to be appropriate to the developmental needs and skill level of students. This means that classes should be appropriately sized to set specific enough goals to be effective for the class. Instruction should be rich and engaging, with adequate equipment and resources, and plenty of opportunity for extracurricular activities that will help with achieving health and fitness outcomes. With younger children, goals should be focused on developing motor skills and coordination, and as they age, they should be given more decision-making opportunity to help students take their health into their own hands as they progress from children to adults.

PURPOSE OF ASSESSMENT AND ITS ROLE IN EFFECTIVE PHYSICAL EDUCATION PROGRAMMING

The purposes of assessment are to determine or measure student learning and to identify strengths and deficiencies or areas of weakness. Assessment results should inform the teacher (as well as students and parents) on the next steps for improvement or growth. Psychomotor, cognitive, and affective assessments are included in effective physical education programs. The teacher should be clear in the expectations, and criteria should be communicated to students prior to assessments. The teacher should also engage in appropriate uses of physical activity and fitness assessment tools. For example, when assessing fitness, results should only be shared with students and parents, not posted on walls for all to see. Assessments should be ongoing (formative) and allow for students to self-assess and engage in monitoring their activities before a final (summative) assessment is given. There should also be adequate opportunities to respond in order to foster growth and learning.

PRESIDENTIAL YOUTH FITNESS PROGRAM

The Presidential Youth Fitness Program (PYFP) is the national fitness test program designed by the United States government. The PYFP adopted FitnessGram testing protocols for its fitness assessments. FitnessGram is a battery of fitness tests designed for students aged 8-17 that measures the five health-related fitness components. These assessments are designed to assess a student's fitness to inform the teacher, student, and parents of fitness levels, strengths, areas of growth, and potential health risks. Fitness outcomes should also inform teachers how to proceed with the physical education program to ensure that meaningful fitness activities and concepts are embedded in the physical education program to help students gain knowledge and understanding of fitness principles to engage in for a lifetime. Fitness assessments should be conducted at regular intervals (e.g., every two, four, and six weeks) to monitor progress and the effectiveness of fitness programming, as these are components that reinforce effective physical education practices.

SHAPE AMERICA'S HEALTH MOVES MINDS

SHAPE America's Health Moves Minds is a national service-learning program that promotes the benefits of physical activity and mindfulness on overall health with a particular focus on mental health, including anxiety (extreme and exhaustive worry that affects mental and physical health) and clinical depression (mood disorder with chronic feelings of sadness). Childhood stress, anxiety, and depression are on the rise, and this program recognizes the relationship of physical activity and health. The program supports and reinforces the physical literacy concept of developing the whole child, which includes the mental, physical, emotional, and social wellbeing of students. Health Moves Minds lesson plans have been created for teachers to implement in K-12 health and physical education programs.

Evaluating the Effectiveness of the Physical Education Program

One technique used to evaluate the effectiveness of the physical education program through data collection is to track students' progress over time. For example, sets, weights, and reps of a student can be tracked to determine if strength or endurance have improved, regressed, or remained the same. The teacher and student can devise a plan (increase weight, sets, reps) to accommodate each scenario. Heart rate data can also be tracked randomly (monitor one class to see if students are working in their target heart rate) or over time to track trends in fitness. For example, taking the resting heart at the beginning, during, and at the end of the semester will inform the teacher and student of intensity levels and allow them to make adjustments accordingly. Taking heart rate over time will also determine the effectiveness of the program, as the resting and exercise heart rate should stay the same or decrease. Students' oral and written responses to quizzes and tests also provide data on what is known, what is unknown, and what needs to be re-taught.

REFLECTING ON TEACHING PRACTICES TO SHAPE FUTURE INSTRUCTION

Reflective teaching helps teachers make decisions that are instructionally and developmentally appropriate. Reflective teachers take inventory (in the form of data) of their own behaviors and of students' strengths, abilities, attitudes, and deficiencies. For example, if the teacher is taking too long to give instructions, he or she can work on giving concise instruction or different delivery methods (e.g., posted on the wall, slideshow, verbal instructions). If students are waiting too long, the teacher may need to increase the number of stations, distribute more pieces of equipment, or reduce group sizes. If students have difficulty performing a task, the teacher should provide modifications to help the students achieve the goals. For example, if students' balls consistently hit the net during serves (tennis or volleyball), the teacher can lower the net, provide cues (toss the ball higher, make contact here), or move students closer to the net.

REFLECTING ON STUDENT ASSESSMENT DATA TO SHAPE FUTURE INSTRUCTION

Student assessment data helps the teacher determine if class activities are aligned with assessments. Assessment data also informs the teacher if assessments are too easy, just right, or too difficult. For example, if the majority of students are unable to meet the objective, then the assessment is either too difficult, inappropriate, or the activities that the teacher designed did not correspond to the assessment. Based on these data points, the teacher can reteach using different methods and activities, provide students with more time to engage in the activities, focus on different skill cues, and create a new assessment that is aligned to the activities taught. If all of the students meet the objective, then the teacher may be extremely effective or administering an assessment that is too easy. In this situation, the teacher can add challenge to help students continuously improve and to increase motivation.

> **Review Video: Assessment Reliability and Validity**
> Visit mometrix.com/academy and enter code: 424680

Advocating for Physical Education

The Every Student Succeeds Act (ESSA) recognizes that health and physical education are integral parts of developing the whole child. Teachers can advocate for schools and communities by applying for state and federal support (funding) to provide quality programming in schools, including school improvement and teacher effectiveness. SHAPE America also has advocacy toolkits for physical education that includes participating in legislation events that have an impact on physical education policies and practices. Fundraising for program needs is another way to advocate for quality physical education programming. Inviting parents, school leaders, and decision-making personnel to observe physical classes is another way to advocate physical education within the community.

OPPORTUNITIES AND RESOURCES FOR PHYSICAL ACTIVITY IN THE SCHOOL COMMUNITY

Additional opportunities for physical health in schools includes after-school physical activity programs, intramural and athletic teams, recess, and physical activity breaks. Some schools have fitness centers, weight rooms, swimming pools, tennis courts, and athletic fields that are open to parents and the greater school community. Information newsletters, flyers, and emails can be created and distributed to notify recipients of opportunities, as well as any specials or discounts. Making PA announcements and networking with the PTA, PTO, and PTSO (parent-teacher association, parent-teacher organization, and parent-teacher-student organization) to organize presentations for parents and the community can also help communicate this information. Teachers can also take students on field trips to local fitness centers, rock climbing walls, and other facilities that offer physical activity opportunities.

PHYSICAL ACTIVITY OPPORTUNITIES AND RESOURCES IN THE COMMUNITY

Local parks, Frisbee and disc golf parks, recreation centers, hiking trails, golf courses, fitness centers, roller skating rinks, bowling, biking, skateboard parks, and swimming pools are additional opportunities for individuals to engage in physical activities. There are also physical activity meet-up groups that are free or have minimal costs (e.g., walking and running groups, tennis groups) where people can build community with others who enjoy similar activities. Most parks have walking or biking trails, and many have playground and exercise equipment. Recreation centers tend to offer team sporting activities (basketball, soccer, volleyball), swimming, group fitness classes, weight rooms, rock climbing, racquetball, and recreational games (shuffleboard, croquet).

Chapter Quiz

Ready to see how well you retained what you just read? Scan the QR code to go directly to the chapter quiz interface for this study guide. If you're using a computer, simply visit the bonus page at **mometrix.com/bonus948/priihpeck5857** and click the Chapter Quizzes link.

Health Education as a Discipline and Health Instruction

Transform passive reading into active learning! After immersing yourself in this chapter, put your comprehension to the test by taking a quiz. The insights you gained will stay with you longer this way. Scan the QR code to go directly to the chapter quiz interface for this study guide. If you're using a computer, simply visit the bonus page at **mometrix.com/bonus948/priihpeck5857** and click the Chapter Quizzes link.

Health Care Agencies, Programs, and Services

PRIMARY HEALTH CARE

Primary health care describes the delivery of health services by entities that manage patients with acute and chronic conditions below a level of specialized care. **Primary care providers** (e.g., family doctors or general physicians, gynecologists, nurse practitioners) are often referred to as "gatekeepers" because they are often the first physician that individuals encounter in the health care system. Primary care providers may be the first physician visited when a person develops symptoms, and they are responsible for diagnosis, treatment, and management of illness or injury. They hold an **extensive breadth of medical knowledge** and frequently deliver patient education. Primary care providers may also **coordinate services** and **identify patient resources**. For example, if a patient requires specialized care or community resources (e.g., food assistance, reduced cost medication), primary care providers may refer them to a specialist or a community organization who provides wraparound services. Primary health care can be delivered at physician's offices or through community agencies (e.g., community health centers and free clinics, health departments).

PREVENTATIVE HEALTH CARE

Preventative health care seeks to prevent disease before it develops and reduce the impact of an illness once it occurs. It is typically divided into primary, secondary, and tertiary prevention.

- **Primary preventative health care** seeks to prevent the onset of illness or injury through legislation, education, and immunization. Lawmakers and government agencies may **implement legislation to reduce risk of injury** (e.g., tobacco tax, seat belt mandate) or **ban hazardous substances and working conditions** (e.g., lead ban). It can also include **interventions** like immunization and mandatory vaccination, health education/promotion, and nutritional fortification.
- **Secondary preventative health care** reduces the impact of disease or injury on an individual by identifying and administering disease treatment as soon as it is detected (e.g., cancer screening, preventative drug therapy).
- **Tertiary preventative health care** describes programs and services that **minimize complications or disability** that result from **chronic disease** and improve quality of life. Examples include diabetes management programs and cardiac rehabilitation. Secondary and tertiary preventative health care may take place within a medical setting but are **frequently implemented in the community** (e.g., community diabetes management classes, free STD testing at health departments, community cancer screenings).

EMERGENCY HEALTH CARE

Emergency health care describes the rapid treatment of acute illness or injury and the prevention of serious complications from disease or death. Emergency health care is typically administered at emergency health care centers (e.g., hospitals, urgent care centers) by trained and licensed physicians. They are responsible for providing **immediate care** to individuals with **serious, sometimes fatal, conditions**. Emergency mental health care programs exist outside of the medical health care system, too. Many community organizations provide mental health first aid to intervene when an individual experiences a mental health crisis to reduce the risk of resultant harm. Federal and state entities and non-profit organizations (e.g., FEMA, DHHS, American Red Cross, Salvation Army) may deploy emergency health practitioners and services when a community experiences a natural disaster or infectious disease outbreak. Their role is often to provide emergency aid and mitigate the damage caused by the emergency.

COMMUNITY AND NATIONAL HEALTH CARE NEEDS AND GOALS

Community health care needs and goals are typically outlined in annual **community health assessments** (CHA). CHAs are often developed by state, local, or tribal government bodies to examine key health indicators within the communities they serve. Quantitative and qualitative data on risk factors, social determinants of health, and morbidity and mortality rates are collected and analyzed to identify health needs. Findings are paired with information on community assets, key partners, and essential services to establish health goals. National health care needs and goals are commonly identified through the US Department of Health and Human Services' (USDHHS) **Healthy People program**. Similar to local community health assessments, goals and objectives are identified through data collection, but needs and goals are redefined every ten years instead of annually. Both engage stakeholders and assets within their reach to address identified health needs.

HEALTH-RELATED SOCIAL, POLITICAL, AND ECONOMIC ISSUES

According the Bureau of Labor Statistics, medical costs have increased an average 2.1% annually over the past ten years. Over the same time period, the cost of commercial health insurance premiums rose 5.8% annually. **Rising medical costs** impact an individual's access to health care. Individuals may delay or avoid seeking care due to cost, which can have devastating impacts on their long-term health and wellbeing. **Uninsured and underinsured families**—who are often more likely to simultaneously experience poverty and poor health—are disproportionately affected by rising health care costs. Those who lack sufficient health care coverage are more likely to accumulate medical debt, delay or forgo treatment, utilize emergency health care instead of primary care services, or ration medical supplies and medication. Thus, health care delivery often transitions from primary care and prevention to late-stage treatment of injury and disease or emergency health care treatment.

FACTORS INFLUENCING COST, AVAILABILITY, ACCESSIBILITY, AND USE OF HEALTH CARE
INDIVIDUAL FACTORS

Social determinants of health (SDOH) describe the social and economic conditions that influence health outcomes (e.g., economic and housing stability, education, food access, the physical environment, social norms and attitudes, and culture). Those with low **socioeconomic status**—one's economic position compared to others—have diminished access to health care and worse health outcomes than their peers. **Low financial security** may influence their decision to seek care and the type of care they receive. A person's **cultural background** and **health attitudes** can impact their perception of health, as well as their accessibility to and use of health care. The cultural background of one delivering care can impact **how well health information is communicated** and the **patient's treatment adherence**. One's cultural background can influence their

understanding of the causes, severity, and treatment regimen of illness or injury and may also influence their health attitudes. For example, historically marginalized groups who have experienced medical maltreatment and discrimination are often more reluctant to use health care services. **Age** can influence health care use. For example, youth may lack access to care since their caregivers are responsible for their medical decisions. Older adults may use health care more frequently, yet their mobility can impact access.

SOCIETAL FACTORS

Economic trends can impact an individual's access to health care. During **economic recessions** or downturns, employers may revise coverage and benefits to reduce costs. Economic downturns are also associated with **increased unemployment**. One's loss of financial security and employee-sponsored insurance can influence their **accessibility to services and their willingness to seek care**. Widescale unemployment and changes in coverage associated with economic downturn can impact health care delivery. Inability to pay for services can lead hospitals to avoid clinical and technological upgrades or avoid hiring new health care professionals, which can diminish the health care quality. Medicare and Medicaid are federal insurance programs for seniors and disabled individuals and those with low income, respectively. Government policies like **Medicaid expansion** increase coverage and affordability of health care. **Price regulation** (e.g., price caps on prescription drugs and hospital service costs) enforced through government policy can reduce health care costs, improve affordability and accessibility of care, and increase use of health care services.

Environmental Health

IMPACT OF POLLUTION

The health impact of pollution differs by the type of pollution.

- **Air pollution** is a compilation of hazardous gases and particles from sources like wildfires, particulate matter, vehicle emissions, and manufacturing byproducts. They can cause respiratory infections, cardiovascular disease, and cancer. **Smog**—a type of air pollution—can obstruct sunlight and impair visibility.
- **Water pollution** describes chemical or bacterial substances that contaminate water, including wastewater contamination (e.g., sewage, chemical solvents, or grease runoff), agricultural fertilizers or pesticides, plastic, and oil. Health impacts include complications from **waterborne diseases** (e.g., diarrhea, vomiting), gastrointestinal diseases, skin irritation, or cancer. Water pollution, specifically **nitrate pollution**, can cause **hypoxic conditions** that create **uninhabitable marine ecosystems**, which can be detrimental to fishing industries and ecosystem health. Oil spills and plastic pollution can also cause harm to marine ecosystems.
- **Noise pollution** refers to disruptive sounds—typically over 85 decibels—that produce harmful effects on human and animal health. Examples include vehicle and air traffic, construction and event sounds, and industrial or manufacturing noises. Noise pollution can cause stress and anxiety, sleep disruption, hearing loss, and memory and attention challenges. In animals, it can impact mating and migratory patterns, predator avoidance, echolocation, and behavior.

IMPACT OF OVERCROWDING

Overcrowding describes the presence of excessive people in a space that impacts comfortability and health. Overcrowding is associated with **emotional distress, anxiety, and depression**. It can also increase an individual and a community's risk of infectious disease. A higher volume of residents in an area with limited space makes it **easier for diseases to spread** and puts many at **increased risk of disease-related mortality**. Overcrowding can **place stress on existing resources** (e.g., land, water, food) and **infrastructure** (e.g., sanitation and sewage, roads and transportation pathways). This may **increase resource scarcity and risk of accidents or injury**. Overcrowding can place strain on **interpersonal relationships** that may contribute to poor interactions with others. Overcrowded schools can **impact the quality of academic institutions and their capacity to deliver educational services**, which can have lasting impacts on one's academic and professional success. Communities experiencing overcrowding may lack sufficient economic opportunities for all residents and may suffer from an overloaded health care system.

IMPACT OF HAZARDOUS WASTE

Improperly managed or stored **hazardous waste** can impact human and environmental health. Hazardous waste may be **toxic** (e.g., carcinogens, mutagenic substances), **reactive** (e.g., corrosive or ignitable waste like batteries), **infectious** (e.g., needles or bandages), or **radioactive** (e.g., nuclear waste). Hazardous waste can cause cancer, organ failure, developmental defects or genetic mutations, and behavioral changes. Hazardous waste can lead to **reproductive complications** in humans and animals and can cause widescale **mortality** in contaminated environments. For example, exposure to toxic waste can cause massive death of marine life and organisms in a lake. Corrosive and ignitable hazardous waste can also lead to **explosions** and **fires** that endanger human and animal life. **Bioaccumulation**—the gradual buildup of chemicals and hazardous waste within a biological organism—can cause serious health complications throughout the food chain. For example, **mercury contamination** from industrial emissions and runoff can accumulate within the tissues of coastal fish. As pregnant mothers consume the mercury-laden tissues, the fetus receives secondhand exposure to mercury, which can lead to possible developmental and infant cognitive impairments. Oftentimes, hazardous waste impacts whole communities or specific demographic groups to produce inequitable health outcomes.

REDUCING ENVIRONMENTAL HAZARDS

Water purification describes the process of removing hazardous substances and contaminants from water. Purifying water improves its quality, reduces risk of waterborne disease transmission, and limits exposure to chemical compounds that cause irritation or cancer. **Emissions controls** regulate the acceptable amount and types of pollutants emitted by combustion engines and industrial processes. For example, federal and state automobile emissions regulations may enforce design requirements among vehicle producers, and testing requirements among automobile operators. They are intended to prevent the excessive release of harmful pollutants into the environment and reduce the health impacts of acute or chronic exposure to noxious emissions. Responsible **waste management** can prevent adverse impacts of exposure to toxic substances, medical waste or infectious diseases, and water or air pollution. An example of a waste management practice is recycling or composting to reduce the release of plastic waste and carbon dioxide or methane into the environment. Waste management can also include the responsible disposal of medical waste through sterilization, incineration, and transportation to non-municipal landfills.

PROTECTING THE ENVIRONMENT

Engaging in **policies and practices** that protect the environment can reduce exposure to harm and improve an individual's health outcomes. Healthy ecosystems and physical environments can **ensure access to resources** that fulfill human needs (e.g., clean water, arable farmland, renewable energy, sufficient natural materials for manufacturing). Protecting the environment is also important for **maintaining community health** and **promoting health equity**. Too often, destructive environmental practices take place in under-resourced and marginalized communities.

By implementing policies and practices that protect ecosystem health, **governing bodies can ensure equitable access** to environmental goods and services and the health and wellness benefits of living in a healthy environment. Protecting the environment also **safeguards the wellbeing** of plants and animals and preserves the environment for future generations.

CONTRIBUTING TO IMPROVING COMMUNITY AND ENVIRONMENTAL HEALTH

Environmental advocacy refers to the practice and promotion of environmentally sustainable practices and environmental stewardship, and the mobilization of people to influence policy and behavior. Examples of environmental advocacy include reducing waste (e.g., recycling, composting, using renewable resources, purchasing used or repurposed items or biodegradable materials), reducing emissions and industrial pollution (e.g., using alternative modes of transportation like bikes or trains, eating a plant-based diet), and reducing impact (e.g., conserving water and electricity). Advocacy can also include **petitioning** and **protesting** to effect larger systemic change. Altogether, environmental advocacy encourages the use and adoption of sustainable practices to improve the health and wellbeing of all beings within the ecosystem. **Environmental volunteerism** refers to community service that benefits the environment (e.g., community tree plantings, community river cleanups, starting a community gardens). Volunteering improves the natural environment and can improve an individual's sense of place and belonging. It also provides free labor for overburdened community and non-profit organizations which may improve their capacity to further serve their community.

Influences on Health Decisions and Behaviors

BELIEFS

An individual's **health beliefs** can impact his or her **desire to seek medical services** and can **predict** whether he or she engages in a certain health behavior. According to the Health Belief Model, six theoretical constructs interact to influence a person's health beliefs:

- **Perceived susceptibility** describes how vulnerable a person believes he or she is to a disease, condition, or other health problem.
- **Perceived severity** refers to an individual's perception of the severity of the illness if he or she doesn't seek treatment.
- **Perceived benefits** describe a person's perception of the effectiveness and advantages of the actions he or she must take to prevent or treat an illness.
- **Perceived barriers** refer to the obstacles one believes impede his or her ability to perform a health-promoting action.
- **Cues to action** describe external (e.g., health campaign or PSA on the dangers of smoking) or internal stimuli (e.g., a persistent cough that prompts one to go to the doctor) that provoke action.
- **Self-efficacy** is an individual's confidence in how capable he or she is to perform a health-promoting action.

Each of these constructs influence a person's understanding of disease risk, how important or easy it is to act, and whether he or she can maintain health behaviors.

ATTITUDES

A person's **health attitudes** are formed by the **perceived quality** of his or her health and his or her favorability toward various aspects of health. For example, a person with a **positive health attitude** may consider his or her health very important, so he or she might participate in health-enhancing behaviors like exercise. On the other hand, someone with a **negative health attitude** may refrain from engaging in behaviors that improve his or her health and well-being. Often, one's health attitudes are informed by one's **participation in health-enhancing practices** (e.g., a person who exercises frequently and eats nutritious foods will have positive health attitudes). Positive health attitudes may shift one's beliefs about his or her vulnerability to disease and his or her belief that health-promoting behaviors can be maintained. The beliefs and attitudes of others can greatly influence health attitudes.

KNOWLEDGE

Health knowledge refers to a person's comprehension of disease etiology, transmission, treatment, and risk. An individual is more likely to have **low health knowledge** if he or she has low educational attainment and is a non-native speaker, older, or belongs to a lower socioeconomic group. Individuals whose caregivers or peers have low health knowledge may be more likely to have low health knowledge as well. A person with a **high degree of health knowledge** is more likely to engage in health-promoting behaviors and disease-prevention practices. One's health knowledge can greatly influence one's **health literacy**, which is the ability of a person to find, comprehend, and appropriately apply health information. For example, people with **poor health literacy** may rely on false health information disseminated through social media websites to inform their decision to get a COVID-19 vaccine. They may also **lack the critical thinking skills** to adequately **assess the validity** of the health claims and information they consume. Poor health knowledge may impact their perceived susceptibility to the virus and thus influence them to make poor health decisions.

SKILLS

Health skills refer to the tools a person uses to maintain good health. The ability to identify and seek out **reliable health information** and the ability to **assess the external influences** (e.g., peers, media) that promote positive or negative health behavior are two important health skills. These skills help a person **make informed decisions** that reflect his or her personal beliefs and attitudes. **Goal setting** is another health skill that empowers an individual to achieve his or her health aspirations by setting reasonable targets and action. Through successful goal setting, a person gains the confidence necessary to make positive health decisions. **Advocacy and negotiation** are health skills that encourage healthy decisions and behaviors. A person who is skilled in health advocacy **feels comfortable asserting** his or her beliefs and opinions when making health decisions. For example, a person may advocate for himself or herself by remaining resolute when faced with pushback from physicians or contempt from peers. **Negotiation and refusal skills** empower a person to make decisions that result in improved health and well-being.

PEERS

Both **implicit and explicit social pressure** from peers can encourage or reinforce healthy decisions and behaviors. **Explicit social pressure** describes direct, often verbal pressure to engage in a certain health behavior, whereas implicit social pressure refers to unspoken pressure by peers or society (e.g., observing friends who participate in fad diets). An individual with **positive peer influence** is more likely to make safe and health-promoting decisions than a person with **negative peer influence**. For example, a person who surrounds himself or herself with physically active peers may be more likely to engage in regular exercise than a person whose peers are sedentary. He or she may receive verbal encouragement, feedback, or advice from those peers that inspires him or her to engage in healthy behaviors. By surrounding oneself with individuals who make healthy decisions, a person may also observe the positive effects of exercise on a friend's health or identify achievable actions he or she can adopt to improve his or her health. Peers may also **expose a person to new experiences** (e.g., playing a new sport, trying a new food) that influence them to make positive health decisions and implement positive health behaviors.

ROLE MODELS

A **role model** is a person who can exhibit desirable attributes and shape the decisions or behaviors of others. The role model may lead by example or influence others' health choices through advice, guidance, or encouragement. Role models may also **influence a person's perception and attitude** toward health behaviors. For example, a person with a role model who maintains a healthy relationship with food, consumes nutritious foods, and encourages his or her mentee to maintain a healthy diet is likely to mirror those health behaviors. A **positive role model** may serve as an example of how health-promoting decisions and behaviors lead to good outcomes. Research indicates that adolescents with positive role models are **less likely** to make unsafe or risky choices (e.g., unsafe sex, drug use), receive higher grades in school, make healthier decisions about nutrition and exercise, and have higher self-esteem. The **benefits** of role models are **amplified** if a person has a **personal relationship** with his or her role model.

Health Problem Solving and Decision Making

USING PROBLEM-SOLVING SKILLS IN HEALTH-RELATED CONTEXTS

Problem-solving is a process through which a person finds solutions to complex issues. It begins with **identifying and defining** the problem. This can be accomplished through a health care practitioner's diagnosis or a self-evaluation of one's health status. A person's health problem can be defined by determining the causes and contributing or mitigating factors. For example, a person may be diagnosed with prediabetes after a blood sugar test performed by his or her primary care physician. That person may work with the doctor to identify the lifestyle and environmental factors that led to the condition (e.g., family history, diet, physical inactivity). The next step in problem-solving is **generating potential solutions**. A person might make a list of treatment options and rank them based on preference, each solution's advantages and disadvantages, and the person's capacity to perform each solution. Once a treatment plan or solution is decided upon, it should be **implemented and evaluated**. The **measured outcomes** of a solution can determine whether it was effective in addressing the health problem and if the treatment plan should be revised.

USING DECISION-MAKING SKILLS IN HEALTH-RELATED CONTEXTS

The **DECIDE model** is a tool for making decisions regarding one's health, and it begins with **defining the problem**. A person should consider his or her **health status** and each of the **determinants of health** (e.g., the social, economic, environmental, lifestyle, and genetic factors) when defining the problem. The second step is to **establish the criteria**. One should contemplate what **outcomes** he or she hopes to achieve and avoid, and by determining such criteria, he or she will be able to **brainstorm possible solutions**. Third, one must **consider the possible choices** using that criteria and **weigh the advantages and disadvantages** of each possible solution. He or she should also consider how each possible solution **aligns with his or her values**. Next, a person should **identify the best solution**. The best solution may be one that aligns most with what he or she deems important or valuable or the one that is most practical to implement. The fifth step is to **decide and act**, and the final step is to **evaluate and monitor the solution**. A person should monitor one's health and continuously reflect on one's progress to assess how his or her choices impacted his or her health outcome(s). Doing so can also be helpful for the person as he or she prepares to make future health-related decisions.

DECIDE Model

> **D**efine the problem
> **E**stablish the criteria
> **C**onsider the possible choices
> **I**dentify the best solution
> **D**evelop and implement the solution
> **E**valuate the solution

CHARACTERISTICS AND BENEFITS OF RISK ASSESSMENTS

A **health risk assessment** (HRA) is an appraisal of an individual's health and risk factors. It can be performed by health care professionals to evaluate one's health status, determine health risks, and track health changes between doctor visits. It is also used in health research to assess population-level health data (e.g., health disparities). HRAs are used to identify one's **physiological and mental health status** and **assess the lifestyle and environmental factors** that increase or mitigate risk. Health status may be determined through **self-reported questionnaires** or through **biometric data**. Questions about one's personal medical history, family history, and lifestyle factors (e.g., smoking status, exercise and eating habits) can be used to identify risks. Qualitative data may be collected to **assess health beliefs and attitudes**, which can also be used to evaluate risk. Results from HRAs can be used to create **individualized feedback** and **tailor health plans** for reducing health risks and enhancing and maintaining health, **evaluate the efficacy** of health interventions, and **inform the type of programs** needed to address poor health outcomes.

REDUCING HEALTH RISKS AND ENHANCING/MAINTAINING HEALTH

Once health risks have been identified through a health risk assessment (HRA), an individual can use the findings to adopt health behaviors that **enhance and maintain health**. For example, a person whose HRA identifies a family history of breast cancer might conduct daily breast self-exams, schedule regular cancer screenings, and adopt lifestyle-related behaviors that mitigate the risk of cancer (e.g., weight control, abstaining from alcohol use, exercising). These behaviors can **prevent and detect** cancer early to improve and maintain health. **Biometric data findings** from HRAs can also be used to **adjust health habits**. For example, a person whose HRA determines he or she has high blood pressure can engage in daily exercise, eat nutritious and heart-healthy foods, practice stress-reducing activities (e.g., meditation, mindfulness) and quit smoking. These health risk-reducing behaviors can mitigate risk of complications due to high blood pressure and enhance overall physical, mental, and emotional health.

PLANNING, DECISION-MAKING, AND GOAL-SETTING SKILLS

The **DECIDE model** can be used to make decisions regarding one's health. A person with prediabetes seeking to make health behavior changes should **define the problem** first (e.g., poor diet, overweight). He or she should then consider what he or she would like to **achieve** (e.g., weight loss without a restrictive diet) and **brainstorm possible solutions** to accomplish the overall goal (e.g., changing eating patterns, abstaining from alcohol, exercise). Once he or she has identified and implemented the best solution, he or she should **monitor progress** (e.g., regular weigh-ins, A1C checks). **SMART goals** are specific, measurable, achievable, relevant, and time-bound and help an individual plan and successfully implement health goals. For example, a SMART goal for someone who seeks to lose 30 pounds could be to walk at least 30 minutes five days a week for six months. This goal includes a specific and appropriate exercise for weight loss, a measurement to assess progress (e.g., 30 pounds), and the method and rate of weight loss are achievable within the time frame. The SMART goal also has a **start date and deadline.**

PROBLEM-SOLVING AND DECISION-MAKING SKILLS AND PROCEDURES

The root causes of a person's, family's, or community's poor health outcomes can be determined through the **problem-solving process**. A person with **strong problem-solving and decision-making skills** may develop a more thorough and appropriate plan for enhancing his or her personal health than one who does not. The ability to identify and evaluate health problems, brainstorm solutions, and implement health behavior changes will better prepare a person to effectively manage his or her health. A **collective** (e.g., family, community) **approach** to problem-solving and decision-making can often be an effective way to solve a complex health problem properly and efficiently. The **diversity** of opinions, experiences, and assets of a larger group of people may **reveal novel ideas and improve the efficacy** of the solution. To **enhance collective health**, it is important that the opinions, beliefs, and values of all involved are regarded fairly. All affected by the health decision must be included in the problem-solving and decision-making process.

SEEKING ADVICE AND GUIDANCE
HEALTH CARE PROFESSIONALS

Health care professionals are well-versed in **disease etiology**, and they are often the **primary point of contact** for disease diagnosis, treatment, and prevention. Although they generally have a deeper understanding of medical science than the average person, their expertise is often limited to their **specialty**. Primary care providers hold a broad knowledge of medicine, yet they **lack the ability** to diagnose and/or treat a person with advanced health needs. **Specialists** are trained in a specific field of medicine (e.g., neurology, oncology, psychiatry) and can perform **specialized care**. Since health care professionals may have **differing interpretations** of an individual's health or treatment options, a person making an important health care decision should **seek a second opinion**. Asking for a second opinion can **corroborate the accuracy** of the initial findings and **confirm** the most appropriate treatment options. It can also equip a patient with the skills and knowledge to make informed decisions.

FAMILY MEMBERS

While health care professionals provide indispensable medical expertise to patients, a person might hold a **family member's advice** and recommendations in **higher regard** than a physician's. Family members are often more attuned to a person's health beliefs, attitudes, and goals, so they can provide appropriate and responsive advice. They may also be more aware of the social and environmental factors that contribute to an individual's health outcomes or decisions because of their shared experiences. Family members may **see each other far more often** than a health care provider, so they are **more likely to notice changes** in a person's health and **suggest actions**. The close ties and personal relationships that a person shares with their family members may make them **more likely to disclose sensitive health information or health concerns**. Thus, family members are a **crucial component** of medical decision-making. However, a family member who is misinformed or holds inaccurate health beliefs may provide poor advice and guidance.

DEVELOPING PERSONAL PLANS FOR MAINTAINING AND ENHANCING HEALTH
BENEFITS

A **personal health plan** details a person's health goals and the steps needed to achieve those goals. The plan is guided by an individual's personal health vision. Personal health plans often contain a **detailed account** of one's health objectives to achieve his or her goals, a timeline, and a list of benchmarks to track progress. Since personal health plans **contain clear and actionable goals**, they are useful tools for **maintaining accountability** and **sustaining momentum**. When a person **achieves the health goals** detailed by the plan, he or she may feel **empowered and motivated** to continue working. The framework that personal health plans provide enables a person to make better decisions regarding his or her health. Additionally, the practice of creating and adhering to a personal health plan requires **regular reflection**. A person who practices self-evaluation may be more equipped to **make better health decisions** and **advocate** for his or her health needs with others.

PROCEDURES

The first step an individual should take to develop a personal health plan is **assessing his or her health status**. One's health status can be measured through assessments performed by health care professionals (e.g., biometric data collection) or through a self-evaluation of one's health habits. Second, one must **develop relevant and achievable goals** based on his or her health assessment findings. A person's current health status and/or health risks can inform whether one should seek to **maintain or enhance** aspects of his or her personal health. For example, a physically active person who is diagnosed with high cholesterol should create health goals that enhance one's eating behaviors and that maintain one's exercise habits. Next, a person should **create a list of objectives** necessary to reach each goal and **establish a reasonable timeline** in which each objective can be accomplished. Once each objective is achieved, the person should **reflect on his or her progress**. Reflection is crucial to **understanding the barriers and mitigating factors** that impede or support a person in achieving his or her goals.

Sources of Health-Related Information

VALIDITY OF HEALTH-RELATED INFORMATION

ASSESSING

Not all health-related information is **valid** or **trustworthy**. In some instances, the **primary source** of the information (e.g., research studies) may have **flawed study designs** that skew results. The **interpretations** of results by the authors or those citing the research may also be inaccurate. Both can impact the reliability of the information. If the author's intent is to shift the reader's opinion, the health-related information may also be biased. By assessing the validity of health-related information, **one can avoid making a decision based on inaccurate and/or unreliable claims**. An informed decision can **prevent unnecessary or harmful outcomes associated with invalid information**. For example, a person who consumes a weight-loss pill without researching its side effects, exploring its reviews, or without consulting a health care provider may suffer serious health consequences. He or she may also lose money purchasing an ineffective product and may become disheartened if intended results are not achieved.

HEALTH PROFESSIONALS

Health professionals receive rigorous medical training and education through which they acquire a wealth of knowledge about health. They are required to demonstrate their **proficiency** through competency-based exams and certifications from accredited organizations. Thus, health-related information from health professionals can be considered **valid**. Health professionals' level of education and specialty can **impact their knowledge** of the subject matter and their level of expertise. For example, a gastroenterologist is a far more reliable expert on stomach and digestive diseases than a nurse. Health professionals' **personal gains or biases** may also **cloud their judgement**, which can **impact the validity** of the health-related information or guidance they provide. Therefore, it is important for health care consumers to **practice good judgment** when considering their physician's advice (i.e., one should seek a second opinion). A person can **access health information** from health professionals through regular visits with his or her primary care provider and published educational materials (e.g., pamphlets, flyers) that are accessible in his or her doctor's office.

GOVERNMENT AGENCIES AS A SOURCE OF HEALTH INFORMATION

Government agencies (e.g., Centers for Disease Control and Prevention, National Institutes of Health) have a vested interest in the health of the nation. A **healthier population** can improve a nation's economic productivity and produce a more educated and larger workforce. Since they serve the public, **government agencies have a responsibility to release accurate and valid information**. Those who conduct government health research are often beholden to rigorous requirements throughout the research process that ensure the credibility of their findings. A person can access health information from government agencies through federal and state government websites. Most **government websites** end in ".gov." Examples of government agency websites include www.CDC.gov, www.NIH.gov, www.medicaid.gov, https://www.dshs.texas.gov/. Government agencies often release health information that employs plain language (e.g., clear, easy to comprehend) to ensure that their constituents can understand it. They may use infographics, pamphlets, videos, social media, or written text to present health information.

HEALTH-SPECIFIC GOVERNMENT AGENCIES PROVIDING VALID HEALTH INFORMATION

- The **Centers for Disease Control and Prevention** (CDC) is a federal agency that monitors communicable diseases, conducts health research, and produces health guidance materials.
- The **National Institutes of Health** (NIH) and the **US Department of Health and Human Services** (HHS) are federal agencies that conduct health and biomedical research. The HHS also provides many social services and publishes resources about disease prevention, public safety, and emergency preparedness.
- The **Food and Drug Administration** (FDA) and the **Substance Abuse and Mental Health Services Administration** (SAMHSA) are two agencies within the HHS. The FDA primarily enforces federal food and drug regulations, but it also conducts research and development. SAMHSA produces health materials related to mental illness and substance abuse, increases substance abuse and mental health awareness, and improves health care delivery.
- The **Centers for Medicare and Medicaid Services** (CMS) is another HHS agency that administers health insurance to low-income Americans and those over 65 and ensures regulatory compliance.
- The **US Public Health Service** (PHS) consists of nine HHS public health-related agencies that provide rapid response to public health crises and deliver health education.
- The **World Health Organization** (WHO) is an international agency within the United Nations that conducts health research, provides health guidance and standards, and organizes global public health emergency responses.

PRIVATE NONPROFIT AGENCIES

Nonprofit agencies are often reliable sources of health-related information. They are more likely to use **scientifically valid and current research** to substantiate their health claims. They are also more likely to use **quality control measures** to ensure that the information they release is **trustworthy**. For example, an organization may exclusively use peer-reviewed journal articles or federal health information to support its claims. It might also use an editor or fact-checker to ensure the accuracy of its health information. However, since agencies are governed by a board of directors and trustees, **conflicts of interest can arise**. Similarly, although **private organizations** may use credible health research, their interpretation can be presented in a **biased** way. Furthering their mission or organizational interests may be the motive behind the information that they publish rather than presenting unbiased and factual information. Therefore, individuals should seek out information published by organizations that **openly state their mission** and **employ**

neutral references. Nonprofit health information can be found on agency websites (usually those that end in ".org") or in books, pamphlets, articles, or social media.

INTERNET RESOURCES

Health-related information from internet sources is generally the **least valid type of information**. While online, a person reviewing health information should use **caution** unless the resource is sponsored by government agencies, academic institutions, or credible nonprofit organizations (e.g., scientific associations, medical societies). Internet sources not affiliated with a credible agency or organization **may lack quality control measures** (e.g., fact-checking employees, editors) that ensure the reliability of the information. Many credible agencies use the internet to **improve the reach and accessibility** of their published health information. However, health information may be presented **inaccurately or in a biased manner** by others as it is reshared through secondary websites or social media. Therefore, when reviewing health information posted on a website, it is vital that a person research the data source to ensure the validity of the site's claims. Government, academic, and nonprofit organization websites can be identified by their URL ending (**e.g., ".gov," ".edu," or ".org."**). Websites with valid health-related information will have **clearly identifiable authors and contact information**. They may also include information on the last updated or published date and links to the information source.

VALID HEALTH-RELATED INFORMATION AND PRODUCTS

When seeking valid health-related information and products, one should first **consider the sponsor** (e.g., government, nonprofit, academic institution, private company) of the information **and the author(s)**. The entity funding the health research or the creation of health materials may have secondary reasons for publishing the information. For example, a pharmaceutical company that releases a pamphlet on a disease may be interested in selling its product in addition to educating the public. Thus, one should examine the **purpose of the information** (e.g., inform, sell a product, shift opinion) since it can impact the trustworthiness of the resource. The goal or mission of the sponsor can suggest the purpose. The person consuming the health-related information should also consider the expertise and credibility of the author and the **publication date** because current material may be more accurate. **Transparent references and cited sources** listed throughout the resource often indicate that the information is valid. The **quality of the references** used to inform the health material (e.g., peer-reviewed research) can also indicate its validity.

BEST PRACTICES FOR MAKING INFORMED HEALTH DECISIONS

When a person makes an informed health decision, he or she is aware of all possible choices and understands the outcomes of treatment. A person making an informed health decision should first obtain health information from multiple sources. Seeking information from **multiple sources** can help a person better understand his or her health condition and all available choices. Once he or she has acquired valid health information, the person should **synthesize all information gathered**. This entails evaluating the validity of the sources, determining the similarities and differences between the health information collected, and finding connections between the information to form insights. Although factual information is a crucial part of the decision-making process, individual values and health goals can influence a person's ultimate decision. For example, two individuals with the same cancer diagnosis who receive the same information from their doctors may have different health philosophies that impact their treatment. One may opt to pursue chemotherapy to prevent metastasis, while the other may reject it due to religious beliefs. Both are valid health decisions. Therefore, when making a final decision, one should **consider if it aligns with his or her values and health goals**. The person should then **consult his or her health provider** to confirm his or her understanding and discuss next steps.

VALID VS. INVALID SOURCES

Valid health information is factual, unbiased, and almost always based on research. Findings that form **valid health information** can be generated through **rigorous studies** performed by **experts**. Studies whose methodologies, analyses, and findings are **peer-reviewed** by field experts and whose authors perform **reliability and validity testing** can be considered **valid health information**. Examples of valid health information include government websites or medical journals. Although health information from secondary sources (e.g., newspaper articles) is an interpretation of data, materials that include neutral claims about health topics and use multiple primary sources to substantiate their claims are often more valid than those that do not. **Invalid health information** may be **inaccurate or biased**. Information regarding side effects or risks associated with a treatment option or medication may be omitted from invalid health information materials to influence perception. Invalid health information may also be used to purposely shift public opinion about controversial health topics. Common sources of invalid health information can include advertisements by pharmaceutical or medical product companies or personal testimonies.

EVALUATING THE VALIDITY OF HEALTH INFORMATION

The first step in evaluating the validity of health information is **assessing the credibility and relevance of the source**. **Credibility** can be measured by the author's credentials, the use of peer-reviewed, scientifically sound source material, and date of publication. For example, a research article on COVID-19 written by a group of virologists that is published in a peer-reviewed journal is often far more credible than a blog post written by a member of the public. The next step is **assessing for partiality**. The purpose of the sponsoring agency or author in writing the health information can indicate partiality. For example, a federal agency whose mission is to inform the public about measles, mumps, and rubella (MMR) vaccines is a more valid source of health information about the benefits and risks of vaccination than an anti-vaccination association whose motivation is to prevent vaccination mandates. Health materials that use **sensational language** or **omit key pieces of information** from their sources may be **biased**. One should then **review other health materials to substantiate the information**. If the information is consistent with other credible sources, it is likely valid.

IDENTIFYING FRAUDULENT HEALTH INFORMATION AND QUACKERY

Fraudulent health information and quackery both refer to inaccurate and dishonest claims about medicine or medical practices. Such claims come from companies or individuals who allege medical expertise and intentionally deceive others to promote a service or product. Health frauds and quackery can **delay proper treatment**, which can exacerbate health problems. Products or services that **claim to be the sole cure** for a medical problem or **claim to cure many different health ailments** are often a form of **health fraud**. Other examples include products that use exotic ingredients, products that lack an endorsement by federal regulating agencies (e.g., Food and Drug Administration), and products or services with **unlikely or too-good-to-be-true health testimonials**. Celebrity and other **nonexpert endorsements** may also indicate health fraud and quackery. A person who suspects fraudulent health information or quackery should consult a credible health source or a medical professional.

ADVERTISING AND MARKETING METHODS USED TO INFLUENCE CONSUMERS

Health-related **marketing and advertising methods** use logos, pathos, and ethos appeals to influence consumers.

- **Logos** refers to an appeal to **reason or logic** and employs scientific facts or statistics. For example, a commercial for a weight-loss medication may advertise that the product is "clinically proven" to cause 60 percent more weight loss than other diet pills. Logical appeals are generally seen as the **most trustworthy** as they should be **based on verifiable facts**. Even without being based on true evidence, the **appeal to logic** may still be effective, which is one reason that customers should **consider truthfulness** when considering a product.
- **Pathos** is a technique that appeals to the consumers' **emotions or senses**. For example, a commercial for depression medication that depicts depression's impact on a person's life, relationships, and emotional well-being can elicit an emotional response. Advertisers may use a variety of film techniques (e.g., lighting, music, B-roll) to evoke a stronger emotion.
- **Ethos** refers to an appeal to **credibility**. Advertisements that appeal to ethos often include **credible experts to influence consumers**. For example, a commercial for an energy drink that features an endorsement from a doctor and an athlete may imply that the drink is safe and effective.

MARKETING CLAIMS USED TO INFLUENCE BEHAVIOR

Health-related claims about health care products and services can **elicit trust** if the claims are backed up by scientific research. The use of factual evidence and statistics in marketing advertisements reassures the consumer that the product or service is safe and proven to work. Claims about health care products and services can also **create an emotional response** that prompts a consumer to act. Consumers may form an attachment to the product or service or feel **compelled to adopt new health behaviors**. Emotional appeals may also **produce a fearful response** among consumers, which can lead to product or service avoidance. Health-related claims about health care services and products that use **bandwagon tactics** (e.g., a person performs a health behavior because others are doing it) use **social pressure** to influence behavior. Claims may imply that the product or service is used and well-liked by many, which can motivate a person to conform.

Informed Decision-Making Processes

MAKING DECISIONS ABOUT PRODUCTS OR SERVICES

A person seeking to make a decision about a health care product should first **compile relevant and credible health information regarding all possible products or services**. He or she should then **consider his or her personal values, health goals**, and the pros and cons of each option. Before making a final decision, the individual should **discuss the decision with a health care provider and/or family and friends**. For example, a person who hopes to stop smoking cigarettes should first research all feasible smoking cessation aids (e.g., nicotine gum and/or patches, vaping, anti-craving prescription medication). Next, he or she should consider the pros and cons of each (e.g., cost, ease of access, addictive potential, side effects) and whether the product fits his or her goals (e.g., gradual cessation, reducing reliance on nicotine). Third, the person should discuss the potential decision with his or her physician and/or family and friends. Finally, the person should make a decision and monitor his or her progress.

MAKING DECISIONS ABOUT A HEALTH BEHAVIOR

The **ABCDE decision-making rubric** can be used to make a decision about health behaviors. A decision about adopting a new health behavior is scored in five criteria: **a**ims, **b**enefits, **c**apacity, **d**ata-driven, and **e**ffectiveness.

- **Aims** refer to the extent to which the behavior aligns with a person's health goals.
- **Benefits** describe the number of potential benefits.
- **Capacity** is the extent of one's ability to adopt a new behavior.
- **Data-driven** describes the amount of credible research regarding the behavior.
- **Effectiveness** is how well the behavior will address the health problem.

The person would score the behavior on a scale. **The higher the final score, the better the decision**. For example, a person hoping to lose weight may opt to increase his or her exercise. The behavior aligns with the goal and has numerous benefits, so he or she may assign a 5 to aims and benefits. If the person lacks the time to exercise throughout the week and the funds to afford a gym membership, he or she might score capacity at 2. Exercise is well-researched and proven to reduce weight, so data-driven and effectiveness may be scored at 5. The final score is a 22, which indicates that this decision is achievable and well-thought-out.

ABCDE Decision-Making Rubric					
Aims	1	2	3	4	5
Benefits	1	2	3	4	5
Capacity	1	2	3	4	5
Data-Driven	1	2	3	4	5
Effectiveness	1	2	3	4	5
Composite Score Range	5 low	10	15 mid	20	25 high
Score:					

USING HEALTH INFORMATION FROM HEALTH PROFESSIONALS

Individuals making a decision about a health service, product, or behavior should **consult their health care provider first**. Providers can **advise patients** on the actual risks or benefits of health-related products, services, and behaviors. They can **provide factual and clear information** that aids in **informed decision-making**. However, a health professional's interpretation of the efficacy of a service, product, or behavior may differ, so it is important that consumers **seek a second opinion**. Consumers should **evaluate the similarities and differences** between the information they receive and **synthesize their findings**. Those making health-related decisions can use health information from health professionals to corroborate claims in advertisements for health services, products, or behaviors. For example, a person who is considering the ketogenic (keto) diet—a low-carbohydrate and high-fat diet—can consult his or her physician to determine if the diet is appropriate for his or her health goals and health status. He or she can use information from the provider to identify which health claims about the keto diet or keto products are trustworthy.

USING HEALTH INFORMATION FROM GOVERNMENT AGENCIES

A person making a decision about a health service, product, or behavior can use health information from government agencies to make an informed decision. Health-related information from government sources (e.g., federal agencies, local health departments) is reliable and trustworthy. Resources provide credible health facts and statistics; accurate information on specific diseases, conditions, or treatments; advice on healthy behaviors; and helpful information on where to locate community health resources. Information from government agencies can be used **to prompt**

discussion about health concerns or treatment options with health care providers. Government health resources are typically presented in plain and accessible language, which can **help consumers better comprehend information** from physicians and health claims. Comparing well-documented facts to claims can help a person **spot fraudulent or inaccurate health information**. For example, a diet pill advertisement may boast that its special ingredient will help consumers lose up to 20 pounds per week without any lifestyle changes. A person can compare information about fad diets and best practices from the USDA, NIH, FDA, or CDC to assess the validity of the product's alleged results.

USING HEALTH INFORMATION FROM PRIVATE NONPROFIT AGENCIES

A person making a decision about health services, products, and behaviors can use **health information from private nonprofit agencies** to inform his or her choices. Nonprofit agencies that synthesize credible source material to produce health information can be viewed as **credible**. They may also **conduct research** or **initiate advocacy** campaigns on health-related issues. Agencies that specialize in health-related issues often have in-depth information on a consumer's area of interest. They may have useful health materials or trainings that educate consumers about health topics and available resources for health care. For example, the **American Heart Association** (AHA) has wide-ranging materials on heart health, provides CPR training and courses on maintaining heart health, and publishes guidance on heart-healthy activities (e.g., recipes, fitness routines). Information from the AHA can be used to make decisions about adopting new behaviors, diet products, or heart health-related services (e.g., nutrition counseling, support groups).

USING HEALTH INFORMATION FROM INTERNET RESOURCES

A person making decisions about health services, products, and behaviors can use internet resources to **research health conditions and treatments** and **connect with health-related resources**. Reliable health-related websites can provide a plethora of information regarding common symptoms of specific illnesses and available treatment options and their outcomes. If used properly, the information can help individuals **discern between a benign and serious health problem**, which can save them time, money, and anxiety. However, the wide generalizability of health information can serve to increase health anxiety instead of relieving it. Reviews by consumers of various health products and services may **help a person identify health frauds or scams**. However, many internet sources promote products or claims that are biased or unsubstantiated by research. Therefore, a person should consult multiple resources and health experts before deciding. **Telehealth applications available through the internet can connect consumers to physicians** and health care professionals. Easy access to experts can provide quick confirmation of the validity of health information to make health decision-making less daunting.

USING INSIGHTS FROM FRIENDS AND FAMILY MEMBERS

Since one's support system (e.g., family members, friends) are **familiar with the individual's personal goals, values, and barriers**, they can provide invaluable insights about health decisions. Due to their proximity to the individual, family members may be **more aware of the impact** that a health decision can have on a person's daily life or long-term health. Shared behavior alterations with family members and friends are often easier and more effective than when one adopts a new health behavior alone. **One's support system can provide motivation, accountability, and advice**. The family of a person seeking to lose weight may help him or her cook healthy meals or accompany him or her on daily walks. Their involvement may help a person feel more supported in his or her goal. Family-wide involvement may also be necessary for difficult health decisions. For example, a person with a substance use disorder may consult family about treatment options. Family involvement may reduce distress and treatment dropout.

Health Care Systems and Services

HOSPITALS

The **primary role of hospitals** is to provide patients with medical care and support. Hospitals provide **emergency or trauma health care to patrons and host a range of specialized services** (e.g., radiology, oncology, psychiatry, gynecology). At a hospital, an individual may also receive such medical treatments and procedures as a surgery, an MRI or X-ray, radiation, or dialysis, among many others. Depending on the level of care needed, patients may stay overnight or for longer durations. In addition to providing patient care, **some hospitals provide training to medical residents and conduct health research.** Hospital staff often assist patients in identifying community resources to maintain good health after discharge. Hospitals are quickly becoming hubs for wraparound services and primary care. Individuals experiencing rising inaccessibility to health care (e.g., uninsured or underinsured, low proximity to primary care providers, reduced capacity of practitioners to provide timely care) are increasingly relying on hospitals and emergency medicine practitioners for primary care.

CLINICS

Clinics are health care facilities that provide routine outpatient care. At clinics, **primary care providers conduct health checkups, provide immunizations, and treat mild to moderate illnesses.** Clinics rarely allow overnight stays, and appointments with medical practitioners can be booked ahead of time. Patients may also have the option of walk-in appointments; however, clinic hours are usually limited to the standard workday. Whereas hospitals generally provide disease treatment, at clinics, physicians may provide preventative health care services (e.g., blood pressure measurements, cancer screenings, vaccinations, or health counseling). **Clinics may also refer to specialized care locations at which medical practitioners perform outpatient care.** For example, a psychiatrist may conduct diagnostic tests, psychiatric treatment, and therapy at an outpatient psychiatry clinic. Some clinics—often referred to as free clinics—provide reduced or free services to the public. These clinics are managed by volunteer physicians, nurses, and administrative staff to serve community members experiencing financial hardship.

HEALTH CARE PROFESSIONALS

Health care professionals are individuals who are licensed to perform medical services. Examples include primary care doctors, physician's assistants, dieticians, pharmacists, registered nurses, and specialty care physicians (e.g., pediatricians, obstetricians, dermatologists). The role of health care professionals varies by specialty, yet overall, they are responsible for **disease prevention, diagnosis, and treatment**. Health care professionals engage in **disease prevention** through health education and health counseling. For example, a primary care doctor whose patient was recently diagnosed with high cholesterol may explain the risks associated with the condition and assess modifiable lifestyle factors. The physician may also assist with drafting a personalized plan of action to prevent the onset of diseases like heart disease and stroke. Health care professionals, like dieticians and pharmacists, also provide disease treatment. For example, a dietician may provide medical nutrition therapy for a person with Crohn's disease to manage nutrient loss, while a pharmacist may supply immunosuppressants to control symptoms.

BENEFITS OF REGULAR MEDICAL CHECKUPS

Medical checkups are annual comprehensive exams performed by a primary care provider. A medical checkup is a valuable preventative and diagnostic tool that can **delay the onset of disease, treat diseases early, and improve or prolong well-being**. It typically consists of a physical exam, a review of one's medical history, blood tests, and health counseling. Regular medical checkups can **reduce one's risk of developing an illness and can lead to the early detection of a disease**.

Identifying a disease early can increase the success of treatment and reduce the risk of health complications. Patients with **existing health conditions** can be **monitored regularly** to track disease progression and adjust treatment strategies if needed. **Long-term benefits** of regular medical checkups include a longer lifespan, lower health care costs, and greater health knowledge.

BENEFITS OF REGULAR DENTAL CHECKUPS

Dental checkups are biannual exams conducted by a dentist and a dental hygienist. They typically consist of a **dental cleaning** (e.g., plaque and tartar removal, polishing) and an **oral exam**. Fluoride application and dental X-rays may also take place to prevent tooth decay, identify cavities or potential cavities, and monitor tooth migration. The dentist will also evaluate a patient's head and neck, soft tissue (e.g., tongue, cheeks), and gums to **identify possible oral health problems or diseases** like mouth cancer. Regular dental checkups can **prevent the onset or exacerbation of tooth decay or gum disease**. Both, if left untreated, can result in costly medical bills, infection, and tooth loss. The dentist can provide information on how to maintain proper dental hygiene and refer patients to other providers (e.g., orthodontists, prosthodontists, oral surgeons) for specialized care.

Cultural Influences on Healthcare

INFLUENCE OF CULTURAL BACKGROUND

A person's **cultural background** can influence his or her decision-making when selecting a health care provider because it can influence one's understanding of the causes of a disease and the type of treatment one is seeking. Cultural influences can be difficult to pinpoint, but **they are related to geographic location, family history, religious values, language, and social interactions**. They can be subtle or strong but often still affect one's choices. Individuals with **stronger cultural values** often prefer to have a practitioner who **shares or is empathetic with their beliefs**. Practitioners should be careful to consider cultural backgrounds and values when dealing with a patient. Individuals pursuing health care services should be **encouraged** to consider and **disclose** their cultural values to receive the best care possible as **tailored to their beliefs**.

TYPES OF CULTURAL INFLUENCE

Cultural influences **can both promote or discourage a person's reliance on health care services and products**. For instance, individuals on a sports team or within a health-conscious peer group may be more willing to take vitamins, purchase protective gear, exercise, and eat well. In some family dynamics, an individual might be **expected** to "push through" being sick, rather than visit a doctor, take medicine, and take time to recover. A patient holding **homeopathic or traditional religious-based health beliefs** may opt for alternative medical practitioners (e.g., acupuncturists, shamans) in addition to or in lieu of conventional providers. In some **traditional cultures**, individuals may believe that spirits or sorcery are the causes of illness instead of bacteria and viruses. As a result, these individuals may choose to forego conventional medicine for spiritual treatments. For example, one traditional practice originating in East and Southeast Asia is called **cupping**, which is the use of suction created from heated cups to draw negative forces out of the body.

INFLUENCE OF SOCIOECONOMIC STATUS

Socioeconomic status can influence a person's likelihood of seeking health care services and the type of care that he or she receives. Individuals with **lower socioeconomic status (SES)** may be less likely to seek health care due to the cost of services. Those with low SES are more likely to be uninsured or underinsured, which can impact the providers they are able to see, the services that are or are not covered by their insurer, and the cost of their co-pay. A person with low financial security may lack the funds to select more efficient health products or higher-quality treatment options. Low or no-cost community resources (e.g., free clinics) and federal health insurance programs (e.g., Medicaid) can ease some of the financial restraints that impact the health and well-being of those with low SES. Research indicates that a person's SES is correlated with his or her **health literacy**, which is a person's ability to locate, comprehend, and apply health information properly. Individuals with low SES are more likely to have poorer health literacy, which may impact their medical decision-making and health care service selection.

INFLUENCE OF INFORMATION ACCESS

Access to health information can influence an individual's health attitudes and awareness of the health products, services, or providers available to him or her. **A person who has adequate access to accurate health information is better able to make informed health care decisions.** For example, a person with greater access to information about the causes of and management strategies for autoimmune diseases may be better able to make decisions regarding treatment options. He or she may also be able to identify more types of disease management options than those detailed by his or her provider or identify new health care practitioners to consult. With **greater access to health information**, a person may be better able to identify credible sources and recognize untrustworthy health claims. He or she may be more capable of selecting legitimate health care products and services than a person without adequate access to information. **Access to health information can be influenced by low health literacy or environmental barriers.** Individuals residing in rural areas and individuals with low socioeconomic statuses or low technology literacy may lack access to digital health information available through affordable or reliable internet.

Advertising and Marketing in Healthcare

ADVERTISING AND MARKETING TECHNIQUES USED

Testimonials and statistics are commonly used health product and health service promotion techniques. **Health testimonials** utilize an endorsement by a celebrity or a trusted individual (e.g., health care professional, current user of the health product or service) to convince the consumer to purchase the product or service. **Statistics** are used to appeal to a person's logic. People often trust numbers and research—even if the statistics are inaccurate or unclear. Advertisements may also utilize a **personal appeal** that is intended to evoke an **emotional response** (e.g., joy, sadness, fear) that inspires the consumer to select or purchase the health product or service. For example, many hospitals and health care-related organizations released advertisements that urged the public to get vaccinated during the COVID-19 pandemic. They used strong emotional imagery, such as footage of vaccinated individuals reuniting with their family members after a substantial social distancing period and/or speeches from nurses and doctors describing their experiences, to **evoke empathy**. Most advertisements will use a combination of multiple techniques to enhance the consumer response and increase the likelihood that the public will purchase a product or service.

DETERMINING IF ADVERTISING CLAIMS ARE ACCURATE

A consumer can **determine the accuracy** of an advertised service or product by **evaluating the legitimacy of its claims**. A review of a product's claims can be conducted through conversations with trusted peers or through independent research (e.g., examining consumer reviews, exploring available research about the product's or service's efficacy, reviewing similar products). For instance, a person seeking a personal trainer to lose weight might consult some fitness-related groups or his or her provider, friends, or family to determine the best service for his or her health goals or to identify possible trainers. **Feedback from trusted sources** can help someone determine if a trainer's advertised services are accurate and trustworthy. **Consumer reviews** often provide a spectrum of responses about various aspects of a health product, service, or provider. Consumers can assess desirable or undesirable attributes of a health care product by reviewing similar health products and doing so may **reveal inconsistent advertising claims** if a product promises results not achievable by similar products. Reviewing research about different health care goods can help **identify trustworthy products** and **reveal the legitimacy of claims**.

DETERMINING IF ADVERTISING CLAIMS ARE MISLEADING OR DECEPTIVE

Consumers should **avoid products or services that claim to be a cure-all or quick fix**. Very few products can be used to cure a wide range of diseases or treat illnesses in a short period of time. Products or services that list a suspiciously long list of ailments they treat or promise unreasonable desirable outcomes (e.g., "lose 15 pounds in two weeks," "eliminate type 2 diabetes") are likely **misleading or deceptive**. Testimonials can also be used to make misleading or deceptive claims about a health product or service since they are difficult to dispute. **Endorsements from credible health care professionals** are often more trustworthy than a testimonial from a single product user. A person should **pay attention to websites or advertisements with sensational titles and quotes that have been shortened** (e.g., "this product helped me lose weight …") as these may be used to garner attention and misrepresent the truth. **Reviewing the statistics cited and/or any graphs or diagrams** depicted in the health product advertisement can help a person determine whether a claim is accurate or misleading.

Evaluating Health-Related Products

EVALUATING AND SELECTING HEALTH-RELATED PRODUCTS, TREATMENTS, AND SERVICES
CRITERIA

When evaluating and selecting health-related products, treatments, and services, one should consider the following criteria: cost, insurance coverage, quality, and legitimacy.

- **Cost and insurance coverage** can often be prohibitive factors when selecting a health product, treatment, or service. **A review of one's budget and the funds necessary** to sustain the intended health outcomes can help one determine if the product or service is a good choice. **A review of one's health insurance coverage** is also necessary to determine affordability as some products, treatments, or services may not be covered.
- The **quality of a product** can reveal its **effectiveness** for treating a health condition or attaining a health goal. An **evaluation of the product's formula** can imply adequate quality. Oftentimes, **approval from a federal regulatory agency** like the Food and Drug Administration (FDA) is a good indicator of a product's reliability.
- The **legitimacy of a product** can be determined by **identifying the credentials and authority** of the seller and product. A **credible seller** is licensed by a legitimate certifying entity, such as the National Association of Boards of Pharmacy (NABP). Reviews or ratings from other consumer protection organizations, like the Better Business Bureau (BBB), can reveal the legitimacy of health-related businesses.

SKILLS

The following skills are important to use when **evaluating and selecting health-related products, treatments, and services**: health literacy, financial literacy, and negotiation skills.

- The Centers for Disease Control and Prevention describes **health literacy** as one's ability to locate, comprehend, and utilize health information and services. Health literacy is helpful for those evaluating and selecting health-related products, treatments, and services because those with high health literacy are **better at locating credible information and discerning between accurate and misleading claims**. They are also often **better at making informed health decisions** and **advocating for their health needs and goals**.
- Since cost is a significant factor when selecting a health product or service, high **financial literacy** can help an **individual budget** for his or her health care and **identify cost-effective solutions** to health care problems.
- **Negotiation skills** are important for **confidently communicating** one's health goals, one's service or product preferences, and one's health needs. Health literacy and a strong understanding of one's personal health status or needs can be beneficial when practicing negotiation skills in health care.

CRITERIA FOR EVALUATING AND SELECTING HEALTH PROVIDERS

Criteria for successfully evaluating and selecting health care providers includes staff medical knowledge, insurance coverage, cultural competence, and treatment management recommendations. These criteria can be used to **identify whether the physician is the right fit**; however, one should consider other important attributes prior to visiting. The extent of a **provider's medical knowledge** can be ascertained through a **review of his or her credentials** (e.g., licensing, certifications) and through **reviews by current or former patients**. There are many provider review websites that use overall patient satisfaction to rank or score health care professionals. These websites also often include information on licensing and certification, insurance coverage, and languages spoken. **Insurance coverage** can significantly lower the cost of health services. To determine whether a provider is in-network, one should consult his or her insurer directly. A provider's **cultural competence** can influence the type of care provided and impact the patient's overall experience. A physician who practices culturally competent care treats more than physical health; he or she meets the social, cultural, and linguistic needs of his or her patients.

INTERPRETATION OF SIGNS AND SYMBOLS

Sign/Symbol	Interpretation
	Flame: Includes flammable materials and gases and those that are self-heating or self-reactive.
	Corrosion: Includes substances that can cause skin burns, metal corrosion, and eye damage.

Sign/Symbol	Interpretation
	Health hazard: Includes carcinogens, toxic substances, and respiratory irritants.
	Poison: Includes materials, gases, or substances that are extremely toxic and may result in death or severe illness.
	Irritant: Includes material, gases, or substances that are irritants to skin, eyes, and/or respiratory tract, acutely toxic, or have a narcotic effect.
	Biohazard: Includes biological substances, such as body fluids, that pose a threat to humans. Appears on sharps containers that hold contaminated needles.

Consumer Health Protections and Laws

LOCAL LAWS, REGULATIONS, AND AGENCIES RELATED TO CONSUMER HEALTH

Local laws and regulations related to consumer health are often created and enforced by county, tribal, or district-level officials and divisions. Individuals on **local boards of health** are responsible for **establishing and enforcing public health policy** to ensure the protection of human health within their jurisdiction. They may also **make recommendations** for health policy and initiatives to other governing bodies (e.g., the city council). Similarly, local **boards of commissioners** help enforce regulations and ordinances; they are granted the authority by state legislators to impose fines or other penalties for noncompliance. Some counties have a local **office of consumer protection** to protect consumers from scams and deceptive business practices. Each county has a **division of public health** that develops policy and enforces local laws and regulations to protect public safety and wellness. Other local divisions (e.g., water quality division) also provide education, enforce local laws, and monitor the compliance of private and public businesses and consumers. Local policy and agencies related to consumer health can be found on local government websites.

STATE LAWS, REGULATIONS, AND AGENCIES RELATED TO CONSUMER HEALTH

An **attorney general** is a government official who supervises consumer protection initiatives in the areas he or she represents. His or her **responsibility** is to conduct investigations, manage licensure and certifications of service providers, prosecute those who violate consumer protection laws, and advocate for constituents. Consumers can **file a complaint** against a business if they suspect a health fraud or scam. Most states have a **department of consumer affairs** dedicated to

investigating consumer protection violations, educating consumers, licensing professionals, and providing support. The **Deceptive Trade Practices Act** is a law observed by states like Texas, Illinois, Minnesota, and Nebraska that prohibits business fraud and misleading advertising. State and local **departments of justice** and **departments of agriculture and consumer services** are responsible for protecting against fraud and ensuring product safety.

FEDERAL LAWS, REGULATIONS, AND AGENCIES RELATED TO CONSUMER HEALTH

The **Federal Trade Commission (FTC)** is a government agency that is responsible for consumer protection. The FTC's **Bureau of Consumer Protection** is designed to enforce federal consumer protection laws and deliver consumer education. The **Pure Food and Drug Act of 1906** was the first of many consumer protection laws in the United States. Along with creating the FDA, the law banned mislabeled foods, required food and drug labeling (e.g., ingredients on packaging), and established food and drug testing. The **FDA** is a federal agency that oversees the safety of food, pharmaceutical goods, and medical devices. The Consumer Product Safety Act of 1972 established the **Consumer Product Safety Commission (CPSC)**. The CPSC assesses complaints regarding consumer protection, coordinates product recalls, and creates safety standards to minimize consumer harm. However, **other federal agencies** like the US Bureau of Alcohol, Tobacco, Firearms, and Explosives, the US Department of Agriculture, and the US Environmental Protection Agency are responsible for enforcing protective laws, monitoring compliance, and providing education for various health-related products.

HOW LAWS, REGULATIONS, AND AGENCIES PROTECT CONSUMERS

Health-related consumer protection laws and regulations are often **created in response to violations** against the public's safety and security. They are intended to protect consumers against **predatory business practices, deceptive marketing schemes, and poor production or health practices**. For example, in response to the rampant use of toxic substances in food, the addition of addictive drugs to medical products, and quack medicine during the late 19th century, the United States passed the **Pure Food and Drug Act of 1906**. **Consumer protection agencies** are created to regulate business practices, investigate potential violations of consumer protection laws, award and monitor licensure of health care providers, and educate the public about consumer protection. Many federal agencies that were not exclusively created for consumer protection now contribute to it through monitoring, enforcement, and education and engage in consumer protection advocacy.

Coordinated School Health Model

A **coordinated school health model** is a systematic approach intended to maximize the health and well-being of the school community through the delivery of health education, programs, and services. All aspects of health (e.g., physical, social, emotional, intellectual) are addressed through coordinated school health programs. Coordinated school health models can **improve academic achievement, interpersonal relationships, and student success**. A school that utilizes a coordinated school health model simultaneously addresses multiple health areas like a comprehensive health education curriculum, preventative health care, nutrition services, staff health promotion, and psychosocial health opportunities. **Adaptations to the school environment** are also made to optimize physical, social, and emotional health (e.g., installing play areas or green spaces). **Successful coordinated school health programs** include teachers, administration, school counselors or social workers, nutrition staff, community partners, parents and guardians, and students. The inclusion of each stakeholder throughout the planning, implementation, and maintenance of changes is **crucial for buy-in and sustainability**.

ROLE OF THE TEACHER

All teachers play a role in the planning, implementation, and maintenance of coordinated school health education programs. They are responsible for **creating and delivering lessons** that improve student knowledge and **evaluating content mastery**. Schools that are interested in incorporating health promotion in the traditional classroom setting may benefit from the expertise of health and physical education teachers. Teachers are also important for **assessing students' comprehension of health topics** and **collecting student input**, which can be informative for planning effective schoolwide health interventions. The relationships that teachers form with their students' families and guardians can be useful because those relationships can give teachers **valuable parental insights into a student's health**. Parent-teacher relationships may also be helpful for identifying parents interested in helping plan and support a coordinated school health education program.

COMPONENTS

The Whole School, Whole Community, Whole Child Model (WSCC) is a popular coordinated school health model that consists of 10 components:

- **Health services** like primary care delivery, referrals, and immunizations are performed at schools to promote student health.
- Through **health education** and **physical education**, students learn how to evaluate and improve their health, prevent illnesses, and set health goals.
- The **physical environment** (e.g., school, land, surrounding community) is safe. For example, hazardous substances are secured, smoke alarms and fire extinguishers are operational, and the campus is visually welcoming.
- The **psychosocial climate** is designed to optimize academic performance and improve social relationships and student engagement. For example, learning and behavior expectations are clear, cultural differences are celebrated, and school activities are inclusive and reflective of the student body.
- **Nutrition services** ensure students receive nutritious foods while at school to maximize student success.
- **Counseling and social services** enhance student psychosocial health, connect students to mental health services, and deliver mental health care.
- **Employee wellness** programs promote healthy practices to improve staff well-being and job satisfaction.
- **Community involvement** and **family engagement** create buy-in, pool community resources, inform needed health programs, and reinforce healthy behaviors beyond the classroom.

EXAMPLE

CATCH (Coordinated Approach to Child Health) is a widely used coordinated school health program. The program's goal is to **improve the nutrition and exercise habits of students, staff, families, and the community**. This goal is accomplished through **engaging representatives** from all stakeholder groups: health and physical activity educators, health and nutrition services, counseling and social services, staff wellness and healthy school environment initiatives, and families and community members. **Teachers incorporate healthy living** into the lessons that they deliver to students. More **opportunities for moderate to vigorous physical activity** are incorporated into gym classes and traditional classrooms (e.g., games, activity breaks). **Consistent health messaging** is displayed through signage around school campuses, and health campaigns (e.g., "get ur 60" and "get ur H20") encourage the adoption of healthy behavior. Schools host CATCH family events to **engage parents and broaden the reach of health education to families and**

community members. Each school implements environmental changes: school gyms are open to students before and after school, and sugar-sweetened beverages are replaced with water.

RELATIONSHIP BETWEEN HEALTH EDUCATION AND OTHER COMPONENTS

A comprehensive health education program can improve the success of other components of a coordinated school health program. Students with strong health literacy and knowledge may be better able to **identify** their personal health problems, **communicate** their health concerns to adults, and **advocate** for necessary school health services. Health education may also make students more **amenable** to participating in school health initiatives or programs. A strong student comprehension of physical, social, and emotional health may **impact health attitudes, beliefs, and knowledge among family members and the broader community**. Students who receive adequate health education are more likely to **select** healthier foods from nutrition services and **engage** in physical activity during their allotted exercise periods. They also may be more likely to practice health behaviors that promote emotional health, which can amplify the benefits of counseling and social services.

PLANNING AND IMPLEMENTING COORDINATED SCHOOL HEALTH MODEL

Prior to implementing a school health education program, planners should first **define the population** and **establish health goals**. Next, they must **assess the needs, assets, and capacity** the school has for a health education program. Needs and assets can be identified through a thorough review of school demographics, community and school health data, existing curricula, health knowledge and literacy data, and key informant interviews. Findings should be used to **select health education priorities, create program objectives**, and **determine effective interventions**. Program objectives must be **specific and measurable**. This can be accomplished by clearly stating who is participating in implementation and evaluation and how much or what kind of change is expected. Objectives should also include the **anticipated outputs or outcomes** and how each component of the intervention **contributes to the program's overall goals**. Those planning interventions should consider the school's **capacity for change** (i.e., the number of resources available to implement a program, how realistic the objective is). A school health education program will take time to properly plan, implement, and evaluate. While evaluation findings are not always positive, they create an opportunity to identify barriers to program success and future adaptations to implement.

IMPORTANT STAKEHOLDERS

A **diverse team** that represents all aspects of school health should be included throughout the planning and implementation process of a health education program. A **health assessment** performed prior to the program's implementation can identify key stakeholders. Important actors in a school health education program include faculty, administrators, health care professionals, parents or caregivers, and students.

- **School faculty** provide insight on students' needs and abilities, and they deliver health education to students.
- **School administrators** are important figures in program decision-making and can aid in improving the capacity of a school to effectively implement and sustain a health education program.
- As the recipients of health education programming, **students** can provide valuable information regarding the success of health education initiatives.
- **Parents and caregivers** can provide input about health education programs and help continue education outside of the classroom.

- **Health professionals** may assist in the planning and delivery of health education to ensure that accurate and appropriate material is presented to students.

The inclusion of stakeholders throughout the planning and implementation process can ensure the sustainability of health education programs.

BEST PRACTICES FOR MAINTAINING A SCHOOL HEALTH EDUCATION PROGRAM

A successful school health education program is typically **evidence-based and responsive** to the identified health priorities of the intended population. If program planners **include key stakeholders** (e.g., faculty, administration, caregivers, students, health professionals) throughout the entire process, outcomes are more likely to be attained because a **shared vision** is more likely to be established. Stakeholder inclusion keeps intended recipients of a health education program engaged, accountable, and informed. **Partnerships with local coalitions and community health leaders** can sustain efforts outside of school and secure necessary resources (e.g., funding, space, volunteers) to ensure program success. **Partnerships** can also strengthen the capacity of the school to implement and support the health education program. **Program monitoring and evaluation** help identify problems early, ensure acceptable delivery of the intervention and use of resources, assess program outputs and outcomes, and stay organized.

CONSIDERATIONS FOR IMPLEMENTING HEALTH EDUCATION CURRICULA

An **in-depth review of district-level stances on health concepts** (e.g., comprehensive sex education) **and health philosophies** should occur prior to implementation. The use of procedures that are **compatible with school policy** can ensure that the concepts taught and information delivered are permissible. Policy is often implemented to protect students and faculty and establish acceptable practices for delivering culturally and developmentally appropriate material. Policy can also guarantee that a school's established health priorities are reflected in the curricula. School health policy should be regularly reviewed to ensure that it accomplishes its intended health goals. It is also important to **review state-level education standards related to health**. They can help set clear and measurable learning goals, plan accessible and engaging lessons, measure achievement, and support instruction.

School Health Advisory Councils

SCHOOL HEALTH ADVISORY COUNCIL (SHAC)

A **school health advisory council (SHAC)** is composed of individuals that advocate for the health and education priorities of a community. The individuals are often **appointed by school district leaders** to advise on school health-related programs and interventions. **Common representatives** may include health and physical health educators, nutrition services staff, social workers, school psychologists or counselors, and administrators. However, an SHAC can include others who are beneficial for understanding and improving student health. The members have a **direct influence** on the health and well-being of students and can **contribute insights** from their daily interactions with students. They can provide an **accurate depiction of student needs** and the resources available within and outside of school to meet health needs. Individuals on SHACs are also important communication links and advocates for the groups that they represent. They can help **solve conflicts** and **clear up misconceptions** that may arise from a newly implemented health initiative.

MANDATES REGARDING SHACS

Mandates regarding SHACs are often enacted by local or state boards of education. These mandates ensure that **local values and interests are reflected in all health education programs and**

curricula. The statutes often mandate that school districts consult the SHAC prior to altering or adopting a new health education curriculum. Every state education code varies, and here are some of the areas that different education statutes might say that SHACs are responsible for providing recommendations on:

- The number of hours of instruction
- Health education graduation requirements
- Appropriate policies, procedures, and initiatives related to preventative health
- Appropriate methods of health instruction related to sexual health, opioid abuse, and violence
- Strategies for integrating school health services, counseling, a safe and healthy school environment, and employee wellness
- Opportunities for collaboration with community organizations and parental engagement and awareness

There are often provisions about **who must be included in an SHAC**. For the most part, SHAC members must represent classroom teachers, school counselors, school administrators, students, health care professionals, the business community, law enforcement, senior citizens, faith-based organizations, nonprofit health organizations, and local domestic violence programs.

LOCAL HEALTH ADVISORY COUNCILS

A local SHAC's primary role is to **advise the school district on health-related programs and initiatives**. For example, a school district seeking to lower school dropout rates may assemble an SHAC composed of teachers, social workers, academic counselors, administrators, and local education coalitions or organizations to illustrate the problem and offer solutions. SHACs help **collect data on health needs of students and the school community**. Findings from student assessments, informal discussions with students or caregivers, or independent research on student health and development can contribute to a more complete understanding of student health. Individuals on SHACs are often experts in their respective fields, which can add to the group's **comprehension of barriers or motivators** to implementing health education programs (e.g., policy, research, experience). Members of SHACs also have an **in-depth understanding** of the available school or community resources needed or available to address the health problem. Their insight can ensure program fidelity and sustainability.

Strategies for Involving Parents and Guardians

Parent or caregiver involvement when planning and implementing a school health education program can contribute to its success. When **school staff coordinate with parents**, health promotion and messaging can be delivered in a clear and consistent manner outside of school. Research by the CDC indicates that parents are motivated to engage in their child's education if they believe that their involvement will enhance their child's well-being. Therefore, school health education planners should **clearly state how parents' involvement in health initiatives will benefit student health and education outcomes**. School staff should collaborate with parents to **create a shared school health vision** and **create opportunities for parental feedback** regarding student health (e.g., survey, public forums, interviews). Health education programs and initiatives should incorporate opportunities for parental engagement. For example, parents can provide support through volunteering and leading events or delivering at-home learning. To sustain parental involvement, **a variety of engagement opportunities should be offered to parents** and any **health education events must be hosted at an accessible location and time**.

STRATEGIES FOR INCORPORATING LOCAL CULTURE

The compatibility of a health education program with local culture can determine its success. Local culture refers to a **geographic area or group with a shared identity** (e.g., race, ethnicity, religion). It **encompasses language, beliefs, attitudes, values, customs, and ways of communicating**. Therefore, it is important to **incorporate multiple dimensions of culture** when identifying school health needs and planning interventions. A school health education program that is designed in **coordination with local cultural norms** can improve the community's receptivity and ease regarding the adoption of positive health behaviors. A **situational analysis**—an evaluation of the learner, teacher, school environment, and societal values—can be conducted to understand the local culture regarding health. Findings can **provide context** for local health beliefs and **inform effective strategies** for teaching concepts in a culturally appropriate manner. The inclusion of local community leaders in developing health education programs can illuminate unique health beliefs and strategies for implementation.

STRATEGIES FOR ADDRESSING LOCAL NEEDS AND INTERESTS

Since SHACs comprise representatives from the school and local community, they can provide useful information about local needs and interests. A **community health needs assessment** provides comprehensive information about a community's health needs, challenges, and health status. **Health needs assessments** utilize quantitative data (e.g., health statistics, demographic data) and qualitative data (e.g., key informant interviews, focus groups, formal surveys, observation) to identify local needs, assets, and interests. Knowledge gained from a health needs assessment can help school health education program planners develop a **community health improvement plan** (CHIP) to create programming that **addresses local needs and interests**. Insights from local health departments can reveal information about the health status of the community, barriers to health care access, and available community resources to address health needs. Health departments' annual community health needs assessments provide a snapshot of community health and what the health department's **key health priorities** should be.

Health Education Curriculum

CONTENT AREAS OF HEALTH INSTRUCTION

The four major content areas of health instruction are community health, nutrition, mental health, and sex education.

- The purpose of **community health instruction** is to prevent illness and injury through health-management strategies and promote a healthy physical environment to improve well-being. Students learn where to access health-related services and resources, as well as how to advocate for the health and well-being of their community.
- Through **nutrition education**, students learn about maintaining a balanced diet and healthy body weight and how to create and implement health goals.
- Through **mental health education**, students learn about how to identify various mental illnesses and maintain positive relationships and what resources are available for seeking help.
- Students learn about the consequences of engaging in sexual contact and internal and external influences that affect sexual behavior through **sex education**. They may also learn about consent and how to identify and effectively communicate their needs and feelings.

In each major content area, students learn **essential concepts** and **how to analyze influences**, **access valid information**, **communicate effectively**, **make good decisions**, **set goals**, and **practice health-enhancing behaviors**.

SCOPE PLAN FOR HEALTH INSTRUCTION

A **scope plan** is a long-range planning tool that helps an educator identify what a student should know by the end of an academic period. It is often accompanied by a sequence plan. A scope plan includes the **objectives** and **educational milestones** that must be accomplished during the school year for students to demonstrate proficiency in the content covered. A **matrix** is the most used format for scope plans. The purpose of a scope plan is to create a structured and intentional learning experience for students and ensure compliance with content standards. The general components of a scope plan include the **grade group** or level, **education topics** (e.g., community health, nutrition, mental health, sexuality education), **developmentally appropriate skill expectations**, and **performance indicators**. Scope plans should **align with national or state education standards**. They should also **address local health needs or interests** and the developmental status or abilities of the intended audience.

SEQUENCE PLAN FOR HEALTH INSTRUCTION

A **sequence plan** is a long-range planning tool that an educator can use to arrange the order of the content that is to be taught. It is useful for **scaffolding learning** and helps educators plan which materials and learning experiences (e.g., activities) are needed to support student learning throughout the unit. Components of a sequence plan include a list of **activities or objectives** to be completed, the **order** they must be completed in, and the **length of time** required to complete each. The order should flow logically, and each objective should be completed in a reasonable amount of time. Sequence plans are complemented by scope plans. When implemented together, scope and sequence plans create a well-planned instructional framework that covers all required standards in a fixed amount of time.

USE OF SCOPE PLAN AND A SEQUENCE PLAN

Together, a health education scope plan and sequence plan **detail the order and rigor of concepts to be taught by the end of each school year**. The knowledge and skills that students acquire become more complex as students progress through subsequent grade levels. Health educators can **use these plans to create lesson units that address multiple health skills** (e.g., decision-making, goal setting) and **reinforce previously acquired health knowledge**. For instance, a scope plan and a sequence plan may place a nutrition unit after units on body systems. Its position will reinforce health concepts from previous lessons and present new information to improve comprehension. A scope plan and a sequence plan can also be helpful for teachers planning across grade groups. A health instructor could use them to **distribute health knowledge and skills at developmentally appropriate age periods**. For example, a health instructor may introduce information about reproductive health and physical changes in adolescence during sixth grade and expound upon those concepts in eighth grade (e.g., discuss STIs in depth) and tenth grade (e.g., discuss forms of contraception). In this scenario, the concepts are reinforced, and more complex information is introduced at developmentally appropriate times.

INTEGRATING THE HEALTH EDUCATION CURRICULUM WITH OTHER CONTENT AREAS

Integrating the school health education curriculum with other content areas like language arts, science, and social studies **promotes cross-curricular learning and produces a more authentic and collaborative educational experience**. To effectively integrate the school health education curriculum, instructors must know the academic standards and instructional strategies for each curricular area. This can reveal any similar methodologies or concepts that could aid in integration. A **concept map** can help teachers chart learning priorities for each curricular area and identify connections between content areas. Teachers can reinforce skills from other content areas, plan thematic units, or engage in project-based learning (PBL). **Thematic units** consist of cross-curricular lessons unified by a theme or topic, and **project-based learning** is an inquiry-based instructional strategy in which students learn through collaborative problem-solving. For example, a health teacher could reinforce narrative writing skills and peer pressure knowledge by asking students to write stories about a time they applied refusal skills. A thematic unit created by social studies and health teachers could explore cultural and geographical nutritional practices and perspectives. Science and health instructors could create a project in which students learn and apply disease knowledge and laboratory skills to test local water sources for E. coli.

Planning for Health Instruction

REFLECTING THE SKILLS AND ABILITIES OF ALL STUDENTS

A **thorough assessment of all students' abilities** at the beginning of the academic period is necessary for planning inclusive health instruction. This includes an evaluation of students' content knowledge and preferred learning styles (e.g., visual, auditory, kinesthetic, and reading and writing). By **appealing to students' learning styles** and **implementing a range of instructional modalities**, teachers can create engaging lessons that reflect the skills and abilities of all students. Health teachers can adapt the **delivery of content**, the options for how students **process material** and **demonstrate competency**, and the **learning environment** to teach students with varying abilities. For example, material in a unit on nutrition can be taught using a variety of methods such as the interactive MyPlate tool, songs, collage artwork, and cooking demonstrations. **Multiple instructional methods** ensure that the lesson is **accessible to all**. Demonstration of content mastery can also be adapted. For instance, a student tasked with demonstrating mastery of refusal skills could be evaluated through a traditional assessment, a writing assignment, a theatrical skit, or an oral exam. Each option allows students to exhibit comprehension of the material through strengths-based methods.

Visual learners	Learn best by seeing and reading: Provide written directions, picture guides, or demonstrate procedures. Use charts and diagrams. Provide photos and videos.
Auditory learners	Learn best by listening and talking: Explain procedures while demonstrating and have the learner repeat. Plan extra time to discuss and answer questions. Provide audiotapes.
Kinesthetic learners	Learn best by handling, doing, and practicing: Provide hands-on experience throughout teaching. Encourage the handling of supplies and equipment. Allow the learner to demonstrate. Minimize instructions and allow person to explore equipment and procedures.

REFLECTING THE NEEDS AND DEVELOPMENTAL LEVELS OF ALL STUDENTS

Instructors should **assess content knowledge, educational history, and challenges** when planning health instruction that reflects the needs and developmental levels of all students. These criteria can be evaluated through **beginning of year assessments**, **student surveys**, and **parental input**. Information from evaluations can reveal any knowledge deficits, barriers to learning, and effective strategies utilized by former teachers and/or parents. It can be used to make appropriate instructional or learning environment modifications to meet student needs. Instructors should also **explore health needs and interests** prior to instructional planning. In addition to student and parent surveys, data from the Youth Risk Behavior Surveillance System (YRBSS) and community health data can produce insights on age- and community-specific health needs. **Differentiated instruction** may be used to tailor material to meet the needs and developmental levels of students simultaneously. Regular monitoring of student growth can illuminate deficits in academic progress and opportunities for adaptation. Flexible and responsive shifts in instructional strategies ensure that material is reflective of student needs. A deep understanding of an age group's standard abilities and capacity for learning, as well as the developmental objectives for each age group, is also necessary for responsive instruction.

REFLECTING THE INTERESTS OF ALL STUDENTS

Interest-based strategies for health instruction include encouraging students to identify content and materials related to health topics, allowing students to develop assessment methods, and giving students time to reflect on and practice their strengths. Health instructors could also incorporate strategies or concepts from **other content areas** and present material that **responds to real-world situations**. For instance, a health teacher implementing student-centered design during a unit on risk prevention and management could allow students to collaboratively explore stressors that contribute to conflict and different types of conflict management strategies. Each student can explore the material through a preferred method (e.g., reading a textbook chapter, analyzing data, watching an informational video, or listening to a podcast) and present his or her findings to the class. Students can **demonstrate mastery** of the material **through methods that reflect their academic preferences** (e.g., written report, awareness campaign, play, website) or personal interests. For example, a group of students interested in sports could create a pitch for a basketball intervention program to increase physical activity among their peers. Game-like activities like **choice boards**—a matrix of learning activities that students choose from—and **cubing**—rollable cubes with different activities on each side—**promote choice and honor student interest**.

REFLECTING THE CULTURAL BACKGROUNDS OF ALL STUDENTS

Materials and visual aids that depict cultural diversity can **promote inclusion** within the classroom. For example, a health instructor can opt for health posters, videos, or other learning materials that include figures of diverse backgrounds, such as people of different ethnicities, races, nationalities, and genders. **Representation** creates a learning environment in which **all feel welcomed and accepted**. Teachers can also create learning activities that are **culturally relevant** to students. Instructors can include key health practices and cultural perspectives related to health and well-being among different communities to stimulate interest and celebrate cultural differences. Instructors can **incorporate works from notable figures in different cultures** or **use relevant cultural activities to foster interest**. One may consider presenting vocabulary terms in different languages alongside English. Students should be **encouraged to share their cultural perspectives** about health topics to garner understanding among their classmates. However, it is important that instructors **do not mandate or coerce students to contribute**. Teachers should **model respectful speech and tolerance of alternative perspectives**. For example, a health instructor should use a **neutral tone** and **impartial language** when presenting information about sex education. Despite the teacher's opinion, the material should be accurately and respectfully introduced.

Implementing Health Education Curriculum

EFFECTIVELY IMPLEMENTING AND INTEGRATING A SCHOOL HEALTH EDUCATION CURRICULUM

Learning the **district's academic standards** and **school policy** related to health education is the first step in effectively implementing and integrating a school health education curriculum. A **needs**

assessment should be conducted to evaluate learning needs and strengths and any assets for or barriers to learning among students. For example, a needs assessment could identify that a community's robust anti-bullying campaign contributes to student knowledge regarding interpersonal relationships and refusal skills. It could also reveal a lack of student knowledge regarding nutrition and physical health due to staffing issues and poor exercise facilities. Both insights can be helpful for instructors when implementing a health education curriculum. Instructors should also review the effectiveness and adaptability of existing curricula. Next, the curriculum developer(s) must **use findings to establish intended outcomes or objectives**. Information can be organized in a **scope plan** and a **sequence plan**, and planners can begin **developing instructional methods, activities, and assessments**. The curriculum should be **reviewed, tested, and revised** to ensure that it meets the school's and district's requirements and the needs of the students. Evaluation through a combination of formative and summative assessments can determine the impact of the curriculum (e.g., effectiveness, reach, clarity).

ACCURATE AND AGE-APPROPRIATE SOURCES OF INFORMATION ABOUT HEALTH

Students in **different developmental stages** have **different informational needs** related to health topics and need to be able to access accurate and age-appropriate health information. Accompanying textbooks and learning materials provided by the school or school district often serve as appropriate sources of information and are readily available for student use. **School health practitioners** (e.g., school nurse, school psychologist or social worker, nutritionist) are sources of knowledge related to health and community resources. They can **direct students to age-appropriate and accurate resources** and may have literature (e.g., brochures, one-pagers) that students can use. Physicians may have health-related information for **different age groups**. Physicians are often trained to pare down information to make it more **accessible** and **developmentally appropriate**. **State and federal governmental agencies** (e.g., Centers for Disease Control and Prevention, Food and Drug Administration, local public health offices) distribute reliable, easy-to-read materials that are appropriate for all ages. **Health education teachers** are also reliable sources of accurate and age-appropriate sources of health information. They are often content experts, and instructors can also teach students and families how to recognize accurate sources of health information through media literacy.

INCORPORATING ACCURATE AND AGE-APPROPRIATE RESOURCES AND MATERIALS

Textbooks are often purchased to complement each content area's curriculum. Although teachers should use a variety of media in instruction, **textbooks function well to introduce or reinforce health education concepts**. For example, students could use textbooks to learn important vocabulary terms at the beginning of a unit, or they could use them to explore a topic more in-depth during a learning circuit. **School health practitioners**, **physicians**, or **child health advocacy groups** can be invited to speak during class to discuss a topic with students. They can also be a source of knowledge for a student's independent research or provide age-appropriate health materials to integrate into lesson units. Students can use resources from **federal and state governmental agencies** or trustworthy **nonprofit agencies** to process or reinforce information learned in a lesson. Many agencies distribute written materials (e.g., brochures, one-pagers, websites) for children. Some have health-related games, videos, or podcasts to make the learning material more engaging. A health education teacher should incorporate multiple types of resources and materials into health instruction to model responsible information consumption.

Student Health Knowledge and Behaviors

SHAPING STUDENTS' PATTERNS OF HEALTH BEHAVIORS

A person's knowledge about health-related topics has an **impact on the behaviors that he or she engages in and on his or her motivation to change behaviors**. For instance, a student with **poor nutritional health literacy** may lack knowledge about healthy eating habits or the health effects of a poor diet on physical and emotional health. Without adequate knowledge, the student may **fail to understand the importance** of adopting new health behaviors. Knowledge is acquired through many sources (e.g., education, peer discussions, social media), yet it is important that students receive **adequate experience learning how to assess the validity of health information to ensure the information they receive is accurate**. Health skills are also influential in shaping health behavior, especially one's self-efficacy. **Self-efficacy** refers to a person's belief in his or her ability to adequately enact healthy behaviors. For example, a student with low self-efficacy may believe that they would not be able to refuse alcohol if offered by a peer. If the student received knowledge and opportunities to practice applying refusal skills in a health education course, he or she would be more likely to refuse negative health behaviors if prompted.

HOW ATTITUDES SHAPE STUDENTS' PATTERNS OF HEALTH BEHAVIORS

Health attitudes refer to an individual's **favorability of a health behavior** (e.g., smoking, drug use, exercise). They are **influenced by knowledge, experience, observation, and relationships**. For example, a student that has substantial knowledge of the dangers of drug use or has had a negative experience because of drug use may be more likely to have a negative health attitude about drugs. Alternatively, a student whose friends habitually use drugs may have a more positive attitude towards drug use. The **origins of a health attitude** can influence the strength of an attitude and a person's willingness to change his or her health behaviors. For instance, a person who had a traumatic experience at a doctor's office may have a strong aversion to seeking health care. A person whose family or peers believe that health care visits are expensive or inconvenient may also avoid seeking health care. Both may avoid receiving an annual checkup, but the attitude of the individual who experienced a traumatic event is far less likely to change compared to the person whose attitude is shaped by peer influence.

HELPING STUDENTS LEARN AND APPLY SKILLS

Students should learn the importance of regularly examining personal health behaviors and influences. **Recurrent reflection** can help students assess their health status and the factors that influence their well-being. This can reveal opportunities for behavior adaptation that are necessary for maintaining good health. **Continuous learning** and strong **health literacy** skills can help students identify accurate and trustworthy sources of health information and build student knowledge about health-related topics. **Robust knowledge about health** (i.e., valid, reliable, and evidence-based health information) is useful for assessing how a behavior contributes to one's overall health and strategies for maintaining good health. Health instructors that teach students **SMART goals** (specific, measurable, achievable, relevant, and time-bound) can help students learn how to maintain health behavior changes. SMART health goals position students for long-term success. They are effective at motivating students to remain focused and improve self-efficacy. Students who learn problem-solving skills and skills for building social support networks can more effectively respond to derailed health behavior goals, temptation, or barriers to success.

HELPING STUDENTS LOCATE, READ, COMPREHEND, AND RETAIN CONTENT

The ability to locate, read, comprehend, retain, and apply content-related information from a range of texts and technologies is referred to as **information literacy**. It can transform a student into a more confident and discerning learner. Instructors should teach students that when locating credible texts and technologies, they should **assess the credibility** of the author or publisher, review the citations used in the resource, identify potential biases, and evaluate when the resource was published. Instructors should teach students **active reading strategies** (e.g., posing pre-reading questions, identifying unfamiliar words, taking notes, creating diagrams, summarizing the main idea of the text). **Active reading strategies** can help students comprehend and retain information regardless of the source. **Reciprocal teaching** is a strategy in which students act as the instructor. This practice can aid in comprehension and retention as students must locate, read, comprehend, and apply content-related information from a resource. Information is then relayed to their peers in an age-appropriate and engaging manner. **Project-based learning** incorporates all skills into a final product. Students must independently locate, explore, retain, and apply information to solve a real-world problem or situation.

Effective Communication in Health Education

ADDRESSING SENSITIVE OR CONTROVERSIAL HEALTH ISSUES

Sensitive or controversial health subjects include issues related to sex, substance use, abuse, and death. Health instructors who are knowledgeable about school policy and state academic standards can more **effectively address sensitive or controversial health topics**. Sticking to the required health objectives as outlined by state education curricula or policy can prevent noncompliance and act as a well-structured framework to guide teachers through challenging topics. Prior to planning the lesson(s), instructors should consider their own **biases**, **misinformation**, and **questions** about the sensitive topic. This can ensure that teachers adequately plan for student questions and practice presenting information in a nonjudgmental way. Teachers may also **prepare a list of resources** (e.g., age-appropriate materials, list of community health practitioners) that students can access outside of class. **Sensitive subjects should be presented without bias** (e.g., neutral language and tone) and **devoid of the teacher's personal perspective** about the topic. All information shared must be **factual and sourced from credible texts, and all perspectives should be presented**. Students should be given opportunities for reflection to sort through any triggering content, process the material, and express any lingering thoughts and questions.

IMPORTANCE OF MODELING POSITIVE HEALTH BEHAVIORS

Social networks can have a profound impact on health behaviors. The perceptions of those whom one values can influence one's health habits or choices. For example, a child may abstain from underage drinking because his or her parents disapprove of alcohol use. The health attitudes, knowledge, and behavior of individuals within a person's social network can also shape behaviors. A teenager whose peer group lacks knowledge about the dangers of vaping, has a positive attitude toward smoking, and actively participates in vaping may be more likely to adopt the behavior. Peer and parent influences are often the most impactful relationships among youth; however, teachers and other respected adults or role models (e.g., coaches, pastors, tutors) can also influence one's health behaviors. Teachers should routinely model healthy behaviors to increase exposure to healthy habits. For example, a teacher can regularly eat a healthy lunch at school, exercise, or practice healthy communication skills.

USING COMMUNICATION SKILLS AND STRATEGIES

When teaching health material, teachers can use **precise and accurate health terms to avoid miscommunication**. Clearly and honestly responding to student questions about health topics can **foster effective communication among students**. Teachers can **model positive and effective communication** by building supportive relationships with and among students, motivating students and praising positive behavior, accepting and implementing student feedback, and actively listening to and resolving any problems. An instructor who creates opportunities for **student self-advocacy** can reinforce communication skills. For example, a teacher who encourages students to describe their preferred learning styles, health interests, strengths, and weaknesses provides space for students to actively communicate their needs. Granting students multiple methods for providing feedback or reflecting on content during a unit can encourage them to assert themselves or process thoughts and emotions.

Assessment in Health Education

IDENTIFYING CRITERIA AND METHODS FOR EVALUATING STUDENT LEARNING

Teachers can use content and process criteria to evaluate student learning about health. Both types of criteria are effective at evaluating student learning, yet, when applied together, they provide a more holistic assessment. **Content criteria** describes the extent of a student's knowledge about a topic, and **process criteria** assesses how proficient a student is at completing a skill. A health instructor can use **formative** and **summative assessments** to evaluate student knowledge of a health topic before, during, and after a lesson unit. **Content criteria** can be generated directly from academic standards or learning objectives outlined through scope and sequence plans. These assessments are most used to **measure student knowledge and growth**. **Skill proficiency** is a type of content criteria, but is usually assessed through **performance-based assessments** (e.g., application of refusal skills, creating a health goal). Process criteria can be assessed through student **self-assessment**. For example, a student can evaluate his or her own performance on a project. Self-assessments allow students to reflect on their strengths, weaknesses, and abilities. Information can be used to evaluate lapses in health knowledge and guide future instructional strategies. Regardless of the assessment, students should receive a grading rubric and understand the purpose of the evaluation.

APPLYING STUDENT ASSESSMENT RESULTS

Results from student assessments can be used to adjust teaching strategies, identify or adapt instructional tools, differentiate instruction, and tailor lessons to meet the needs of all students. For example, a **summative assessment**, which is an assessment that takes place at the end of a unit, may reveal that most students performed poorly on the topic of communicable and noncommunicable diseases overall. If the assessment was **standards-based**, an instructor can determine which learning objective(s) students did not master. He or she should reflect on the methods used to teach the learning objectives that students mastered or did not master and any accompanying materials or instructional tools (e.g., diagrams, games, written text). The instructor can use his or her findings to research alternative instructional methods to implement in subsequent lessons. **Results** from assessments can also be used to **tailor instruction** among individual students or subsets of students that perform poorly. When used in conjunction with information on student demographics, health needs, community culture, and learning styles, this information can help an instructor create **differentiated learning opportunities** that are relevant, engaging, and accessible to all students.

> **Review Video: Formative and Summative Assessments**
> Visit mometrix.com/academy and enter code: 804991

Professional Foundations of Health Education

CONTINUING EDUCATION
NCHEC

One resource for continuing education knowledge and credits is the **National Commission for Health Education Credentialing (NCHEC), Inc.**, accredited by the National Commission for Certifying Agencies (NCCA). NCHEC offers workshops, seminars, and conferences in various health education topics, e.g., lung summits sponsored by the American Lung Association; conferences on annual public health, annual mental health and aging, and breastfeeding; seminars and workshops on teen contraceptive counseling approaches, age-related dementia, creating aging-friendly communities, trauma, and addiction; nutritional training, medical school tobacco treatment specialist trainings, wellness and health coaching workshops and certification courses, family planning health worker courses, asthma educator certification courses; and programs on Medicare, diabetes, women's gender-specific treatment, technology use integrating sexual and reproductive health with primary care, behavioral healthcare in the criminal justice system, worksite wellness certification and health promotion, nonprofit finance, project management, etc. Health educators can also take self-study courses for wellness coaching certification training and information about physical activity, nutrition, weight control, injury prevention, skin assessment, wound care, suicide prevention, grief, mental health, PTSD, substance abuse, addiction recovery, peer education, teen health risk behaviors, weight control, trauma, prevention, health equity, program evaluation, qualitative research, social media, etc. from diverse sponsors, for certification, knowledge, and credits.

SOPHE

The **Society for Public Health Education** (SOPHE) is a national nonprofit organization dedicated to providing **continuing education** for health and education professionals. It includes an affiliate membership program with local chapters. SOPHE is designated by the National Commission for Health Education Credentialing (NCHEC) as a multiple event provider of Continuing Education Contact Hours (CECH). SOPHE is approved by the National Board of Public Health Examiners as a provider of renewal credits for the Certificate in Public Health. SOPHE is one of the largest continuing education providers for Certified Health Education Specialists (CHES). Health educators can take advantage of continuing education opportunities SOPHE offers, including attending local chapter events; attending the SOPHE Annual Meeting; pursuing eLearning including taking online courses, Journal Self-Study Tests, playing back meeting webcasts, marketing and promotion videos, archived webinars, and streaming live webinars; publishing and/or reviewing manuscripts in SOPHE Journals; and participating in Journal and Meeting Calls for research. Health educators can create accounts and profiles at SOPHE's updated Center for Online Resources and Education (CORE), log in, and earn CE credits via courses and other activities.

PROFESSIONAL DEVELOPMENT OPPORTUNITIES FOR HEALTH EDUCATORS

Resources offering health educators **PD opportunities** include National Education Association's (NEA) Educational Support Professionals (ESP) PD; US Centers for Disease Control and Prevention's (CDC) Division of Scientific Education and Professional Development (DSEPD); ShapeAmerica.org, aka American Association for Health, Physical Education, Recreation, and Dance (AAHPERD); American Public Health Association (APHA)'s Center for PD, Public Health Systems and Partnerships; and health and education departments of many state and private universities and colleges. Shape America offers a webinar series covering topics including Adapted Physical Education (APE); APE for autism; sport coaching; Common Core State Standards (CCSS); Early Childhood Education (ECE); PE e-learning, etc.; a Researcher's Toolkit; a Distinguished Lecture

Series; and workshops on fitness, PE, and the Presidential Youth Fitness Program (PYFP). The CDC Learning Connection includes thousands of public health learning products and continuing education (CE) courses, many free, through CDC TRAIN; online educational resources; Quick-Learn Lessons for mobile devices; and links to Facebook and Twitter posts on public health topics. NEA offers its ESP National PD Conference; Leaders for Tomorrow program; and trainings in results-oriented job descriptions, crisis action plans, leadership, air quality action plans, collective action, mentoring, and school community team-building.

OHDSI

An interdisciplinary collaborative initiative among disciplines including biomedical sciences, physics, informatics, epidemiology, computer science, and statistics; and multiple stakeholders including healthcare providers, academics, medical product manufacturers, payers, and government agencies is the **Observational Health Data Sciences and Informatics Program (OHDSI)**. Its purpose is to use large-scale analytics to demonstrate the value of **observational health data**. With its coordinating center headquartered at Columbia University, OHDSI has developed an international network of observational health databases and researchers. In 2014, at the EDM (Electronic Data Methods) Forum in San Francisco, OHDSI released Achilles, its first open-source software application. OHDSI has produced a two-minute YouTube video to welcome new participants, and has published a paper in the Drug Safety periodical. Those who can benefit from participating in the OHDSI community include: scientists exploring large-scale data methodologies; clinical researchers using OHDSI's network for answering clinical questions; members of organizations that have healthcare data, for more effectively using their data; members of healthcare systems, for improving the efficiency and quality of healthcare using OHDSI's tools; and software designers and developers, for contributing to projects to enhance patient health.

The Observational Health Data Sciences and Informatics Program (OHDSI) includes participation from multiple disciplines and stakeholders. Participants are developing **open-source software tools** to analyze, characterize, and evaluate health data; medical product safety; healthcare quality; comparative effectiveness; and for predictive patient-level modeling. They are also developing an **international data network** to use large-scale analytical methods for extracting evidence from observational health data. OHDSI's Columbia University center will house open-source summary statistics to share throughout the network, enabling all stakeholders to learn from real-world evidence. OHDSI aims to evaluate the reliability of the evidence it produces by systematically assessing observational analysis methods performance. This collaboration holds weekly webinar teleconferences where members present current research including proposals, works in progress, and final products for collaboration, feedback, and review. At these meetings they also review funding and publication opportunities and topics of shared interest. OHDSI has formed specific workgroups for design and implementation of the Observational Medical Outcomes Partnership Common Data Model, version 5 (OMOP CDMv5) specifications and vocabulary standard; data characterization; patient-level prediction; population-level estimation; the knowledge base; a phenotype library; and visualization/communications.

VALID, RELIABLE ONLINE DATABASES

The US Department of Health and Human Services (HHS) includes the National Institutes of Health (NIH). The NIH offers a number of **public databases** that users can search for valid, reliable **health-related data**. These databases include: NIH RePORTER, the database of RePORT (Research Portfolio Online Reporting Tools); NIDB (NeuroInformatics DataBase) Resources; the NCBI (National Center for Biotechnology Information) Literature Databases; PubMed Central; PubMed Medline; Research.gov; Community of Science (COS); Science.gov; World Wide Science; and ClinicalTrials.gov. The Centers for Disease Control and Prevention (CDC) have interactive database systems on their website for these topics: birth defects and developmental disabilities; child and adolescent health; chronic disease; crosscutting; diabetes; disabilities; environmental health; global health; health risk behavior; HIV, STIs, and viral hepatitis; infectious disease; influenza; injury; maternal and child health; occupational safety and health; oral health; and population. The World Health Organization (WHO) has an online database of survey information from health and human rights organizations, established through collaboration with the Harvard School of Public Health's Program for International Health and Human Rights. WHO also offers an online library catalogue, WHOLIS, for searching WHO's printed publications collection from 1948 to the present, historical medicine and public health monographs, and international health literature.

YRBSS DATABASE

The YRBSS is the (National) **Youth Risk Behavior Surveillance System** used in the National Youth Risk Behavior Survey conducted by the Centers for Disease Control and Prevention (CDC). Data from this survey are available online in ASCII and Access® file formats for download and use. The YRBSS website also offers SPSS® and SAS® programs for converting ASCII data into datasets compatible with SPSS® and SAS® use. Users can access YRBS national high school data files from as far back as 1991 online, including user's manuals for each year. Every year of data has its own format library. The website includes instructions for using the data files in the different formats, plus methodology of the YRBSS; a review of analysis software; best practices and guidance for combining YRBS data from multiple years, for conducting trend analyses of the data, and interpreting trend data; for groups to conduct their own YRBS surveys; and frequently asked questions (FAQs).

SHAPEAMERICA RESOURCES AND AMA DATABASE LICENSING AND DATA ACCESSING PROCEDURES

The **American Alliance for Health, Physical Education, Recreation, and Dance** (AAHPERD.org), aka **ShapeAmerica**, offers databases and other resources, including: a database with regularly updated information about available research and program grants from the NASPE (National Association for Sport and Physical Education); a database where research fellows can enter and update their information; a database of grassroots contacts, through its Legislative Action Center Tutorial PDF; and its Library/Shared Files Exchange for lesson plans, assessment tools, etc. from which educators can access, contribute, and share. The AMA has offered healthcare community access to its Physician Masterfile for over 60 years to benefit the medical industry and public good. Today, **Database Licensees** contract with the **AMA** to arrange access to a variety of databases containing health-related research activities and marketing services. Medical schools, hospitals, pharmaceutical manufacturers, medical supply and equipment companies, consultants, insurance companies, market research firms, and commercial organizations all use the AMA Masterfile. The AMA reviews data requests from Database Licensees daily to monitor licensing agreement compliance. Physicians can restrict their prescription information from pharmaceutical sales representatives, and request no contact and no release restrictions to their AMA Physician Masterfile records.

CSHP

A **coordinated school health program** (CSHP) should include comprehensive health education (K–12); health services; psychological and socials services; safety initiatives/safe environment; physical education; nutritional services; and partnerships with local public health staff, parents, and state and community agencies and organizations. The purpose of the CSHP is to recognize that **academic success** and **physical and emotional health** are linked and that all components must be integrated and work together for the benefit of the students' health and well-being as well as health promotion for the staff. The CSHP helps to focus attention on behaviors that have a negative impact on students' health and achievement, such as risk-taking behaviors. Some of the goals of this program include better attendance, improved academic outcomes, fewer dropouts, fewer behavior problems (including bullying/violence), better nutrition, increased physical activity, and increased participation by family, educational staff, and other members of the community.

HEALTHY PEOPLE 2020

Healthy People 2020, enacted in 2010 and released by the US Department of Health & Human Services, is a 10-year guide to national public health practice and objectives. *Healthy People 2020* is based on previous initiatives, including *Healthy People 1990, 2000*, and *2010. Healthy People 2020* is particularly relevant to the health educator because many funding sources are tied to these objectives and educational materials are developed in support of them. Additionally, one section specifically addresses **adolescent health** with the goal of improving the "development, health, safety, and well-being of adolescents and young adults." This section addresses public health and social problems (such as unintended pregnancies), environmental influences on behavior and outcomes, and emerging issues. *Healthy People 2020* can be used to guide the focus of instruction because it includes a framework for health promotion and disease prevention and measurable objectives, such as increasing the proportion of students who graduate with a regular diploma after four years of high school.

RESOURCES FOR CURRENT KNOWLEDGE IN HEALTH SCIENCE RELATED TO ADOLESCENT HEALTH

Resources for keeping informed about current knowledge in health science include the following:

- **Internet**: The government has many websites devoted to current knowledge, such as CDC.gov. A valuable online resource is the E-Updates and News in Adolescent Health provided by *the Office of Adolescent Health* (HHS). Major news sites, such as CNN.com, have daily health news. *Medical News Today* provides links to medical news articles.
- **Professional journals**: Journals such as the *Journal of School Health* and the *American Journal of Health Education* provide health information of particular interest to health educators.
- **Public health/Local health agencies**: These agencies provide updates to the community about issues of current concern, such as outbreaks or emerging infections.
- **Professional organizations**: Organizations such as the American School Health Association (ASHA) and the American Association for Health Education (AAHE) carry out research and provide information and support to members as well as sponsoring state and national conferences, various workshops, and informative websites.

ROLE OF HEALTH EDUCATORS IN ADVOCATING FOR HEALTHY SCHOOL ENVIRONMENT

The health educator has the primary role of communicating, promoting, and **advocating** for a healthy school environment and should take every opportunity to do so, beginning with **increasing awareness** within the classroom through a variety of means: panel discussions, guest speakers, demonstrations, project-based learning, debates, experiments, and role playing. The health educator should carry out an **assessment** and report to the school board about the school's environment, highlighting areas in which the school is performing well as well as those that need improvement. The health educator must also establish close working relationships with **administrators**, whose support is critical, and with teachers and other staff members, stressing how their roles are made easier in a healthy school environment and ways in which they can support taking steps to improve the situation at the school. The health educator should monitor and report progress.

Chapter Quiz

Ready to see how well you retained what you just read? Scan the QR code to go directly to the chapter quiz interface for this study guide. If you're using a computer, simply visit the bonus page at **mometrix.com/bonus948/priihpeck5857** and click the Chapter Quizzes link.

143

Health Education Content

Transform passive reading into active learning! After immersing yourself in this chapter, put your comprehension to the test by taking a quiz. The insights you gained will stay with you longer this way. Scan the QR code to go directly to the chapter quiz interface for this study guide. If you're using a computer, simply visit the bonus page at **mometrix.com/bonus948/priihpeck5857** and click the Chapter Quizzes link.

Fitness and Exercise

COMPONENTS OF FITNESS

There are 3 main components of **physical fitness**: flexibility, muscular strength and endurance, and cardiovascular fitness.

- **Cardiovascular fitness** improves the ability of the heart and lungs to deliver oxygen and fuel to the body during exercise. It also helps burn calories to achieve a healthy **body composition** (the total amount of fat mass compared to muscle and bone mass). Cardiovascular fitness is usually divided into two types: **moderate intensity** (50-70% of the maximum heart rate) and **vigorous intensity** (70-85% of the maximum heart rate). Examples of cardiovascular fitness include **aerobic** activities like brisk walking, running, bicycling, and swimming.
- **Muscle-strengthening activities** like lifting weights or exercises that use body weight for resistance help improve strength and endurance and are useful for achieving and maintaining a healthy body composition. Strength training tends to be **anaerobic**, as the muscles consume more oxygen than the replenishment rate.
- **Flexibility** exercises, like stretching and yoga, improve range of motion. Well-balanced exercises are comprised of activities that address all 3 components of fitness.

METHODS FOR ASSESSING FITNESS

Cardiovascular fitness is often assessed through a calculation of one's at-rest heart rate, their target heart rate zone, and a running or jogging test like the Cooper Test. The **target heart rate zone** is a guide for assessing the **intensity** of exercise for an individual's age. By measuring the number of heartbeats per minute during exercise, one can assess whether they need to increase or decrease the intensity of their workout. The **Cooper Test** assesses cardiovascular fitness level based on age and sex by measuring how far a person is able to run in 12 minutes. **Muscular** strength and endurance are often assessed through **pushup and sit-up tests**. These tests measure the number of pushups and sit-ups one is able to do in one minute. This amount is compared to the average number for individuals of the same age and sex. **Flexibility** is commonly assessed through the **sit-and-reach test**, which measures the distance a person is able to reach from a sitting position. The distance reached is used to determine the flexibility of their legs, hips, and lower back.

TYPES OF EXERCISE

There are 4 main types of exercise: endurance, flexibility, strength, and balance.

- **Endurance exercise** generally refers to aerobics. Aerobic exercise refers to exercises that actively oxygenate the involved muscles at a sustainable rate. **Aerobic exercise** is usually cardiovascular in nature as well, as the heart rate increases to sustain the increased need for oxygen.
- **Flexibility exercises** stretch the muscles and tendons to improve and maintain the body's limberness. Examples include yoga and Pilates.
- **Strengthening exercises** build up the muscles through the use of weight resistance and repetitive motion.
- **Balance** exercises like heel-toe-walking and standing on one foot focus on steadiness to maintain stability.

INFLUENCE ON DIFFERENT BODY SYSTEMS

- **Aerobic** exercises enhance **cardiovascular system** functioning to improve the condition of the heart, lungs, and circulatory system. They are beneficial for reducing the risk of heart disease and stroke, lowering blood pressure, and raising "good" HDL cholesterol.
- **Strength training** increases the amount of force that a person's muscles can resist, and stimulates bone growth, which is essential for musculoskeletal system functioning.
- **Flexibility** exercises also improve musculoskeletal health by stretching an individual's muscles to reduce risk of muscle damage and improve their range of motion.
- **Balance** exercises improve overall steadiness to prevent falls and age-related damage to muscles and joints. Types of flexibility and balance exercises, like yoga and tai chi that use meditation and breathing exercises to reduce stress, can also improve cardiovascular system health.

HEALTH BENEFITS OF PHYSICAL ACTIVITY

Regular physical activity provides numerous **health benefits** throughout the life span, especially weight control. In **childhood and adolescence**, regular physical activity improves cardiorespiratory fitness, strengthens bones, contributes to muscle development, lowers symptoms of anxiety and depression, improves cognition and brain development, and prevents heart disease, diabetes, obesity, and cancer later in life. In **adulthood and old age**, regular physical activity reduces the risk of heart disease and stroke, and developing type 2 diabetes, hypertension, and some cancers. In **older adults**, regular physical activity reduces the risk of falls or injuries from falls, and delays the loss of physical functioning and muscle mass related to old age. It is also associated with improved physical function, mental health, and overall quality of life in individuals managing existing chronic conditions like arthritis and type 2 diabetes.

MAINTAINING AND IMPROVING FITNESS

Assessing and recording an individual's baseline physical fitness is the first step in creating strategies to maintain and improve fitness. A person's results provide information on their **starting point** to use to measure their progress and establish fitness **goals**. Measure pulse rate, running distance, number of pushups or sit-ups, sit-and-reach distance, waist circumference, and/or body mass index (BMI) to assess baseline fitness. Create **SMART fitness goals** by creating goals that are specific, measurable, attainable, realistic, and time-bound (SMART) in order to create actionable steps to gauge one's progress and maintain motivation. Individuals should select fitness activities that engage all components of physical fitness (cardiovascular, strength, flexibility, and balance). All activities selected should be appropriate for fitness goals and physical capabilities. Individuals should monitor their progress by retaking the physical fitness assessments every few months and comparing them with the baseline. Exercise progress can be used to create new fitness objectives that reflect evolving healthy lifestyle goals.

Personal Health Plans

DEVELOPING AND FOLLOWING A PERSONAL HEALTH PLAN

Maintaining adequate nutrition, exercise, and an appropriate body weight are key parts of improving overall wellness. A **personal health plan** (PHP) is a personalized roadmap to achieve health and wellness goals. To develop a personal health plan, one should complete a **personal health inventory** to evaluate their overall health and find their starting point. For example, an individual can assess whether they are at a healthy weight by calculating their **body mass index** (BMI) and their **waist circumference**. Regularly reflecting on and assessing nutritional habits is a crucial component of developing a personal health plan. Keeping a food and beverage diary that tracks daily food and beverage consumption can help one identify their current intake patterns. An activity log can track physical activity throughout the day. Pedometers, fitness watches, or smartphone fitness applications can also be used to track activity levels. **SMART goals** (specific, measurable, attainable, realistic, and time-bound) can help an individual create actionable steps to achieve their health and wellness goals based on their personal health inventory. Finally, **new habits** can be reinforced and unhealthy behaviors replaced through regular **reflection and positive self-talk**.

Overview of Disease and Illness

COMMUNICABLE DISEASES

Diseases are divided into two types: communicable and noncommunicable. **Communicable diseases** are illnesses caused by infectious agents transmitted from an infected person or animal to other people or animals. They are caused by **pathogens** like bacteria, viruses, and fungi. Transmission can be **direct contact**, which occurs through contact with an infected person via blood or bodily fluids, touching (e.g. staphylococcus), kissing or sexual contact (e.g. gonorrhea, HIV), or contact with fecal or oral secretions (e.g. hepatitis A), or **indirect contact**, which occurs without human-to-human contact but through contact with contaminated surfaces or objects (e.g. Norwalk virus), food (e.g. salmonella, E. coli), water (e.g. cholera), insect bites (e.g. malaria, yellow fever, and plague), or air (e.g. tuberculosis, measles). Most communicable diseases are acute—which means the disease and symptoms appear over a short period of time—and occur seasonally.

NONCOMMUNICABLE DISEASES

Noncommunicable diseases (NCDs) are diseases that are not contagious or transmittable to other people. They contribute to far more deaths worldwide than communicable diseases—approximately 70% of all deaths. Unlike communicable diseases, NCDs are long-lasting, slow progressing **chronic illnesses** that are often a result of poor lifestyle choices (e.g., type 2 diabetes, emphysema, and cardiovascular disease) or genetic mutation (e.g., cystic fibrosis, sickle cell anemia, lupus, and cancer). They are not the result of a pathogen; rather, they result from multiple risk factors that are further divided into modifiable risk factors, environmental risk factors, and non-modifiable risk factors. **Modifiable risk factors** are personal behavior or lifestyle choices that can be reduced or controlled by intervention like diet, physical activity, smoking, and alcohol or drug use. **Environmental risk factors** result from the physical environment and contribute to health outcomes like pollution, radiation, noise, and climate change. **Non-modifiable risk factors** cannot be reduced or changed like age, gender, family history, and race.

> **Review Video: Gene Mutation**
> Visit mometrix.com/academy and enter code: 955485

VIRUSES AND HOW THEY ARE TRANSMITTED

A **virus** is a microscopic entity that uses living organisms like animals, plants, or bacteria to replicate. Viruses **reproduce** by attaching themselves to their host's cells and reprogramming them to make new copies of the virus, effectively spreading as they go. The most common virus **transmission** methods are through droplets generated from coughing and sneezing, fecal contamination of food or water, contact with skin rashes or lesions, contact with contaminated surfaces, and bites from an infected animal vector. Once infected, the virus can cause damage to one or multiple body systems.

BACTERIA AND HOW THEY ARE TRANSMITTED

Bacteria are single-cell microorganisms that can live inside and outside of the body. They are larger and more complex than viruses and can **reproduce** on their own. Although most bacteria are harmless and even beneficial, those that cause illness in humans are called pathogenic bacteria. **Pathogenic bacteria** are infectious but not always contagious, which means that they cause sickness when they enter the body but are not always spread from person to person. Bacteria are **classified** by their gram-negative or gram-positive status—the ability to produce an **endotoxin** that causes tissue damage or death— and their need for oxygen, genus, and shape (spheres, rods, and spirals). Similar to viruses, bacteria can be **transmitted** through coughing and sneezing (e.g., pertussis), contact with infected people (e.g., impetigo, chlamydia), animals or insects (e.g., Lyme disease), contact with contaminated surfaces (e.g., cellulitis), and food or water (e.g., salmonella).

FUNGI AND HOW THEY ARE TRANSMITTED

A **fungus** is an organism that feeds on **decaying organic matter**. Although fungi are often found outdoors in soil and plants, they can also be found on and inside of the body. Fungi **reproduces** through the spread of microscopic spores. When an individual inhales or touches fungal spores, they may contract a lung and skin infection. Fungal infections are rarely transmitted from one person to another. There are two types of fungal infections: opportunistic and primary.

- **Opportunistic fungal infections** spread aggressively, but typically only impact individuals with weak immune systems.
- **Primary fungal infections** can develop in individuals with functioning immune systems, but are slow to develop. and usually emerge once a person has inhaled fungal spores.

Fungal infections can be local or systemic.

- **Local** infections only affect one area of the body. For example, a local fungal infection may only show up on the nail that was infected–not any other part of the body. Common locales for local infections also include the skin, genitals, and mouth.
- **Systemic** infections can affect many areas of the body or multiple organs at one time.

PARASITES AND HOW THEY ARE TRANSMITTED

Parasites are organisms that live in or on their host and feed on their host while causing it harm. There are three main types of parasites that cause disease in humans: protozoa, helminths, and ectoparasites.

- **Protozoa** are rapidly reproducing microscopic single-celled organisms that invade the body's tissues to obtain nourishment. They are spread through a variety of ways, but are most often transmitted by contact with human feces (e.g., giardia, cryptosporidium).

- **Helminths** (worms) are macroscopic multi-celled organisms that live in and outside of the body and cause infection. They are transmitted by eggs spread through fecal contamination and are most common in tropical and subtropical regions. Examples of parasitic diseases include Guinea worm disease, Chagas disease, and trichomoniasis.
- **Ectoparasites** are large multi-celled organisms that live on or feed off of skin (e.g., ticks, mosquitos, fleas, lice). They are vectors of infectious viral and bacterial diseases like Lyme disease, typhus, encephalitis, malaria, etc.

Communicable Diseases

RISK FACTORS FOR CONTRACTING COMMUNICABLE DISEASES

An individual's **risk** of contracting a **communicable disease** varies based on their overall health, vaccination status, personal hygiene, number of people they live and work with, socioeconomic status, and condition of their housing. Those who frequently come into contact with wildlife and other potential vectors (e.g., mosquitos) are at **higher risk** of contracting a communicable disease. Certain populations are at **higher risk** of becoming severely ill (i.e., hospitalization, ventilator, death) once they are infected. This includes individuals who are 65+ years old or under 2 years old, individuals experiencing health and social inequities (e.g., racial and ethnic minorities, low socioeconomic status), and people with medical conditions like cancer, chronic lung disease, diabetes, and heart conditions. Individuals living in communities with poor water and sanitation, insufficient public health surveillance, poor waste management, and inadequate government regulations regarding food and water safety are at higher risk of contracting a communicable disease. Communities with high exposure to climate-related catastrophes and few health professionals or medications are more susceptible to disease outbreak and inadequate disease management.

METHODS FOR TREATING DIFFERENT TYPES OF COMMUNICABLE DISEASES

- **Bacterial diseases** are treated with **antibiotics**, which kill bacteria or slow their development to allow for the immune system to respond.
- **Viral infections** can be prevented with **vaccines**. When given a vaccine which contains an agent (e.g., weakened forms of the microbe, proteins) that resembles the virus, the body mounts an **immune response** and produces **antibodies** that will terminate the active form of the virus in the future. If already infected with a virus, **antiviral medications** can be used to treat the infections. They do not destroy the pathogen, but inhibit further development of the virus.
- **Fungal infections** are treated with **antifungal medications** that attack the fungal cell membrane to either kill fungal cells or prevent them from reproducing.
- **Parasites** are treated with **antiparasitic drugs** that kill the parasite.

PREVENTATIVE MEASURES REDUCING SPREAD OF COMMUNICABLE DISEASE

The most effective way to **limit the spread** of many communicable diseases is through **quarantine** and **physical distancing**. **Vaccines** also prevent many infectious diseases. Keeping up to date on vaccinations, getting vaccinated before traveling, and getting the recommended vaccinations during childhood are important for reducing transmission. **Practicing good hygiene** (i.e., hand washing after using the bathroom, before and after eating, treating a wound, touching others' hands or an animal, or coughing/sneezing) can prevent the spread of bacteria, viruses, and parasites. **Safe food handling and preparation**, such as washing utensils and surfaces during food preparation, washing fruits and vegetables before eating, and cooking/storing food at proper temperatures, are also effective strategies for preventing the spread of many foodborne illnesses. **Cleaning surfaces**

regularly with soap and water, especially the bathroom and kitchen, can reduce the spread of many diseases that are transmitted indirectly. Finally, **reducing stress** can prevent disease transmission as chronic stress can suppress the immune system and make a person more susceptible to infection.

Non-Communicable Diseases

ASTHMA

Asthma is a noncommunicable disease. While the exact **cause** of asthma is unknown, genetics, allergies, respiratory infections, and contact with allergens or environmental irritants are likely to contribute to the development of asthma. Those with asthma experience **recurring symptoms** like chest pain, chest tightness, and shortness of breath. Individuals with an **asthmatic parent** are more likely to develop asthma. A **childhood respiratory infection and allergies** can increase the risk of asthma. Working or living in **environments** in which one comes into contact with **irritants** like industrial or wood dust, chemical fumes, and solvents can lead to the development of asthma. Smoking, secondhand smoke, and air pollution can also lead to asthma. Additional **social factors** like poverty and poor access to health care can exacerbate asthma symptoms.

DIABETES

Diabetes is a noncommunicable disease that affects how the body uses a sugar called glucose. There are three types of diabetes: type 1 diabetes, type 2 diabetes, and gestational diabetes.

- **Type 1 diabetes** is caused by an autoimmune reaction which causes the body to destroy cells in the pancreas that make **insulin**. The pancreas is unable to produce insulin, and glucose is unable to move out of the blood and into the cells which results in **very high blood sugar levels**. **Risk factors** for type 1 diabetes include family history of diabetes and exposure to a viral infection that triggers the autoimmune disease.
- In **type 2 diabetes**, cells become **resistant** to insulin and sugar builds up in the blood. **Risk factors** for type 2 diabetes are being overweight or obese, family history of diabetes, physical inactivity, race and ethnicity, older age, gestational diabetes, abnormal cholesterol, and high blood pressure.
- **Gestational diabetes** is a pregnancy-induced condition in which the pancreas is unable to produce enough extra insulin to overcome the hormone-induced insulin resistance. This must be a new-onset condition that presents in the second or third trimester of pregnancy to be diagnosed.

CANCER

Cancer is a noncommunicable disease that occurs when there are **DNA mutations** within a cell that inhibits growth and replication. The new cancerous cells crowd out non-cancerous cells and damage body tissues. The most common **causes** and **risk factors** are related to environmental exposure, radiation exposure, infections, age, family history, and various lifestyle factors. Exposure to carcinogens, asbestos, and benzene in the home and workplace environment can lead to cancer. As people age, they are exposed to more **carcinogens** and the body loses its ability to find and destroy cancerous cells, which can lead to the development of cancer. **Radiation** from the sun or medical treatment, viral infections that affect the DNA or suppress the immune system (e.g., HIV, human papillomavirus), and **genetic susceptibility** can also cause cancer. **Major lifestyle risk factors** like tobacco use, alcohol use, physical inactivity, obesity, diets high in processed and red meats, sun exposure, and unsafe sex can increase the risk of cancer.

HEART DISEASE

Heart disease refers to numerous conditions that affect heart health (e.g., coronary artery disease, arrhythmias, congenital heart defects, heart valve disease, heart infection). The causes of heart disease depend on what kind of heart disease a person has. For example, **coronary artery disease** is caused by a buildup of plaque in arteries. **Heart infection**—also called endocarditis—is caused by bacteria, viruses, and parasites. **Cardiomyopathy**—the thickening of heart muscle—can be caused by damage from heart attacks, drugs, or genetics. **Risk factors** for heart disease include old age, sex, family history, smoking, poor diet, high blood pressure and cholesterol, diabetes, obesity and overweight status, physical inactivity, stress, and poor dental health.

METHODS FOR PREVENTING NONCOMMUNICABLE DISEASES

Primary disease prevention seeks to prevent disease or injury before it occurs through restricting exposure, modifying existing risk factors, and increasing resistance to disease before exposure. Examples of noncommunicable primary disease prevention include adjusting poor eating habits, tobacco cessation, exercising and weight loss, using legislation to ban substances associated with a disease or health condition (e.g., asbestos, lead paint), and implementing legislation to mandate safe and healthy practices (e.g., workplace health standards, restrictions on air pollution emissions, tobacco regulations).

METHODS FOR EARLY DETECTION OF NONCOMMUNICABLE DISEASES

Secondary prevention aims to reduce the impact of existing disease or injury through early disease detection and treatment and developing strategies to prevent reinjury or reoccurrence of disease. A common secondary prevention method is the implementation of regular **cancer screening tests** to detect early-stage disease (e.g., regular mammograms to detect breast cancer, colonoscopies to detect colorectal cancer, and pap smears to check for cervical cancer). Another method is **genetic counseling** to assess the likelihood of a person or their relative developing a genetic condition or disease and help them explore treatment options. Genetic counseling can be conducted before and during pregnancy to address concerns that can affect infant health (i.e., birth defects, genetic conditions, abnormal test results, maternal infections). It can also be used to address concerns about genetic disorders in childhood like abnormal newborn screening results, birth defects, or intellectual and developmental disabilities. Genetic counseling is often used in adulthood to assess symptoms of a condition or family history of a hereditary condition (e.g., hereditary breast and ovarian cancer, Huntington's disease, sickle cell disease, muscular dystrophy).

Immune Responses

IMMUNE SYSTEM RESPONSE TO AN ANTIGEN

Many different organs, cells, and proteins make up the **immune system**. The immune system defends the body from **pathogens** and removes harmful substances from the body. When a foreign substance—called an **antigen**—enters the body and attaches to immune system cells, the immune system begins mounting a response. Examples of **common antigens** include bacteria, fungi, viruses, allergens, and pollutants. Once eliminated, the immune system stores information about the pathogen and how to eliminate it to maintain protection for future encounters.

FEVERS

A **fever** is a temporary rise in body temperature above the **normal range**, which is within 1 degree above or below 98.6 degrees Fahrenheit. Although commonly thought to be bad for the body, a fever is an example of one of the many **helpful defense mechanisms** that the body employs to respond to disease. When the immune system identifies an antigen, it sends biochemical substances called **pyrogens** to a part of the brain called the **hypothalamus**. In response, the hypothalamus commands the body to produce and retain more heat. An elevated body temperature creates an **inhospitable environment** for pathogens like viruses to replicate or temperature-sensitive bacteria to survive. Fevers also speed up and strengthen immune cell response by altering their surface proteins to improve their ability to reach the infection site. Since fevers help the immune system fight disease, it is not always necessary to suppress them. However, if a fever exceeds the safe temperature threshold or is accompanied by unusual behavior, medical attention should be sought.

ANTIBODY FORMATION

Antibody formation is an example of a process that the immune system uses to respond to disease. **Antibodies**—also referred to as immunoglobulins—are proteins that the immune system manufactures when it identifies an antigen in the body. Antibodies are created by **white blood cells** called B lymphocytes or **B cells**. B cells bind to antigens and produce antibodies that are circulated throughout the body. The released antibodies ambush all antigens like the one that prompted the body to mount an immune response. The body continues to produce antibodies until it eliminates all detected antigens, but antibodies may remain in the body for up to several months.

The white blood cells of the immune system include the following:

WBC	Type	% of WBCs	Causes of Increase	Causes of Decrease
Basophils (black or purple)	Granulocyte	1%	Asthma, chronic myelocytic leukemia, Crohn's disease, dermatitis, estrogen, hemolytic anemia, Hodgkin's disease, hypothyroidism, polycythemia vera, and viruses	Allergies, corticosteroids, hyperthyroidism, pregnancy, and stress.
Eosinophils (orange-red, double-lobed nucleus)	Granulocyte	1-3%	Allergy, asthma, or parasitic infestation	Cushing's disease or glucocorticoids use
Lymphocytes (dark, large nucleus surrounded by thin cytoplasm rim)	Agranulocyte	15-40%	Antigens or chronic irritation	AIDS
Monocytes (lavender)	Agranulocyte	2-8%	Myeloproliferative process, like an inflammatory response or chronic myelomonocytic leukemia (CMML)	Hairy cell leukemia
Neutrophils (pink cytoplasm, dark nucleus)	Granulocyte	50-70%	Burns, kidney failure, heart attack, cancer, hemolytic anemia	Leukemia and abscess

Autoimmune Responses and the Immune System

Occasionally, the body mistakes its own cells as antigens during an immune response and attacks healthy, harmless cells in the body. This process is called an **autoimmune response**. When an individual has an **autoimmune disease**, their immune system is unable to distinguish between foreign cells and healthy cells and releases proteins called autoantibodies to attack parts of the body (e.g., the pancreas attacked in type 1 diabetes) or the whole body (e.g., lupus). The exact cause of autoimmune responses is unknown, but scientists theorize that family history, sex, diet, prior infections, and exposure to chemicals may contribute to developing an autoimmune disease. Examples of **common autoimmune diseases** are rheumatoid arthritis, psoriasis, ulcerative colitis, and psoriatic arthritis.

> **Review Video: Immune System**
> Visit mometrix.com/academy and enter code: 622899

Factors Influencing Disease Risk

Environmental Factors Affecting Health and Disease

Environmental factors have a significant impact on health and disease. In fact, 70-90% of chronic disease risk can be attributed to **environmental factors** like air, water, and soil pollution, exposure to harmful chemicals, metals, and nanomaterials, climate change and natural disasters, and ultraviolet radiation. Exposure can **disrupt bodily function** and cause health problems like respiratory diseases, cardiovascular diseases, and certain types of cancer. The health impacts of and exposure to the previously mentioned environmental factors can be exacerbated by an individual's **socioeconomic** and **biological characteristics**. This places people with low incomes, those living or working in heavily polluted or poorly environmentally-regulated areas, children, pregnant women, and immunocompromised individuals at increased risk of poor health and/or disease due to environmental factors.

Influence of Laws and Policies on Disease Prevention

Health laws and policies are important preventative measures to address health-related issues.

- **Health policies** are plans, decisions, and actions that achieve health goals. They can be implemented at the local, state, and national level or codified within a clinical environment.
- **Health laws** are legally binding regulations that can lead to consequences if not followed. Local, state, and national legislation are necessary for eliciting changes that reduce disease.

When legislation to address factors contributing to disease is enacted at each level, it can have a **profound impact** on disease prevention. For example, local smoke-free restaurant and business ordinances, state-wide tobacco tax increases, and a national program like the National Tobacco Control Program influence the ease with which individuals can acquire tobacco and consume it and limits broad exposure to harmful pollutants that tobacco contains.

STAGES OF PREVENTION AND INTERVENTION ALONG THE CONTINUUM OF CARE

The continuum of care includes all aspects of care that influence outcomes. The primary components are prevention, intervention, and recovery/maintenance during which the person is monitored for compliance.

Prevention	Intervention
May be aimed universally at the entire population, at selected groups, or at-risk individuals, and it usually involves long-term goals. Primary: Aims to prevent disease occurrence and may include educational campaigns (no smoking, use seatbelts), vaccinations. Secondary: Aims to identify and reduce impact (screening mammograms, BP checks). Tertiary: Aims to prevent/delay disease progression (support programs).	Usually aimed at specific groups or individuals and often involves specific treatments (such as surgery, chemotherapy, medications) to alleviate a problem or disorder. Goals may be long term, or they may be time limited with the aim to resolve the problem as quickly as possible.

Interrelationships Between Components of Health

PHYSICAL, MENTAL, EMOTIONAL, AND SOCIAL HEALTH

Overall health is a combination of physical, mental, emotional, and social health.

- **Physical health** refers to a person's exercise level, diet and sleep.
- **Mental health** refers to emotional, psychological, and social heath, as well as how an individual thinks, feels, acts, copes, and interacts with others or the world around them.
- **Emotional health** is a component of mental health; it refers to a person's ability to cope with emotions.
- **Social health** is another component of mental health which refers to the ways in which a person interacts or relates with others.

Each of these components of health are deeply intertwined and can influence each other. For example, an individual with chronic pain may experience sleep disturbances which lead to depression and associated symptoms of depression like social isolation, excessive or undereating, etc.

INFLUENCE OF CHILD ABUSE AND NEGLECT

Child abuse and neglect can have a significant impact on an individual's short and long-term health. Injuries inflicted by abuse or neglect can contribute to poor **short-term** physical health outcomes. In the **long-term**, chronic abuse and neglect negatively affect **brain development**, which can lead to **cognitive delays** or **learning disorders**. Additionally, child maltreatment is associated with chronic pain, obesity and eating disorders, heart disease, and hypertension in adulthood. The impact of abuse and neglect on **mental health** can persist into adulthood. Child maltreatment is associated with post-traumatic stress disorder (PTSD), attention deficit hyperactivity disorder (ADHD), anxiety, depression, anti-social personality disorder, and borderline personality disorder. Child abuse and neglect can also influence **emotional and social health**, as children do not develop vital communication skills or coping mechanisms. As a result, they are prone to drug and alcohol abuse and tend to have difficulty maintaining healthy relationships. Since the components of overall health are interconnected, poor outcomes in one dimension can influence others and contribute to inferior overall health.

INFLUENCE OF SUBSTANCE ABUSE ON OVERALL HEALTH

The effects of **substance abuse** are cumulative, and the impacts of substance abuse extend beyond individual health and wellbeing. When an individual begins to abuse illicit and licit substances, their physical, mental, and emotional health diminishes. In the **short-term**, they are more likely to experience direct effects like injuries (e.g., car accidents, drug-related violence) and overdose. **Persistent use** increases the risk of cardiovascular disease, stroke, liver failure, HIV/AIDS, hepatitis B and C, lung disease, problems with memory and decision-making, and an array of mental disorders (e.g., depression, anxiety, mania, drug-induced psychosis). Substance abuse **strains social relationships** with peers and family members. Due to stigmatization and withdrawal, users often disengage from relationships with friends and family. These **direct consequences** of drug abuse are interrelated and can exacerbate poor health in other dimensions of overall health. **Indirect effects** of substance abuse include the impacts felt by those close to users. They can experience financial and emotional hardship as they witness their loved one struggle with substance abuse, which can result in poor physical, social, emotional, mental, and economic health among non-users.

Changes in Mental and Emotional Needs Throughout Life

ATTACHMENT THEORY

Emotional attachment is characterized by feelings of closeness and affection and refers to the connections and bonds individuals form with others. According to **attachment theory**, emotional attachment patterns shift throughout the life span, with the first 3 years being the most formative for developing healthy emotional attachment. Children who have a responsive and dependable primary caregiver are far more likely to have healthy attachment patterns, good self-esteem and self-reliance, healthy romantic relationships, and trust in others more easily than those who experience early abuse, neglect, or abandonment. As people age, friends, romantic partners, and life experiences begin to influence attachment more than primary caregivers. Thus, interactions in personal relationships and negative life events can influence adult attachment. For example, bullying, death of a loved one, divorce, or domestic abuse can cause insecurity, anxiety, or avoidance in a person with secure attachment.

DECISION-MAKING THROUGHOUT THE LIFESPAN

Changes in decision-making can be attributed to brain development throughout the life span, life experiences, and changes in motivation. The **frontal lobe**—a part of the brain that controls personality characteristics, decision-making, and movement—develops throughout childhood and adolescence and typically reaches maturation at age 25. As **new brain connections** are formed, children and adolescents adopt new behaviors and make decisions characterized by overestimation of rewards, underestimation of possible risks, and egocentrism. **Social relationships** with peers and caregivers also influence decision-making for youth. The results of new behaviors and how decision-making is modeled creates brain circuits that are retained into adulthood. Behaviors that elicit positive feedback from others during development are also retained throughout adulthood. As frontal lobe development slows, decision making becomes more **stable**. Decision making—specifically, perceived risk and reward—becomes more **balanced**. As the brain ages, older adults are increasingly unable to hold on to multiple thoughts and struggle to make decisions that require consideration of many options. They become less concerned about bad outcomes that result from their decisions and more focused on the good outcomes.

PERCEPTION OF LIFE AND DEATH

As people age, their **perceptions of life and death** shift due to cognitive development, social influences, and personal experiences.

- **Infants** cannot comprehend death, yet they can be physically impacted by maternal separation. Infants separated from their mothers tend to lose weight, sleep less, display less energy, and no longer coo or smile.
- During **early childhood**, young children struggle to understand death. They believe death is temporary and/or reversible and may believe that the death resulted from their actions or misbehavior.
- In **middle and late childhood**, children begin to understand that death is permanent and universal. Throughout adolescence, teenagers begin to think abstractly about death and ponder existence. However, their lack of realistic understanding of life and death and perceived invincibility is evident by their risky behaviors.
- **Adults** begin to report increased anxiety and fear about death, peaking in middle adulthood.
- **Older adults** generally fear death less than younger adults. They often have fewer caregiving responsibilities and usually become more comfortable with death as they experience it more frequently with age.

Factors that Affect Mental and Emotional Health

EFFECT OF HEREDITY ON MENTAL AND EMOTIONAL HEALTH

Heredity—or genetics—can affect mental and emotional health. Although a specific mental illness gene has not been identified by researchers, it is well known that if an individual has a biological family member with a diagnosed mental health disorder, they are at an **increased risk** of developing one. However, their inherited susceptibility to mental illness does not mean that they will inevitably develop one or that they will develop one with the same severity as their family member. **Mental illness** occurs from an interaction between genetic, social, and environmental factors. These factors can either trigger an illness in someone who is genetically susceptible or serve as protective factors. Hereditary factors include **single gene expression** which occurs when one gene activates and triggers a mental illness, and **epigenetic expression** which describes how a person's genes change in response to environmental stimuli. Some mental illnesses, like schizophrenia, anxiety, depression, bipolar disorder and addiction, have a **higher genetic predisposition** than others; however, the development of these illnesses results from a combination of environmental, social, and genetic factors.

EFFECT OF PERSONAL EXPERIENCE ON MENTAL AND EMOTIONAL HEALTH

Personal experiences during childhood and throughout adulthood can profoundly affect mental and emotional health. Individuals who **experience adverse childhood experiences (ACEs)**, such as abuse or neglect, violence, divorce, or caretaker mental illness, are at risk for developing depression, anxiety, substance abuse, and other poor health behaviors as they mature. Conversely, those who experience **positive childhood experiences (PCEs)** like healthy interactions with caregivers and other adults and household stability tend to have better coping skills and higher self-worth, self-efficacy, and optimism. Personal experiences in adolescence and adulthood can also affect mental and emotional health (e.g., separation or divorce, living with chronic illness, death or loss of a loved one, job transition, moving, substance abuse, and unhealthy relationships).

EFFECT OF ENVIRONMENTAL FACTORS ON MENTAL AND EMOTIONAL HEALTH

While there are many **environmental factors** that contribute to mental health and wellbeing, an individual's **social and physical environment** can increase their susceptibility to mental illness. **Physical environmental factors** can influence a person's neurochemistry or cause distress. Examples of biology-altering environmental factors include food insecurity, poor housing conditions (i.e., living in a home with asbestos or lead), exposure to pollution in childhood, and parental substance abuse. Other examples include natural disasters, climate change-related events, and living in a community with unsafe drinking water. **Social environmental factors** refer to racial and ethnic, relational, and economic conditions that influence an individual's mental health and wellbeing. Examples include isolation, prejudice (e.g., racism, sexism, homophobia, xenophobia), experiencing war, community violence or crime, poverty, and social stigma.

Mental and Emotional Disorders

ANXIETY

An **anxiety disorder** is mental health condition in which an individual experiences intense, excessive, and persistent worry. An anxiety disorder is different from regular nervousness because it—like other disorders—inhibits a person's ability to cope with everyday stressors and negatively impacts their social and occupational functioning. Anxiety may induce heart palpitations, chest pain and tightness, difficulty breathing, cold or sweaty hands, and muscle tension. Panic, fear, and unrest are common among those experiencing anxiety. Nightmares, sleep disturbances, and turbulent thoughts can also be caused by anxiety. **Chemical imbalances** resulting from severe or chronic stress, **environmental stressors**, and **heredity** are common risk factors for anxiety. Though there are multiple types of anxiety disorders, they differ in their characteristics and triggers. However, despite their differences, the symptoms of each are persistent and interfere with daily activities or relationships.

DEPRESSION

Depression is mental health condition that is characterized by persistent feelings of sadness and hopelessness. Depression may be short-term or long-term, known as **acute** or **chronic depression**, respectively. Individuals who are depressed **lose interest** in things they used to find enjoyable and may experience concurrent feelings of **worry or frustration**. Those with depression may experience trouble falling or staying asleep, chronic pain, memory loss, and difficulty thinking or concentrating. Factors like atypical chemical levels and faulty mood regulation due to injury or abnormal brain development can make a person prone to depression. An individual with a family history of depression can be more susceptible to depression. Life events (e.g., unemployment, domestic abuse, childhood neglect, chronic illness) and environmental factors (e.g., natural disasters, community violence, war) can incite and exacerbate depression.

EATING DISORDERS

An **eating disorder** refers to a condition in which an individual engages in persistent **unhealthy dietary behaviors** to alter their appearance or quell emotional distress. Since there are many types of eating disorders, the symptoms vary. However, those with eating disorders may exhibit inexplicable weight changes, mood swings, food rituals to eliminate food-related anxiety, and avoidance (e.g., isolating while eating, refusing to eat certain foods). Those with a **family history** of eating disorders, adverse childhood experiences, and a history of dieting are vulnerable to developing an eating disorder. **Major life changes** and **mental health disorders** like obsessive compulsive disorder (OCD), depression, and anxiety can increase susceptibility to developing an

eating disorder or worsen an existing one. **Social pressure** to be thin and certain personality traits such as perfectionism or low self-esteem are additional causes of eating disorders.

SUICIDE

Suicide occurs when an individual self-inflicts a fatal injury with the intent to die. An individual who is considering or planning to commit suicide may withdraw, isolate, and increasingly talk about death. No single, specific cause leads to suicide. It often results from converging risk factors and stressors that cause **hopelessness** or **despair**. Individuals with existing mental health conditions, especially conditions that cause persistent feelings of hopelessness and despair like chronic illnesses, adverse childhood experiences, and traumatic brain injuries are at **higher risk of suicide**. Access to firearms and drugs, chronic relationship or financial stress, and upsetting or traumatic live events are risk factors for suicide. Witnessing or experiencing another person's suicide and previous suicide attempts can significantly increase the risk of suicidal ideation and suicide. **Protective factors** reduce the likelihood of a negative outcome. Examples of protective factors that reduce the risk of suicide include healthy relationships, accessible mental health care, and limited access to weapons or lethal drugs.

OBTAINING ASSISTANCE FOR MENTAL AND EMOTIONAL PROBLEMS

Seeking professional help is the best way to address an unmanageable mental health problem. Primary care doctors, physician assistants, and nurse practitioners can help refer individuals to a mental health provider or counsel them on alternative solutions or resources. Psychologists, therapists, and social workers are trained experts who provide counseling, psychological testing, and mental health education to improve coping skills. **Psychiatrists** prescribe medications to manage mental health symptoms. Another method for obtaining assistance for emotional problems is through **support groups**—a space where individuals share their experiences, troubles, and coping strategies. These resources are accessible in-person or online and are facilitated by community organizations, churches, private institutions, hospitals or healthcare providers, etc. **Mental health services** are often available through community outpatient, inpatient, and residential treatment facilities, universities, teaching hospitals, churches, and non-profit organizations.

Managing Anxiety and Grief

MANAGING ANXIETY

Psychotherapy and medication are often first-line treatments for anxiety; however, there are a number of **coping strategies** to manage anxiety. Strategies for reducing stress levels and anxiety generally include promoting overall health, avoiding stressors, and effectively processing existing stress.

Promoting overall health by following exercise routines, pursuing a balanced and healthy diet, and healthy sleep patterns all play a role in promoting healthy stress levels and reducing anxiety. Meditation, stretching, and relaxation are also known to help with reducing stress levels and easing the symptoms of anxiety. Similarly, healthy and lasting relationships are key aspects of a healthy life and tend to help reduce stress.

Those suffering from excess stress and anxiety should avoid **stressors** and **promotors of stress**. Alcohol, recreational drugs, smoking, and caffeine can contribute to anxiety, as each of these acts to artificially alter mood. It also helps to **identify stressors** in life that can be avoided or altered, such as challenging and unhealthy relationships, work, and home environments. One method for identifying stressors is to keep a **stress journal** and look for patterns of what is correlated with anxiety over time.

MANAGING GRIEF

Grief is an emotional response to loss. It can result from death of a friend or loved one, divorce or breakup, job loss, miscarriage, loss of a friendship, etc. Common **reactions** to grief include denial, shock, despair, anger or guilt, sadness, vulnerability, physical pain, or apathy. The **grieving process** is unique to each person and takes time. Research suggests that individuals with adequate **social support** and **healthy habits** can recover from loss better than those without. **Maintaining physical health** is an important part of managing grief. Establishing and continuing in exercise, sleep, and eating routines can keep an individual productive and motivated. Limiting alcohol and drugs and eating nutritious foods can keep a person healthy and active. **Maintaining connection** with trusted confidants or others experiencing loss can help an individual cope with the loss and prevent isolation. **Visiting a physician or mental health professional** may be beneficial to address the fear, guilt, depression, or anxiety associated with loss. Trained professionals can help build resilience and develop coping and grief management strategies through evidence-based treatments.

SUICIDE PREVENTION

Like other mental health conditions, **preventative strategies** are most effective for suicide prevention. **Improvements** made to an individual's mental health care coverage and accessibility can make it easier to receive treatment from trained mental health professionals. **Limiting access** to lethal weapons and drugs can thwart attempts. Social emotional learning programs, mental health first aid training programs, and crisis intervention programs can help individuals experiencing suicidal ideation. These kinds of programs are typically hosted by community-based or religious organizations with the intention of improving social support and community connectedness to prevent isolation. **Health promoting activities** that foster physical, social, and emotional wellbeing can improve a person's mood, strengthen their support networks, and develop coping mechanisms to intercept suicidal thoughts or attempts. **Postvention strategies** are activities or treatment for individuals who have attempted suicide or experienced the suicide of someone they know. They are crucial strategies for minimizing repeated or imitative suicide risk.

Family Structures and Roles within a Family

DIVERSE FAMILY STRUCTURES

Contemporary families are not limited to the traditional nuclear definition of two or more biologically related individuals. Family living arrangements have **changed drastically** in the last few decades due to **demographic shifts** (e.g., life expectancy), fewer marriages, increases in the number of divorce and remarriage, postponed childbearing, increases in childrearing outside of traditional nuclear marriages, and rises in singlehood. Today, families are far more **diverse** than they used to be, and the **definition** of family has shifted significantly. The dimensions of family diversity can differ by race and ethnicity, socioeconomic status, gender, sexual orientation, family structure, and family process. Families may be related by birth, chosen, or made circumstantially through adoption, guardianship, or marriage. The **family process**, or interpersonal dynamics (e.g., support, decision-making, communication) between family members, varies based on family demographics, societal and cultural influences, family history, and family structure. Families can be connected through shared identities or experiences, cultures, or emotional commitment. Families may also be connected through **reciprocal relationships**, which refers to mutually beneficial and complementary actions. They may provide emotional and economic support, discipline, and affection.

INFLUENCE OF FAMILY STRUCTURE AND DYNAMICS

Family structure and dynamics can have a profound impact on social relationships with others and individuals' overall health. It is through their observations of relationships among parents, siblings, extended family members, caregivers, etc., that children first perceive acceptable social dynamics and healthy relationships. **Sociological factors** like gender, age, sexuality, religion, economic status, race, and ethnicity can influence the practices and dynamics within a family. The quality of interfamilial relationships is of specific importance as it can impact social and physical wellbeing. **Interpersonal stressors**, such as frequent arguments and overly critical or demanding family members, and external stressors, such as lack of time or economic hardship, can contribute poor mental and physical health. However, **social support** (e.g., giving advice, providing care) is a protective factor against many poor health outcomes like immune system dysfunction and depression. A **diverse family structure** may strengthen family members' social networks and access to social support. For example, a multigenerational household in which grandparents assist in fulfilling family functions can reduce internal and external stress on primary caregivers.

FACTORS INFLUENCING RELATIONSHIPS WITHIN FAMILIES

Relationships can be influenced by the composition of family members, family structure, roles and expectations, values, family events or hardship, family member personalities or traits, and past and present relationships. **Changes in family structures** (i.e., the combination of family members) can impact dynamics and roles within a family. Shared or conflicting behavioral, moral, and cultural **values** can influence the health of familial relationships. **Family hardship**, **events**, and **trauma** can negatively affect a family and its function. For example, financial hardship can induce stress among family members that strains relationships. Trauma can lead to emotional turmoil and lasting effects on future generations that influence family dynamics. **Family personality traits** and **past and present relationships** can influence how family members feel towards each other and how they interact. Each family member holds a unique role within the unit that influences how they interact and communicate with others. **Roles** can influence individual's self-concept and perceived importance within the family. They may also influence family members' expectations of the individual which could impact self-confidence, self-efficacy, and emotional health.

INDIVIDUAL ROLES AND RESPONSIBILITIES WITHIN A FAMILY

The **Family Systems Theory** posits that each family member occupies a distinctive role and level of influence within the family unit. A person's **family role** refers to the authority they hold and responsibilities or expectations assigned to them. As an individual ages and family dynamics shift, their role within the family changes. Typically, family roles are intended to maintain function and satisfy needs; however, roles may have a positive or negative impact on the family. Equitably assigned and allocated roles ensure that family members are able to accomplish their responsibilities and avoid conflict within the family unit. Explicitly defined and fairly allocated roles can help families develop healthy family roles and responsibilities.

Promoting Healthy Interactions Among Family Members

EXPRESSING NEEDS AND WANTS APPROPRIATELY

Families must **balance** the needs and wants of many different people, which can lead to **conflict**. Respectfully **communicating** one's needs and wants can help to nurture physical and emotional wellbeing and improve interpersonal relationships. **Expressing** needs and wants appropriately can demonstrate self-respect and respect for others. Practicing **assertiveness** can help a person communicate their thoughts and feelings in a positive way and advocate for themselves. Expressing needs also promotes mutual respect, trust, and intimacy within a person's relationships. Individuals who **withhold** their wants and needs can develop feelings of resentment, frustration, and abandonment. This can impact their emotional wellbeing and how they interact with others.

PRACTICING SELF-CONTROL

Self-control describes the ability of an individual to **manage** their emotions or impulses. An individual with too little or too much self-control may develop depression, anxiety, or isolation. Those with **too little self-control** may be quick to blame others and have difficulty controlling emotions, which can cause conflict in their relationships. Individuals with **too much self-control** may be rigid in their beliefs and opinions, overly focused on details, struggle to display feelings, and can be overbearing in relationships. These qualities can create **distance** in relationships and make resolving conflict difficult. **Practicing self-control** can help an individual control impulses and negative reactions that may cause emotional distress or physical harm. It is also helpful in managing thoughts, emotions, and actions in order to become more productive and achieve a greater goal. Employing self-control strategies can help an individual achieve positive outcomes and maintain healthy, respectful relationships with others.

BUILDING TRUST

Building trust among family members promotes healthy interactions and strengthens relationships. **Mistrust** may cause family members to limit their involvement and vulnerability. It can lead to fragmentation within the family unit and conflict. Boundaries, accountability, and communication are key components of building trust and promoting healthy interactions among family members.

- **Boundaries**—clear limitations and expectations—create a shared understanding of acceptable behavior among family members.
- Respected boundaries can prevent conflict, but **accountability** for overstepped boundaries is important for repairing trust and mitigating conflict.
- An important aspect of trust-building is establishing strong **communication** skills. The ability to express one's feelings, wants, and needs, and the openness of their family members to accept what they share, can build trust among the family.

EXPRESSING AFFECTION

Expressing **affection** and **positive attention** promotes healthy interactions among family members. **Receiving regular affection** is associated with improved overall social, emotional, and physical wellbeing. Parental warmth and affection are associated with improved brain development, higher self-esteem, improved educational performance, stronger family communication, and fewer psychological and behavioral challenges. Affectionate behaviors elevate levels of a hormone called **oxytocin** in the body, which encourages bonding and calms those giving and receiving affection. **Positive attention** between family members builds connection and strengthens individual self-confidence. Expressing and receiving affection and positive attention can create close bonds between family members. Benefits resulting from positive interactions between family members can extend beyond the immediate relationship. For example, healthy intrafamilial relationships can improve an individual's ability to navigate social situations, increase compassion, and make them better able to relate to others.

SETTING LIMITS

Setting limits promotes healthy interactions among family members. **Limits**, or relational boundaries, are personal guidelines and rules that people set for themselves in relationships. These limits identify acceptable ways for others to behave around them and reasonable ways to respond when their boundaries are overstepped. An individual with **healthy boundaries** values their own feelings and opinions, refuses to compromise their values for others, appropriately shares personal information, communicates their personal wants and needs, and accepts when others decline their requests. Setting limits allows a person to practice **self-respect** and **communicate their needs** in relationships. The practice of establishing and respecting limits promotes healthy interactions because it enables family members to demonstrate trust and respect, avoid conflict that may arise from physical and emotional space intrusion, and share responsibility and power.

Effects of Family Problems on an Individual

INFLUENCE OF ABUSE

Abuse refers to repeated harmful or injurious actions. It can have a significant impact on an individual's physical, emotional, and social health, especially when it occurs within a family unit. Individuals who experience abuse may sustain **immediate physical injuries**, but abuse can also result in **long-lasting physical ailments**. Individuals who experience abuse during early childhood may experience **stunted brain development and function**. Individuals who experience abuse are at **higher risk** of diabetes, respiratory and cardiovascular illness, and diminished vision and functional capacity. Abused individuals frequently experience persistent isolation and fear which impact their **emotional and social health**. They are far more likely to experience memory problems, impaired self-control, and mental health conditions (e.g., depression, anxiety) than their non-abused peers. Their **impaired mental state** can result in educational and learning challenges, which can influence academic attainment and job readiness if unaddressed. The **social health** of abused individuals can also be affected; those who experience abuse are more likely to develop attachment disorders and poor social skills. This can impact an individual's ability to form positive relationships. Abuse can contribute to poor decision-making and coping skills which may result in unsafe sexual activities, substance misuse, crime or violence, and future perpetration or victimization of abuse.

INFLUENCE OF DIVORCE

Divorce refers to the termination of a legally recognized marriage. It can **drastically impact** an individual's physical, emotional, and mental health. **Self-reported health** is much lower among divorced individuals, and they have a greater overall **mortality rate**. Divorced individuals are more likely to develop heart disease, diabetes, cancer, and mobility challenges (e.g., climbing stairs, walking). They tend to report higher amounts of anxiety, depression, isolation, and stress than the general population. The individual health effects are not solely limited to those receiving a legal separation or divorce. **Children of divorced caregivers** have a higher perceptibility to illness and increased injury rates. They are more likely to become divorced as adults than their peers. Children of divorce are at **higher risk** of experiencing depression, anxiety, poor academic performance, substance use/abuse, early sexual activity, poor social maturation, and premature mortality.

INFLUENCE OF DEATH

Experiencing death can influence all dimensions of health. Those who experience the death of their family member may experience **diminished health outcomes** as they grieve the loss of their loved one. Specifically, grieving individuals report chronic fatigue, compromised immunity, chronic pain, digestive issues, and inflammation. Individuals experiencing the death of a loved one can develop sleep disturbances which may increase feelings of depression or anxiety. Levels of **cortisol**, a hormone associated with stress, are much higher following the loss of a loved one. High levels of cortisol for an extended amount of time can raise blood pressure and increase risk of heart disease. Grief from the death of a loved one can increase an individual's risk of developing anxiety, panic disorders, substance abuse, post-traumatic stress disorder, depression, and suicide. The death of a family member can have significant impacts on the interaction between living family members as their family structure shifts. Following the death, many note a loss of personal or relational identity and difficulty connecting to others. The loss of a family member may continue to cause poor emotional and physical health outcomes among the bereaved long after their death.

NATURE OF CONFLICT IN FAMILIES

Family conflict refers to disagreements or opposition among family members. Compared to other forms of relationship conflict, family conflict tends to be **more intense and complex** because of the duration of the familial relationships and the **strong emotional attachments** that exist among family members. Therefore, the nature of family relationships can intensify conflict and make managing family conflict more challenging. Conflict may be verbal, physical, sexual, financial, or psychological. **Conflict style**—the tactics and routines families use when conflict arises—can influence the intensity, duration, and severity of family conflict.

CAUSES OF CONFLICT IN FAMILIES

There are many causes of family conflict.

- **Financial difficulties** can be a major source of family conflict. Inability to pay bills or afford food and uncertainty about economic security can cause stress among family members.
- **Unemployment** can also have the same effect.
- **Marital and relational challenges** like infidelity, separation, or divorce can trigger conflict among family members.
- **Child rearing** is a major stressor; disagreements about discipline, caregiver responsibilities, children's assertion of independence, and sibling rivalry or disputes can lead to contention and conflict.
- **Poor communication** about wants and needs, the distribution of responsibilities, unresolved issues, and the inability to express needs and wants can lead to misunderstanding, disconnection, and conflict.
- **Intrusive relatives or friends** can also lead to conflict as family members struggle to manage extramarital and familial dynamics.
- **Contrasting beliefs, opinions, and values** can lead to disagreement and resentment among family members.
- **Differences in gender and age** can cause behavior that seem unreasonable to the other party. Specifically, gender stereotypes or generational and cultural differences may fuel conflict between family members.

CONSEQUENCES OF CONFLICT IN FAMILIES

Family conflict **impacts all family members involved** and influences **multiple dimensions of health**. Family conflict can contribute to mental health problems like anxiety and depression. Parental or caregiver conflict reduces children's **emotional security** and can lead to emotional dysregulation and poor reactions to future conflict. **Intergenerational conflict** can sever supportive ties that provide crucial aid and companionship to family members. **Physical health impacts** of conflict include digestive problems, heart disease, sleep disturbances, high blood pressure, immune system suppression, and premature aging. Children who are involved in conflict may adopt unhealthy or risky behaviors (e.g., substance use, unprotected sex) and may develop poor attachment styles and unhealthy interpersonal relationships. **Chronic and severe conflict** can exacerbate health problems as family members grow increasingly overwhelmed and exhausted. **Social health** can also be affected by family conflict. Conflict strains relationships which can lead to resentment among those involved and distrust of others. The dissolution of families due to conflict can result in a loss of social contact between family members. This can cause stress as the family adjusts to a shift in structure and loss of emotional and financial support.

Supporting Students with Family Problems

HELPING STUDENTS COPE WITH FAMILY ABUSE AND NEGLECT

Abuse refers to the intentional harm or coercion directed by one person toward another. **Neglect** refers to the failure of a caregiver to fulfill a child's basic needs in a manner that threatens a child's health and wellbeing. Abused and neglected victims are often **reluctant** to open up about their experiences, so **identifying indicators** of abuse and reporting it is crucial to preventing it. Educators who are aware of the appropriate behaviors exhibited by children at each developmental stage are more capable of recognizing conduct that indicates abuse and intervening quickly. **Structured classrooms** provide a safe space in which abused and neglected children can cope with unhealthy behaviors in the family. For example, **consistent classroom routines** and schedules can counteract a turbulent home life. At school, students are able to engage in productive coursework that fosters a sense of achievement and develop healthy relationships with others outside of their family. Classroom activities that promote **social emotional learning**—the process of developing problem-solving, interpersonal, and emotional management skills—can help students establish **positive coping mechanisms** and strengthen their ability to **self-advocate**.

HELPING STUDENTS COPE WITH FAMILY ALCOHOLISM

Alcoholism refers to a compulsive and uncontrolled dependence on alcohol. Children of alcoholics (COA) may be exposed to unsafe physical conditions and are at risk of violence or abuse, neglect, and emotional distress. **Age-appropriate information** about alcoholism and its secondary risks can help COA comprehend addiction. Information can be shared during lessons or through a classroom library that contains relevant books or articles on addiction. A readily accessible classroom **list of school and community resources** or professional counselors can help educators connect students and their families to support. COA are at higher risk of emotional and behavior challenges. Therefore, **skill-building opportunities, collaborative learning projects, and social emotional learning activities** can help them develop necessary coping skills to navigate alcohol-related conflict and receive constructive attention from others. Educators who model consistency and positive communication can build the trust and self-confidence of COA that they may lack at home.

HELPING STUDENTS SEEK HELP IN DEALING WITH FAMILY PROBLEMS

As **mandatory reporters**, educators are generally required by federal and state law to report suspected maltreatment, although some reporting laws vary from state to state. Once reported, Child Protective Services investigates and identifies services to prevent future maltreatment. **School protocols** and **staff development programs** are effective strategies for identifying and reporting suspected cases of maltreatment; they eliminate obstacles for reporting and quickly connect students with appropriate resources or referrals. **Wraparound initiatives** refer to comprehensive services aimed at meeting the needs of children and families to foster student wellbeing. Examples include mental and physical health care, food and nutrition services, and community education and training. Wraparound initiatives can connect students and families to mental health professionals who can deliver counseling and treatment. They are also helpful for providing financial relief and social supports that cause and/or worsen child maltreatment. Research suggests that students who participate in **school-based programs** that offer training in life skills, parenting, and problem-solving openly communicate about maltreatment and seek help more readily.

Healthy and Unhealthy Interpersonal Relationships

HEALTHY RELATIONSHIPS

Regardless of the kind of relationship, four characteristics that are necessary for all healthy relationships are mutual respect, boundary setting, open communication, and trust.

- **Mutual respect** is expressed when an individual values and affirms another's feelings and opinions—regardless of whether they are different.
- **Setting healthy boundaries** establishes expectations for how individuals in a relationship should be treated and holds them accountable if boundaries are violated.
- **Open communication** ensures that both parties feel that they can share their feelings honestly and without judgment or interruption. Open communication is achieved through consistent, intentional, and honest discussions between both parties.
- **Trust** refers to security and fidelity; a relationship in which both parties trust one another elicits openness and honesty.

Along with the four mentioned above, there are a few characteristics that are particularly important in intimate and familial relationships. **Equality**, **compatibility**, and **shared decision-making** are crucial for developing and maintaining strong **romantic relationships. Accountability**, **support**, and **showing appreciation** are especially important for **optimal family functioning and family cohesiveness**.

UNHEALTHY RELATIONSHIPS

Qualities of an **unhealthy relationship** include control, disrespect, dependence, and dishonesty.

- **Control** within a relationship refers to an unequal distribution of influence and displays of dominance by one party towards another. A controlling person may use **coercive or intimidating tactics** to exert power over another or isolate them from their friends or family. They might also exhibit hostile or antagonizing behavior or resort to violence and intimidation to maintain control.
- **Disrespect** refers to insulting or humiliating behavior that devalues one's thoughts, feelings, opinions, or identity. It can cause one to feel undervalued or underappreciated.
- Although healthy relationships require interdependence—shared and equitable dependence of two people on each other—the level of **dependence** may be unbalanced in unhealthy relationships. This can result in relationships that are unfulfilling, one-sided, and mutually destructive.
- **Dishonesty**—deceit or intentional withholding of information—can erode trust and mutual respect.

Together, these characteristics can contribute to unhealthy behaviors such as jealous and unfounded accusations, picking fights, lying or withholding information, stealing or destruction of property, threatening self-harm or suicide with the intent to control another person, and committing sexual or physical violence.

BUILDING AND MAINTAINING HEALTHY INTERPERSONAL RELATIONSHIPS

Mutual respect is developed as both parties practice open communication, respect boundaries, show interest in the other's interests, show appreciation, and encourage one another. Building mutual respect can be accomplished through **consistent and reliable actions** (e.g., follow through with promises). **Healthy boundaries** are established through **open communication** about an individual's needs and expectations. This may be accomplished when both parties assert their limitations or ground rules for the relationship, communicate when a boundary is breached, and identify mutually agreed upon consequences for violated boundaries. Open communication can be accomplished when both parties are **transparent** about their thoughts, feelings, beliefs, etc., and participate in respectful discourse. It can also be achieved when both parties are **approachable** (e.g., inviting behavior and positive language) and **receptive to feedback**. **Trust** can be developed through transparency, vulnerability, and willingness to accept and apply criticism. Expressing one's feelings and demonstrating vulnerability can **improve intimacy and connection** between both people. Relationships are **not static**; they change as a person grows and develops. Therefore, to maintain a relationship it is important for one to **check in** with their partner, friend, coworker, etc., regularly to ensure that both feel **content**, **respected**, and **fulfilled**.

Peer Relationships

A **peer relationship** refers to an established interpersonal connection between two individuals who share a developmental (e.g., age) or situational identity (e.g., school, work). Peer relationships are often influenced by early interactions with caregivers or family members and can be positive or negative. Those in a **positive peer relationship** may encourage each other to make positive, healthy decisions, reinforce healthy behaviors, and support one another. Those in a **negative peer relationship** may pressure or encourage one another to make poor decisions and reinforce unhealthy choices. The interactions that occur within peer relationships can influence an individual's identity, attitude, and ethics. Social skills, in-group norms, and socially-acceptable behavior are **learned through observation and peer interaction**. Additionally, peer interactions and peer reactions to an individual's behavior can promote or discourage health and behavior choices. The quality of peer relationships, peer status (e.g., popularity), and fear of social rejection can impact the level of peer influence on an individual.

PEER PRESSURE

Peer pressure refers to the external influence that members of a person's reference groups have on their behavior or decision-making. It can be **direct** or **indirect** (e.g., a teenager is directly pressured to drink a shot of liquor by a peer vs. a teenager is tempted to drink when surrounded by peers who are drinking at a party), and **negative** or **positive**.

- **Negative peer pressure** is associated with poor health outcomes. Specifically, it can result in depression, poor self-confidence, increased anxiety and stress, and sleep disturbances. Depending on how hazardous the activity is, it may also increase an individual's risk of injury.
- **Positive peer pressure** can encourage healthy behaviors that result in improved social, mental, and physical wellbeing outcomes.

The effect of peer pressure is especially powerful among **adolescents**, who are more **vulnerable** to social desirability and reinforcement than adults.

RESPONDING TO PEER PRESSURE

Having a diverse set of **ready-to-use strategies** is important for responding to negative peer pressure. Those who **plan ahead** and **practice** their refusal skills are often far better at responding to peer pressure when it occurs. An example is confidently saying, "no," or explaining how one's pressuring actions or language makes another person feel. Other examples of responses may include the use of humor to deflect, an excuse to leave the situation, a change of subject, or the use of a secret code with another person to swiftly exit the situation. **Remaining calm and unwavering** in one's decision is important for resisting negative peer pressure or persuasion. A clear understanding of one's **values and morals** (e.g., right and wrong decisions) can make it easier to refuse peer pressure and to discern between a healthy and unhealthy choice. Maintaining healthy relationships with positive influences can prevent negative peer pressure and reinforce making constructive choices.

Group Relationships and Dynamics

GROUPS, GROUP DYNAMICS, AND SOCIAL SUPPORT NETWORKS

A **group** is an aggregate of individuals who work interdependently to accomplish a common goal or outcome. They share a **collective identity** and adhere to an explicitly or implicitly **defined structure**. Groups can be **primary**, meaning small and connection-based, **secondary**, meaning large and objective-based, or **reference**, which vary in size and influence an individual's beliefs and behaviors. Group cohesion is reliant upon the fulfillment of various roles and **group dynamics**, which refers to the interactions within groups. A **social support network** refers to an individual's friends, family, and peers who provide reciprocal support and guidance. While groups are centered around a common goal, they tend to be more open and fluid when compared to social support networks. Social support networks are usually made up of more stable relationships and do not typically change very quickly.

HEALTH CONSEQUENCES OF GROUP INTERACTIONS

An **in-group** is a group an individual belongs to along with likeminded or similar individuals, and **out-group** is a group that one does not identify with. In-group members may feel acceptance and belonging; however, **in-group/out-group bias** can lead to in-group favoritism or out-group exclusion/discrimination. Out-group members may feel rejection and disdain towards in-group members. The **black sheep effect** describes instances when an in-group member displays divergent beliefs or norm-violating behavior. As a result, they may be judged or denied membership. The **group-subgroup interaction** describes how an individual can belong to two groups—a group and a subgroup—that both shape and reinforce an individual's beliefs and behavior. For example, an individual who belongs to a religious family and a religious club that share complementary values should experience reinforcement from both groups. Membership in compatible groups may minimize emotional turmoil or conflict that can arise from discordant group beliefs. Group **mutual exclusivity** describes an inability of one to belong to two or more groups with incompatible characteristics or values. For example, a person who belongs to an academic club and sports team may feel pressured to choose between them.

Social and Communication Skills

DEMONSTRATING TOLERANCE, EMPATHY, CONSIDERATION, AND RESPECT

Practicing tolerance, empathy, consideration, and respect can enhance a person's interactions and improve the health and wellbeing of their relationships.

- **Showing tolerance** to others is expressed by conveying **fairness** and **acceptance** of a person or their beliefs regardless of disagreement or personal grievances. Practicing tolerance in relationships ensures that both parties feel included and accepted, which can improve the connection between both people and promote mutual respect.
- **Empathy** refers to a person's ability to understand or experience another person's point of view. Showing empathy in relationships can build trust between two people. It can also provide reassurance and validation, improve communication, and create more effective solutions to conflict.
- **Being considerate** of others is expressed through kind and accommodating—sometimes anticipatory—actions. Like tolerance and empathy, consideration demonstrates a respect for others. It is a display of self-control and shows others that one values them.
- **Demonstrating respect** in a relationship shows the other person that an individual admires and values them. It is exhibited through positive language and actions, honesty, encouragement, and acceptance. Respect builds trust and security within a relationship.

RESPONDING APPROPRIATELY TO CRITICISM

Although receiving feedback is a crucial part of self-improvement and relationship building, **criticism** can sometimes be difficult to accept. **Responding appropriately to criticism** is a type of communication skill that can prevent or mitigate conflict and foster self-evaluation. A person who responds appropriately to criticism acknowledges the **intent** of the criticism (e.g., constructive, destructive), **accepts accountability** while asserting themselves when necessary, and **inquires to gain understanding** and develop an **improvement plan**. Responding appropriately to criticism establishes a pathway for **improved communication** between the two parties. If effectively and appropriately communicated, criticism presents an opportunity for both people involved to demonstrate mutual respect, understanding, and empathy.

LISTENING SKILLS

Listening skills are important social and communication skills that maintain healthy and bidirectional communication within a relationship. **Active listening** is a listening skill that refers to attentive, responsive, and reflective listening. It consists of **verbal and non-verbal cues** to show engagement and non-judgment (e.g., nodding, body language, eye contact, paraphrasing). If practiced, listening skills can improve one's **empathy** and **tolerance** of another person's perspective, which can encourage others to open up. It is also a useful skill when engaging in conversation with others, which can be beneficial in building relationships.

DISCUSSING PROBLEMS

Discussing problems in a relationship is an essential part of building and maintaining healthy communication. **Constructive problem solving** is achieved when issues are discussed early, talked about honestly and productively, and received by an engaged and empathetic listener. Discussing problems or conflicts provides clarity to both parties. It also reduces **rumination**—obsessive and negative thoughts or feelings about a particular situation—that can lead to emotional or social distress. Discussing problems with another person can also present **different perspectives** that aid in problem solving and promote healthy conflict resolution. Since it requires **vulnerability** and **empathy** from both parties, discussing problems can maintain and strengthen **trust** in existing relationships.

CONFLICT RESOLUTION SKILLS

Conflict refers to disagreement or incompatibility between individuals or groups. **Conflict resolution skills** are communication strategies that prevent relationship disputes or avoid escalation. Though the method varies depending on the type of relationship, most effective conflict resolution strategies are rooted in **healthy and effective communication, empathy, and self-awareness**. Developing conflict resolution skills can help individuals navigate conflicting and contrasting perspectives or volatile situations resulting from conflict. Utilizing conflict resolution can **strengthen relationships** once a disagreement has occurred and **prevent escalation** or future conflict. Conflict resolution can improve the quality of relationships by promoting **reciprocal respect** for others' perspectives and shared problem solving.

ASSERTIVENESS

Assertiveness is a communication strategy in which an individual firmly and clearly **communicates their needs** and **respectfully advocates** for themselves. Compared to other communication styles—passive, aggressive, and passive-aggressive—assertive communication is the **healthiest** and **most effective** form of communication. Assertiveness is important for improving situations involving **interpersonal interactions** because it promotes the integrity and rights of both people involved. Assertive communicators address conflict early on, engage in active listening, and set/respect boundaries. As a result, all those involved are able to express their feelings honestly and confidently before conflict arises or escalates. Since assertiveness improves self-advocacy and prevents conflict, it can **reduce individual and relationship stress**.

REFUSAL SKILLS

Refusal skills are communication strategies that help an individual confidently refuse when they are confronted with a decision and remain resolute when pressured. They are a crucial component of **resisting peer pressure** and **preventing risky or hazardous situations**. Refusal skills are especially important for avoiding substance use/misuse, preventing injury, and protecting personal space and privacy. Refusal skills allows individuals to identify, assert, and uphold their **personal boundaries**, which can aid in establishing and maintaining healthy communication with others. Refusal skills are important for anyone at any age, yet they are particularly essential for children and adolescents, those with low self-efficacy, and individuals with low self-confidence, since all can increase an individual's susceptibility to peer influence. During childhood and adolescence, youth begin to form an identity and cultivate their psychosocial skills; this makes them very susceptible to peer influence. During this time period, they are often exposed to new, potentially dangerous, or risky experiences and situations (e.g., drug use, sexual activity) that necessitate refusal skills. Individuals with **low self-esteem** or **low-self efficacy** may struggle to assert themselves or develop strategies for refusal.

Conflict Avoidance and Resolution

CONFLICT RESOLUTION STYLES

There are five conflict resolution styles.

- An individual with an **avoiding** conflict management style may **withdraw or circumvent** an issue to prevent conflict. They may ignore a problem or person until the dispute is resolved or repeatedly evade a conversation to avoid conflict.
- One with an **accommodating** style of conflict management may **yield** to the needs or desires of others to manage conflict. These individuals may allow others to make decisions for them that conflict with their needs in order to keep the peace.
- An individual with a **competing** style uses **firm, dominating**, and **uncooperative** conflict management—often at the expense of another person. They may be headstrong and unaccommodating to the needs or desires of others.

- An individual with a **compromising** conflict management style works together with others to find **middle ground** and to create a resolution that is **mutually accepted by all parties**. Often, all participants must make concessions to appease the other and not everyone is pleased with the solution.
- Similar to compromising style, a person who uses a **collaborative** style is cooperative. However, one with a collaborative style seeks to find an **innovative resolution** in which all who are involved are engaged throughout the process and are satisfied with the result.

MEDIATING AND RESOLVING CONFLICT

Conflict resolution refers to the informal or formal process of resolving conflict between two parties. It involves identifying the source of the conflict, contributing factors, and triggers, and creating a resolution. It is important that all involved feel **motivated to express their honest feelings and perspectives** without judgment or retribution. Active listening and assertive communication throughout the process are necessary to ensure that all involved feel affirmed and fairly represented. Successful conflict resolution occurs when both parties create a solution that settles their dispute. Conflict resolution can be achieved through **mediation**—the use of a neutral third party to guide those involved to resolution. In this style of conflict resolution, participants engage in a structured and facilitated process to reach a mutually agreed upon solution. The mediator works with both parties to identify the problem and strengthen understanding of both parties' perspectives. They work with participants to determine a shared goal and strategize potential solutions needed to reach one. Often, both parties create a formal plan that includes steps for achieving resolution and accountability measures needed to end the dispute.

AVOIDING UNSAFE SITUATIONS

One must practice **situational awareness** at all times in order to avoid unsafe situations. This requires that an individual stays **alert** (e.g., abstaining from mind-altering substances, minimizing distractions) and pays attention to others' odd behavior (e.g., staring, loitering or stalking, persistent attempts at conversation, unwanted advances).

- **Avoiding isolation** can offer protection from unsafe situations and ensure that there are others around who can provide aid if an unsafe situation occurs.
- **Maintaining visibility** (e.g., staying in well-populated areas) can be a deterrent to crime and unsafe situations since perpetrators often seek out an isolated victim in a secluded area.
- **Maintaining communication** with others and sharing one's location or plans with a loved one can increase the likelihood of intervention before a situation occurs or provide quick assistance if necessary. A lack or sudden halt of communication can signal to others that something is wrong and that they should intervene.
- Valuable items in plain view make an individual a target for crime; **keeping valuables hidden** or left in a secure place can prevent unsafe situations.
- **Avoiding conflict** or deescalating disputes can prevent injurious or fatal confrontations.

BULLYING, RIDICULE, AND HARASSMENT

Bullying refers to deliberate acts of intimidation or harm by one individual against another. Bullying may be physical, verbal, social, and cyber. **Ridicule**—the act of mockery and humiliation—and **harassment**—threating or intimidating behavior—are examples of bullying. Cultivating healthy and **nurturing relationships** with others can prevent bullying; those engaged in healthy relationships are far less likely to be the subject of bullying, harassment, or ridicule. Having friends or **surrounding oneself with others** is a deterrent to bullies, as they frequently seek out those who are isolated or vulnerable. Individuals should **avoid conflict and unsafe situations** (e.g., isolation, no adult supervision, bullying "hot spots") that could put them at risk. When faced with

169

bullying, ridicule, or harassment, an individual can respond by **confidently and assertively telling their bully or harasser to stop**. However, they should remain calm and refrain from using intimidation or any other behavior that could escalate the situation. If possible, one can **remove themselves** from the situation or ignore any negative behavior. An individual can also **tell an adult or authority figure** who can mediate the situation and prevent further conflict.

Human Sexuality

SEXUAL ACTIVITY

Sexual activity refers to intimate relations or behavior through which a person expresses their sexuality; it can be **solitary** or between **two or more individuals**, and can be **penetrative** (e.g., anal, oral, vaginal) or **non-penetrative** (e.g., oral, touching). Poor adherence to safe sex precautions and engagement in high-risk sexual behavior (e.g., unprotected sex, early sexual initiation, multiple partners) can result in consequences that may impact a person's physical or emotional wellbeing. **Physical consequences** of sexual activity are **unplanned pregnancy**—unintended or mistimed pregnancy that results from misuse or non-use of contraception—or **sexually transmitted infections (STI)**—infections that are transferred from an infected person to a non-infected person through semen, blood, or vaginal fluids. **Emotional consequences** like **sexual regret** are largely dependent on one's emotional wellbeing (e.g., existing depression, anxiety, or low self-esteem), assertiveness and refusal skills, sexual negotiation skills, perceived reputational damage, and knowing one's partner prior to sexual contact.

ABSTAINING FROM SEXUAL ACTIVITY

An individual who practices **abstinence** refrains from engaging in sexual activity; it is the **most effective way to avoid risks associated with sex**. Abstaining from sexual activity outside of a committed relationship prevents the risk of unintended pregnancy and minimizes one's risk of contracting a sexually transmitted disease. Remaining abstinent outside of a committed relationship can reduce stress or concern associated with sexual activity (e.g., fear of contracting STIs, pregnancy). It also reduces feelings of guilt, shame, or regret that can be associated with casual sex. Abstinence is associated with **improved emotional wellbeing** for those who harbor negative feelings or experiences involving sexual activity, or individuals for whom sexual activity is a source of **anxiety**. It can help an individual develop greater self-confidence and self-worth. Abstinence is often associated with better academic outcomes and improved focus on school or work. Choosing not to engage in sexual activity outside of a committed relationship can improve one's ability to develop and maintain non-sexual or non-romantic relationships.

INFLUENCE OF PEER PRESSURE

Sexual decisions refer to one's choices about whether to participate in sexual activity, and with whom, when, or what kind of sexual activity they engage in. Decisions about sexual activity are **heavily influenced by indirect peer pressure and direct peer pressure**. Of the two, indirect peer pressure has a greater impact on one's decision to engage in sexual activity—especially among adolescents. Two examples of the impact of indirect peer pressure on decisions to have sex are **perceptions about peer sexual activity** and **peer approval**. An individual who believes that their peers are engaging in sexual activity may feel an indirect or unspoken pressure to have sex and is more likely to engage in sexual activity. Perceived peer approval (e.g., whether their friends would approve or disapprove of engaging in sexual activity) can also influence one's decision about sexual activity. Direct peer pressure or **sexual coercion**—nonphysical pressure imposed on a person (e.g., ridicule, lying, repeated requests or harassment)—can influence one's decision to engage in sexual activity.

INFLUENCE OF PERSONAL VALUES

An individual's personal values can guide their beliefs and decisions about sexual activity. **Sexual values**—personal beliefs regarding one's sexuality and sexual activity—are **not static** and are continually shaped by many factors. Family, friends, culture, media, personal experiences, and religion are the **most influential**. Those with **strong sexual values** are often more aware of acceptable or appropriate sexual behavior, which may make them better able to communicate their wants and needs to their partner, make decisions regarding their sexual activity or health, negotiate sex, assert themselves when their values are violated, or refuse unwanted sexual advances. Those whose behaviors and actions align with their personal values often have **improved self-confidence and sense of empowerment**. Strong sexual values may lead to more fulfilling and healthier relationships, especially if they are clearly communicated to one's partner. Those with poor or no sexual values may struggle to make decisions about if, when, where, how, and with whom they engage in sexual activity. This can put them in a dangerous situation or result in emotional distress, abuse, or unintended consequences like pregnancy or STIs.

INFLUENCE OF MEDIA

Media refers to the various channels through which information and messages are communicated (e.g., television, newspaper, music, photographs, videos, social networking websites or apps). Media serves as a **primary source of information** regarding sex and sexual activity for many; however, **inaccurate information** and **unhealthy portrayals** about sexuality and sexual activity relayed through media can negatively influence sexual decisions. This can significantly impact one's **perception** about healthy relationships, consent, potential consequences of sexual activity, sexual or gender stereotypes, sexual objectification, and sexual violence. The content and messages about sexual activity can also influence an individual's **ideas about sexual norms**. For example, suppose a television show depicts popular male characters making inappropriate comments or unwanted sexual advances directed at passive female characters without consequence. In that case, viewers may develop a warped view of acceptable sexual behavior. Unbiased and realistic portrayals of sexual activity and comprehensive sex education are **protective factors** that counteract the effects of negative media messages.

MAKING RESPONSIBLE DECISIONS

An individual can make responsible decisions about sexual activity through abstaining from or limiting substance use, media literacy, comprehensive sex education, positive and healthy relationships with peers, and parent-child communication. Substance use can impact one's decision-making and place them at risk of many adverse outcomes (e.g., sexual abuse or rape, pregnancy, STIs). **Abstaining from or limiting substance use** can help an individual think and act clearly as they make decisions about their sexual activity or health. **Improving one's media literacy** can make them better prepared to identify biased or inaccurate information about sexual activity and relationships. Additionally, **comprehensive sex education** increases a person's knowledge of sexual health and improves their ability to protect and advocate for themselves when making decisions about sexual activity. **Positive and healthy relationships with peers** can reduce pressure to initiate sexual activity and secure peer guidance and support for making responsible decisions regarding their sexual health. **Open communication between parents and children** about sex and reproductive health can promote healthy sexual behaviors and prevent negative sexual health outcomes.

Healthy Skills for Dating Relationships

EXPRESSING AFFECTION

Affection can produce mutual feelings of trust and security between two people in a relationship. However, expressing or displaying affection inappropriately can cause **discomfort**. Affection can be expressed through physical touch, words of affirmation, gifts, quality time, and acts of service. **Physical touch** can be sexual or non-sexual (e.g., holding hands, hugging). Expressing physical affection appropriately requires **consent**—mutually agreed-upon and respected **boundaries** related to physical contact or sexual activity. In a caring relationship, the type of and degree to which different kinds of affection are expressed should be appropriate for the needs and wants of both partners. Affection should never be **forced or coercive**. It is important that the individual receiving affection honestly and clearly express whether they like or dislike of the action. Open and honest communication can **prevent inappropriate displays of affection** and ensure both parties feel fulfilled and comfortable.

REFUSING SEXUAL ADVANCES

An individual can refuse a sexual advance by clearly and **directly saying "no"** to the person making the advance. Ambiguous or passive responses to advances can lead to **misunderstanding** between the two involved. It could also contribute to future advances or an unsafe situation. One should **avoid explaining their refusal** or **implying that certain circumstances contributed to their decision** (e.g., relationship status, other people around, too busy) as that may signal that the person making the advance should try again or use other strategies to convince them. Using **body language** and **maintaining personal space** are nonverbal gestures that reinforce an individual's refusal. **Avoiding isolation** or **preventing unsafe situations** (e.g., substance use, accepting drugs or alcohol from strangers) can make it easier for one to refuse sexual advances. If there are more people around, the perpetrator is less likely to make unwanted sexual advances. Additionally, stating one's discomfort around others when sexual advances are made can add **social pressure** to comply and group accountability when one's refusal is not respected. **Separating oneself, avoiding conversation, and limiting interaction** with the individual making sexual advances can help prevent further contact.

DATING RELATIONSHIPS

Each person's role within a dating relationship depends on their partner's needs. For example, a person whose partner is experiencing emotional distress may fill the role of confidant, while one whose partner is struggling to meet their financial commitments may fill the role of supporter. One's role also requires fulfilling the three components of love as determined by Robert Sternberg's **Triangular Theory of Love: intimacy, passion**, and **commitment**. It is one's responsibility is to act in a way that fosters connectedness, excitement, and loyalty. These components can be fulfilled through **identifying and asserting one's boundaries, respecting their partner's boundaries, demonstrating empathy, sharing responsibility, communicating clearly and honestly**, and **compromising when necessary**. Setting and respecting boundaries cultivates loyalty and strengthens a pair's connection. Demonstrating **empathy** can imbue intimacy and passion between two people. Sharing responsibility with one's partner can show commitment and nurture the bond between both people. **Communication** strengthens mutual understanding, which can foster connectedness. **Compromising** shows one's commitment to and support of the other's wellbeing, which can bolster the connection between two people.

Legal and Ethical Implications of Unacceptable Behaviors

LEGAL AND ETHICAL IMPLICATIONS OF SEXUAL HARASSMENT

Sexual harassment refers to unwanted sexual advances, explicit or implicit requests for sexual favors, or verbal or physical sexual transgressions (e.g., sexual jokes or comments, unwanted touch). Committing sexual harassment is **implicitly unethical** and can result in **emotional damage**, such as emotional distress (e.g., fear, humiliation, anxiety, depression) among victims and fear of damage to their interpersonal relationships, reputation, or security – especially if committed by a person with **authority**. It can create a **hostile environment** for all involved. The legal implications of sexual harassment depend largely on the context in which it occurs. Most employers have internal disciplinary policies for **addressing sexual harassment**. For example, employers can demote or terminate harassers. Victims can also file charges with government and state agencies (e.g., the Equal Employment Opportunity Commission) to ensure that their employer adequately disciplines the harasser. In school settings, students are protected by **Title IX provisions** which prohibit sexual harassment; many school districts have clearly outlined consequences for sexual harassment. Victims of sexual harassment can sue harassers in civil court, but most acts of sexual harassment are not criminally punishable until they become sexual assault.

LEGAL AND ETHICAL IMPLICATIONS OF ACQUAINTANCE RAPE

Rape is forceful or nonconsensual sexual intercourse. **Force** refers to the exertion of physical or coercive tactics to overcome a person, and **consent** refers to clear, informed, reversible, and enthusiastic assent to sexual activity. **Acquaintance rape** describes nonconsensual penetrative sex that occurs between a perpetrator and victim who know each other. Although rape is often committed by an attacker whom the victim knows, acquaintance rape is far **less likely to be reported** than rape involving strangers. Victims may experience emotional distress, embarrassment, or self-blame. They may fear not being believed by others who know both the rapist and the victim. Since victims may have a **preexisting personal bond** with their attacker, they may avoid reporting their experience to keep their attacker safe or prevent conflict among their mutual connections. As with other forms of rape, victims may be subject to **secondary victimization**—implying that a victim is partially or entirely responsible for the outcome (also known as **victim blaming**), which can affect emotional wellbeing and reporting. Rape is a criminal offense, and the severity of the punishment depends on the victim's age and the use of violence or substances to override consent.

LEGAL AND ETHICAL IMPLICATIONS OF STATUTORY RAPE

Statutory rape is sexual intercourse between an adult and a person under the **age of consent**—the age at which an individual is competent to consent to sexual activity. It can refer to chronological age or mental age. Statutory rape is considered rape because a minor is **legally incapable of consenting** to sexual activity, thus the sexual act is deemed **coercive**. Consequences of statutory rape may include poor emotional wellbeing among victims (e.g., depression, low self-esteem, anxiety), loss of sense of security and safety, and disrupted capacity to form healthy, trusting interpersonal relationships. Statutory rape laws are intended to protect victims from overt abuses of power and authority. It is a criminal offense; however, criminal punishments for statutory rape vary from state to state since each state defines age of consent differently. The victim and perpetrator's age and the act committed determine the severity of the punishment. For example, nonforcible sexual activity that occurs between two partners—one 18 and the other 17—will carry a far lesser sentence than rape of an individual under the age of 13 by an adult in a position of authority.

LEGAL AND ETHICAL IMPLICATIONS OF SEXUAL ABUSE

Sexual abuse describes any coercive or forceful sexual activity by one person upon another that occurs **without consent**; it includes but is not limited to groping or unwanted touching, rape and attempted rape, refusing condoms or access to contraception, threat or pressure by one person to engage in sexual activity, sexual contact with someone incapable of consent (e.g., unconscious or on drugs/drugged), and purposeful transmission or nondisclosure of STIs. The trauma that results from sexual abuse can lead to a number of **adverse mental health outcomes** like depression, anxiety, and PTSD. Those who experience sexual abuse are far more likely to develop substance abuse and attachment issues. Children who experience sexual abuse are twice as likely to experience intimate partner violence and sexual abuse in adulthood. As with other forms of sexual assault, victims may experience **secondary victimization** by their peers or institutions whom they confide in. Since sexual abuse is broadly defined, the legal implications of sexual abuse vary. Acts such as rape and child sexual abuse carry severe criminal punishment, while unwanted touching or nonconsensual sharing of personal sexual images have few, if any, legal ramifications.

> **Review Video: Ethical and Professional Standards**
> Visit mometrix.com/academy and enter code: 391843

Sexually Transmitted Diseases

CHLAMYDIA

Chlamydia is a bacterial sexually transmitted disease. It can be **spread** through penetrative sex (e.g., vaginal, anal), oral sex, and transmitted to an infant during birth. Typically, those with chlamydia experience **no or mild symptoms**; however, symptoms can include painful urination and sex, abdominal pain, abnormal discharge, and bleeding between menses. **Rectal infections** may cause soreness, anal discharge, or bleeding. **Antibiotics** are used to treat chlamydia. If chlamydia is untreated, the bacteria can ascend into a woman's reproductive organs (e.g., uterus, fallopian tubes) and cause **pelvic inflammatory disease** (PID) and accompanying infertility. Women with chlamydia are at higher risk of scarring in their fallopian tubes and **ectopic pregnancies**—a pregnancy that occurs outside of the uterus (i.e., in the fallopian tube, abdomen, ovary, or cervix). Using condoms and dental dams and having few sexual partners can **reduce one's risk** of contracting chlamydia, but the most effective way to prevent transmission is through abstinence. Sexually active individuals should get regularly tested for STIs.

GONORRHEA

Gonorrhea is a bacterial sexually transmitted disease that can be **treated** with antibiotics. It is **spread** through semen and vaginal fluids during penetrative and oral sex. Pregnant women may also pass gonorrhea to their infants during childbirth. Similar to chlamydia, gonorrhea can present **without symptoms**. In fact, most women have no symptoms at all or have mild symptoms that are often mistaken for a bladder or yeast infection. Those who do have symptoms may experience painful urination, abnormal discharge, and bleeding between periods. **Rectal infections** can cause discharge, pain or soreness, and itching. If untreated, gonorrhea can spread to a woman's reproductive organs and cause PID. This may result in infertility, ectopic pregnancy, or chronic pain. A person with gonorrhea is at **higher risk** of contracting or spreading HIV (Human Immunodeficiency Virus), since having an STI like gonorrhea, herpes, and syphilis alters one's genital, rectal, and oral cell lining–making it easier for the virus to infect its host. The best way to prevent and minimize risk of gonorrhea is through abstinence, condom use, and regular STI testing.

HIV

Human Immunodeficiency Virus (HIV) is a sexually transmitted virus that has **no cure**. The virus infects and destroys white blood cells called **helper T cells** and severely limits the immune system's ability to fight disease. There are three stages of infection: acute HIV infection, chronic HIV infection, and AIDS. **Acquired Immune Deficiency Syndrome (AIDS)** refers to the final and most severe stage of HIV. AIDS occurs when the body no longer has enough T cells to fight off illness effectively, usually ending in death due to illnesses that the body could have otherwise fought off. The virus remains contagious throughout each stage. HIV is transmitted through certain bodily fluids—blood, semen, vaginal fluids, breast milk, and anal mucous. One can **contract** HIV through penetrative sex, shared needles, pregnancy/childbirth, breastfeeding, or contact with infected fluids via open cuts or sores. HIV can be managed through **antiretroviral therapy** (ART), which reduces the viral load, slowing the progression and minimizing risk of transmission. HIV prevention includes abstinence, condom use, regular STI testing, and **pre-exposure prophylaxis** (PrEP) or **post-exposure prophylaxis** (PEP). PrEP and PEP induce antibody production to prevent transmission and reduce risk of transmission after exposure, respectively.

Contraception

METHODS OF CONTRACEPTION

Contraception refers to various methods aimed at preventing **conception**—the fertilization of an egg by sperm. **Long-acting reversible contraception** (LARC) include hormonal or copper intrauterine devices (IUDs) and arm implants. Hormonal IUDs and implants release **progestin**—synthetic progesterone that prevents egg release and fertilization by thickening cervical mucous and thinning the uterine lining—into the bloodstream. Copper IUDs inhibit sperm movement to prevent entry into the uterus. **Hormonal contraception** refers to shots, patches, oral tablets, and rings used to prevent pregnancy; they include progestin-only or combined hormonal contraception (i.e., containing both estrogen and progestin). Both prevent fertilization by thickening cervical mucous and thinning the uterine wall to make it more challenging for sperm to travel to the egg and implant. **Barrier methods** like male and female condoms, diaphragms, sponges, and spermicides block and kill sperm. Permanent contraception refers to **tubal ligation**—closing the fallopian tubes to prevent fertilization—and **vasectomies**—blocking the supply of sperm to semen. **Abstinence** and natural methods (e.g., **fertility awareness-based methods or FAM, withdrawal,** and **breastfeeding**) can also be used to prevent pregnancy.

HORMONAL CONTRACEPTIVES

Combined hormonal contraceptives can make periods lighter and shorter, reduce risk of uterine or ovarian cancer, reduce acne, and minimize period symptoms caused by fibroids and endometriosis. **Progestin-only hormonal contraceptives** can reduce or stop menstrual bleeding and unlike combined hormonal contraceptives do not increase the risk of heart disease, blood clots, or high blood pressure. They are best for those who are sensitive to estrogen. Most hormonal contraceptives ease menstrual symptom and duration. No hormonal contraceptive protects against STIs. **Oral tablets** are 91% effective. They must be taken at the same time every day, so they may be troublesome for forgetful people. **Implants**—small rods inserted in the arm—are 99% effective. They last about three years and are removed easily. **Injections** are given every three months, so they are a good option for those who prefer a long-acting contraception. They are 94% effective, but they may cause weight gain and bone loss. **Vaginal rings and patches** last approximately one month and are 91% effective. Similar to implants and injections, rings and patches do not interrupt sex but can be less effective if not put in/on correctly. Patches may cause skin irritation and are visible.

LONG-ACTING REVERSIBLE CONTRACEPTION AND BARRIER METHODS

LARCs can remain in one's uterus for up to twelve years and can be easily taken out. They do not impact fertility once removed and can be used as a form of emergency contraception. They are 99.2-99.9% effective, depending on the type. Hormonal IUDs can reduce menstrual bleeding and symptoms (e.g., cramps, anemia), but they may result in **secondary amenorrhea**—the absence of a previously regular period. **Copper IUDs** contain no hormones and cause no amenorrhea. Although very rare, LARCs may cause PID or ectopic pregnancy, and most people experience temporary pain during insertion. LARCs do not protect against STIs. In general, **barrier methods** are less effective at preventing pregnancy than LARCs or hormonal contraception; however, some can prevent STIs (e.g., condoms) and do not affect menstruation. Most require no prescription and are an effective alternative for breastfeeding women and those who are sensitive to hormonal contraceptives. However, barrier methods are only effective at preventing pregnancy if correctly used each time. Some can cause **genital irritation** (e.g., spermicide, sponge, latex condoms) or **toxic shock syndrome** (e.g., cervical cap, diaphragm, sponge). The effectiveness of barrier methods ranges from 73-86%.

NATURAL METHODS AND PERMANENT CONTRACEPTION

Fertility-based awareness methods (FAM) refers to tracking the number of days that one is fertile or infertile to prevent pregnancy. FAMs are no-cost and involve no devices or medications to prevent pregnancy. However, they do not protect against STIs and are only 76-88% effective. **Withdrawal**—otherwise known as the pull-out method—describes the removal of the penis from the vagina before ejaculation. It is typically 78% effective at preventing pregnancy but does not protect against STIs. Exclusive **breastfeeding** prevents ovulation and induces lactational amenorrhea. It can be just as effective as hormonal contraceptives (~98%) but does not protect against STIs and requires that one breastfeeds every 4-5 hours to be effective. **Abstinence** is 100% effective at preventing pregnancy and STIs. **Permanent contraception** (e.g., sterilization via tubal ligation and vasectomy) are surgical procedures that prevent pregnancy. **Sterilization** is 99% effective at preventing pregnancy and is hormone-free. However, sterilization is expensive, invasive, irreversible, and not protective against STIs.

Community Health

COMMON COMMUNITY HEALTH PROBLEMS

The extent of poverty and access to health care services can lead to community health problems like poor nutrition, violence, and unplanned pregnancy. **Community poverty** is associated with distribution of wealth and resources, access to economic opportunity and livable wages, and quality of educational opportunities. Limited financial security can lead to hunger and food insecurity among families, which is associated with **poor nutrition** and **poor health outcomes**. Limited job opportunities and poor academic attainment associated with community poverty can increase the risk of participation in/exposure to **crime and violence** and **unplanned pregnancy**. Limited proximity to health care facilities and providers can influence a community's **access to health care**. Inadequate access to care may result in **poor health education** and promotion, poor health literacy, and insufficient delivery of care. Thus, community members may be **more susceptible to health problems** like poor nutrition and unplanned pregnancy.

ADDRESSING COMMON COMMUNITY HEALTH PROBLEMS

Upstream solutions (e.g., policy changes, access to affordable housing, and adequate education) that **improve the social determinants of health** are the most effective way to address poor health outcomes; however, they are also often **most expensive and time-consuming strategy**.

Community programs like violence prevention awareness campaigns and drug abuse prevention and treatment programs can address community health problems. **Violence prevention awareness campaigns** can provide information to the broader community on the signs and symptoms of violence or abuse and identify resources to escape violence. Similarly, **drug abuse prevention programs** may provide education on the different types of drugs, their effects, and the consequences of drug misuse/abuse. They may also provide helpful information on confronting a friend or family member who is misusing drugs. Both awareness campaigns and prevention programs **empower and motivate individuals** to avoid behaviors that lead to common health problems. Community **drug abuse treatment programs** provide affordable and accessible health care to reduce risk of drug related illness, injury, or death.

INFLUENCES ON INDIVIDUAL AND COMMUNITY HEALTH
MEDIA MESSAGES

Media messages can **negatively and positively influence** health behaviors and health outcomes. The validity of information delivered through media—television, social media, radio, newspapers, etc.—is not always **verified**. The spread of false or inaccurate information and the messages' deliverer can change or reinforce individuals' health beliefs and practices. For example, false reports and health claims by influential individuals about the origin of the COVID-19 virus, its mode of transmission, and its vaccine efficacy influenced many Americans to discriminate against Asian Americans, renounce masks, and refuse vaccination. As a result, the US experienced a surge in violent crimes against Asian Americans, COVID-19 infections and deaths, and hospitalization rates. However, media messages can also be **powerful tools to improve health outcomes**. Media can be used to **spread valid and verified information quickly and communicate tailored messages effectively to different groups of people**. The anti-smoking truth campaign utilized many different forms of media to elicit a response and shift public opinion of tobacco. It influenced individuals, specifically youth, to reject tobacco and mobilized communities to enact programs and policies aimed at curbing tobacco use.

TECHNOLOGICAL ADVANCES

Technological advances have significantly **improved health care** precision, delivery, access, and use. Technological advances have improved physicians' ability to accurately diagnose illness or injury (e.g., MRI, genetic testing) and perform minimally invasive and low-risk procedures (e.g., robotic-assisted surgery, endoscopy cameras). **Health care delivery and accessibility** is also improved through technological advances. For example, telehealth and telemedicine provide opportunities for patients to receive care remotely. Various applications and platforms allow patients to **track symptoms or bodily function** (e.g., diabetes testing, symptom tracking) and **order prescription medication** directly to their homes. Technological advances have also improved the ability of epidemiologists to **monitor and track infectious disease**, as well as **measure the occurrence of chronic disease**. As a result, they can mitigate disease transmission and improve short and long-term health outcomes.

EFFECTS OF MANDATORY VACCINATIONS

Vaccinations are one of the **most effective** means of preventing disease spread. **Mandatory vaccinations** are not literally compulsory, but are vaccinations that are required as a condition of participating in certain jobs or attending school, with some exceptions. For example, the Polio vaccine and the MMR (Measles, Mumps, and Rubella) vaccine are required for children attending public schools. Those who refuse to comply or present proof of vaccination may be **barred from attendance**. However, **religious and medical exemptions** may preclude certain students from receiving a vaccine. Employer-mandated vaccinations and vaccine mandates for travel are largely dependent on **regional and state policy**. The immunity that one gains from vaccination can

reduce risk of injury or illness due to infectious diseases and disease-related deaths. **Mandatory vaccinations** increase vaccination rates among individuals, which can **reduce the risk of disease transmission**. Mandatory vaccinations, like the smallpox and polio vaccinations, are attributed with **disease eradication**. The improvements in health outcomes and reductions in disease spread are associated with **lower community mortality rates** and **reduced burden on community health care providers**.

EFFECTS OF WORKPLACE SAFETY REGULATIONS ON COMMUNITY HEALTH

Workplace safety regulations are implemented to protect the health and wellbeing of employees. They are intended to **minimize risk of harm or death** from accidents, work-related injuries, or exposure to hazardous materials. Minimizing injuries reduces individual and employer's expenses related to health care costs and productivity losses. The **Occupational Safety and Health Administration (OSHA)** is a federal agency that regulates safe working conditions through statute and regulation enforcement, inspections, compliance assistance, and training. They **impose workforce safety regulations** that require personal **protective equipment** (PPE) and **hazard prevention** (e.g., exposure limits, infectious disease protections, fall and accident prevention measures). Compliance with OSHA standards can also **protect the general public** from health hazards or accident risks. For example, regulations related to the prevention of infectious diseases (e.g., Hepatitis vaccine), monitoring of accidents (e.g., reporting injuries), and communicating hazards (e.g., using wet floor signs) help minimize exposure to illness or injury in public spaces.

Components of Nutrition

NUTRIENTS THE HUMAN BODY NEEDS TO FUNCTION

There are 6 main nutrients that the body needs to function: water, carbohydrates, protein, fat, vitamins, and minerals.

- **Water** regulates the body's temperature, transports nutrients to cells, and removes waste products.
- When **carbohydrates** are digested, they are broken down into glucose which is used to fuel the brain, heart, kidneys, and nervous system. They come from grains, fruit, starchy vegetables, and dairy.
- **Protein**, which helps build and repair the body's tissues, is found in meat, seafood, eggs, dairy, and beans.
- **Fats** or lipids produce energy for the body, insulate and protect vital organs, and support cell function. They are often found in foods like meat, dairy, nuts, seeds, and oils.
- **Vitamins** and **minerals** can be found in many different food groups and carry out many tasks to keep the body functioning.

IMPORTANCE OF CALCIUM FOR BONE GROWTH

Calcium is a type of **mineral** that is most often associated with **bone and tooth health**. The body cannot make calcium, so it must consume calcium-rich foods like dairy milk and fortified plant-based milks (e.g., almond, oat, soy, rice milks), milk products like cheese and yogurt, canned fish with bones, leafy greens (e.g., broccoli, kale, mustard green, spinach), and legumes. Once digested, the body deposits the calcium in the **bones**, where 99.5% of the total calcium in the body resides. Thus, calcium is crucial for bone and tooth growth, development, and maintenance. Calcium is also an important mineral for muscle relaxation and contraction, blood clotting, blood pressure, and nerve functioning. Without enough calcium in the diet, the body will remove calcium from where it is stored in the bones, which can lead to **weak and fragile bones**.

IMPORTANCE OF IRON FOR RED BLOOD CELLS

Iron is a type of **mineral** that is primarily necessary for **transporting oxygen** around the body. It makes up a large part of **hemoglobin**, which is a substance in the red blood cells that carries oxygen from the lungs to the rest of the body. Iron is found in two forms: heme and non-heme. **Heme iron** comes from animal flesh (meat, poultry, seafood), while **non-heme iron** is found in plant-based sources like grains, seeds, legumes, leafy greens, and nuts. Without iron, the body is unable to make enough healthy oxygen-rich red blood cells to deliver oxygen to all parts of the body. This can cause fatigue and a weakened immune system. Individuals at **higher risk of iron deficiency** include menstruating or pregnant women, children, and kidney dialysis patients.

IMPORTANCE OF VITAMIN A FOR VISION

Vitamin A (also called retinol or retinoic acid) is a **fat-soluble vitamin** that can be found in many foods. Although both are organic substances that are made by plants or animals, **fat-soluble vitamins** do not dissolve in water, while **water-soluble vitamins** dissolve in water. The resulting effect is that fat-soluble vitamins are stored in the body's tissues; high and frequent intake can lead to accumulation of vitamins in body tissues that lead to toxicity. Vitamin A is crucial for **vision and eye health**. Specifically, it helps the eye see in low-light conditions, protects the cornea (the outermost layer of the eye), and lubricates the eye. Vitamin A assists in producing and distributing T-cells to protect the body from infection. There are two different sources for vitamin A: preformed vitamin A and provitamin A carotenoids. **Preformed vitamin A** can be found in fish, organ meats like liver, dairy products, and eggs. **Provitamin A carotenoids** are plant pigments that the body converts into vitamin A inside of the liver. They are highest in yellow, orange, and red fruits and vegetables.

Dietary Practices

COMPONENTS OF A WELL-BALANCED DIET

There are **6 essential nutrients** that the body needs to function properly: carbohydrates, protein, fat, vitamins, minerals, and water. Although **calorie requirements** differ by age, sex, activity levels, and weight goals, a well-balanced diet consists of meals that contain appropriately proportioned amounts of the six essential nutrients.

- **Carbohydrates** should make up most of the diet (60%), since they meet most of the body's energy needs.
- Because **protein** is vital to repairing cells and tissue, approximately 25% of daily calories should be derived from it.
- **Fats** are also a major source of energy and vitamins and should provide 15% of daily calories.
- Fruits and vegetables are important sources of **vitamins** and **minerals**.
- Drinking at least 8 cups of water per day can satisfy requirements for **water consumption**.

The best way to achieve a **well-balanced diet** is through A) minimizing consumption of refined simple carbohydrates (sucrose and glucose), saturated and trans fats, and salt, and B) eating a diet rich in foods like whole grains, lean protein, unsaturated fats, and fruits and vegetables.

HEALTHY VS. UNHEALTHY DIETARY PRACTICES

Healthy dietary practices include healthy weight management and regular eating patterns. These include meeting appropriate caloric and nutritional needs for health goals, drinking sufficient amounts of water, and avoiding foods that are high in calories from sugar, fat, and sodium. **Unhealthy dietary practices** are exemplified by frequent dieting or unhealthy weight management, obsessive or no exercise, and disordered eating (binge eating, purging, or restricting). **Fad diets**—diets that become popular for a short period of time and make unreasonable and unfounded claims for rapid weight loss—consist of many unhealthy dietary practices. They typically promote rapid weight loss, highly restrictive diets, and the consumption of nutritionally imbalanced foods. **Eating disorders** (e.g., anorexia nervosa, bulimia nervosa, binge eating, orthorexia) are also comprised of many unhealthy dietary practices like binge eating, skipping meals, avoiding specific foods, self-induced vomiting, laxative misuse, and use of diet pills. Dieting, especially fad dieting, is a significant predictor for developing an eating disorder. Understanding the progression of behaviors that lead to eating disorders or fad dieting is crucial in preventing them.

INFLUENCE OF DIET ON PERSONAL HEALTH

A **healthy diet** is important for maintaining physical, mental, and social wellbeing. Eating well-portioned nutritious whole foods can positively impact the body. For example, eating plenty of fruits and vegetables, whole grains, nuts, and lean meats is associated with improved blood pressure levels, inflammation, and insulin sensitivity. Eating the appropriate number of calories for a person's age and physical activity level can improve energy levels and sleep quality—both integral to weight management. Positive moods and mental clarity are associated with healthy eating patterns (i.e., eating when hungry and stopping with satisfied). Healthy dietary practices and good nutrition are also linked with positive social development and friendliness among children.

CONTRIBUTION OF USDA'S FOOD PYRAMID AND MYPLATE TOOLS

Developed by the US Department of Agriculture (USDA), the **Food Pyramid** is a visual representation of the types and suggested quantities of foods that individuals should eat to satisfy their daily nutritional requirements. Although categories are depicted both horizontally and vertically, foods are positioned in the pyramid based on the **recommended servings per day**. Grains, fruits, and vegetables are located at the **base** of the pyramid, and meat, dairy, and fats are located at the **top** of the pyramid. The USDA also uses the **MyPlate tool** as another visual representation of a plate to illustrate what constitutes a healthy meal. The plate is separated into four groups—fruits, vegetables, protein, and grains—with a small circle to the right of the plate to represent dairy. Unlike the food pyramid, fats and sugars are omitted from the MyPlate. Both of these tools show how eating balanced meals is important to sustaining a healthy diet.

Dietary Choices

INFLUENCE OF FOOD LABELS AND PROMOTIONAL CLAIMS

Food labels are located on most packaged foods. The nutrition facts label is required to be on each food package to help buyers make quick and informed food choices. It breaks down the number of calories, carbohydrates, fiber, protein, and vitamins per serving of food, which makes it easier to read and evaluate nutritional information and compare the nutrition among similar foods. Although food labels contain key information about a food's serving size, nutritional information, and ingredients, they can be difficult to interpret without sufficient knowledge about nutrition. **Front-of-package labels (FOP)** include symbols or graphics that feature the product's favorable nutritional aspects (e.g., lower in calories) but omit less favorable aspects (e.g., high in saturated fats). These labels tend to **overrate** how healthy a product is and can **mislead** buyers if they do not also read the nutrition facts label. Additionally, promotional claims about a product's health benefits are often featured on the front of products. They highlight the health benefits of the food, but can also mislead buyers about the overall healthfulness of a product.

FACTORS INFLUENCING NUTRITION AND CALORIE REQUIREMENTS

Nutritional and caloric requirements vary based on factors related to age, activity level, and pregnancy status. **Metabolism** decreases with age as the body's ability to digest and absorb nutrients slows down. As a result, overall energy requirements decrease throughout the lifespan. However, although older adults need fewer calories, they require similar or higher nutrient needs compared to younger adults because their nutrient absorption declines. Aging is also associated with **changes in physiology** that impact the ability to chew, swallow, and sense thirst or hunger. Nutritional requirements also differ based on the frequency, type, duration, and intensity of physical activity. Those who engage in **high levels of physical activity** require more carbohydrates, protein, and water than the average person to fuel the brain and muscles during exercise, build and repair muscles, and replenish fluids lost to sweat. **Pregnant individuals** require more calories and higher amounts of folic acid, iron, calcium, and vitamin D to promote healthy fetal development.

FACTORS INFLUENCING FOOD CHOICES

There are many different factors that influence food choices.

- **Cultural background** can contribute to which foods you eat and how they are prepared. For example, individuals who adhere to Hinduism believe that the cow is a sacred animal and do not consume beef.
- **Family eating patterns** have a significant influence on food choices. During childhood, meals are prepared and eaten with family members. From these interactions, children observe eating behaviors, food selection patterns, and food preferences that shape their eating habits.
- **Peer behaviors** also have a sizable influence on food choices, especially as the degree to which parental influence on food choices diminishes with age. Children's desire to fit in with their peers contributes to the adoption of new food choices and preferences.
- **Food advertising** is intended to influence food choices through a variety of media, especially in children and adolescents. There are many advertising techniques that food and beverage companies use to influence food choices. These may include inflated claims about a product's health and nutrient content, appealing songs or catchphrases, celebrity endorsements, and promotional discounts. They may also use targeted techniques to attract children, such as free toys or prizes, cartoon characters, and colorful packaging.

MAKING HEALTHY FOOD CHOICES

Mindful eating is a strategy for making healthy food choices that consists of focusing on one's sensory awareness and the experience of eating. Practices include heeding **signs and signals** from the body (i.e., stomach growls or low energy) rather than eating to quell feelings of sadness or boredom, eating foods that make a person feel healthy and energized rather than those that are emotionally comforting, and avoiding eating while multitasking. Keeping a **daily food journal** is also an effective and motivating strategy for making healthy food choices. By writing down what one eats and their emotional state when they eat each meal, individuals are better able to understand their eating habits. Planning and preparing meals in **advance** is an effective way to make sure that meals are balanced and reflect healthy food choices. It eliminates impulsive eating patterns and promotes mindful eating.

DIETING, EXERCISING, AND MAINTAINING A HEALTHY WEIGHT

Physical activity and healthy eating are essential to achieving and maintaining a **healthy weight**. The amount and type of exercise needed depends in part on an **individual's health goals**. For example, one may participate in cardiovascular—also called **aerobic and endurance**—exercise to lose weight (e.g., running, swimming, biking), or **anaerobic exercise** to strengthen muscles and improve bone health (e.g., weightlifting). Healthy eating is a long-term strategy to achieve a healthy weight characterized by balance and moderation, while dieting consists of restricting or limiting calories or certain foods. Dieting often takes place in combination with exercise to reduce weight among obese and overweight people. An individual is able to maintain a healthy weight by eating diverse foods in the required quantity for their health goals and exercise practices.

Health Hazards and Factors that Contribute to Safety Concerns

BIOLOGICAL AND CHEMICAL HAZARDS TO HEALTH AND SAFETY

Biological hazards (e.g., viruses, bacteria) and chemical hazards (e.g., non-biological substances like acids) can be found in the home, school, and community. **Biological hazards** like bacteria and viruses are **transmitted** through contaminated objects, droplets, or contact and can spread disease among the residents of a school, home, or community. Poor or dated building infrastructure may contribute to **exposure** to various molds or materials like asbestos and lead, which can cause moderate to severe **allergic reactions** and the development or exacerbation of **asthma**. The risk of exposure to biological hazards increases in communities with high population density and high contact potential with wild animals or insects (e.g., ticks, bats, rodents). **Chemical hazards** may arise from use of **cleaning supplies**, **chemical agents** used in science labs, **mishandling of medications**, **lead exposure** from contaminated pipes or paint, **rodent control supplies** (e.g., super warfarin), or **carbon monoxide** leaks. If ingested or inhaled, chemical hazards can cause serious health problems.

ENVIRONMENTAL AND EQUIPMENT HAZARDS TO HEALTH AND SAFETY

Environmental hazards refer to natural conditions that cause adverse health effects and can impact the health and safety of a home, school, or community. These include **extreme weather** events like earthquakes, hurricanes, heat waves, freezes, blizzards, and floods. Environmental hazards can also result from **pollution** (e.g., oil spills, sewage leaks). **Equipment hazards** result from misuse or malfunctioning of a machine or device. Fires, electric shock, or drowning are unfortunate outcomes of equipment hazards. Fires may be caused by heat generating appliances (e.g., ovens, dryers) or electronics used for an extended amount of time, cooking mishaps (e.g., oil fires), faulty electrical wires, unattended candles or fires, and smoking. **Improper use of pool equipment or poor supervision** at pools and in bathtubs can lead to drownings, especially among those who are unable to swim or those who are incapacitated in or near water.

AVOIDING AND PREVENTING UNINTENTIONAL INJURIES
DRIVING AN AUTOMOBILE

Unintentional injuries refer to those that are not deliberate and are typically accidental. They can often be prevented by adherence to safety rules and precautions.

- **Following all traffic laws** pertaining to automobile safety can prevent unintentional injuries.
- **Staying alert and cautious** while driving can ensure that other drivers, bicyclists, or pedestrians who may not be attentive remain safe and free from injury.
- Proper and consistent **use of seatbelts and car seats** can protect all passengers from car accident-related injuries or fatalities.

- Practicing safe driving measures (e.g., maintaining a **safe speed**, keeping a **safe distance between cars**) and abstaining from erratic driving behavior can prevent unintentional injuries while driving an automobile. Additionally, avoiding alcohol or substance use before/while driving can prevent injury or death.
- **Limiting distracted driving**—any activity that limits the driver's focus and attention (e.g., texting or talking on the phone, eating or drinking, using a music player or navigation device)—can help keep all passengers safe from unintentional injury.

BICYCLING

Similar to drivers, it is imperative that all bicyclists **adhere to local traffic laws** to prevent unintentional injury or fatality. Individuals should:

- Use hand signals, hand bells, or electronic devices to **signal their intention** to turn, pass, or brake.
- **Bike in a predictable manner** (e.g., no weaving or abrupt stops) and avoid substance use while biking.
- Since bicycles are often harder for automobile drivers to see, it is important that riders **exercise caution** on shared roads and **stay alert**. To stay alert, bicyclists should refrain from using cellular or navigation devices and listening to music. Staying alert while riding can also prevent injury that may occur from objects in the road, stationary objects, potholes, uneven surfaces, etc., that can cause a rider to lose control of their bicycle.
- **Using traffic lanes designated for bicycles** or sidewalks can prevent injury that may occur from sharing lanes with motor vehicles.
- W**ear protective gear** (e.g., helmets, protective glasses) and reflective gear to protect themselves and maximize their visibility while on the road.
- Bicycles should be appropriate for the rider's height and weight, and should receive regular maintenance to prevent unintentional injury.

SWIMMING

Prior to entering the water, it is important that one **learns how to swim** and/or properly wears a well-fitted **floatation device**. Individuals should:

- **Swim in supervised areas** patrolled by a lifeguard, and swim with or around another person whenever possible.
- **Obey all rules and safety regulations** and always make sure that it is safe to swim. Regardless of the location, swimmers should prepare to exit the water if thunder or lightning occurs. When at a natural body of water, swimmers should avoid swimming in fast-moving water or choppy waves. They should also practice caution when walking in the water as there may be submerged objects.
- **Enter water feet first** will protect swimmers from head or neck injuries associated with diving.
- **Refrain from alcohol or substance use** and swimming after eating to prevent unintentional drowning.
- Learn **resuscitation techniques** to prevent unintentional injury or death from drowning.

FATIGUE

Fatigue refers to drowsiness or tiredness; it can significantly impair one's motor functioning, concentration, and psychological health. It can result from reduced sleep duration and quality, strenuous or stressful work conditions, and long or demanding work hours. Those who are fatigued **may experience** mood changes, communication and processing delays, irritability, reduced concentration, diminished memory, and impaired decision making. Each of these traits can

increase the risk of injury as a person may exhibit irrational behavior and make poor or uncharacteristic choices. Fatigue is associated with **greater accident and injury rates** in fields like health care, emergency response, military, education, and manufacturing. Fatigue is also associated with **higher risk** of motor vehicle accidents, job error, poor productivity, and illness.

USE OF ALCOHOL AND DRUGS

An individual who engages in **risk-taking behavior** makes potentially harmful or hazardous choices that can endanger themselves or others. Examples of risk-taking behavior include substance use, dangerous or impaired driving, or unsafe sex. Those who make risky behaviors often make **impulsive**, thrill-seeking choices that place them at **high risk** of sustaining injury or injuring others. Use of alcohol and drugs **impairs** a person's **decision-making abilities** and **psychomotor functioning**, which can cause an individual to engage in risk-taking behavior and have poor control over their physical motions. Research shows that as alcohol consumption increases, an individual's function and inhibitions decrease while their tendency toward risky behavior increases. For example, an inebriated person may lack the ability to recognize how impaired they are and become increasingly confident that they can return home safely. While driving, they will likely experience delayed reaction time, poor concentration, and an inclination to drive erratically. Their behaviors increase their risk of self-injury or injury to others.

Personal Responsibility in Avoiding Risky Behaviors

PERSONAL RESPONSIBILITY IN PREVENTING INJURY

Although **unintentional injuries** may occur due to others' poor or risky choices, individuals should act responsibly to minimize and prevent the risk of injury. One should always try to understand and respect the **safety rules and expectations** of their school, workplace, etc. In doing so, they can **maximize safety** for all and prevent potential hazards that result from non-adherence. Each person has a right to **opt out** of unsafe or risky behavior, and it is the responsibility of all to ensure that everyone involved has the ability to **communicate their concerns or refusal**. Maintaining effective communication with others can ensure that all feel confident and comfortable to speak up when they feel their safety is threatened. An individual should **utilize refusal skills** to establish boundaries or guidelines for what they will or will not do in order to maintain safety. **Peer pressure** is a powerful and coercive force, yet individuals should **always reject participation** in unsafe behavior—despite its real or perceived consequences—and maintain common sense to avoid situations that could result in unintentional injury. **Awareness of personal risk** is important for preventing injury. This involves being alert and aware of one's surroundings and being mindful of situations that may put others at risk.

Risky behaviors	Harmful behaviors
Critical—Public or private criticism, purposefully humiliating the person.	Aggressive/Abusive—Any type of hitting, shoving, pushing, or physical violence.
Irresponsible/Immature—Constant problems (social, financial) and discord.	Controlling/Possessive—Attempts to control another person's life and to isolate the person from others.
Noncommunicative—Difficulty expressing feelings and being open with others.	Volatility—Unpredictable bouts of anger and rage.
Self-centered—thinks only in terms of personal needs.	Manipulative—Pressuring someone to do something or using guilt or threats to get one's way.

SAFE AND UNSAFE BEHAVIORS

The **leading cause of death** for individuals under the age of 44 in the United States is unintentional injury. **Infants** are extremely curious but have little to no concept of danger and lack motor functioning. Thus, they are at higher risk of choking or falling and need constant supervision from a caregiver. From ages 4-9, **young children** begin to learn about the concept of danger from others or past experience and improve their self-control, yet they still **lack a mature ability** to recognize dangerous situations and employ strategies to prevent injury. They also begin to **gain confidence**, which makes them more likely to engage in risky behavior without the knowledge of their own limitations. During **adolescence**, teenagers begin to exhibit risk-taking behavior due to **peer pressure** and **lack a clear sense of mortality**. They are at far more **risk for injury**, and their behavior can have **lasting implications** for their adult health (e.g., adolescent substance abuse and increased risk of cancer, addiction, or permanent injury).

RECOGNIZING AND AVOIDING POTENTIALLY DANGEROUS SITUATIONS

Maintaining personal safety requires that one recognize and avoid **potentially dangerous situations**. A potentially dangerous situation is any event or experience in which a hazardous or harmful outcome is possible, and the individual(s) involved feel uncomfortable or unsafe. A person can protect themselves from potentially dangerous situations by **avoiding areas where criminal activity often occurs** or those who engage in criminal activity. **Maintaining situational awareness**—the awareness of the physical and social happenings around a person—at all times can ensure that an individual **recognizes possible threats to safety** before they happen and takes actions to prevent them. Avoiding situations or crowds in which others begin to act aggressively or erratically can prevent a potentially dangerous situation from occurring.

PREVENTING AND RESPONDING TO DATING VIOLENCE

Dating violence refers to physical, emotional, or sexual abuse within a romantic relationship. An important first step to preventing dating violence is to **understand the characteristics of healthy/unhealthy relationships** and the early warning signs of intimate partner violence (e.g., excessive communication, jealous or controlling behavior, gaslighting). **Learning and practicing skills** to communicate effectively, manage emotions, and refusing behaviors that make one feel uncomfortable can reduce the risk of dating violence. Developing **positive relationship-building skills** and **self-respect** during childhood and adolescence can prevent the victimization or perpetration of dating violence. **Assertiveness and boundary setting** are effective strategies to respond to dating violence. Both encourage an individual to **advocate** for their needs and **respectfully decline** any unwanted activity or behavior. Educating communities on **bystander**

intervention can help individuals identify intimate partner violence and empower others to take action to support those affected.

PREVENTING AND RESPONDING TO GANG VIOLENCE

Gang violence refers to any violence—physical, emotional, sexual—committed by members of a gang (e.g., assault, rape, intimidation). Violence may be directed **internally** (e.g., initiation) or toward other gangs and innocent bystanders. The most effective way for a person to prevent gang violence is to **remove oneself from the threat of violence**. If possible, one should **avoid locations** where gangs have a strong presence and **avoid association** with gang members. They should **avoid engaging in criminal activity and exhibiting aggressive behavior** when in public or online that may incite violence. Establishing healthy relationships with others who are not affiliated with a gang or do not commit criminal acts can prevent an individual's exposure to gang violence. If inadvertently exposed to gang violence, one should respond by **leaving the situation** or **alerting emergency responders** or law enforcement. At the organizational and community-level, **early and collaborative intervention** by community groups, school staff, law enforcement, parents, and local government is necessary to address risk factors for gang initiation and violence.

PREVENTING AND RESPONDING TO HATE CRIMES

A **hate crime** is any violent act or criminal offense directed at a person because of their identity (e.g., race, ethnicity, religious affiliation, gender, sexuality, or disability). **Federal legislation** like the Matthew Shepard and James Byrd, Jr. Hate Crimes Prevention Act and the Emmett Till Anti-Lynching Act dictate that individuals who commit hate crimes may be liable to prosecution. Additionally, **state and local legislation** exists as a preventative and protective measure against hate crimes. If an individual experiences or witnesses a hate crime, it is important to **alert emergency responders and law enforcement** immediately. Victims and witnesses should respond with **caution** as offenders may exhibit violent behavior; however, it is important for bystanders to **de-escalate** the situation and support victims of hate crimes. **Education on hate crimes and its impacts** and **critical-thinking skills** are important preventative measures to address hate crimes. Those who are able to identify hate crimes and assess discriminatory speech, material, or actions may be better able to prevent and respond to it. Improving **media literacy** is also an important strategy for preventing hate crimes since they increasingly happen online.

Emergency Response Planning

HOME SAFETY PLANS

A **home safety plan** is a set of procedures and preventative measures intended to lower the risk of danger at home. Home safety plans can **minimize injuries or fatalities** and **provide a sense of security** among those who live in the home. When revisited and practiced routinely, home safety plans can **alleviate the confusion or chaos** that often accompanies breaches to home safety. A home safety plan typically includes an emergency contact list and a detailed checklist of what to do if an emergency happens. An **emergency contact list** may include numbers of caregivers, family members or friends, neighbors, and emergency responders; it is intended to improve communication in case of a safety concern. Home safety plans may also include a **detailed checklist** of what to do in response to an emergency or safety concern (e.g., fire, tornados, burglary, unknown visitors, injury, power outage). Home safety plans can also include a **list of important information** or tools located in the home. This list can include information regarding when to replace the batteries in smoke/carbon monoxide detectors, how to check home alarm systems, and the location of fire extinguishers and stockpiles of emergency supplies (e.g., extra food, water, first aid kit).

EMERGENCY RESPONSE PLANS

Emergency response plans include a set of procedures for unexpected threats to health and safety. It is similar to a home safety plan but includes **detailed information regarding emergency response and recovery**. Emergency response plans typically include an emergency contact list, a list of external emergency resources, responsibilities for each household member, evacuation plans, and important information about where to locate emergency supplies. An **emergency contact list** can include contact information for caregivers or other family members, friends, neighbors, and emergency response teams. It can also include a **list of resources** an individual can access in case of an emergency (e.g., natural disaster shelters). Emergency response plans can also include a **list of instructions** for responding to various emergencies (e.g., fires, sudden weather event, intruder). Emergency plans may also include **designated roles and responsibilities** necessary to ensure the safety of all (e.g., who will contact first responders, administer first aid, acquire the emergency supplies). Emergency response plans often include **evacuation plans**—diagrams of the safest and quickest exit routes—and emergency supplies information. The location and contents of emergency supplies (first aid kit, food, water, clothing) is often listed in an emergency response plan.

CPR

Cardiopulmonary Resuscitation (CPR) is a first aid procedure that is performed when an individual's heart stops beating—also known as **cardiac arrest**. CPR consists of chest compressions that restore blood flow to the rest of the body, and rescue breaths that allow the blood that is being circulated to be oxygenated. If administered correctly, a person's **chance of survival is 2-3 times higher** when they receive CPR. If a mouth mask is not available to provide rescue breaths for ventilation, mouth-to-mouth breaths are not recommended and instead, only chest compressions should be administered. This prevents the risk for infection. Regardless of the mode of CPR being administered, an AED should also be utilized to determine the heart rhythm, whether a shock may restore spontaneous circulation based on that rhythm, and (if a shock is warranted) deliver that shock. Considerations for these interventions include the following:

- **Hands only CPR** is the recommended method for the general public. Those performing hands only CPR should push hard and quickly on the person's chest—usually at a rate of 100-120 compressions per minute. The depth of the compression varies depending on the depth of the victim's chest.
- **CPR with mouth-to-mouth breaths** should be done at the ratio of 30 chest compressions and 2 breaths that result in chest rise, with compressions always starting first. Pulse checks should occur every 2 minutes for no longer than 10 seconds.
- Portable machines called automatic external defibrillators (AEDs) monitor heart activity and can administer an electric shock to the heart to force it to beat again when deemed necessary. This technology can be used by anyone, as it clearly directs each step of the process audibly, to include applying the chest pads, pausing CPR for rhythm checks, and either resuming CPR or clearing the patient for a shock, then resuming CPR.

CONSCIOUS CHOKING

A **conscious choking** person may be awake or reactive yet is unable to breathe, cough, or speak due to a foreign object lodged in their throat. Their skin and lips may begin to flush and turn blue. It is vital that first aid be administered immediately, since an **obstructed airway** can prevent oxygen from reaching the brain. If a person is no longer able to speak, cry, laugh, or cough forcefully, the rescuer can use the "five-and-five" method or the Heimlich maneuver to clear their airway. The **"five-and-five" method** consists of 5 back blows between the victim's shoulder blades with the palm of the hand and 5 abdominal thrusts. Back blows and abdominal thrusts should be repeated until the object is dislodged. The **Heimlich maneuver** is performed by a person standing behind

187

the victim, administering quick abdominal thrusts with a closed fist, until the object is dislodged. Those providing **choking first aid to infants** should administer thrusts with two fingers on the breastbone in a seated position and with the infant resting on their forearm. If at any point the victim becomes **unconscious**, the rescuer should begin performing CPR immediately until help arrives.

Legal and Illegal Drugs

CATEGORIZATION OF DRUGS

Drugs are substances that produce a psychological or physiological effect in the user. Drugs can be **categorized** by their effects as depressants, stimulants, hallucinogens, inhalants, and opioids.

- **Depressants** slow down or depress parts of the central nervous system (CNS), which can have a sedative and relaxing effect on users. Examples include alcohol, cannabis, and barbiturates.
- **Stimulants** activate the CNS, increasing users' heart rates and blood pressure and improving their alertness. Examples include cocaine, caffeine, methamphetamine, and Adderall. Nicotine, a compound found in tobacco, is considered both a depressant and stimulant.
- **Hallucinogens** affect an individual's perception of reality; they can influence sensory experiences and mood. Examples include LSD and psilocybin. Inhalants are drugs—often everyday household items—that cause brief euphoria when inhaled. Examples include aerosol sprays, gasoline, and nitrous oxide.
- **Opioids/opiates** are highly addictive drugs—also referred to as **narcotics**—that are used to treat pain and incite feelings of euphoria. The term "opiates" is often used interchangeably with "opioids," but opiates (e.g., opium, morphine, heroin) refers to drugs extracted from plants while opioids (e.g., oxycodone, fentanyl) are often synthetic.

The category that a drug is placed in has no influence on its legality nor how it is ingested.

LEGAL VS. ILLEGAL DRUGS

Legal drugs are lawfully prescribed and used, whereas possessing, selling, and using **illegal drugs** is considered unlawful and carries strict penalties depending on the drug class. For example, possession of drugs that are **highly addictive** and carry a higher potential for abuse like opioids carry a much heavier criminal penalty than possession of alcohol by an underage individual. Additionally, possession and use of some drugs without authorization (e.g., prescription) and use of some drugs in public or unauthorized spaces is illegal. A drug's legality does not make it any less addictive or harmful to the individual ingesting it. For example, legal substances like alcohol and tobacco can be very addictive and have a high risk of harm. Some drugs are legal for those with a prescription but illegal for those without, such as some stimulants (e.g., Ritalin), steroids, some opioids (e.g., morphine, oxycodone), and some depressants (e.g., Xanax). **Common illegal drugs** are stimulants like cocaine, depressants like cannabis, narcotics/opiates like heroin, and hallucinogens like LSD. **Over-the-counter drugs** and herbal supplements are legal and mostly accessible to all yet can carry a high risk of harm if overconsumed (e.g., Aspirin) or unregulated (herbal supplements).

SHORT-TERM EFFECTS OF DRUGS

Short-term effects of the appropriate use of prescribed drugs can alleviate health ailments, but their **misuse** (e.g., exceeding recommended doses, unauthorized use) can result in serious complications. Effects can also differ by the type of drug that an individual takes. **Short-term**

physical effects of **depressants and opioids** are feelings of drowsiness, lethargy, hypoventilation, and potential unconsciousness. **Stimulants** may cause increased blood pressure and heart rate. The altered perception of reality that **hallucinogen** users experience may increase their risk of serious bodily harm. **Short-term psychological effects** vary. **Stimulant and hallucinogen** abuse can cause hyperfocus, irritability, or paranoia. Some drugs—specifically, those that induce feelings of euphoria—produce a neurochemical reaction that releases excessive amounts of dopamine from the brain. **Dopamine depletion** can lead to depression and emotional numbness following drug use. Misuse or abuse of drugs can alter one's mental state, which can result in erratic behavior or poor decision-making and **social effects**. Their behavior may deter those around users and **alienate** them from their friends and family. The emotional impacts paired with undesirable physical sensations from hangovers or withdrawals can prompt an individual to use again to ease the symptoms.

LONG-TERM EFFECTS OF DRUGS

Chronic use of drugs can increase their addictive potential and cause internal organ damage. **Long-term physical effects** of **stimulants** include cardiovascular disease and dopamine depletion. Long term physical effects of **depressants** include chronic fatigue and respiratory distress. Depressant withdrawal—specifically, alcohol and benzodiazepine withdrawal—following heavy abuse is especially dangerous, as it can lead to seizures, hallucinations, delirium tremens, and even death. Beyond opioids' high addiction potential, long-term effects of **opioids** include brain and liver damage. The ingestion method can also have long-term effects. Drugs that are inhaled (e.g., tobacco, cannabis) can cause respiratory complications and cancer. Drugs that are **snorted** can cause permanent damage to the nose, and drugs that are **injected** can cause collapsed veins and heart and blood vessel injections. **Hallucinogens** can cause **psychological effects** like persistent psychosis and disturbing flashbacks that can impact a person's emotional wellbeing. Long-term psychological effects of persistent **stimulant** use include dopamine depletion-induced depression, poor emotional and impulse regulation, memory loss, and paranoia. Since addicted drug users tend to be more irritable, secretive, and prone to isolation, their social relationships often become strained. Other long-term **social effects** include failed role obligations and estrangement from family members or friends.

LONG-TERM EFFECTS OF DRUGS ON PREGNANT WOMEN AND ADOLESCENTS

Drug use during **pregnancy** can impact the **short and long-term health** of both the mother and the fetus. Illicit drug use can result in **miscarriage** and **stillbirth**. It may also result in birth defects, sudden infant death syndrome (SIDS), or a number of developmental disabilities. Mothers who use **intravenous drugs** are at **higher risk** of developing HIV and other bloodborne diseases, which can be passed along to their fetus. Fetuses exposed to **alcohol** during pregnancy are at **higher risk** of birth defects, cognitive developmental disabilities, and emotional/behavioral problems. Mothers who **smoke** while pregnant may expose the fetus to hazardous chemicals and **raise the risk** of preterm birth or stillbirth. **Drug use** during pregnancy can also cause **infant withdrawal**, which can lead to serious health complications for the infant. Substance use during adolescence can increase users' risk of chronic mental health problems (e.g., depression, personality disorder, suicide), memory loss, proclivity to commit crimes, and developmental delays. Use of drugs during adolescence can also have significant impacts on relationships. Friends and families may struggle to support their loved one, which can place a strain on relationships.

ADDICTION

Addiction often results from chronic and frequent drug abuse; as one's **tolerance** for a drug increases, their physical and psychological **dependence** often grows. **Physical addiction** refers to one's **physiological need** to maintain the homeostatic function they have developed through repeated use. With chronic use, the body grows **accustomed** the presence of the substance and adapts its functions to accommodate. Chronic exposure to drugs can cause **neurophysiological and neurochemical changes** that affect the basal ganglia, extended amygdala, and prefrontal cortex. These changes impact one's ability to feel pleasure and make it more difficult to stop using or practice sound decision making. **Psychological addiction** refers to an individual's **drive** to use substances despite their negative consequences to biological, emotional, and psychosocial health. It often includes an accompanying impairment of judgment and insight. **Physical and psychological addiction are often interrelated**. A person's psychological addiction to a drug can be caused by their physical dependency, and their physical addiction can be reinforced or strengthened by a mental craving.

Chemical Dependency

Factors that contribute to **chemical dependency** are an individual's environment, genetics, mental health, and the manner of their drug use. Chemical dependency is strongly influenced by social environment, specifically **spheres of social influence** (e.g., peers, family). Peer and family drug practices and attitudes can impact an individual's decision to try and continue to use drugs. Another aspect of an individual's environment that contributes to chemical dependency is emotional turmoil from one's career. Those in **high-stress jobs** (e.g., military, medicine) may use drugs frequently to ease the anxiety and stress that can accompany their careers. According to a 2012 study in the journal Nature, **genetic heritability** of addiction ranges from 42-79%, depending on type of drug and gender. **Mental health** disorders often contribute and co-occur with chemical dependency. Substance use may be used to cope with symptoms of psychiatric illness, and the dopamine rush from stimulants or dulling effect of depressants may ease emotional disturbances caused by mental illness. An individual's **drug of choice** can influence chemical dependency. Drugs with high addictive potential, like opioids, can lead to dependency much faster than other types of drugs.

Drug Use and Intervention

Factors Influencing Use and Abuse of Legal and Illegal Drugs
Home

- **Early exposure** to drugs by caregivers can make an individual more familiar with drugs, their effects, and how to procure them.
- **Regular use by caregivers** or others whom the individual looks up to or admires may imply that drug use is acceptable or condoned behavior.
- **Presence of drugs** and easy accessibility to drugs in the home can increase one's risk of experimenting or regularly using drugs.
- **Poor caregiver involvement** and supervision can increase the risk of early drug use and addiction.
- **Family history of addiction** can increase one's risk of developing a substance abuse disorder.
- **Early use of drugs** can alter an individual's brain development to make them more prone to drug addiction.
- The **quality of an individual's relationships** with family members can be both a risk and protective factor. Those who grow up in hostile or abusive environments and/or have poor relationships with their family members are more likely to develop drug addiction.

School and Community

An individual's **peers** at school and in the community can **significantly influence** their decisions to try or regularly use drugs. Pressure from peers and peers' favorable attitudes towards drugs may lead to **early initiation** of drug use and sustained use. The **accessibility and availability** of drugs in one's community can also impact their decision to use drugs. Although no causal relationship exists between poverty and drug use, those who experience **poverty** are more likely to develop drug addiction. One explanation for this is that individuals living in impoverished communities may have greater exposure to drugs than those living in wealthier areas. Since **educational attainment** is a protective factor for drug abuse, under-resourced schools with little academic support for students may fail to adequately intervene. Bullying and gang activity are also risk factors for drug use, so schools without sufficient drug, gang, or bullying policies and intervention programs could influence one's drug use/abuse.

PREVENTING THE USE AND ABUSE OF LEGAL AND ILLEGAL DRUGS

The most effective strategy for preventing the use and abuse of drugs is **abstinence**. An individual with well-developed **refusal skills** may be better prepared to refrain from trying drugs, especially when confronted with peer pressure. **Establishing healthy relationships with non-users** and developing a strong and supportive network can prevent individuals from using or abusing drugs. A strong **knowledge of the effects of drugs, addiction risk factors** (family history, mental illness), and **how substance abuse develops** may prevent drug use and abuse. Those with mental illness can prevent drug use/abuse by **seeking mental health care**. Mental health professionals can work with patients to develop healthy **coping skills** and provide guidance or assistance in identifying drug use prevention resources. Since stress can be a contributor to drug use or abuse, developing **stress management skills** can help prevent drug use. Since drug abuse can develop from a growing tolerance and overuse of prescribed medications, maintaining **one's physical health** is also important for preventing drug use.

PROMOTING INDIVIDUAL RESPONSIBLE DRUG USE

Responsible drug use describes use that **minimizes harm** for the individual and others. **Designated driver programs** promote the use of sober drivers to safely shuttle intoxicated passengers home. Typically, the designated driver **abstains from drinking** at a social event in order to drive themselves and their friends safely. For illicit drugs, individuals can **check the purity and strength** of the drugs they intend to ingest to make sure it is not unexpectedly laced or cut with anything. This can prevent unknown effects or overdose. Users can also **avoid mixing drugs** to avoid unknown or hazardous interactions. Harm reduction strategies are often implemented at the organizational and community-wide levels to prevent the spread of disease and encourage safe, responsible drug use. An example is **supervised injection sites** which gives users a safe location to inject drugs with sterile supplies without fear of injury or arrest. Users may also carry medication like Naloxone when using drugs to reverse opioid overdoses.

INTERVENTION AND TREATMENT METHODS FOR DRUG ABUSE

Addiction is considered a mental health disorder, so intervention and treatment often require the assistance and case management of a licensed professional. **Counseling and therapy** can prevent the escalation of drug use to abuse. **Behavioral interventions** can improve a user's **motivation** to change their behavior and grants them the skills necessary to increase their self-efficacy. Therapists or counselors can help identify any **underlying mental health disorders** or **abnormal thought patterns** that preceded the drug use or addiction. Counseling may consist of individual, family, or group sessions, and different styles of therapy may be used (e.g., cognitive behavior therapy, dialectical behavior therapy, motivational interviewing). Treatment is multifaceted and tailored for each person. Those with mild or moderate drug addiction may be able to seek treatment in **outpatient settings** (e.g., addiction specialist office, support group meetings), while those with severe addiction may require **inpatient** treatment (e.g., hospital, rehabilitation centers). **Supervised withdrawal** is used to safely treat those with moderate to severe addiction. It

Mometrix

describes the administering of medications to prevent severe, life-threatening symptoms of withdrawal. **Peer support groups** (e.g., Alcoholics Anonymous, Narcotics Anonymous, Self-Management and Recovery Training or SMART) may be used as both and intervention and treatment strategy.

CONFRONTING OR HELPING WITH ANOTHER PERSON'S SUBSTANCE ABUSE

Discussing one's concerns with a **substance use specialist**, medical professional, or counselor can help identify the most appropriate strategy for **confronting** another person's substance abuse. Seeking **mental health care** may also be helpful for the friend or loved one of a user, because one person's addiction can greatly impact others. A person who is experiencing substance abuse may **fail to recognize** their behaviors. **Sharing one's observations** and information about the signs and symptoms of abuse in a non-confrontational and considerate manner may be a helpful intervention strategy. It is important to provide those struggling with substance abuse with encouragement, reassurance, and praise. **Positive reinforcement** is key to sustaining motivation. Since those struggling with addiction are often exposed to unsafe conditions or environments, **developing a safety plan** with the user can be helpful for maintaining their physical health and safety. The safety plan can also consist of a list of identified individuals who can offer support if the user experiences temptation.

DRUG USE/ABUSE AND HEALTH AND SAFETY PROBLEMS

Since drugs may alter one's physical and psychological states, they can lead to a myriad of health and safety problems. The **loss of judgment and sound decision making** associated with drug use may result in non-use of contraception, which can lead to **unplanned pregnancies**. Poor decision making, slowed reaction time, the and propensity for risk taking that accompany drug use may result in **motor vehicle crashes** or other injuries. Some drugs, specifically depressants and opioids, can cause lethargy, numbness, or unconsciousness. This can cause life-threatening or fatal injuries. For example, if the user is operating heavy machinery, they may fall asleep and lose control of their vehicle or device. If the user is swimming, they may become too tired, fall unconscious, and drown. Use of drugs by injection can expose users to **diseases** like HIV and Hepatitis C, which are transmitted through exposure to blood of an infected person.

Promoting Drug-Avoidance Programs in the School and Community

ASSERTIVENESS, REFUSAL SKILLS, AND PEER PRESSURE

Although they may be reluctant, those who experience **peer pressure** are more likely to use drugs. The **desire to fit in or bond** with others and **avoid perceived embarrassment** may make it more difficult to say no. Therefore, **strong refusal skills** are crucial for building the confidence to advocate for oneself when faced with peer pressure. An individual who practices refusal skills may feel more comfortable expressing their feelings about substance use and resist insistent peers. Refusal skills can be practiced in different ways: saying no, using humor to deflect, suggesting another activity, showing concern, leaving the conversation, etc. **Assertiveness** is an effective strategy for clearly and respectfully communicating one's disinterest in using drugs and standing their ground when pressured. An assertive individual would maintain their refusal in a respectful and dignified way and use both verbal and body language to communicate to others. They may make sure that they are not judgmental of their peers' choices and refrain from being overly critical or disparaging.

SCHOOL-BASED EFFORTS TO ADDRESS HEALTH RISK BEHAVIORS

Health risk behaviors refer to factors that increase an individual's predisposition to poor health outcomes and raises a person's risk of harm or injury (e.g., tobacco and drug use, unprotected sex). Poor academic performance and lack of involvement in school activities can lead to health risk behaviors like drug use. Therefore, school-based efforts (e.g., tutoring, participation in after school activities, clubs, and leadership opportunities) to **address academic performance and commitment** can reduce the risk of drug use. Since unhealthy relationships and isolation can place an individual at risk of drug use/abuse, school-based efforts to improve the culture and connectedness among students and **educate students** about healthy relationships can be powerful intervention strategies. This can include anti-bullying and harassment initiatives or curriculum, opportunities for school bonding (e.g., school events, extracurricular activities), and positive behavioral incentive programs. Schools may also use **peer or adult mentorship programs** to connect students to a support network. Educational opportunities that speak to the dangers, pressures, and effects of drug use may help shift students' attitudes towards drug use.

COMMUNITY-BASED EFFORTS TO ADDRESS HEALTH RISK BEHAVIORS

Community-based efforts to address health risk behaviors related to drug use can be achieved through education, messaging, and resource identification. **Educational campaigns** that discuss the factors which contribute to drug abuse, the short and long-term effects of drug use, and resources for treatment can confront drug use at the community level. Educating community members on how to successfully navigate peer pressure and temptations through social skill development classes may help address drug use. A **community-wide anti-drug messaging campaign** can help **shift local norms** regarding drug use. If a community cohesively works together to change how drug use is perceived, they may be able to change attitudes and behaviors among users or potential users. It is important that **anti-drug messaging maintains respectful and non-judgmental** language to ensure that recipients do not experience shame or embarrassment. **Free programs** that occur during times when drug use risk is high (e.g., after school) can be powerful interventions since they decrease accessibility during key times. A readily accessible **compilation of resources** for drug users/abusers with information on where individuals can seek assistance or treatment may catalyze an individual's decision to stop using.

PROMOTING STUDENT PARTICIPATION

The most effective way to improve student participation in school-based and community-based efforts is to **include students in planning, implementing, and evaluating** efforts. If included, they are more likely to produce initiatives that reflect current student attitudes toward drugs. Their role may lead to more appropriate and effective efforts. Their stakeholder status is also likely to encourage their participation in the program and their promotion of the efforts to their peers. Providing opportunities for **student feedback** is important for ensuring participation. If students feel that their voices and opinions are **valued**, they may be **more likely to feel involved**. Participation in school and community-based efforts is more likely if **tactics that elicit fear or shame in recipients are not used**. Efforts that are accessible to **students** and their families and **provide incentives** are more likely to gain participation among students. For example, a program that occurs from the end of the school day to 6 p.m., provides a bussing option to students' homes, and provides food to students and their families will have greater participation than one that lets out at 4 p.m. with no food or transportation.

Chapter Quiz

Ready to see how well you retained what you just read? Scan the QR code to go directly to the chapter quiz interface for this study guide. If you're using a computer, simply visit the bonus page at **mometrix.com/bonus948/priihpeck5857** and click the Chapter Quizzes link.

Praxis Practice Test #1

Want to take this practice test in an online interactive format?
Check out the bonus page, which includes interactive practice questions and much more: **mometrix.com/bonus948/priihpeck5857**

1. The teacher consistently provides direct verbal and demonstrative feedback to beginning students. What is the purpose of using these feedback strategies?

 a. To diversify feedback delivery
 b. To help students practice the desired outcome
 c. To help students perfect the desired outcome
 d. To help students understand the desired outcome

2. Which of these resources for coordinated school health approaches includes information on the connection between school health and academic achievement and on school health assessment and planning?

 a. The Centers for Disease Control (CDC) Web site's Coordinated School Health Publications and resources page
 b. "School Health 101 Packets" offered by the National School Boards Association
 c. School health coordination guidelines from some state education departments
 d. The LISTSERV provided by the Comprehensive Health Education Network (CHEN)

3. Which of the following is an example of how emotional/behavioral factors can affect young children's levels of physical activity and fitness?

 a. A child diagnosed with ADHD is physically so overactive that he becomes exhausted.
 b. A child diagnosed with asthma needs monitoring for breathing problems in exercise.
 c. A child diagnosed with diabetes needs exercise watched and coordinated with diet.
 d. A child diagnosed with disabilities needs adaptive equipment for physical activities.

4. Regarding indications that a student should be evaluated to determine eligibility for adapted physical education (APE), which of the following (in addition to referral) correctly states a criterion?

 a. The student performs at his or her ability level in group settings but not on an individual basis.
 b. The student's social behaviors impede his or her or others' learning more than half of class time.
 c. The student has scored below average in at least one part of the state physical fitness test.
 d. The student scored at least one standard deviation low on the norm-referenced test used.

5. What type of communication might a person use to reinforce messages and information conveyed in his or her casual speech?

    a. Verbal communication
    b. Written communication
    c. Visual communication
    d. Nonverbal communication

6. A new teacher is planning health lessons for the school year. What is the recommended first step to ensure that his curriculum aligns with the school's academic expectations?

    a. Consult the Common Core standards for healthful living
    b. Refer to the Society of Health and Physical Educators (SHAPE America) national standards and grade level outcomes
    c. Review the National Commission for Health Education Credentialing (NCHEC) competencies
    d. Familiarize himself with district standards

7. Among fundamental movement skills (FMS), which two are both part of the same main category?

    a. Locomotor and manipulative
    b. Manipulative and rotation
    c. Rotation and balance
    d. Balance and stability

8. A spectator passes out during the football game and the CPR certified PE teacher is called to help. Which of the following steps should the PE teacher do first?

    a. call 911
    b. check the scene
    c. check for breathing
    d. start CPR

9. Which of the following is an equitable fitness assessment?

    a. standardized fitness testing
    b. standards-based fitness goals
    c. fitness reflection journals
    d. peer-assessments

10. What is a confounding variable in research?

    a. A characteristic that cannot be quantified
    b. A factor that distorts the relationships between the causes and effects of phenomena
    c. The condition that a researcher manipulates to produce a result
    d. The outcome of an experiment

11. Which of the following has been shown to foster lifelong physical activity?

    a. Competence in physical activities
    b. Modeling physical activity
    c. Participating in organized sports
    d. Having active parents

12. Which of the following practices is NOT an example of a population-level intervention to prevent chronic diseases?
    a. A local public health department launches a healthy eating campaign.
    b. A tobacco company prints warning labels on its products.
    c. A city votes to implement a soda tax.
    d. A group of coworkers form a running group that meets up twice a week to exercise.

13. Katherine felt her body over rotate during the shotput. Which of the following types of feedback describes Katherine's experience?
    a. knowledge of performance
    b. knowledge of results
    c. positive transfer
    d. negative transfer

14. The prefrontal cortex begins to mature during which developmental stage?
    a. Early childhood
    b. Middle childhood
    c. Late childhood
    d. Adolescence

15. Which of the following best describes the order of periodization used for sports conditioning?
    a. Transition, preparation, competition
    b. Preparation, competition, transition
    c. Competition, transition, preparation
    d. Preparation, transition, competition

16. Which of the following is an acute response to aerobic exercise?
    a. lower resting heart rate
    b. increase in ventilation
    c. constant cardiac output
    d. decrease in stroke volume

17. According to experienced PE teachers, which of the following is true about classroom management in PE classes for the elementary grades?
    a. Making eye contact is more important than learning student names for rapport.
    b. Post gym rules and consequences clearly and deliver consequences consistently.
    c. Stay on the move constantly throughout class; do not have your back to the wall.
    d. Making positive comments reinforces good behavior but does not encourage it.

18. Among the most prevalent challenges to kindergarten through Grade 12 physical education, which has recently become even more challenging than the others?
    a. Inadequate resources and parental support
    b. Overly large class sizes and teacher burnout
    c. Violence, student drug abuse, and discipline
    d. Reductions in school curriculum times for physical education

19. Which of the following methods would be LEAST useful for assessing student performance of physical education skills?

    a. Observational checklists
    b. Rating scales of skill level
    c. Written-response exams
    d. Performance data graphs

20. Which safety rule is unique to golf, archery, and racquet activities?

    a. Maintaining distance from striker or shooter
    b. Avoiding facing the person striking or shooting the object
    c. Keeping one's eyes on the object
    d. Looking before releasing or striking

21. Of the following assessment approaches, which one is traditional rather than alternative?

    a. Students write down their personal fitness plans.
    b. Students perform a series of dance movements.
    c. Students show learning by playing a sports game.
    d. Students label the team's positions on a diagram.

22. After expressing her dissatisfaction with the unfair distribution of household chores to her parents, a young woman is told that children should be "seen and not heard." This expectation affects how comfortable she feels speaking up about injustices that she faces. Which type of factor most describes this influence?

    a. Genetic
    b. Cultural
    c. Environmental
    d. Intrinsic

23. Which of the following describes the most appropriate physical education self-assessment activity for kindergarten through Grade 2 students?

    a. Students write entries in journals describing the fitness activities they are doing.
    b. Students pictorially illustrate their activities in each of several fitness categories.
    c. Students keep notebooks of progress notes and give them to teachers regularly.
    d. Students record their progress on index cards they give to teachers at intervals.

24. In addition to physical activity, which of the following activities has been shown to help manage stress?

    a. Drinking red wine
    b. Getting adequate sleep
    c. Watching television
    d. Drinking caffeine

25. What is the purpose of using a drum to teach dance?

    a. Better control of the tempo and effort
    b. Provide students with creative alternatives
    c. Allows students to take turns using the drum
    d. Closer alignment to convey the movement concepts

26. Among the life skills of values clarification, decision-making, communication, and coping skills, which of the following responses to stressful life events MOST reflects decision-making skills?

    a. Considering positive aspects of the situation
    b. Evaluating the pros and cons of the situation
    c. Expressing your feelings about the situation
    d. Positive behaviors to deal with the situation

27. The teacher has noted that Robert is extremely competitive and regularly argues with classmates during invasion games. Which of the following strategies can minimize conflict and foster a healthy environment for all students?

    a. banning Robert from invasion games
    b. substituting Robert out each occurrence
    c. assigning Robert to time-out
    d. contracting a behavioral plan with Robert

28. To create positive and supportive classrooms with respect for diversity, which of these is an effective educator practice?

    a. Invite parent, teacher, and staff to collaborate for students.
    b. Praise finished student products more than effort/progress.
    c. Analyze past successes; then focus on them for self-esteem.
    d. Avoid providing suggestion boxes as this only invites abuses.

29. Ms. Johnson is in a panic because Mr. Oliver took the heart rate monitors she needs for class. Which of the following heart rate monitoring strategies can the teacher use?

    a. taking the pulse rate at the radial artery
    b. using the talk test
    c. checking rate of perceived exertion
    d. asking students how they feel

30. According to attachment theory, a person whose parents rejected his or her social-emotional needs during childhood is most likely to develop which of the following attachment styles that is characterized by independence, intolerance of close relationships, and evasion of emotional situations?

    a. Secure attachment
    b. Anxious attachment
    c. Disorganized attachment
    d. Avoidant attachment

31. Which of the following describes how dances aid in development of respect for diversity?

    a. Every student can participate
    b. Every student's culture can be included
    c. Every locomotor movement can be used
    d. Every non-locomotor movement can be used

32. Which of the following exercises helps strengthen the lower back?

    a.   Lat pulls
    b.   Rear deltoid raises
    c.   Lateral raises
    d.   Deadlift

33. Mr. Sulliman is planning a lesson unit on the 10 major body systems and introduces the essential question, "How do the body systems interact to fulfill a person's needs?" He then separates students into groups and gives each group an array of manipulatives and instructional resources to collaboratively explore the essential question. Students are given a list of questions to spark conversation about the material and invited to share their insights. Which instructional strategy is Mr. Sulliman implementing?

    a.   Guided discovery
    b.   Role playing
    c.   Brainstorming
    d.   Direct instruction

34. Social responsibility and ethics theory suggest that a person has a duty to act in a way that benefits and protects the best interests of the local community. Which of the following examples best represents directly fulfilling this civic responsibility to one's community?

    a.   A person receives the flu vaccine to reduce rates of transmission in his family.
    b.   A member of a local congregation tithes 10 percent of her income to support her church program.
    c.   A regional grocer donates a portion of the business's earnings to a local food bank to increase food access to low income populations.
    d.   A person reduces the number of products he or she purchases that contain single-use plastics to reduce plastic pollution.

35. Which technique aids in the refinement and integration of locomotor skills?

    a.   Utilizing demonstrations
    b.   Incorporating movement concepts
    c.   Leading and following
    d.   Isolation of locomotor skills

36. When designing, choosing, modifying, and sequencing game activities, what should PE teachers have as their main purpose(s)?

    a.   To ensure that students remain occupied
    b.   To enhance skills practice and enjoyment
    c.   To ensure student behavior management
    d.   To enhance student enjoyment primarily

37. Bernice works in a rural county health department. After conversations with community members, she learns that many residents are unaware of health-related resources in the area. Residents also note that inadequate public transportation and limited hours at the local health clinic prevent many from accessing primary health care (e.g., wellness screenings). Which of the following opportunities for health education advocacy could Bernice use to respond to community feedback?

    a. Health professional conference
    b. Community resource guide
    c. School assembly
    d. Health fair

38. Which of the following statements best describes Bandura's social learning theory?

    a. Learning through touch
    b. Learning through reading
    c. Learning through mental imagery
    d. Learning through observation

39. Which of the following combined motor skills is on the upper end of the skill progression continuum?

    a. Skipping baseline to baseline
    b. Running 400 meters
    c. Dribbling a soccer ball
    d. Jumping over an obstacle

40. What is a common misconception among teenagers that health educators should correct?

    a. That conception cannot occur by body rubbing without vaginal or vulvar sperm contact
    b. That conception will not occur without penetration and ejaculation inside the vagina
    c. That teenage males should put on condoms before sex and wear them continuously
    d. That kissing or oral or anal sex will not cause pregnancy if no sperm touches the vulva or vagina

41. When does physical education instruction necessarily require giving feedback to students?

    a. When a skill requires specific correction
    b. When a skill gets environmental feedback
    c. When a student has experience with a skill
    d. When a teacher can comprehensively demonstrate a skill

42. A male student wants to join the dance team. His parents are extremely dissatisfied and think boys should play football. What strategy can the teacher use to support the student without offending the parents?

    a. Respectfully tell the parents they are misinformed
    b. Suggest that the student participate in both
    c. Discuss the risks of playing football
    d. Discuss the physical benefits of dance

43. Of the following choices, which one most describes a stage of motor learning associated with the age period of adolescence?

    a. Purposeful movements develop beyond simple reflexes.
    b. Motor patterns of increasing complexity are developing.
    c. Motor patterns gain increasing automaticity and fluidity.
    d. Ability, motivation, and practice influence development.

44. Among physical proficiencies that affect individual performance, which type of strength is most involved in the activity of kayaking?

    a. Static strength
    b. Trunk strength
    c. Dynamic strength
    d. Explosive strength

45. Which of the following sport skills contain similar jumping patterns?

    a. High jump and long jump
    b. Volleyball spike and basketball lay-up
    c. Basketball jump shot and high jump
    d. Vertical jump and volleyball spike

46. In a public school's PE risk management and emergency procedure plans, which is typically among the provisions?

    a. If any students are injured, the school nurse offers the initial first aid.
    b. All physical educators carry emergency first aid kits during PE classes.
    c. Not all physical educators need have current first aid and CPR certificates.
    d. PE teachers may not know which students lack treatment permission.

47. Which of the six essential nutrients helps repair and build tissue?

    a. Carbohydrates
    b. Fats
    c. Protein
    d. Minerals

48. What is a result of regular and substantial alcohol use?

    a. It impairs judgment over the long term but not in the short term.
    b. It distorts the perceptions but not the senses of vision or hearing.
    c. It damages both the cardiovascular and central nervous systems.
    d. It causes liver damage but not impotence or stomach disorders.

49. Some physical education programs have been cut and threatened with elimination. Which of the following physical activity resources are available to students from diverse communities?

    a. Basketball courts
    b. Tennis courts
    c. After school programs
    d. Parks and recreation centers

50. A _____ assessment is a formal evaluation that is administered to students at the end of a lesson unit to assess student learning. Student performance is usually measured by an academic standard or benchmark.

    a. Formative
    b. Norm-referenced
    c. Performance
    d. Summative

51. Relative to inclusion of students in instructional decisions, which statement is correct about how these affect student motivation for learning?

    a. Students perceiving teacher control of instruction tend to develop internal motivations.
    b. Students perceiving ownership of content and learning have more external motivation.
    c. Students perceiving some control of learning are more likely to be internally motivated.
    d. Students perceiving that teachers control all instruction are unaffected by punishments.

52. Which of the following are techniques used to ensure equal opportunities for students to participate, learn, and succeed in physical education class?

    a. Inviting administrators to observe classes
    b. Inviting parents to observe classes
    c. Appointing student captains
    d. Modifying activities

53. The teacher is concerned that he talks too much during instruction, which reduces student engagement. How can the teacher assess if his concerns are accurate to determine if changes should be made?

    a. Ask another PE teacher for instructional feedback
    b. Ask the principal to conduct an informal observation
    c. Employ an Academic Learning Time assessment
    d. Have students assess instructional delivery

54. Which of the following helps establish student responsibility and self-control?

    a. Playing a team sport
    b. The course guide or syllabus
    c. Parental feedback
    d. Expectations and assessment

55. Identify the communication strategy used in the following scenario: a teacher helps two students identify the root of their dispute and guides them as they set boundaries that satisfy the needs and wants of both students.

    a. Mediation
    b. Negotiation
    c. Active listening
    d. Arbitration

56. Research finds that motor skills training, endurance training, and strength training all share which neuroplasticity effects in common?

    a. New blood vessel formation
    b. Motor map reorganization
    c. Spinal reflex modification
    d. New synapse generation

57. According to experts, what is true about the primary functions of nonverbal communication?

    a. Nonverbal communication serves a function of performing social rituals.
    b. Nonverbal communication shows personalities rather than relationships.
    c. Nonverbal communication is used to replace, not help, verbal interaction.
    d. Nonverbal communication is not used like words for expressing feelings.

58. Which of the following is MOST accurate regarding the components of a coordinated school health program?

    a. School health education should be comprehensive.
    b. Physical education is separate from such a program.
    c. School health services are only for emergency care.
    d. Community and family are not part of this program.

59. A community health assessment (CHA) contains information about a community's health status, needs, assets, and barriers to well-being that is collected by state, local, and tribal health entities. CHAs are often used to influence local and state health policy. Each of the following factors that impact health policy is assessed in a CHA EXCEPT:

    a. Demographics (e.g., age, race, gender)
    b. Socioeconomic status (e.g., poverty rate, academic achievement)
    c. Total community health-related expenditure
    d. Available community resources

60. Which of the following best sums up the theory of deliberate practice?

    a. Practice makes perfect
    b. Natural athletes require little practice
    c. Long bouts of practice are most effective
    d. Reflection is a necessary aspect of practice

61. When using an assessment instrument meant to measure aerobic endurance, physical education teachers find that maximum student repetitions are limited not by their becoming winded but by specific muscle fatigue. After obtaining the same results over repeated administrations, they conclude that this test measures muscular endurance instead. What have they discovered about this test?

    a. The test is neither a reliable nor valid test.
    b. The test is a valid test, but it is not reliable.
    c. The test is a reliable test, but it is not valid.
    d. The test is valid and reliable, but misused.

62. Regarding physical, emotional, and social factors that influence personal physical health, which of the following is true?

    a. Anxiety and depression cause sleep and diet problems but not cardiovascular troubles.

    b. Stress and family dysfunction cause emotional problems, not physical illness.

    c. Air pollution can aggravate asthma but is not actually found to cause asthma.

    d. People can overeat and be overweight, and yet still suffer from malnutrition.

63. In three stages of motor learning, which of these is characteristic of the associative stage?

    a. Understanding an activity's goal and nature

    b. Making attempts that include major errors

    c. Making fewer and more consistent errors

    d. Effortless automaticity in performance

64. According to the Centers for Disease Control (CDC), what is a valid guideline for writing clear, relevant health education materials appealing to diverse audiences?

    a. Engage the audience by saving the most important information for later.

    b. A good rule is to keep the number of main ideas in each document to ten.

    c. Use prescriptions rather than proscriptions for giving action instructions.

    d. Avoid audience boredom by alternating rapidly among various subjects.

65. Which of these accurately reflects research findings on gender differences in early childhood motor development?

    a. Preschool girls are found to be equally muscular as, but more physically mature than, boys are in preschool.

    b. Preschool boys exhibit both more strength and coordination in large-muscle gross-motor skills than girls do.

    c. Preschool girls exhibit more fine-motor skills, but less gross-motor coordination, than boys do in preschool.

    d. Despite certain differences, preschool motor development between genders is more similar than different.

66. In the majority of US states and territories, which of these professions are identified as mandated reporters of child maltreatment?

    a. Probation or parole officers, substance abuse counselors, and film processors

    b. Camps and recreation and youth center employees, directors, and volunteers

    c. School, health care, child care, mental health, and law enforcement employees

    d. Domestic violence workers, humane or animal control officers, and college faculties

67. After tracking his teaching behaviors, Mr. Green realized that taking attendance for 40 students takes up a lot of time, which reduces student engagement. How might Mr. Green alter his attendance taking method to increase the opportunities for students to respond?

    a. set a time-limit to take attendance

    b. practice taking attendance faster

    c. take attendance during the warm-up

    d. take attendance in squad lines

68. A middle-aged man wants to reduce his risk of heart disease. Which preventative strategies should he consider using to reduce or prevent the onset of heart disease?

    a. Aim to eat 3.5 oz (about 99.22 g) of red meat per day
    b. Use smokeless tobacco instead of cigarettes
    c. Eat foods that lower his LDL cholesterol levels
    d. Aim to lose 30 lb

69. Which of the following is a recommended strategy for physical education teachers to plan effective class behavior management?

    a. Announce at least ten expectations to the students in oral format.
    b. Enforce expectations occasionally for intermittent reinforcement.
    c. Define expectations in terms of what they want students not to do.
    d. Define expectations in terms of what they want the students to do.

70. Using the skill of rallying a tennis ball against a wall as an example, which assessment method is quantitative rather than qualitative?

    a. Having students demonstrate correct grip rallying a ball against a wall
    b. Observing students demonstrate sideways position in rallying the ball
    c. Counting the numbers of times in one minute that students rally the ball
    d. Seeing that students keep the racquet heads up while rallying the ball

71. Which of these is an effective strategy for physical education teachers to enhance students' perceived physical competence?

    a. Specify the number of trials to complete during a certain time period.
    b. Specify the length of time for practicing but not the number of trials.
    c. Specify the technical errors students make in instructional feedback.
    d. Specify a certain activity without varying it to keep students on task.

72. What is the first step in beginning a needs assessment?

    a. Establish the roles and responsibilities of the research team
    b. Design the data collection methodology
    c. Identify and engage stakeholders
    d. Determine the purpose of the needs assessment

73. When should teachers and students primarily apply a rubric?

    a. After learning
    b. During learning
    c. Before learning
    d. During all these times

74. Of the following major health behavior theories, which one is another name for the stages of change model?

    a. The behavioral change model
    b. The transtheoretical model
    c. The public health model
    d. The health belief model

75. A/an _____ teaching style creates a classroom in which students are highly involved and engaged, yet the teacher has very little control over his or her students.

   a. authoritarian
   b. permissive
   c. authoritative
   d. indulgent

76. Which statement is true about children and environmental health risks?

   a. Children's body systems are more robust and resilient than adults' are.
   b. Children are liable to be more vulnerable to environmental health risks.
   c. Children take in fewer toxins from the air, water, and food than adults.
   d. Children's normal behaviors expose them to fewer toxins than adults'.

77. Which of the following is the best reason for a self-assessment assignment?

   a. To refine skills
   b. To assess learning preference
   c. To aid the teacher in the summative assessment
   d. To practice the summative assessment

78. Tom is driving Louisa home after their first date. As they approach Louisa's house, Tom begins to make unwanted sexual advances toward Louisa. Which of the following is the LEAST effective strategy for refusing sexual advances?

   a. Louisa remains quiet and hopes that Tom will pick up that she is uncomfortable.
   b. Louisa tells Tom that she is not interested.
   c. Louisa makes a joke to diffuse the tension.
   d. Louisa exits the car and heads to a neighbor's house until Tom leaves.

79. All of the following are true regarding wind energy, EXCEPT:

   a. Wind turbines use space inefficiently, but they have low operational costs.
   b. Wind is not a reliable source of energy in all geographic locations.
   c. Wind turbines are expensive to manufacture and install.
   d. Wind turbines are a threat to wildlife.

80. A part of which of these human body systems regulates the body temperature?

   a. Lymphatic
   b. Circulatory
   c. Integumentary
   d. Musculoskeletal

81. Which statement is correct regarding apparatus and procedures for testing sports equipment, specifically helmets?

   a. Auto crash simulation headforms are used to test linear impact from head collisions in football.
   b. Drop towers for testing helmet impact performance also apply with head collisions in football.
   c. The stretch in a helmet retention system is tested the same as the retention system's strength.
   d. The mouthguard on a helmet is designed to protect the teeth, not the brain from a concussion.

82. Which of the following is NOT a good way to maximize participation in a physical education class?

    a. Let each student choose his or her own activity, as long as it is physical.
    b. Group the students according to skill level.
    c. Set up different activity stations for students to use.
    d. Change the rules of games to suit different skill levels.

83. Research-based strategies to motivate students are reflected by which teacher behavior?

    a. They are interested in students' learning but are not personally interested.
    b. They are role models, leading student motivation and passion by example.
    c. They need not believe in students' abilities as long as they indicate interest.
    d. They eschew the personalization of subject content for individual students.

84. Of the following, which is accurate regarding personal hygiene in adolescence?

    a. The majority of teens experience acne regardless of skin care habits.
    b. Teens should not need to shampoo hair more but do so out of vanity.
    c. The same oral hygiene they used as children should suffice for teens.
    d. Teens who learned good bathing habits as children need not change.

85. Among signs of domestic abuse, physical violence, isolation, and psychological symptoms of being abused, which of the following is more specifically a sign of domestic abuse than of the others?

    a. Constantly reporting one's locations and activities to the partner
    b. Often exhibiting or trying to hide injuries, claiming accidents
    c. Marked changes in a person's personality traits or behaviors
    d. Few or no public outings, no car or money use alone, or no visiting with others

86. Fresh water is a finite resource, yet reserves are being depleted far faster than they can be naturally replenished. Which of the following water conservation methods has the potential to preserve the greatest volume of water?

    a. The US government provides a federal subsidy to support the installation of drip irrigation and subsurface irrigation systems on US farms.
    b. A county enforces lawn watering restrictions from all water sources.
    c. A housing development installs leak detection systems in all newly constructed homes.
    d. A farmer plants native crop varieties to reduce the need for artificial watering.

87. Which of the following strategies fosters teamwork?

    a. Having team captains
    b. Goal setting
    c. Meeting with players individually
    d. Watching videos of gameplay

88. When learning new PE skills, students need more _____ feedback; when they have developed more competence and confidence in certain PE skills and can analyze their own performance, they can make better use of _____ feedback.

    a. Extrinsic; intrinsic
    b. Intrinsic; extrinsic
    c. Positive; negative
    d. Constructive; corrective

89. Jessica goes to the gym locker room after completing her workout and finds a woman lying on the ground. After she checks the scene for safety, she checks for responsiveness, breathing, and bleeding. The woman does not appear to be conscious or breathing, and Jessica cannot feel her pulse. Jessica calls 911 and places the woman on her back. Jessica is not CPR-certified. What is the next step the 911 operator should direct Jessica to take?

   a. Immediately initiate chest compressions while calling for help
   b. Conduct a blind swipe of the mouth to remove any possible foreign objects
   c. Deliver a cycle of 100 chest compressions before checking for signs of life
   d. Find and attach an automated external defibrillator (AED)

90. Each of the following is an example of an effective way to assess learning needs EXCEPT:

   a. A teacher conducts in-depth interviews with parents to determine students' cognitive abilities and preferred instruction strategies.
   b. A teacher administers a post-assignment survey to identify students' experiences learning and applying the content.
   c. A teacher uses prior knowledge gleaned from previous interactions with individuals of a cultural group to assess learning needs.
   d. A teacher conducts a learning needs assessment for each student to evaluate content knowledge and preferred learning styles at the beginning of the year.

91. The National Health Education Standards (NHES) were developed in response to what?

   a. Standards being developed in hospitals
   b. Standards being developed in education
   c. Standards being developed in public health
   d. Standards being developed in private practice

92. Which of the following is the dominant movement concept when performing a leap?

   a. rhythm
   b. force
   c. time
   d. levels

93. Which of the following do experts recommend to foster teacher collaboration?

   a. Cultivating senses of individual responsibility in all faculty members
   b. Recruiting experienced teachers for induction and mentoring only
   c. Recruiting experienced teachers in professional development only
   d. School leaders' earmarking resources for supporting collaboration

94. Student-centered instructional approaches have been shown to be more effective than teacher-driven approaches. Which of the following student-centered approaches has been shown to increase motivation?

   a. Choice
   b. Direct instruction
   c. Competition
   d. Traditional

95. Which choice reflects expert advice to teachers on communicating with parents?

  a. Communicating expectations undermines parent expectations.
  b. Focus communications with parents to be about their children.
  c. Select one communication method and use it with all parents.
  d. Measure communication results and adjust plans accordingly.

96. Regarding feedback that physical education teachers and coaches give students and athletes, which of the following is an example of prescriptive feedback rather than descriptive feedback?

  a. "You can do this!"
  b. "Follow through!"
  c. "That was great!"
  d. "Way to play ball!"

97. Use the DECIDE model to respond to the following question: Jonathon has noticed that he and his partner, Charles, have been fighting regularly lately. Jonathon shares his observation with Charles who tells Jonathon that he feels like Jonathon prioritizes work over their relationship. After talking more, they decide that they would like to increase the amount of time they spend together each week to ensure that both parties' needs are met. They would also like to avoid future related conflicts. After they discuss their needs, what is the most appropriate next step?

  a. Consider the amount of time each will dedicate and the types of activities they can do together
  b. Identify the best solution that meets both of their needs
  c. Determine the root cause that is contributing to their conflict
  d. Develop a schedule and implement a plan to spend more time together

98. Among the following divisions of biomechanics that involve physics concepts, which one is MOST closely related to Newton's first three laws of motion?

  a. Coplanar vectors
  b. Kinematics
  c. Kinetics
  d. Forces

99. Which of the following is an appropriate method used to assess heart rate (HR) intensity during exercise?

  a. Continuous aerobic activity
  b. Talk test
  c. Percentage of maximum heart rate
  d. Recovery heart rate

100. The MyFitnessPal, Endomondo, and Fitbit digital fitness apps all share what in common?

  a. Sync
  b. Recipes
  c. Audio feedback
  d. Social networking

101. Of the following, which accurately reports research findings related to how physical fitness affects academic achievement?

- a. Cardiovascular fitness and body mass index (BMI) correlate positively with test scores in achievement.
- b. More physically fit children react more quickly but not necessarily more accurately.
- c. Children burn more calories during active gaming than teacher-led fitness activities.
- d. Intense exercise is followed by a significant temporary decline in cognitive function.

102. Which of the following activities helps students conceptualize the different levels?

- a. Animal walks
- b. Nature walks
- c. Jumping rope
- d. Tag games

103. Janice is assigned to write a paper for her health class about heart disease. Which of the following is NOT an example of a valid source of health information?

- a. An American Heart Association article about Heart-Check certification
- b. A well-known health enthusiast's post summarizing the CDC's recommendations on heart-healthy exercises
- c. A peer-reviewed journal article about the relationship between diabetes and heart disease
- d. A fact sheet on frequently asked questions about heart disease from the Office on Women's Health at the Department of Health and Human Services

104. What has research discovered about the adolescent decision-making process?

- a. Conformity with parental or peer norms is unrelated to teen decision making.
- b. Demographic rather than family or personal variables influence teen decisions.
- c. Adolescents tend to be oriented toward the future regarding long-term goals.
- d. Real-life practice is necessary for teens to transfer cognitive skills to decisions.

105. Which of these infant reflexes normally disappears at the latest ages?

- a. Babinski reflex
- b. Stepping reflex
- c. Grasping reflex
- d. The tonic reflex

106. The teacher has little time to go over each health-related fitness component in isolation. Which of the following activities can the teacher use to implement the health-related fitness components when short on time?

- a. resistance training
- b. interval training
- c. fartlek training
- d. circuit training

107. A PE teacher evaluates student performance in archery by measuring student accuracy in hitting a standardized target from a specified distance. This represents which kind of assessment?

    a. Norm-referenced
    b. Process assessment
    c. Criterion-referenced
    d. Biomechanical objectives

108. For large classes, which of the following assessments should be used to assess motor skills?

    a. Checklist
    b. Peer assessment to save time
    c. Self-assessment
    d. Video analysis of skill proficiency

109. The teacher has created progressive activities where students easily find success in skill acquisition before moving on to more complex skills. Which of the following concepts is developed through this practice?

    a. emotional development
    b. self-regulation
    c. motivation competence
    d. autonomous development

110. Which of the stages of change is depicted in the following scenario: a person weighs the pros and cons of changing his or her eating habits to lose weight?

    a. Action
    b. Contemplation
    c. Preparation
    d. Precontemplation

111. Which of the following distinguishes etiquette between individual and team sports?

    a. personal vs. team fouls
    b. no coaching vs. coaching
    c. no noise vs. loud noise
    d. no penalty cards vs. yellow and red cards

112. Which of the following BEST describes how participation in physical education can improve a student's self-esteem?

    a. It can teach students new or improved skills.
    b. It can foster a sense of wonder at human athleticism.
    c. It can teach students to take turns when playing sports/games.
    d. It can cause the release of endorphins, natural "feel good" chemicals.

113. Among movement skill competencies reflecting developmental standards, which is most suitable for students in the fifth grade?

    a. Moving creatively to varied musical rhythms using simple dance steps
    b. Jumping rope to the tempo of music, both singly and with a partner
    c. Bouncing, passing, and catching a ball, matching a musical rhythm
    d. Expressing feelings, ideas in rhythmic motion with, without music

114. Students have physical education two days a week and are not meeting physical activity recommendations. Which of the following are realistic community resources that provide physical activity opportunities for all students?

    a. parks and recreation
    b. hiking trails
    c. rock climbing
    d. fitness centers

115. A physical education teacher has included an objective for student heart rates to reach a target range when they play a sport. The teacher discovers the majority of students did not reach that target. Which teacher response to this discovery is the best example of using reflection to inform instruction?

    a. The teacher decides students were not playing hard enough and gives them a pep talk.
    b. The teacher experiments with having the students play the next game at faster speeds.
    c. The teacher changes the rules of the game so all students will participate more actively.
    d. The teacher might do either (B) or (C) or even both of these but is less likely to use (A).

116. At the beginning of the school year, the administration sent families a survey in which they were asked to contribute ideas and opinions regarding the curriculum and ways to improve the school environment. Which of the following is most likely the intended result of sending out this survey?

    a. Maintaining frequent communication with students' families
    b. Reinforcing classroom learning at home
    c. Encouraging families to participate in school-based decision-making
    d. Inviting families to share information about their children that would enhance the learning experience

117. What is a valid claim when comparing Rosenshine and Stevens' model of direct instruction with the Direct Instruction method of Engelmann and colleagues?

    a. Both are teacher directed, but only one is skills oriented.
    b. Both are face-to-face, but only one uses small groups.
    c. Both use task analysis, but only one is sequenced.
    d. Both teach explicitly, but only one is generic.

118. Among the following common areas of negligence in physical education, in addition to first aid emergencies, which one can teachers and coaches MOST mitigate by enlisting the help of students?

    a. Instruction
    b. Supervision
    c. Transportation
    d. Class environments

119. A first-year teacher has started at a school without a curriculum or lesson plans. Where should the teacher go for resources to help select developmentally appropriate activities for instruction?

    a. Contact former physical education teachers
    b. Consult state and national guidelines
    c. Ask a veteran teacher
    d. Ask the principal

120. Suzanne is exploring contraception options. She is sexually active with her long-term partner but does not plan on having children for the foreseeable future, so she would prefer a long-lasting and low-maintenance method. She also would rather use a nonhormonal contraceptive. Which type of contraception is the most appropriate for her preferences?

    a. Female condom
    b. Depo-Provera shot
    c. Progestin implant
    d. Copper intrauterine device (IUD)

121. When a physical education teacher gives a defense cue of "Match up" to students during basketball practice, what does this mean?

    a. Students always should pair up with another player on the court for defense.
    b. Students should stay near to offensive players that they defend on the court.
    c. Students should defend players more like them in size than fitness or skill level.
    d. Students should defend players similar to them in size, fitness, and skill level.

122. Which of the following is NOT appropriate educational material from a professional organization, agency, or association that meets the needs of diverse audiences?

    a. A scholarly article from the Journal of the American Medical Association
    b. A closed-caption video on how to perform CPR from the American Heart Association
    c. An interactive map that provides state-level data about health behaviors from the CDC
    d. An infographic about positive nutrition habits from the US Department of Agriculture

123. From birth to the age of 2 years, children typically grow to ___ times their newborn weights.

    a. Three
    b. Four
    c. Two
    d. Five

124. The teacher chooses squad lines to take attendance so she can easily see if students are absent. Which of the following is a limitation to this approach?

    a. squad lines are outdated
    b. squad lines are teacher-centered
    c. squad lines take too much time
    d. squad lines can lead to behavioral problems

125. PE teachers who collect and interpret more student data than just fitness scores can use these data to do which of the following?

    a. To show they are teaching, regardless of whether students are learning
    b. To show what students should practice, not what they already know
    c. To show which students need more help, not those making progress
    d. To show parents, principals, school boards the value of PE programs

126. Which of the following is an example of a responsible decision-making model?

    a. Objectives and Key Results model
    b. SODAS and ICED models
    c. Decision tree
    d. SMART framework

127. Which kinds of physical education activities are both appropriate for boys and girls to participate in together and are less dependent on team assignment by student skill levels?

a. Activities that involve participant body contact
b. Activities that require more upper-body strength
c. Activities that require agility and lower-body strength
d. Activities of all these types

128. A young woman is drinking for the first time and consumes five alcoholic drinks within a one-hour period. Which consequence is LEAST likely to result from her risky behavior?

a. Extreme dehydration
b. Alcohol addiction
c. Self-harm
d. Unintentional injuries

129. A physical education program has a 4:1 student-equipment ratio, a large teaching area, a class size of 38-42 students, and students are engaged at least 50% of the time. Which of the following elements of an effective physical education program is present and appropriately accounted for in the example?

a. equipment ratio and teaching area
b. class size and student engagement
c. student engagement and equipment ratio
d. student engagement and teaching area

130. Which of the following best describes the relationship between ability and skill for motor performance?

a. Abilities are genetic characteristics that are the same for all.
b. Abilities are learned traits that promote skill development.
c. Abilities are genetic characteristics that impact one's ability to learn a motor skill.
d. Individuals with low ability cannot improve motor skills.

Answer Key and Explanations

1. D: Beginning students make lots of errors and focus heavily on skill cues, so the teacher needs to be intentional and direct with instruction to help the student understand the movements of the skill. As students begin to understand the movement as illustrated in improvement, the need for direct feedback and demonstrations are reduced.

2. A: The Coordinated School Health Publications and Resources page on the Centers for Disease Control's (CDC's) Web site includes information on the connection between school health and academic achievement and on school health assessment and planning. The National School Boards Association's "School Health 101 Packets" (B); the school health coordination guidelines published by state education departments (C), for example, the Connecticut State Department of Education and the Maine Departments of Education and Health and Human Services; and the Comprehensive Health Education Network's (CHEN's) LISTSERV, which publishes an online mailing list for national, state, and local school health professionals all provide basic information on coordinated school health approaches.

3. A: A child with Attention Deficit Hyperactivity Disorder (ADHD) who becomes exhausted from engaging in excessive physical activity is an example of an emotional (and behavioral) condition that can affect levels of physical activity and fitness. A child with depression who avoids physical activity is also an example of this. The need to monitor a child with asthma for breathing problems during exercise (B) is an example of how a physical factor can affect physical activity and fitness levels, as are the need to monitor the exercise of a child with diabetes and coordinate it with the child's diet (C), and a physically disabled child's need for adaptive equipment (and/or alternative instructional methods) to participate in physical activities (D).

4. B: In addition to referrals, criteria indicating that a student should be evaluated to determine eligibility for adapted physical education (APE) include that the student performs below his or her ability level in group settings (A); has social behaviors that interfere with his or her or others' learning more than one-third of class time (B); has scored below average in two or more parts of the state physical fitness test used by the school district (C); and scored 1.5 or more standard deviations below the norm on the norm-referenced test used (D) by the school or district.

5. D: Verbal communication is the primary means of communication, whereas nonverbal communication is frequently used to reinforce messages or convey unspoken information (e.g., raising eyebrows to show surprise, maintaining eye contact to show active listening). Nonverbal communication consists of body language and facial expressions, and it can be intentional or unintentional.

6. D: Each district may have its own set of academic standards that educators are expected to follow. The local district must also satisfy state and national standards, so the local standards are the strictest level of standardization and the most helpful for a teacher to be familiar with to ensure he or she is meeting the school expectations. District standards may be based on SHAPE America's standards. Common Core does not have health-related standards, and the NCHEC competencies refer to the roles and responsibilities of Certified Health Education Specialists (CHES).

7. C: The three main categories of fundamental movement skills (FMS) are locomotor (A), manipulative, (A and, (B), and stability (D). Within the main category of stability are included the subcategories of rotation, (B) and (C), and balance, (C) and (D). Activities like spinning, twirling, rocking, bending, and turning demonstrate rotation. Balance can involve both stationary and movement activities. Both rotation and balance are components of stability. Locomotor skills involve activities like walking, running, and so on. Manipulative skills include activities like throwing, catching, hitting, batting, kicking, and transporting objects.

8. B: The PE teacher should first check the scene for safety. Next, she would check the spectator for signs of consciousness, e.g., talking, breathing, and pulse. If there is no breathing, the PE teacher would identify and instruct someone to call 911 and include the assessment. If there is an AED available, that request would also be made followed by CPR until the AED arrives, medical personnel arrive, and/or the PE teacher is too tired to continue performing CPR correctly.

9. C: Allowing students to reflect on their individual fitness is an equitable approach as students can focus on their personal goals and needs. Students can develop personal goals, create a plan, determine how to assess/track/monitor, and adjust accordingly. Standardized fitness testing and standards-based fitness goals are not equitable as all students are expected to meet a standard not tailored to the individual.

10. B: Confounding variables are factors that distort the relationship between the independent variable (the cause) and the dependent variable (the effect). For example, confounding variables like metabolic rate, gender, or calorie intake could skew the results of research on the relationship between exercise and weight loss. If confounding variables are not considered, they may lead to inaccurate interpretations of data.

11. A: Competence in physical activities has shown to lead to lifelong physical activity engagement. Modeling is a strategy that can aid in learning how to perform physical activities and build confidence to attempt a movement or skill, but modeling alone has not shown to foster lifelong physical activity. Participating in organized sports can develop competence in specific sports skills, but participation does not equate to competence. Active parents can be role models, but competence needs to be developed to engage in lifelong physical activity.

12. D: Population-level health interventions are strategies that are delivered to a large group of individuals aimed at preventing or addressing known causes of disease. While physical activity is known to reduce the risk of many chronic diseases, the preventative or curative effects are limited to the participating members of the running club. Health promotion, health education, and policy are examples of population-level interventions that can prevent chronic diseases within a population.

13. A: Katherine is aware of her performance, showing that she has knowledge of performance, which is a type of intrinsic feedback used to detect and correct movement skills errors. Knowledge of performance becomes more effective in advanced performers who know why they performed the way they did and are less reliant on teachers and coaches to tell them what went wrong and how to correct it. Knowledge of results is the knowledge of the performance outcome, which is a type of extrinsic feedback. Katherine's throw likely went in the direction that her body rotated, which she would be able to see after the ball lands, which is also terminal feedback or feedback that occurs at the end, which can correct errors. Positive transfer is when skills used in one activity, e.g., serving in volleyball, promotes skill performance in another activity, such as serving in tennis. Negative transfer is when skills used in one activity impedes skill performance in another.

14. D: Adolescence takes place between ages 13 and 18. During this stage, teenagers undergo significant physical changes and hormonal development. Their prefrontal cortexes—the part of the brain responsible for decision-making and judgement—begin to mature. The prefrontal cortex is one of the last regions of the brain to mature and typically finishes around age 25.

15. A: Transition, preparation, and competition are the three phases of periodization used for sports conditioning. The transition, or post-season, phase is when athletes recover and maintain fitness levels through cross-training. During pre-season, the preparation phase is where skill and sport-specific fitness is developed to prepare for the competition phase, where athletes maintain fitness and work on areas for competitive play.

16. B: An increase in ventilation or breathing is an acute or immediate response to aerobic exercise. A lower resting heart rate is a long-term physiological response to aerobic exercise. Cardiac output remains constant during long sessions of aerobic exercise. Cardiac output and stroke volume (the amount of blood ejected from the left and right ventricle due to the contraction of the heart) increases are also acute responses to aerobic exercise.

17. B: Experienced elementary PE teachers advise new teachers to establish rapport with students by learning all their names as soon as possible AND making eye contact (a); establish rules and consequences for breaking them, post these in the gym or classroom, review them periodically as a reminder, and always deliver consequences consistently (b) to keep order; BOTH keep moving during class AND teach with backs to the wall (c) to eliminate blind spots and keep an eye on all students; and make positive comments, both to reinforce students following rules AND encourage students who are not to do so (d).

18. D: Recently, the issue that has become the greatest challenge to kindergarten to Grade 12 (K–12) school physical education (PE) is that time in school curricula for PE classes and activities has been reduced significantly to make time for other academic classes. Inadequate resources and parental support (A); overly large class sizes and teacher burnout (B); and violence, student drug abuse, and discipline problems (C) are also challenges to K–12 PE, but these are also equal challenges to other school subjects and to education in general.

19. C: Tests on which students must write answers are least useful for assessing their performance of physical education skills, which typically must be physically demonstrated. Observational checklists are more useful as teachers can watch students perform the skills to be assessed and mark whether they can do them or not or mark the degree to which they have mastered them. Rating scales of skill level are more useful as teachers can observe student skill performance and then rate the level of mastery or skill they have attained on a scale with degrees between most and least. Graphs of performance data are more useful as teachers can record numbers of successful demonstrations per session as points and connect these to form a line or curve showing progress over time. Graphs also can include a line indicating a criterion for reference, so performance points can be seen above, below, and at this line.

20. A: Students should be taught to maintain distance from the striker or shooter to avoid getting hit with the striking object such as a golf club, arrow, or ball. While students should avoid facing a person shooting in archery, in racquet sports like tennis and badminton, students face their opponents on opposite sides of the net. Keeping eyes on the ball or the target is an important skill cue; however, it is not a safety rule when striking or shooting. There is no time to look around before striking in racquet activities, in contrast to golf and archery, where the golfer or shooter controls these actions.

21. D: Labeling a diagram is an example of a traditional assessment approach. Other traditional approaches include short-answer, constructed-response, and fill-in-the-blank written questions; written matching tests or worksheets; and written multiple-choice or true–false questions. Writing down a personal fitness plan (A) is an example of a written alternative assessment. Additional examples include research papers, essays, stories, poems, anecdotes, journals, logs, checklists, rating scales, brochures, advertisements, rubrics, performance records, newspapers, magazines, projects, pre-assessment inventories, surveys, questionnaires, interviews, editorials, and reflections. Performing dance movements (B) and playing sports games (C) are examples of alternative performance task assessments. Additional examples include locomotor or gymnastics routines, officiating games, making fitness assessments or oral reports, teaching lessons, warm-up routines, showcases, debates, skits, role-plays, or interviews.

22. B: This scenario is an example of how culture influences family dynamics. These dynamics vary widely within societies and often have generational effects. This type of response may condition the children in this family to be more submissive to adults and other authorities in general. The type of response that individuals have to their family dynamics can vary widely, as individuals may either retain their family views or develop contrary beliefs that they bring into their own relationships and new family units later in life. Genetic factors are not conditioned by behavior but are biological and inherited. Environmental factors are a broader category that refer to external influences, including culture, but also include the physical environment and access to resources in society. Finally, intrinsic factors are personal motivations that are not influenced by external situations.

23. B: Physical education (PE) teachers can provide kindergarten through Grade 2 (K–) students with log sheets with a prepared left column and an empty right column. The left side uses simple statements like "I have a strong heart," "I have strong muscles," "I can do movements over and over again," and "I can stretch," accompanied by graphic pictures (a heart, a bicep, a figure with arrows indicating repeated movement, and a figure with arrows or lines depicting stretching) to represent cardiovascular endurance, muscular strength, muscular endurance, and flexibility, respectively. In the blank right side, children make drawings or cut and paste pictures illustrating their activities (e.g., running, lifting, dancing, stretches, etc.) in each category. Teachers can guide this activity and collect the products to get assessment information. Writing journal entries (A), notes (C), or cards (D) is inappropriate for students with the limited writing skills of K–2 levels, as is independently turning in records regularly (C) or periodically (D) on a schedule at these ages.

24. B: Getting adequate sleep has been shown to help manage stress as it restores and calms the body and improves concentration, decision-making, and judgment. Most sleep recommendations are 8-10 hours a night. Short naps have also been shown to have similar benefits, including strengthening the immune system and regulating blood pressure that increases during stressful events. Watching television can aid in escaping stress, but it can have an adverse effect and increase stress depending on what is viewed and the length of screen time. Drinking caffeine has been shown to increase the stress response and interfere with sleep quality. Drinking one glass of red wine has shown stress reduction benefits, but over indulgence of alcohol interferes with sleep quality and duration. Over indulgence of alcohol can also lead to alcohol dependence and alcoholism.

25. A: Hand drums are used to easily control the tempo and effort which are then used to teach movement concepts. It is easy to strike the drum hard and soft to illustrate effort, or fast and slow to illustrate tempo variation, before moving on to music with a set tempo. The tempo of striking the drum can be dramatically slower or faster than music can provide without the technology to alter music tempo.

26. B: Carefully weighing and evaluating the pros and cons of a stressful life situation facilitates making decisions that aid coping with stress and most reflects the decision-making life skill. Considering the positive aspects of the situation (A) most reflects the life skill of values clarification. Expressing feelings about the situation (C) most reflects the life skill of communication skills.

Engaging in positive behaviors that raise self-esteem or develop interests to enable dealing with the situation (D) most reflects the life skill of coping skills.

27. C: Assigning Robert to take a time-out will minimize conflict and foster a healthy environment for all students. Substituting Robert out may send a mixed-message and Robert may not associate the substitution as a result of his behavior as subbing is part of invasion gameplay. To ban Robert from invasion games is an approach that restricts Robert from getting an education; however, a temporary ban may be appropriate for chronic or a certain number of offenses. Calling Robert's parents and developing a contract or behavioral plan with Robert is a strategy used after in-class classroom strategies are unsuccessful. A behavioral plan is co-created with the student or students that includes expectations and consequences for infractions.

28. A: Inviting and involving parents, other teachers, and school staff to collaborate in meeting student needs by solving education and discipline problems is an effective practice for creating positive, supportive classrooms with respect for diversity. Another effective practice is to praise student effort and progress rather than only finished products (b). Teachers should analyze students' past successes with them to learn from them, but then focus on the present (c). Providing suggestion boxes is another effective practice to involve students in classroom decision making, as it gives students a "voice and choice" rather than only inviting abuses (d).

29. A: Ms. Johnson can have students take their pulse at the radial or carotid arteries to measure heart rate. The talk test helps determine if the activities are too easy or intense, but it does not measure heart rate. The rate of perceived exertion is another tool used to determine or evaluate the intensity of exercises but is not a heart rate measurement. Asking students how they feel is a great tool to check in to assess students' responses to activities but is not a tool to measure heart rate.

30. D: Avoidant attachment style typically occurs when a child experiences distant or unavailable caregivers. His or her strong sense of independence and self-sufficiency emerges as he or she learns to self-soothe, yet he or she is often unable to form deep relationships with others when he or she is older. Anxious attachment occurs when caregivers are inconsistent, which causes the child to develop confusion and anxiety. Those with anxious attachment are overly attentive to their partner and constantly seek his or her approval. Disorganized attachment develops when a child experiences trauma or abuse. Individuals with disorganized attachment long for closeness and intimacy, yet they often push others away. Those with secure attachment experience appropriate care and support and will usually cultivate healthy relationships.

31. B: Cultural and folk dances aid in developing respect for diversity as every student's culture can be included or represented through dance. In addition to the dance steps, students are introduced to the meaning behind dances, and historical and cultural facts that pertain to each culture. There are also dances in pop culture that are associated with certain cultural groups such as contemporary line dances. Locomotor movements are activities that children across diverse groups engage or participate in, but these do not inherently foster respect for cultural diversity. Not all students can dance due to mobile disabilities, but respect for other cultures can be gained by learning about others. Non-locomotor movements are inclusive activities that are utilized in dance but do not foster respect for diversity.

32. D: Deadlifts would be the best choice from the list to strengthen the lower back. Deadlifts also strengthen the hamstrings (muscles on the back of the leg). Lat pulls train the latissimus dorsi in the upper back. Rear deltoids and lateral raises are exercise for the shoulders.

33. A: This activity is an example of guided discovery. Guided discovery is a student-centered, inquiry-based instructional strategy that encourages students to explore the material independently or collaboratively.

34. C: Each of the answer choices is an example of a type of social responsibility in which an individual takes responsibility to serve other people. However, only choice C represents an action taken to serve the local community. The person receiving the flu vaccine is doing so for his family, not for his community. Tithing may benefit the larger community if funds are used for community service, but donations to the church vary from church to church and do not directly relate to the community at large. Tithing is also fully elective and related to religious motivations, therefore it is not typically considered a civic responsibility for civilians. A person altering his or her buying habits to reduce the amount of carbon he or she consumes and the amount of plastic released in the environment is an example of individual environmental social responsibility but would not count as civic duty as it does not directly relate to serving the community at hand.

35. B: The movement concepts of spatial awareness, relationships, and effort help refine and integrate skills, as combining these elements increases the locomotor movements' challenge, thus fostering mature movement patterns needed for manipulative activities. Demonstrations, as well as leading and following, aid in the refinement of the basic locomotor movements but will not independently help the student achieve skill integration and refine higher-level skills without incorporating the movement concepts.

36. B: PE teachers should design, choose, modify, and sequence game activities not simply to keep students busy (a) or prevent misbehavior (c). While they should ensure these activities promote maximum student enjoyment, this should not be the only purpose without any learning goals (d). Rather, they should aim for activities to promote student fitness, skill improvement, practice in sport-specific skills, AND enjoyment (b).

37. D: The purpose of a health fair is to provide information about health, share local resources, and offer basic preventative medical screenings for participants. Although the community resource guide is a useful tool for those seeking services, the community expressed a need for medical screenings and basic preventative care. Health professional conferences and school assemblies may be used to deliver health education, but the target population is limited to health practitioners and the school community, respectively.

38. D: Bandura's social learning theory is also known as observational learning theory, where watching someone's performance through modeling and demonstration as well as receiving feedback impact learning. Learning through touch, reading, and mental imagery also aid in learning but are not a part of observational learning theory.

39. C: Dribbling a soccer ball is on the upper end of the skill progression continuum, as it combines a locomotor movement with an object (a manipulative skill), and is one of the most difficult fundamental movement skills. Skipping, running, and jumping are basic locomotor or fundamental movements.

40. B: A common misconception among teenagers is that only vaginal penetration and ejaculation will cause pregnancy. Health educators should inform them that small drops of pre-ejaculate they may not detect can be released before as well as during sex. Pre-ejaculate also contains sperm; males cannot control its release; and vulvar contact alone can cause conception. Thus, there is a smaller but real chance of impregnating a girl without penetrating or ejaculating inside her vagina [a reason to do (C)]. Choices (A), (C), and (D) are all facts, not misconceptions, of which health educators can inform teens.

41. A: While feedback is important in physical education (PE) instruction, knowing when and when not to provide feedback is equally important to effective teaching. PE teachers need to give feedback to give students specific corrections to incorrectly performed techniques, for example. However, when a task furnishes inherent environmental feedback (B),—for example, a student throws a basketball, and it goes through the hoop—additional feedback may be unnecessary. When a student already has enough experience with a skill (C), sometimes PE teachers need not give them feedback. Also, when a teacher's demonstration enables students to see easily how to perform a skill correctly (D), they may need little or no additional feedback.

42. D: Informing parents of the physical benefits of dance, careers in dance, and perhaps male role models in dance may help change their perceptions (stereotypes) that boys/males do not or should not engage in dance. Discussing the risks of playing football could be a strategy, but the parents may find this offensive because they are pro-football and may see the benefits as outweighing the risks. Suggesting that the student participate in both does not necessarily support the student because he does may want to play football. Telling parents that they are wrong will likely be offensive and negatively impact the teacher-parent relationship.

43. D: In Stage 1 of motor learning, babies and toddlers develop beyond simple reflexive movements (e.g., rooting, sucking, startling, Babinski, Moro, palmar, plantar) to fundamental purposeful movements like sitting, crawling, standing, and walking. In Stage 2, young children develop more complex motor patterns (b), like running, climbing, jumping, balancing, catching, and throwing. In Stage 3, older children develop greater automaticity and fluidity in performing the Stage 2 motor patterns (c) while learning more specific movement skills. In Stage 4, adolescents master specialized movements while ability, motivation, and practice influence continuing general and specific motor skills development (d).

44. C: Kayaking is an activity that most involves the physical proficiency of dynamic strength. Static strength (A) is most involved in an activity like weight lifting. Trunk strength (B) is most involved in an activity like pole-vaulting. Explosive strength (D) is involved most in an activity like the standing long jump.

45. D: The vertical jump and volleyball spike have a similar jumping pattern because they are accomplished by jumping upward with two feet. The high jump uses a one-foot take off in a curved position; the long jump also uses a one-foot take-off, but the body propels horizontally with the feet leading. A basketball lay-up uses a one-foot take-off, and a volleyball spike and jump shot use a two-foot take-off.

46. B: School emergency procedures typically provide that injured students are initially offered first aid by physical educators with current first aid certification, and only seen by a school nurse for follow-up as needed (a); that all physical educators carry emergency first aid kits during PE classes (b); that ALL physical educators must have current first aid and CPR certification (c); and that PE teachers and other physical educators have a list of any students who did not return emergency treatment permission forms the first week of school (d).

47. C: Protein is needed to build and repair cells and body tissue. Carbohydrates are the main energy source. Fats also provide energy for the body but also protect organs, support cell function, and absorb nutrients. Minerals and vitamins support growth and development and help body systems function. Water helps regulate temperature, carries nutrients and oxygen, and protects organs like the brain.

48. C: The short-term effects of regular, substantial alcohol use include impaired judgment (A); distortion of perceptions, vision and hearing (B), and emotions; impaired coordination; bad breath; and hangovers. The long-term effects of heavy alcohol use include liver damage, sexual impotence, stomach disorders (D), vitamin deficiencies, skin problems, loss of appetite, loss of memory, damage to the heart and entire cardiovascular system, and damage to the central nervous system (C).

49. D: Parks and recreation centers are resources available to students from diverse communities that are either free, inexpensive, or have sliding scale fees based on socio-economics. Some schools have after-school programs, but not all offer physical activity programs. After school programs also cost extra resources and require that parents provide alternative transportation methods, and not all students live in the communities where they attend school. Basketball and tennis courts are available in some neighborhoods and are generally not supervised unless a part of the parks and recreation centers.

50. D: Summative assessments evaluate student comprehension and learning progress at the end of a lesson unit, academic quarter, or grade level. They are considered formal and high stakes. Formative assessments are usually informal continuous assessments of student comprehension. They are considered low stakes and consist of activities like entrance and exit tickets, sticky note self-assessments, thumbs-up responses, or anonymous polls. Performance assessments measure learning through application of content or tasks. They may be formal or informal. Norm-referenced assessments measure student knowledge compared to the "norm" (e.g., students of a similar age or developmental level).

51. C: Students are found more likely to develop internal motivation for learning and achieving in school when they perceive that they have some control over their own learning. Students who perceive that the teacher controls instruction are more likely to develop external than internal motivations (a); students who perceive ownership of their own learning and the content they learn are more likely to develop internal than external motivation (b). When they perceive that teachers control all instruction, students are more motivated, hence affected, by external rewards and punishments (d) than internal factors.

52. D: Modifying activities ensures equality in participation, learning, and succeeding in physical education. Activities can be modified by making skill activities easier for beginners and increasing skill challenges for advanced learners. Other modifications include increasing or decreasing time in activities, and varying distances, objects, targets, and boundaries. Recording teaching sessions will allow the teacher to evaluate if equity goals are met. Inviting administrators can provide feedback on equity, but it is not a physical education technique the ensures equal opportunities. Parents, unless educators or equity experts, are not in positions to evaluate teacher effectiveness. Parents may, however, observe a class to ensure that their child is being treated fairly. Appointing student captains is a technique used in physical education settings but does not ensure equal opportunities for students.

53. C: While having others observe and provide feedback can be beneficial to improve instruction, teachers should have effective tools that they can implement to assess their own effectiveness. The teacher should employ an Academic Learning Time in PE (ALT-PE) assessment to document the time that he talks during instruction. The teacher can conduct this during class or record the lesson and review the amount of time used talking later. It is inappropriate to ask students to assess a teacher's instructional delivery, as students are there to learn and are not qualified to make such an assessment.

54. D: Expectations, assessment, and accountability help establish student responsibility and self-control. The Teaching Personal and Social Responsibility (TPSR) model employs behavioral expectations where students self-assess their behaviors and progress so they can work to improve in deficient areas. Playing a team sport without rules and expectations does not garner self-control and student-responsibility. The course guide or syllabus contains the rules and expectations, but it does not help students achieve responsibility and self-control. Parents can provide meaningful information regarding their child's learning style and ability, but some parents may enable and engage in practices that limit student responsibility and self-control. Ultimately, the teacher is responsible for creating an environment that develops student responsibility.

55. A: The teacher is acting as a mediator in the scenario. Although mediation and negotiation are both used to resolve disputes between two parties, mediation requires the use of a third party to facilitate resolution whereas negotiation is only between the two disputing parties. Active listening is a tool that one can use when mediating or negotiating since it helps build trust and understanding between parties.

56. C: Research studies find that motor skills, endurance, and strength training all modify the spinal reflexes according to the specific behaviors each task requires. New blood vessels are formed (A) through endurance training but not motor skills or strength training. Motor maps are reorganized (B) through motor skills training but not endurance or strength training. New synapses are generated (D) through motor skills and strength training but not endurance training.

57. A: According to social psychologists, nonverbal communication has these primary functions: performing social rituals (A) like greetings, farewells, and so on; revealing personalities as well as interpersonal relationships (B); supporting verbal interactions (C); and expressing feelings (D).

58. A: A coordinated school health program includes comprehensive school health education addressing physical, cognitive, affective, and social health domains, differentiated for every developmental and age level to promote health knowledge, skills, and attitudes, decrease health risk behaviors, and enhance student health. Physical education is not separate (B) but is an essential component of a coordinated school health program. So are school health services, which include not only emergency care (C) but also prevention, education, referral, and acute and chronic health condition management. Another essential component of a coordinated school health program is family and community involvement (D).

59. C: Total community health-related spending is not included in CHAs. Available community resources, existing health programs and interventions, and other community assets are typically listed in the CHA to display how health issues are addressed. Demographics, socioeconomic statuses, and health data are collected to show a health snapshot of the community. Oftentimes, the data collected is used to demonstrate the need for policy change and how funds should be allocated to improve health outcomes.

60. D: The primary principle of the theory of deliberate practice is that practicing a skill needs to be a focused and reflective process. If the student is not deliberate, or focused on making progress, the student's volume of practice will not be enough to improve their skill level. A secondary principal of deliberate practice is that there needs to be much practice to see effective gains. Regardless of students' ability levels, including the ability level of those who are natural athletes, lots of practice is required to achieve mastery. Short bouts of regular practice have shown to be the most effective method of skill mastery. While some believe that practice makes perfect, performing a skill incorrectly repeatedly will negate mastery of the desired skill. "Perfect practice makes perfect" would be more appropriate.

61. C: According to the description, the test is reliable, meaning that it gives the same results every time it is administered, but it is not valid, meaning that it does not measure what it was intended to measure. Therefore, it is not correct that the test is neither reliable nor valid (A). It is not true that the test is valid but not reliable (B) but, rather, vice versa. The test is not both valid and reliable, and it is not simply misused (D); it is actually not valid because it does not test what it means or claims to test but assesses something else instead.

62. D: Malnutrition is not only caused by eating too little; it is also caused by eating foods that are not nutritious, eating unbalanced diets, and not getting enough of all necessary nutrients. Thus, people can eat too much and become overweight, but if most of the calories they consume are "empty", i.e., they contain few or no vitamins, minerals, protein, healthy fats, or fiber, they can suffer malnutrition. In fact, overconsumption of refined carbohydrates that lack fiber instead of whole grains; saturated and trans fats instead of monounsaturated and polyunsaturated fats; and processed foods instead of fruits and vegetables contribute to both obesity and malnutrition. Anxiety, depression, and other emotional factors can not only disrupt sleeping and eating, but also cause high blood pressure and heart disease (A). Stress and family dysfunction can cause both emotional and physical illness (B). Air pollution is found both to aggravate and to cause asthma (C).

63. C: In the first, cognitive stage of motor learning, learners understand the activity's goal and nature (A) and make initial attempts to perform it that include major errors (B). In the second, associative stage, learners engage in practice to master the timing of the skill, and they make fewer errors that are more consistent in nature (C). In the third, autonomous stage, learners perform the activity effortlessly and automatically (D), enabling them to redirect their attention to other aspects of the skill.

64. C: The Centers for Disease Control (CDC) advises health educators that it is more effective to give positive than negative instructions, for example, "Wear helmets when riding bicycles" rather than "Do not ride bicycles without wearing helmets." They also recommend engaging the audience immediately by stating the most important information first (A); keeping the number of ideas in each document or section to three or four (B); and instead of confusing audiences by alternating among subjects (D), fully developing one idea at a time before proceeding to another one.

65. D: Researchers have observed consistent gender differences in preschool physical and motor development; however, they also observe that in spite of these differences, overall the physical and motor development of preschoolers is more similar than different between genders. In general, the differences are not significant enough to place any emphasis on motor development differences between preschool boys and girls. Some known differences, however, include that preschool boys are more muscular than preschool girls, but preschool girls are more physically mature than preschool boys (A). While preschool boys exhibit more strength in large-muscle, gross-motor skills, preschool girls exhibit more coordination in large-muscle, gross-motor skills (B and C). Additionally, preschool girls are superior to preschool boys in fine-motor skills as well as gross-motor coordination (C).

66. C: As of 2014, 48 US states, the District of Columbia, plus Puerto Rico, the Virgin Islands, Guam, American Samoa, and the Northern Mariana Islands school, health care, child care, mental health, social services, and law enforcement employees are all mandated reporters of child maltreatment. Probation or parole officers are mandated reporters in 17 states; substance abuse counselors are in

14 states; and commercial film processors are in 12 states, Guam, and Puerto Rico (A). Employees, directors, and volunteers of camps and recreation and youth centers (B) are mandated reporters in 11 states. Domestic violence workers and humane or animal control officers are mandated reporters in 7 states and Washington, D.C.; college and university, technical and vocational school faculties, administrators, and other employees and volunteers (D) are mandated reporters in 4 states. Clergy are mandated reporters in 27 states and Guam.

67. C: Mr. Green can reduce the time it takes for attendance by taking it when students are engaged in an activity like the warm-up or instant activity. Setting an attendance time-limit will not likely decrease the time as 40 students need to be accounted for. Mr. Green could practice but practicing a managerial tool takes away from planning for instruction/learning. Squad lines where students sit or stand in the same spot make it easier to see absent students but unless a warm-up or activity is conducted in the squad lines, students have to wait to be engaged in activities.

68. C: High levels of LDL cholesterol can lead to atherosclerosis, or the buildup of plaque, in a person's arteries. If untreated, atherosclerosis can lead to heart disease, heart attack, or stroke. Consumption of red or processed meats, fried foods, and full-fat dairy products can contribute to high levels of LDL cholesterol in the body. It is recommended that those who eat red meat limit their consumption to less than 3 oz one to two times per week. Any form of tobacco can increase the risk of heart disease. Although excessive body fat can increase the risk of heart disease, a person should always consult a doctor to discuss what his or her ideal weight should be to prevent heart disease.

69. D: For effective class behavior management plans, physical education (PE) teachers should define their expectations positively in terms of what they want the students to do, not negatively in terms of what they want them not to do (C). They should limit expectations to five at most, as students will be unable to remember more than that, and put them in writing, not orally (A), posted visibly in locker rooms and on classroom bulletin boards. They also should enforce their stated expectations consistently, not just occasionally (B).

70. C: Quantitative assessments are norm-referenced or numerical, e.g., counting how many times a student can rally a tennis ball against a wall in one minute. However, a complex skill like this takes longer for beginning students to master, so measuring their learning and progress by having them perform the whole skill is not accurate. **Qualitative** assessments, like having students demonstrate key components of the tennis forehand (a), (b), (d) while rallying against a wall, show their progress even before they are ready to play the game.

71. B: To enhance students' perceived physical competence, it is better for physical education (PE) teachers not to specify how many trials to complete during a certain time period (A) but rather to specify the time period for practicing without requiring any specific number of trials (B). This allows students to focus not on how many times they complete the actions but rather on perfecting their technique. Rather than emphasizing technical errors they make (C), it is better to emphasize which things students do well technically, providing positive reinforcement that increases their motivation to practice. Varying assigned activities is more effective to minimize off-task student behavior than not varying them (D).

72. D: School health needs assessments collect data (e.g., achievement data, health status, health attitudes and behaviors of school stakeholders, community input) to determine the perceived or actual health needs and establish strategies for addressing those needs. Results may be used to establish school health goals, determine priorities for school health programs, and assess school health needs. Defining the purpose of the needs assessment (e.g., how it will be used, who will participate, defining the target population) is the first step in conducting a needs assessment.

73. D: A rubric should be used before learning (C), when teachers go over all parts of the rubric with the students to explain how it defines what they are expected to learn, that is, their learning objectives. Then teachers should instruct students to use the rubric during learning (B) to guide their learning experiences, activities, and products according to the learning objectives specified in the rubric. Finally, teachers apply the rubric after learning (A) to assess whether the students have fulfilled the learning objectives it specifies.

74. B: The transtheoretical model is another term for the stages of change model of health behavior. The behavioral change model (A) encompasses multiple theories, including the public health model (C); a planning model containing four steps (defining the problem, identifying the risk, developing and testing prevention methods, and communicating which interventions were effective); and the health belief model (D), which ascertains whether and why an individual will change his or her behavior by evaluating the perception of threat from disease and the net benefits of behavioral change.

75. D: There are four categories of classroom management styles: authoritarian, authoritative, permissive, and indulgent. Each differs based on the level of student engagement and control over the classroom. Teachers with an authoritarian teaching style have high control and low student engagement, which means that the classroom environment is highly structured with few disruptions, yet the teachers make little effort to form bonds with the students. Authoritative teachers have a high level of control over the classroom and are highly invested in each student's success. They set and reinforce behavioral expectations and forms strong connections with the students. Permissive teachers have low control over the classroom and low involvement with students. They often fail to set or maintain classroom rules or punish poor behavior. They are also often ill-prepared for teaching and fail to meet student needs. Teachers with an indulgent teaching style demonstrate a genuine interest and care for their students. Students trust and feel connected to their teacher, which often enhances student engagement. However, teachers with an indulgent teaching style lack the assertiveness and discipline necessary to control their classrooms.

76. B: Children are liable to be more vulnerable to environmental health risks than adults for several reasons. For one, children's body systems are immature and are still developing, making them easier to damage than those of adults, not vice versa (A). For another, children have smaller body sizes than adults do, so they take in more not fewer (C) toxins through the air they breathe, the water they drink, and the foods they eat. Additionally, the normal behaviors of children expose them to more, not fewer (D) toxins than normal adult behaviors do. Children are more likely to handle and mouth unsanitary and toxic substances and objects; to engage in physical contact with others having contagious illnesses; to go without washing their hands before and after using the bathroom, eating, etc.; to expose themselves unwittingly to various environmental toxins; and to lack experience and judgment about exposure.

77. A: Self-assessment is a self-regulation tool designed to help students evaluate skill development and refine skills. Self-assessment allows students to ascertain the quality of their own performance based on skill cues. They focus on the missed cues to refine the performance. The teacher usually administers a survey or inventory of learning preferences, which helps to plan for instruction. Self-assessment is designed for student growth and should not determine student outcomes because that is the teacher's job. The teacher also administers or determines which summative assessment will be used to establish what was learned.

78. A: Assuming that Tom will stop any unwanted sexual advances based on Louisa's nonverbal cues is the least effective strategy. Effective refusal skills include making excuses, making a joke, saying "no," redirecting the conversation, proposing alternative activities, and physically leaving the situation.

79. A: Pros of wind energy include space efficiency, no pollution, and low operational costs. Cons of wind energy include wind fluctuation, threats to wildlife, and the expense to manufacture and install.

80. C: The human skin regulates the body's temperature, and the skin is a part of the integumentary systems, which also includes the hair, nails, and sweat and oil glands. The lymphatic (A) system defends the body against infections and helps the circulatory system by returning fluids to the bloodstream. The circulatory (B) system supplies oxygen and nutrients in blood to all body tissue cells, exchanges oxygenated blood for metabolic waste products, and transports waste for elimination. The musculoskeletal (D) system provides body shape, support, stability, and locomotion, and protects the internal organs via bones and muscles. Bones also store minerals, including calcium, and the bone marrow produces blood cells.

81. A: Companies like Biokinetics (www.biokinetics.com) use different machinery, software, and procedures to test sports equipment like helmets against official standards. While drop tests from towers traditionally test helmet impact performance, this method cannot accurately test football head-to-head collision impacts (b) because players collide at much higher speeds; linear impact tests, with rams hitting auto crash-simulation headforms, are used (a). Different tests and apparatus test helmet retention system stretch rather than strength and stability (c). Helmet mouthguards not only protect teeth, but also brains from concussions (d); headforms with articulating mandibles test this.

82. A: The problem with letting each student choose his or her own physical activity without any further guidelines is that such an approach lacks organization, which can inadvertently suggest that the class is not to be taken seriously and make it more difficult to teach important specific content or skills. One good way of maximizing participation in a physical education class is grouping students according to skill level (B). For instance, having skilled students play with skilled students, or arranging teams so that they have a mix of beginning and more advanced students. Another way to maximize participation is to offer different specific activities at individual stations, making the most use of equipment and appealing to a range of interests (C). Changing the rules of games to better suit student skill levels (D) is also a good way to ensure more student participation.

83. B: Research-based strategies found to promote student motivation include not only teacher interest in student learning, but also teacher personal interest (a) in their students' backgrounds and concerns; teacher demonstration of their own motivation and passion as role models for students (b); teacher belief in students' abilities (c) as well as interest in students; and teacher personalization of content for individual students (d).

84. A: At least 80 percent of adolescents develop acne. This is not due to inadequate or incorrect facial skin care but to hormonal changes. Health educators should inform teen students how to treat and not treat acne. Hormonal changes in puberty also frequently make teens' hair oilier, so they are likely to need to shampoo it more often (B). Many teenagers have to wear braces, which makes oral hygiene more complicated and challenging; additionally, fresh breath becomes more important to them in adolescence. Therefore, the same oral hygiene they practiced in childhood usually will not suffice (C). Hormonal changes also cause increased perspiration, so adolescents need to bathe more often than in childhood (D).

85. A: Constantly reporting one's locations and activities to the partner is a sign of being domestically abused as well as appearing desperate to please the partner; agreeing with all the partner's words and actions; often receiving harassing partner contacts; and mentioning partner possessiveness, jealousy, or temper. Often exhibiting or trying to hide injuries or excusing them as accidents (B) or clumsiness is a sign of being physically abused. Marked personality and behavioral changes (C) are psychological symptoms of being abused. Making few or no public outings, use of the car or money, or visits with friends and family (D) are signs of being isolated by an abuser.

86. A: Agriculture consumes the largest amount of water in the US. Therefore, a water conservation intervention that incentivizes the installation of highly efficient watering systems has the potential for greater impact than the other strategies.

87. B: Setting team goals fosters teamwork since, ideally, all members agree and are committed to working towards the same goal. Team captains help lead and can remind players of the common goals, but this is not the best strategy to foster teamwork, as not all teams have captains. Meeting with players individually is more appropriate for individual goal setting or to inform players of behaviors counter to teamwork, such as not passing the ball. Watching videos can help identify and provide feedback regarding teamwork, but setting goals and expectations must occur for this to be an effective strategy.

88. A: Students need more extrinsic (external) feedback from teachers or coaches when learning new PE skills. When they are more competent and confident with certain PE skills, they can analyze their own performance and make use of this intrinsic (internal) feedback. Choice (b) has this backwards. Students need both positive feedback for reinforcement and encouragement and negative feedback for correction (c), and both constructive and corrective (d) feedback, at all learning stages.

89. D: The first step a person should take when encountering a scenario like this is to call 911 and follow the dispatcher's instructions. Usually, the second step is to find an AED as it can help to guide a trained or untrained person through CPR, monitor vital signs, and administer shocks if necessary. In this situation, After checking for responsiveness, breathing, and pulse and calling 911, Jessica would most likely be guided by the operator through the use of an AED. AEDs are intended to be usable by anyone, even if the individual is not CPR-certified. The American Heart Association recommends that an untrained person administer hands-only CPR. Hands-only CPR consists of chest compressions delivered at a rate of 100 beats per minute and a depth of two inches. Blind swipes of the mouth to remove foreign objects are no longer encouraged due to risks for further lodging the object into the airway. Conventional CPR consists of giving two breaths after every 30 compressions.

90. C: While interactions with individuals of a different cultural group can unearth new perspectives, a teacher should discuss cultural norms and beliefs with current students to assess learning needs. In-depth interviews with parents, pretests and learning needs assessments, and posttests are effective strategies for assessing learning needs. Teachers may also consult previous teachers and content standards to determine a student's actual and anticipated developmental progress and cognitive abilities.

91. B: The original impetus for the National Health Education Standards (NHES) was that health education, physical education, public health, and school health authorities observed standards being developed for other subject-area content in education (B) and decided that the subject area of health education needed similar standards developed. Health educators were not influenced by standards developed in hospitals (A), public health (C) agencies, or private medical practice (D).

92. B: Force or effort is the most emphasized movement concept in the leap as it requires power on the take-off, and force is absorbed on the landing while maintaining body control. Rhythm is the movement concept that helps students develop creative movements to music or sounds, e.g., a drum beat. Time is the movement rate and is used across locomotor movements but is not the leap's dominant movement concept. The leap is performed at a medium or high level.

93. D: Experts recommend that to foster collaboration among teachers, school leaders should earmark resources for supporting classroom observation, planning, and mentoring; cultivate senses of shared responsibility in all faculty members (a); and recruit experienced teachers, both for the induction and mentoring of new teachers (b) and also for teacher professional development (c).

94. A: Student choice has been shown to increase student motivation as it empowers students to make their own decisions rather than the teacher directing instruction. Physical education models of choice include cooperative learning, adventure education, sport education, and Teaching Games for Understanding (TGfU). Direct instruction and traditional teaching approaches are teacher-driven and based on the teacher's decisions. Competitive instruction has been shown to motivate highly athletic students but de-motivate less athletic or competitive students.

95. D: Communicating high expectations of students to parents makes them allies, and enables parents to reinforce teacher expectations at home. Research finds parental expectations strongly predict student achievement. Teachers should communicate about the whole class, not just parents' own children (B). This enables parents to see teachers' viewpoints about decisions not ideal for individual students but best for the group. Teachers should ask parents which communication methods they prefer, and use these (C). They should measure results like parental participation, student preparation, and which methods elicit the highest student and parent responses, adjusting communication plans accordingly (D).

96. B: "Follow through!" is an example of prescriptive feedback, which is specific. It specifies an instruction that corrects or improves what the student or athlete is doing or needs to do. In this example, it tells the student or athlete that, when batting, kicking, throwing, and so on, he or she must follow the movement through for it to be effective rather than stopping it abruptly upon contact or release. The other examples are all descriptive feedback, which is general. It gives students or athletes positive social reinforcement by encouraging or praising their performance in general but does not specify exactly what it was that they did well or need to do better or differently.

97. A: Jonathon and Charles have defined the problem (Charles feels Jonathon is more focused on work than their relationship) and established the criteria (Jonathon and Charles will increase the amount of time they spend together each week to ensure both of their needs are met). The next step in the DECIDE model is to consider the possible choices. Therefore, the next best step is to consider the amount of time they will dedicate each week and the types of activities they can do together.

98. C: Kinetics is the division of biomechanics that studies the forces causing motion. Newton's First Law of Inertia, Second Law of Momentum, and Third Law of Reaction are most closely related to kinetics. Coplanar vectors (A) belong in the biomechanics division of vector algebra. Kinematics (B) is the biomechanics division that describes motion. Kinematics involves physics concepts including mass, center of gravity, inertia, displacement, linear and angular motion, linear and angular velocity, and acceleration. The biomechanics division of forces (D) involves concepts including center of pressure; force line; resultant force; muscular forces, joint forces, joint reaction forces, ground reaction forces, resisting forces, inertial forces, and gravitational forces; and fulcrums, levers, rotation, couples, equilibrium, weight, friction, and mechanical advantage.

99. C: Training at a percentage of the maximum heart rate (MHR) is used to assess heart rate intensity during exercise. For cardiovascular fitness, working at 65 to 85% of the MHR is the recommended range, with beginners starting at the lower limits and advanced exercisers working at the upper limits. Elite endurance athletes or those with high cardiovascular fitness can work at 90% of MHR. Continuous aerobic activity is a method to determine the time and/or distance of the activity. The talk test aids in determining relative intensity based on if one can or cannot talk or sing during cardiovascular activities. If one is unable to talk, the intensity is too high for continuous activity. If one can talk but not sing, the intensity is at a moderate level. If they can sing, the intensity is too low. Recovery heart rate is the time it takes for the heart to return to normal or rest after activity and is one way to measure cardiovascular improvements. The fitter one becomes, the faster the heart rate returns to normal.

100. A: MyFitnessPal is an app that features healthy recipes (B) and an extensive food database, whereby users can enter meals to calculate caloric and nutritional content. The Endomondo Sports Tracker features Audio Coach feedback (C) on user exercise performance. Endomondo and Fitbit both include social networking (D) capabilities for sharing fitness motivation, goals, progress, support, and reinforcement with friends. One thing these apps share in common is that they all sync (A) with each other as well as with other apps, devices, and online tools. MyFitnessPal and Endomondo sync with heart-rate monitors as well as with each other and Fitbit.

101. A: Large-scale state research has found that student cardiovascular fitness achievement and healthy body mass index (BMI) scores correlate positively with student scores on the state academic achievement test of knowledge and skills. Other research has found that children who are more physically fit demonstrate not only quicker reaction times but also more accurate responses (B). Another investigation found that children burn more calories and take nearly twice as many steps during teacher-led fitness activities as during active gaming, not vice versa (C). Other studies show that intense exercise is followed by improvement in cognitive function (D).

102. A: Animal walks help students conceptualize the different levels because there are animals that move or travel at low levels (snakes), medium levels (dog), and high levels (giraffe). As students have often been exposed to animals via books, visits to the zoo, in class, and on TV, they tend to recognize the size and movement patterns. Tag games, jumping rope, and nature walks tend to only occur at a high level with little opportunity to change levels.

103. B: Although the health enthusiast has a keen interest in heart health, he or she is not a credible source of information since the health enthusiast holds no formal certification. Since the information is presented through a personal blog post, the information may be misrepresented, inaccurate, or biased. Valid sources of health information can be found through government websites and materials. Nonprofits and medical or health-related associations are also valid sources of health information.

104. D: According to research findings, adolescents must have practice with making decisions in real life to transfer the cognitive skills they have acquired for decision making to reality. Studies identify that variables influencing teen decision-making skills include their levels of conformity with parental or peer norms (A); demographic characteristics like age, race, ethnicity, gender, social class; and family dynamics, family structure, and personal characteristics like intelligence and temperance as well (B). Research also shows that adolescents tend to be more oriented to the present and short-term consequences and goals and need to be taught future orientation, long-term goals (C), and planning.

105. A: The Babinski reflex occurs when the sole of the foot is firmly stroked vertically: the big toe moves upward and the other toes fan outward. This is normal in newborns and disappears anytime between 1 and 2 years of age. The stepping reflex (B), wherein newborns automatically perform a stepping motion when held upright with their feet on or near a surface, typically disappears around the age of 2 months. The palmar grasping reflex (C), wherein a baby will grasp an offered adult finger in his or her fist, typically disappears around 3–4 months. The tonic reflex (D), wherein newborns assume the "fencing position" with the head turned to one side, one arm in front of the eyes and the other arm bent at the elbow, typically disappears around the age of 4 months.

106. D: Circuit training is an effective method to teach all of the health-related activities when there is limited time, as dedication to each component can be included. Resistance training can be included in circuit training, but performed independently, it addresses only muscular strength and muscular endurance—two health-related fitness components. Interval training is inherent in circuit training as there is a particular time or amount of activity followed by transitional rest periods. Intervals can also be explicit within circuit training but do not guarantee coverage of all health-related fitness components independently and are often used for cardiovascular fitness. Fartlek training is speed training for running and does not provide well-rounded coverage of the health-related fitness components.

107. D: A norm-referenced (a) assessment or standardized test evaluates basic PE skills objectively by comparing student results to those of a normative, representative student sample group. A process assessment (b) is a subjective approach, using observation to identify and correct errors in skill form, mechanics, or style. Product assessments (how fast/high/many/far) are quantitative, hence objective. A criterion-referenced (c) assessment evaluates PE skills against defined performance standards. PE teachers can also evaluate performance using biomechanical learning objectives (d) as in the example described.

108. A: For large classes, a checklist of skills is the fastest method to assess motor skills. This checklist can be in the format of a rubric, with particular performance activities or behaviors to look for, making the assessment efficient to quantify and look for in large groups of students. Peer and self-assessments are excellent strategies to help students gain understanding of skill performance but should not be used for the instructor's evaluation of skills. Video analysis of skills is an effective strategy to assess skills, but this method is slow and time-consuming and not ideal to assess skills when there is a faster method to choose from for large class sizes.

109. C: Motivation competence is developed when students experience success in easier tasks that builds confidence to try more difficult tasks. Self-regulation is awareness of how one learns and acceptance of the responsibility for the learning. Emotional development is the ability to manage feelings and emotions to focus on learning. Autonomous development is when learners perform tasks easily or automatically, as they have mastered the skill and no longer have to think about it.

110. B: Contemplation follows precontemplation—the stage in which a person does not recognize or is uninterested in modifying his or her behavior—and precedes preparation—the stage in which a person commits to changing his or her behavior. Contemplation is the correct answer because the person has already acknowledged that his or her weight is unmanaged, yet has not committed to actively losing it. In this stage, the person reviews the negative aspects of a health behavior and considers the benefits of behavior change.

111. C: In dual and individual sports, the expectation is that noise is minimal during gameplay. In contrast, during team sports, especially invasion games, loud noise is expected and promoted as fans cheer on their teams. In individual sports, there are only personal fouls and in team sports there are personal and team fouls, but these are rule differences rather than etiquette issues. In tennis, coaches cannot coach players during match play, but coaches can coach the entire game during team sports. These are also rules and not matters of etiquette.

112. A: When students learn new skills or improve existing skills, they tend to feel a sense of accomplishment, which can lead to improved self-esteem (higher regard of oneself). This is the best answer. Option B makes a true statement, but wonder at human athleticism is not as clearly linked to improved self-esteem as learning new skills or improving one's skills (a student might feel wonder at a person who is athletically gifted and feel inferior in comparison). Option C can be rejected because there is no clear connection between learning to take turns and improved self-esteem. Option D can be rejected because endorphins, which can be released in the course of exercise, make a person feel good in the sense of being in a good mood, rather than fostering the general condition of improved self-esteem.

113. D: Moving creatively to varied music rhythms using simple dance steps (a) is a movement skill competency suitable for students in the first grade. Jumping rope to the tempo of music, both singly and with a partner (b), is suitable for students in the second grade. Bouncing, passing, and catching a ball to match a musical rhythm (c) is suitable for students in the third grade. Expressing feelings or ideas through rhythmic motion, with and without music (d), is suitable for students in the fifth grade.

114. A: Most communities have parks and recreation centers that provide physical activity programming for children, adults, and families which are usually free, low cost, and/or have sliding scale fees based on income. Parks and recreation leaders have degrees and/or training in providing physical activity services. Some areas have hiking trails but these areas tend to be unsupervised and can be unsafe for children. Special equipment is needed for rock climbing and can be expensive. Some parks and recreation facilities offer indoor rock-climbing walls. Fitness centers are appropriate for high-school-aged students but some are for adults only or require a parental waiver for youth under 18 and require a fee. Many parks and recreation facilities have fitness centers for youth.

115. D: A teacher using reflection to inform instruction is less likely to use (A) as placing the responsibility for meeting the objective entirely with the students betrays a lack of reflection. Reflective teachers evaluate how students respond to their instruction, analyze their own design and implementation of lessons, evaluate the results, and determine how they can change what they do to promote the best outcomes for their students. Thus, the teacher using reflection might see whether having the students play the next game faster (B) will increase their heart rates to the target range, or change the game rules to enhance more active participation by all students (C), or even both of these.

116. C: Including students' families in school-based decision-making helps ensure they feel encouraged to actively participate in the education program. This strengthens positive relationships between the school and family members, which promote student academic achievement and development. By sending out a survey regarding the curriculum and school environment, the administration encourages families to contribute their thoughts, ideas, and opinions regarding decisions that would enhance the learning experience for their children.

117. D: The model described and named *direct instruction* (lower-case) by Rosenshine and Stevens in 1986 is a generic instructional model; the Direct Instruction (capitalized) model pioneered in the 1960s by Siegfried Engelmann and his colleagues is a specific instructional model. However, both share in common the characteristics of teacher-directed, skills-oriented (A), face-to-face, small-group (B) instruction that uses task analysis, deliberate sequencing (C), and explicit teaching (D).

118. B: Physical education (PE) instructors can address negligence in instruction (A) by ensuring they teach students the correct procedures and protocols for safety and for equipment setup, use, and takedown and ensuring students understand and practice how to execute sport and movement activities beforehand. Because PE classes often are large and getting larger, they can address negligence best in supervision (B) by ensuring they continually and actively supervise students throughout all activities and enlisting students to practice peer supervision in addition to supplement teacher supervision. In transportation (C), teachers and coaches are liable outside of school and must obtain written parental consent; follow all school policies, practices, and procedures; and supervise student behavior on buses. In class environments (D), teachers and coaches must be alert for possible dangerous conditions, which can vary daily, and space students to limit hazards.

119. B: The first-year teacher should consult the state- and national-level physical education guidelines. Each state has a physical education association with physical education guidelines, and SHAPE America provides national physical education guidelines, standards, and recommendations. Unless the principal was a physical education teacher, they are not a content expert. Former or veteran physical education teachers may not be abreast of current guidelines, standards, and best practices.

120. D: A copper IUD is a 99 percent effective nonhormonal contraception that lasts up to 12 years. It is the most appropriate option since Suzanne would like a long-term solution that requires little maintenance. While progestin implants are equally effective and last up to five years, implants release the hormone progestin to prevent ovulation and obstruct sperm by thickening cervical mucus. Depo-Provera shots—also called Depo shots or birth control shots—are also 99 percent effective. However, birth control shots must be administered every three months. Female or internal condoms are less than 80 percent effective and must be used every time that a couple has sexual intercourse. Similarly, male condoms must be used every time but are slightly more effective (approximately 87 percent effective). Condoms are the only contraceptive option of those listed that also prevent STD transmission.

121. D: "Match up" as a defense cue in basketball means that students should defend other players who are as similar to them in size, fitness, and skill level as possible—not just in size (C). This cue does not mean to pair up with another player (A). Staying near to the offensive players they are defending wherever they move on the court (B) is indicated to students with a cue of "Shadow" rather than "Match up."

122. A: Although a scholarly article from the Journal of the American Medical Association often contains in-depth research about a health topic, it is not accessible to diverse audiences. The article is likely to include scientific jargon, long block text, and few graphics. Materials and practices that are generally supportive of diverse audiences include those that use closed-captions or transcripts of videos and audio-based materials, use 12-point or larger font, chunk content or use bullet points, omit technical jargon, and use a colorblind-friendly palette. A teacher can make educational material more inclusive by omitting any culturally specific references to idioms and incorporating a range of diverse identities and experiences.

123. B: Typically, between birth and the age of two years, children grow to four times their newborn weights. This is the most rapid period of physical growth. After this, children's growth slows incrementally, decreasing between two and three years and decreasing even more between four and six years.

124. D: Students can get bored sitting in squad lines which increases off-task behaviors or behavioral problems. An active squad line approach and frequently changing squad lines may keep students engaged and lessen boredom and off-task behaviors. Locating absent students is generally a faster approach than taking attendance for all present students. Squad lines are considered vintage or an outdated approach but can be effective for extremely large class sizes and combined with learning outcomes, e.g., active warm-up. Squad-lines may or may not be teacher-centered, which depends on how the squads are created and whether squad line leaders are used. Using squad leaders is a recommendation to speed up taking attendance, provide student-leadership, and reduce boredom.

125. D: A PE teacher can use data that measure student learning to show students are learning, which in turn shows he or she is teaching (a); to show what students need to practice AND what they already know (b); to show which students need more help AND which students are making progress (c); and to show the value of the PE program to stakeholders (d), which can prevent or minimize PE program budget cuts, defunding, or elimination, as well as even promote PE program and funding expansion.

126. B: SODAS (situation, options, disadvantages, advantages, and solution) and ICED (identify the problem, create alternatives, evaluate the alternatives, and decide on the best solution) are decision-making frameworks that guide students through responsible decision-making. Decision trees and other flowcharts can help students visually organize components of a decision-making model; however, they are not frameworks. The Objectives and Key Results model and the SMART framework are used for setting goals.

127. C: Activities that require agility and lower-body strength, which do not involve body contact (A), are most appropriate for coed participation and are less dependent on team assignment by student skill levels. For activities that require more upper-body strength (B), it is more important for physical education teachers to assign teams according to individual student skill levels to prevent injuries. Therefore, (D) is incorrect.

128. B: The woman described in the scenario is binge drinking, which is associated with dehydration, alcohol poisoning, unintentional injury, and risk-taking behaviors. Alcohol is also a mood-altering drug and can lead to intentional self-harm if the person is in poor mental health. Although repeated binge drinking can lead to alcohol addiction, it is unlikely she would develop an alcohol addiction after one instance of binge drinking.

129. D: This physical program meets proposed guidelines in student engagement and the large teaching area. SHAPE America recommends that students are engaged in activity at least 50% of the time. The equipment ratio and class size are ineffective characteristics of a physical education program. Class size recommendations are between 25 and 35 students with a 2:1 student-to-equipment ratio.

130. C: Abilities result from the genetic make-up of an individual, which vary among students in physical education. With practice, most individuals can improve their motor skills, but the degree of improvement is contingent upon their abilities.

How to Overcome Test Anxiety

Just the thought of taking a test is enough to make most people a little nervous. A test is an important event that can have a long-term impact on your future, so it's important to take it seriously and it's natural to feel anxious about performing well. But just because anxiety is normal, that doesn't mean that it's helpful in test taking, or that you should simply accept it as part of your life. Anxiety can have a variety of effects. These effects can be mild, like making you feel slightly nervous, or severe, like blocking your ability to focus or remember even a simple detail.

If you experience test anxiety—whether severe or mild—it's important to know how to beat it. To discover this, first you need to understand what causes test anxiety.

Causes of Test Anxiety

While we often think of anxiety as an uncontrollable emotional state, it can actually be caused by simple, practical things. One of the most common causes of test anxiety is that a person does not feel adequately prepared for their test. This feeling can be the result of many different issues such as poor study habits or lack of organization, but the most common culprit is time management. Starting to study too late, failing to organize your study time to cover all of the material, or being distracted while you study will mean that you're not well prepared for the test. This may lead to cramming the night before, which will cause you to be physically and mentally exhausted for the test. Poor time management also contributes to feelings of stress, fear, and hopelessness as you realize you are not well prepared but don't know what to do about it.

Other times, test anxiety is not related to your preparation for the test but comes from unresolved fear. This may be a past failure on a test, or poor performance on tests in general. It may come from comparing yourself to others who seem to be performing better or from the stress of living up to expectations. Anxiety may be driven by fears of the future—how failure on this test would affect your educational and career goals. These fears are often completely irrational, but they can still negatively impact your test performance.

Elements of Test Anxiety

As mentioned earlier, test anxiety is considered to be an emotional state, but it has physical and mental components as well. Sometimes you may not even realize that you are suffering from test anxiety until you notice the physical symptoms. These can include trembling hands, rapid heartbeat, sweating, nausea, and tense muscles. Extreme anxiety may lead to fainting or vomiting. Obviously, any of these symptoms can have a negative impact on testing. It is important to recognize them as soon as they begin to occur so that you can address the problem before it damages your performance.

The mental components of test anxiety include trouble focusing and inability to remember learned information. During a test, your mind is on high alert, which can help you recall information and stay focused for an extended period of time. However, anxiety interferes with your mind's natural processes, causing you to blank out, even on the questions you know well. The strain of testing during anxiety makes it difficult to stay focused, especially on a test that may take several hours. Extreme anxiety can take a huge mental toll, making it difficult not only to recall test information but even to understand the test questions or pull your thoughts together.

Effects of Test Anxiety

Test anxiety is like a disease—if left untreated, it will get progressively worse. Anxiety leads to poor performance, and this reinforces the feelings of fear and failure, which in turn lead to poor performances on subsequent tests. It can grow from a mild nervousness to a crippling condition. If allowed to progress, test anxiety can have a big impact on your schooling, and consequently on your future.

Test anxiety can spread to other parts of your life. Anxiety on tests can become anxiety in any stressful situation, and blanking on a test can turn into panicking in a job situation. But fortunately, you don't have to let anxiety rule your testing and determine your grades. There are a number of relatively simple steps you can take to move past anxiety and function normally on a test and in the rest of life.

Physical Steps for Beating Test Anxiety

While test anxiety is a serious problem, the good news is that it can be overcome. It doesn't have to control your ability to think and remember information. While it may take time, you can begin taking steps today to beat anxiety.

Just as your first hint that you may be struggling with anxiety comes from the physical symptoms, the first step to treating it is also physical. Rest is crucial for having a clear, strong mind. If you are tired, it is much easier to give in to anxiety. But if you establish good sleep habits, your body and mind will be ready to perform optimally, without the strain of exhaustion. Additionally, sleeping well helps you to retain information better, so you're more likely to recall the answers when you see the test questions.

Getting good sleep means more than going to bed on time. It's important to allow your brain time to relax. Take study breaks from time to time so it doesn't get overworked, and don't study right before bed. Take time to rest your mind before trying to rest your body, or you may find it difficult to fall asleep.

Along with sleep, other aspects of physical health are important in preparing for a test. Good nutrition is vital for good brain function. Sugary foods and drinks may give a burst of energy but this burst is followed by a crash, both physically and emotionally. Instead, fuel your body with protein and vitamin-rich foods.

Also, drink plenty of water. Dehydration can lead to headaches and exhaustion, especially if your brain is already under stress from the rigors of the test. Particularly if your test is a long one, drink water during the breaks. And if possible, take an energy-boosting snack to eat between sections.

Along with sleep and diet, a third important part of physical health is exercise. Maintaining a steady workout schedule is helpful, but even taking 5-minute study breaks to walk can help get your blood pumping faster and clear your head. Exercise also releases endorphins, which contribute to a positive feeling and can help combat test anxiety.

When you nurture your physical health, you are also contributing to your mental health. If your body is healthy, your mind is much more likely to be healthy as well. So take time to rest, nourish your body with healthy food and water, and get moving as much as possible. Taking these physical steps will make you stronger and more able to take the mental steps necessary to overcome test anxiety.

Mental Steps for Beating Test Anxiety

Working on the mental side of test anxiety can be more challenging, but as with the physical side, there are clear steps you can take to overcome it. As mentioned earlier, test anxiety often stems from lack of preparation, so the obvious solution is to prepare for the test. Effective studying may be the most important weapon you have for beating test anxiety, but you can and should employ several other mental tools to combat fear.

First, boost your confidence by reminding yourself of past success—tests or projects that you aced. If you're putting as much effort into preparing for this test as you did for those, there's no reason you should expect to fail here. Work hard to prepare; then trust your preparation.

Second, surround yourself with encouraging people. It can be helpful to find a study group, but be sure that the people you're around will encourage a positive attitude. If you spend time with others who are anxious or cynical, this will only contribute to your own anxiety. Look for others who are motivated to study hard from a desire to succeed, not from a fear of failure.

Third, reward yourself. A test is physically and mentally tiring, even without anxiety, and it can be helpful to have something to look forward to. Plan an activity following the test, regardless of the outcome, such as going to a movie or getting ice cream.

When you are taking the test, if you find yourself beginning to feel anxious, remind yourself that you know the material. Visualize successfully completing the test. Then take a few deep, relaxing breaths and return to it. Work through the questions carefully but with confidence, knowing that you are capable of succeeding.

Developing a healthy mental approach to test taking will also aid in other areas of life. Test anxiety affects more than just the actual test—it can be damaging to your mental health and even contribute to depression. It's important to beat test anxiety before it becomes a problem for more than testing.

Study Strategy

Being prepared for the test is necessary to combat anxiety, but what does being prepared look like? You may study for hours on end and still not feel prepared. What you need is a strategy for test prep. The next few pages outline our recommended steps to help you plan out and conquer the challenge of preparation.

STEP 1: SCOPE OUT THE TEST

Learn everything you can about the format (multiple choice, essay, etc.) and what will be on the test. Gather any study materials, course outlines, or sample exams that may be available. Not only will this help you to prepare, but knowing what to expect can help to alleviate test anxiety.

STEP 2: MAP OUT THE MATERIAL

Look through the textbook or study guide and make note of how many chapters or sections it has. Then divide these over the time you have. For example, if a book has 15 chapters and you have five days to study, you need to cover three chapters each day. Even better, if you have the time, leave an extra day at the end for overall review after you have gone through the material in depth.

If time is limited, you may need to prioritize the material. Look through it and make note of which sections you think you already have a good grasp on, and which need review. While you are studying, skim quickly through the familiar sections and take more time on the challenging parts.

Write out your plan so you don't get lost as you go. Having a written plan also helps you feel more in control of the study, so anxiety is less likely to arise from feeling overwhelmed at the amount to cover.

STEP 3: GATHER YOUR TOOLS

Decide what study method works best for you. Do you prefer to highlight in the book as you study and then go back over the highlighted portions? Or do you type out notes of the important information? Or is it helpful to make flashcards that you can carry with you? Assemble the pens, index cards, highlighters, post-it notes, and any other materials you may need so you won't be distracted by getting up to find things while you study.

If you're having a hard time retaining the information or organizing your notes, experiment with different methods. For example, try color-coding by subject with colored pens, highlighters, or post-it notes. If you learn better by hearing, try recording yourself reading your notes so you can listen while in the car, working out, or simply sitting at your desk. Ask a friend to quiz you from your flashcards, or try teaching someone the material to solidify it in your mind.

STEP 4: CREATE YOUR ENVIRONMENT

It's important to avoid distractions while you study. This includes both the obvious distractions like visitors and the subtle distractions like an uncomfortable chair (or a too-comfortable couch that makes you want to fall asleep). Set up the best study environment possible: good lighting and a comfortable work area. If background music helps you focus, you may want to turn it on, but otherwise keep the room quiet. If you are using a computer to take notes, be sure you don't have any other windows open, especially applications like social media, games, or anything else that could distract you. Silence your phone and turn off notifications. Be sure to keep water close by so you stay hydrated while you study (but avoid unhealthy drinks and snacks).

Also, take into account the best time of day to study. Are you freshest first thing in the morning? Try to set aside some time then to work through the material. Is your mind clearer in the afternoon or evening? Schedule your study session then. Another method is to study at the same time of day that you will take the test, so that your brain gets used to working on the material at that time and will be ready to focus at test time.

STEP 5: STUDY!

Once you have done all the study preparation, it's time to settle into the actual studying. Sit down, take a few moments to settle your mind so you can focus, and begin to follow your study plan. Don't give in to distractions or let yourself procrastinate. This is your time to prepare so you'll be ready to fearlessly approach the test. Make the most of the time and stay focused.

Of course, you don't want to burn out. If you study too long you may find that you're not retaining the information very well. Take regular study breaks. For example, taking five minutes out of every hour to walk briskly, breathing deeply and swinging your arms, can help your mind stay fresh.

As you get to the end of each chapter or section, it's a good idea to do a quick review. Remind yourself of what you learned and work on any difficult parts. When you feel that you've mastered the material, move on to the next part. At the end of your study session, briefly skim through your notes again.

But while review is helpful, cramming last minute is NOT. If at all possible, work ahead so that you won't need to fit all your study into the last day. Cramming overloads your brain with more information than it can process and retain, and your tired mind may struggle to recall even

239

previously learned information when it is overwhelmed with last-minute study. Also, the urgent nature of cramming and the stress placed on your brain contribute to anxiety. You'll be more likely to go to the test feeling unprepared and having trouble thinking clearly.

So don't cram, and don't stay up late before the test, even just to review your notes at a leisurely pace. Your brain needs rest more than it needs to go over the information again. In fact, plan to finish your studies by noon or early afternoon the day before the test. Give your brain the rest of the day to relax or focus on other things, and get a good night's sleep. Then you will be fresh for the test and better able to recall what you've studied.

STEP 6: TAKE A PRACTICE TEST

Many courses offer sample tests, either online or in the study materials. This is an excellent resource to check whether you have mastered the material, as well as to prepare for the test format and environment.

Check the test format ahead of time: the number of questions, the type (multiple choice, free response, etc.), and the time limit. Then create a plan for working through them. For example, if you have 30 minutes to take a 60-question test, your limit is 30 seconds per question. Spend less time on the questions you know well so that you can take more time on the difficult ones.

If you have time to take several practice tests, take the first one open book, with no time limit. Work through the questions at your own pace and make sure you fully understand them. Gradually work up to taking a test under test conditions: sit at a desk with all study materials put away and set a timer. Pace yourself to make sure you finish the test with time to spare and go back to check your answers if you have time.

After each test, check your answers. On the questions you missed, be sure you understand why you missed them. Did you misread the question (tests can use tricky wording)? Did you forget the information? Or was it something you hadn't learned? Go back and study any shaky areas that the practice tests reveal.

Taking these tests not only helps with your grade, but also aids in combating test anxiety. If you're already used to the test conditions, you're less likely to worry about it, and working through tests until you're scoring well gives you a confidence boost. Go through the practice tests until you feel comfortable, and then you can go into the test knowing that you're ready for it.

Test Tips

On test day, you should be confident, knowing that you've prepared well and are ready to answer the questions. But aside from preparation, there are several test day strategies you can employ to maximize your performance.

First, as stated before, get a good night's sleep the night before the test (and for several nights before that, if possible). Go into the test with a fresh, alert mind rather than staying up late to study.

Try not to change too much about your normal routine on the day of the test. It's important to eat a nutritious breakfast, but if you normally don't eat breakfast at all, consider eating just a protein bar. If you're a coffee drinker, go ahead and have your normal coffee. Just make sure you time it so that the caffeine doesn't wear off right in the middle of your test. Avoid sugary beverages, and drink enough water to stay hydrated but not so much that you need a restroom break 10 minutes into the test. If your test isn't first thing in the morning, consider going for a walk or doing a light workout before the test to get your blood flowing.

Allow yourself enough time to get ready, and leave for the test with plenty of time to spare so you won't have the anxiety of scrambling to arrive in time. Another reason to be early is to select a good seat. It's helpful to sit away from doors and windows, which can be distracting. Find a good seat, get out your supplies, and settle your mind before the test begins.

When the test begins, start by going over the instructions carefully, even if you already know what to expect. Make sure you avoid any careless mistakes by following the directions.

Then begin working through the questions, pacing yourself as you've practiced. If you're not sure on an answer, don't spend too much time on it, and don't let it shake your confidence. Either skip it and come back later, or eliminate as many wrong answers as possible and guess among the remaining ones. Don't dwell on these questions as you continue—put them out of your mind and focus on what lies ahead.

Be sure to read all of the answer choices, even if you're sure the first one is the right answer. Sometimes you'll find a better one if you keep reading. But don't second-guess yourself if you do immediately know the answer. Your gut instinct is usually right. Don't let test anxiety rob you of the information you know.

If you have time at the end of the test (and if the test format allows), go back and review your answers. Be cautious about changing any, since your first instinct tends to be correct, but make sure you didn't misread any of the questions or accidentally mark the wrong answer choice. Look over any you skipped and make an educated guess.

At the end, leave the test feeling confident. You've done your best, so don't waste time worrying about your performance or wishing you could change anything. Instead, celebrate the successful completion of this test. And finally, use this test to learn how to deal with anxiety even better next time.

> **Review Video: Test Anxiety**
> Visit mometrix.com/academy and enter code: 100340

Important Qualification

Not all anxiety is created equal. If your test anxiety is causing major issues in your life beyond the classroom or testing center, or if you are experiencing troubling physical symptoms related to your anxiety, it may be a sign of a serious physiological or psychological condition. If this sounds like your situation, we strongly encourage you to seek professional help.

Additional Bonus Material

Due to our efforts to try to keep this book to a manageable length, we've created a link that will give you access to all of your additional bonus material:

mometrix.com/bonus948/priihpeck5857